ARTIFICIAL DREAMS

This book is a critique of Artificial Intelligence (AI) from the perspective of cognitive science – it seeks to examine what we have learned about human cognition from AI successes and failures. The book's goal is to separate those "AI dreams" that either have been or could be realized from those that are constructed through discourse and are unrealizable. AI research has advanced many areas that are intellectually compelling and holds great promise for advances in science, engineering, and practical systems. After the 1980s, however, the field has often struggled to deliver widely on these promises. This book breaks new ground by analyzing how some of the driving dreams of people practicing AI research become valued contributions, while others devolve into unrealized and unrealizable projects.

H. R. Ekbia is associate professor of information science and cognitive science at Indiana University, where he is also affiliated with the School of Informatics. Initially trained as an engineer, Ekbia switched his focus to study cognitive science in order to pursue a lifelong interest in the workings of the human mind. To get a deeper understanding of the questions that AI research and writing posed but hastily tackled, Ekbia in turn began to focus on the philosophy of science and science studies, through which he discovered novel ways of thinking about science, technology, and the human mind.

This broad intellectual background is well reflected in Ekbia's writings, which range over a diverse set of topics on humans, machines, and mediated interactions between the two. Ekbia has taught extensively in the areas of computer science, information science, cognitive science, and science and technology studies. He currently teaches human–computer interaction and social informatics at the School of Library and Information Science at Indiana University.

Artificial Dreams

The Quest for Non-Biological Intelligence

H. R. EKBIA
Indiana University

CAMBRIDGE
UNIVERSITY PRESS

CAMBRIDGE UNIVERSITY PRESS
Cambridge, New York, Melbourne, Madrid, Cape Town, Singapore, São Paulo, Delhi

Cambridge University Press
32 Avenue of the Americas, New York, NY 10013-2473, USA

www.cambridge.org
Information on this title: www.cambridge.org/9780521703390

First published 2008

Printed in the United States of America

A catalog record for this publication is available from the British Library.

Library of Congress Cataloging in Publication Data

Ekbia, H. R. (Hamid Reza), 1955–
Artificial dreams: the quest for non-biological intelligence / H.R. Ekbia.
    p. cm.
Includes bibliographical references and index.
ISBN 978-0-521-87867-8 (hardcover) – ISBN 978-0-521-70339-0 (pbk.)
1. Artificial intelligence. I. Title.
Q335.E356 2008
006.3–dc22   2007045450

ISBN   978-0-521-87867-8 hardback
ISBN   978-0-521-70339-0 paperback

To Doug and Mahin, for nurturing my dreams.

Contents

List of Figures and Tables

FIGURES

TABLES

Preface

The year MMVI marked the fiftieth anniversary of the Dartmouth Conference, where the term "Artificial Intelligence" was accepted as the official label of a new discipline that seemed to hold great promise in the pursuit of understanding the human mind. AI, as the nascent discipline came to be known in public and academic discourse, has accomplished a lot during this period, breaking new grounds and providing deep insights into our minds, our technologies, and the relationship between them. But AI also has failed tremendously, making false promises and often manifesting a kind of unbridled enthusiasm that is emblematic of Hollywood-style pecuniary projects. Like many others within and around AI, I am fascinated by those accomplishments and frustrated by these shortcomings. This book is a reflection on both. Currently, we witness a resurgence of interest in, and application of, AI in areas such as Artificial General Intelligence, Self-Aware Computing, video gaming, data mining, the Semantic Web, human-robot interaction, and so on. The revival makes a critical reassessment of the field a necessary task, which the current work has undertaken to achieve.

For me, this book is the outcome of a journey to pursue a lifelong interest in mind, cognition, and agency. I embarked on the study of Artificial Intelligence in order to understand not only the underlying technology but especially its implications for the way we understand ourselves. My dream was to build bridges between science, technology, and the humanities from the novel perspective of a discipline that cuts across disciplinary boundaries. This turned out to be an alluring, and at the same time revealing, dream. I would have liked to share the experience as much as I want to deliver the outcome, and I hope that the readers find enough material here to be able to reconstruct the journey in their mind. I am especially hopeful that those who have embarked on similar projects with the same degree of hope and enthusiasm will be able to get a sense of the ensuing challenges that could be read between the lines.

This was by no means a lonely journey. Many mentors, colleagues, and friends guided, accompanied, and nourished me in different portions. First and foremost stands Douglas Hofstadter, whose influence on this work can be seen in different places and on different levels – from the instillation of the original dream through his writings and the cultivation of skepticism toward unfounded claims, to his insistence on simple and accessible prose. Most important, Doug's moral and deeply passionate support has always been an invaluable asset.

Brian Smith also has been a great source of inspiration in many ways, not the least of which is in his immensely human and caring spirit. Brian showed me how making trade-offs, which he highlights as a major finding of the twentieth-century science, could be artfully managed in thinking and theorizing – how to be playfully but seriously philosophical, how to be religiously human but atheistically religious, and how to be deeply committed but openly skeptical at the same time.

Many others have also contributed to the development of this work. Tom Gieryn, Lisa Lloyd, and the late Rob Kling were major sources of insights and ideas from science studies, philosophy of science, and social informatics. David Leake started me on the path to become a "real" AI person; Mike Gasser, Rob Goldstone, Bob Port, Linda Smith, Esther Thelen, James Townsend, and others in the cognitive science program at Indiana University provided different perspectives on human mind and cognition. My friends Ron Day, Josh Goldberg, Steve Hockema, and Jun Luo were sources of encouragement and intellectual challenge. Occasional discussions in the early years with Fargonauts Harry Foundalis, James Marshal, and John Rehling, together with the care and support of Helga Keller at CRCC (the Center for Research on Concepts and Cognition), and the moral and intellectual support that I have enjoyed in recent years at my current home, the School of Library and Information Science, especially from Dean Blaise Cronin, have multiplied my sense of belonging to Indiana University and Bloomington.

I owe special thanks to Thomas Roth-Berghofer and two anonymous reviewers for their close reading and very useful comments on the manuscript; to Kristin Centanni, Dean Barrett, and especially Jennifer Brosek for her tremendous help with the manuscript; and to Eric Schwartz, the editor of Cambridge University Press and his team – April Potenciano, Jessica Schwarz, and Ken Karpinski – for their persistent effort to bring this work to fruition. My students at The University of Redlands, Indiana University, and Ferdowsi University of Mashhad have, in various ways, been sources of challenge and inspiration. Shahab Ghavami, a friend of yesteryears, deserves particular mention – he was the one who gave me a copy of Hofstadter's *Gödel, Escher, Bach* in the dark ages of the 1980s, when I was desperately looking for exciting ideas to overcome the social and psychological distress of the time. In the intervening years, from the cold and calm of Gothenburg, Sweden, he has continued to play his role as a provocative, though not always persistent, critic of my ruminations.

Last but not least is my family, who put up with the psychological and intellectual challenges of the years that led to the completion of this writing. This journey would have not materialized without the continuous, patient, and perceptive support of my wonderful wife, Mahin; our sons, Kaveh and Kia, who grew up with the idea of a mentally absent father; and our daughter, Taraneh, whose witty charm and natural intelligence reminds me of the elusive enormity of the AI project.

HRE
Bloomington
December 2007

Perennial Dreams

Cognition is a complex, multifaceted, and multilevel phenomenon. Unraveling it, therefore, is beyond the scope of any single discipline, the capacity of any one method, or the resources of any individual philosophy. Rather, it can emerge from the exchanges and interactions among multiple ideas, methods, models, and philosophies. In our times, cognitive science has nominally taken on the challenge to bring these strands together but, as any cognitive scientist would be willing to acknowledge, the challenge cannot be effectively met without the serious and engaged contribution of neighboring disciplines. Artificial Intelligence (AI) is one such neighbor to cognitive science, but it seems that in recent years the exchange between them has not been as active and extensive as it could be. One reason for this, I believe, is the history of developments in AI and the overall image that this history has created of the field in the scientific community. The main purpose of the current study is to examine and explain this history, not to merely criticize AI, but also to highlight its contributions to science, in general, and to cognitive science, in particular. Interestingly, these contributions are both direct and indirect. That is, there are lessons to be learned from both the content of AI – its approaches, models, and techniques – as well as from its development. We can learn *from* AI by learning *about* it.

To this end, the current study aims to put AI in context and perspective or, more specifically, to explicate the views, ideas, and assumptions it has inherited from the intellectual past (most notably, the Western rationalist tradition), and to discuss the cultural and institutional milieu of AI practices that support and promote those views. Far from a shared understanding, we shall see, these multiple origins have given rise to an enterprise the goal and character of which is constantly contended, negotiated, and redefined. In the end, the picture that will emerge of AI is a colorful fabric of interwoven cultural, institutional, and intellectual threads that can be best understood through the relationships among its components.

AI is a dream – a dream of the creation of things in the human image, a dream that reveals the human quest for immortality and the human desire for self-reflection. The origins of AI, in one form or another, go back to the perennial pursuit of human beings to understand their place in the overall scheme of things, both as creations and as creators. In primitive societies, this quest gave rise to complex rituals, intricate religious beliefs, enchanted objects of worship, and nascent forms of philosophizing. In religious thought, it manifests itself in many guises – from resurrection and reincarnation to mysticism and other belief systems about the unity of the universe. In early modern times, the quest took the form of a question about the "nature" of animals and humans as *machines* (Mazlish 1993: 14). Today's AI is the inheritor and a major perpetuator of this perennial quest. It embodies, in the most visible shape, the modernist dream of a purified world: of a mind detached from the body and the world, of a nature detached from the self and society, and of a science detached from power and politics. As such, AI brings the intrinsic tensions of modernity – for example, the tensions between mind and body, nature and culture, and science and religion (Haraway 1991; Latour 1993) – into sharp relief. It may fail or it may succeed, but the dream will most likely stay with us in the foreseeable future, motivating similar intellectual endeavors aimed at understanding our place in the grand scheme of things. I would therefore like to think of AI as the embodiment of adream – a kind of dream that stimulates inquiry, drives action, and invites commitment, not necessarily an illusion or mere fantasy.[1]

In this introductory part of the study, my goal is to provide a brief overview of the development of AI, to highlight the common patterns of thought, attitudes, and actions observed within the AI community, and to present an initial interpretation of their meaning. In order to place the present work within the broader context of previous studies, I will examine how critics, from within and without, have reacted to this course of development. Finally, I will then try to show how the approach adopted here can contribute to the improvement of the field and its image in the scientific community.

MAINSTREAM AI IN A SNAPSHOT

AI has a short but intriguing history. Since its inception half a century ago, the discipline has had many periods of unbridled optimism followed by periods permeated by the spirit of failure. As Crevier (1993) aptly put it, this is indeed a "tumultuous history." One of the general patterns that emerges

Table P.1. Salient examples of the disruptive view of change in the history of AI.

The Approach	"Is nothing but"	"Has nothing to do with"
Physical Symbol System	Token manipulation	Body and environment
Supercomputing	Speed of Computation	Human society
Cybernetic	Control and Software	Body
Knowledge-intensive	Knowledge	Control structure
Case-based	Reminiscence	Logic
Connectionist	Neuron-like computation	Symbols and rules
Dynamical	Continuous state change	Discrete computation/ representation
Neo-robotic	Physical interaction	Representation

from the current study, for instance, is that every so often a new paradigm appears on the scene with the explicit claim of overthrowing the previous ones, and of replacing them with fresh new ideas, methods, and models that will overcome or bypass the previous problems altogether. Although this kind of punctuated development is not unfamiliar in the history of science,[2] it takes an unusually "revolutionary" character in the history of AI, in the form of all-or-nothing statements about the essence of intelligence, cognition, and mind. Most commonly, such statements take one or both of the following forms:

- Intelligence is nothing but X
- Intelligence has nothing to do with Y

where X and Y vary depending, respectively, on the specific approach that is being advocated and on the approach(es) against which it has been launched. Table P.1 provides examples of the Xs and Ys that we will see throughout the coming chapters, representing the disruptive view of change prevalent within the AI community.

What turns out in each approach, however, is that none of these black-and-white dichotomies are borne out in the real world. Consequently, almost all of these so-called revolutions, after being so starkly advocated, gradually dissolve into a ripple, turn into limited reforms, and are ultimately absorbed in "mainstream AI," regenerating and reinforcing some of the old assumptions, techniques, and tensions, albeit under new guises and with new labels. As a result, the most outstanding feature of mainstream AI is that it has diverged enormously from the original vision of understanding human cognition (Sloman 2005a).

Despite the initial fervor and the revolutionary claims, therefore, the overall picture that emerges of AI is much like that of the social anarchism of late-nineteenth- and early-twentieth-century Europe. Anarchists advocated a social system without hierarchy and governance. A major tenet of their ideology was, therefore, the elimination of power, oftentimes by resorting to force and social "shocks" such as assassination. One of these shocks, the terror of the Hapsburg Crown Prince, actually triggered World War I. Although these shocks had transient political impacts, the activities of anarchists could not do much in changing the social status quo, and anarchists themselves were gradually divided, with the majority of them joining one of the more traditional poles of the political spectrum. This is what typically happens to all the "new" approaches in AI: they begin with claims that have the disruptive character of a shock, only to gradually merge into the existing poles with the passage of time. What is the explanation for this state of affairs?

SCIENCE AND ENGINEERING IN TENSION

> The moment of truth is a running program.
>
> – Herbert Simon (1995)

The intensity of the debates in AI reflects an internal tension within the field that derives from its scientific and engineering practices. Following a three-step scheme established by Turing in his design of universal machines (see Chapter 1), Artificial Intelligence seeks to do three things at the same time:

1. as an engineering practice, AI seeks to build precise working systems.
2. as a scientific practice, it seeks to explain the human mind and human behavior.
3. as a discursive practice, it seeks to use psychological terms (derived from its scientific practice) to describe what its artifacts (built through the engineering practice) do.

The first two practices highlight the fact that AI, as a way of *knowing* and a way of *doing*, straddles the boundary between science and engineering. On the one hand, its object is typically the building of artifacts that perform specific tasks. On the other hand, those same artifacts are intended as a medium to model and explain an aspect of human behavior. These dual objectives have been present in AI ever since its inception. Herbert Simon, one of the pioneers of AI argued, "far from striving to separate science and engineering, we need not distinguish them at all.... We can stop debating whether AI is science or engineering; it is both" (1995: 100). The engineering principle of "understanding by building" is a strong driving force in AI, and accounts for a good deal of its appeal among its advocates. In the modernist eye, the fact that AI theories and models of cognition are physically instantiated in computer systems provides them with an aura of being "real" – a quality that seemed to be missing from previous psychological theories. In fact, the role of technology is what distinguishes AI from any previous attempt to study human behavior (Varela, Thompson, and Rosch 1991: 5). It is what, according to some accounts, generates within AI (and cognitive science) a potential for rigor, clarity, and controlled experimentation (Crevier 1993: 247), as well as a certain degree of "honesty," which is acknowledged even by the staunchest of AI's critics (Dreyfus 1992). However, as I intend to show, engineering and scientific principles often clash with each other, generating a gap that needs to be filled by the third practice.

This third practice, which acts like a bridge, is more subjective than the other two. The term "discursive practice" refers to a crucial activity of AI practitioners – namely, their pervasive use of a discourse that connects the performances of their artifacts to their scientific claims.[3] In other words, what makes AI distinct from other disciplines is that its practitioners "translate" terms and concepts from one domain into another in a systematic way.[4] Thus, on the one hand, AI practitioners talk about their artifacts using a vocabulary that is canonically used to describe human behavior – in short, they anthropomorphize machines. On the other hand, they think of human beings as (complex) machines. Therefore, it is common to hear engineering terms applied to human behavior by some AI people. Charles Babbage, widely considered as a pioneer of modern computers, was aware of the power and appeal of this cross-domain translation. In 1838, he conceded that "in substituting mechanism for the performance of operations hitherto executed by intellectual labour [...] the analogy between these acts and the operations of mind almost forced upon me the figurative employment of the same terms. They were found at once convenient and expressive, and I prefer to continue their use" (in Schaffer 1994: 208).

The point is not that there is something inherently wrong or exceptionally ad hoc in this practice – for that is essentially what analogies do, and analogies may well constitute the core of human cognition (Hofstadter 2001). Nor is it even that AI practitioners are totally unaware of these translations. The problem is that this use of metaphorical language is often done without due attention to the vague and imprecise nature of the cross-domain allusions (Agre 1997a: 45–46).[5] The danger of this inattention is that it propagates a noncritical attitude, which can interfere with technical (scientific and engineering) practice (Varela et al. 1991: 133). In sum, my claim is that AI seeks to accomplish three things at the same time: a way of doing, a way of knowing, and a way of talking – and I will henceforth call these the *three practices of AI*.

These practices pull the field in different directions, generating a body of models, metaphors, and techniques that, judged by AI's history, keeps moving in cycles of fads and fashions (Ekbia 2001). This happens because the discursive practice simply cannot fulfill the role expected of it: not only does it fail to bridge the gap between engineering and scientific practices, it widens the gap by introducing more and more layers of anthropomorphic language, metaphorical imagery, and technical terminology. Indeed, the history of AI includes a number of "revolutions" that were launched against a governing paradigm (logic, computation, representations, etc.), but that in the end only reinforced some of that paradigm's fundamental assumptions in a more disguised form. Various intellectual, institutional, cultural, and socio-economic threads have heavily contributed to the entrenchment of this situation, as I will show in the coming chapters.

Furthermore, the interdisciplinary character of AI complicates the situation even further.[6] People coming from different disciplines bring with them various intuitions, assumptions, and widely disparate understandings of the same concepts and practices. Differences can begin even at the most basic level – for example, the characterization of "intelligence," which is the most fundamental notion in the field – and they then extend to other, more complex theoretical notions such as "symbol," "syntax," "semantics," "representation," and so on. The result, as we shall see, is pervasive crosstalk, unjustified redundancy displayed in reinvented wheels, mutually estranged research centers, rival research projects that work on the same topics, and, most pervasively, muddled and misleading claims.

The thesis advanced here is, therefore, that the pressures of multiple practices, together with the intellectual, cultural, and institutional threads mentioned earlier, generate great tension inside the field of AI. Engineering practice, for instance, is performance-based – what matters is the working of a system based on physical specifications. Human behavior, however, follows a different "logic" – it doesn't merely function physically; it also seeks truths, follows rules, pursues goals, wills good, and seeks beauty. A theory that attempts to explain or model human behavior will therefore have far more complicated criteria for success than engineering does. The main challenge for AI is, therefore, to how to compromise among these competing logics.

A CRITICAL STANCE

It seems to me that the historical analysis of scientific discourse should, in the last resort, be subject, not to a theory of the knowing subject, but rather to a theory of discursive practice.
– Michel Foucault, *Order of Things*

This work is a critique of AI, and a critique can take different shapes and forms. In art or literature, for instance, criticism usually means "critical appreciation," and a critic is someone with the skills and sensibility to understand a piece of art or literature as well as the process of its production. This kind of critique may not lead to unconditional praise, but it is not usually taken as a debunking of either art or literature (Biagioli 1999: xiii). A different kind of critique is that conducted by the practitioners of science studies in their analyses of science. Although not typically described as "criticism" by the practitioners, these analyses are usually seen by scientists as negative attacks on their enterprise as a whole. Biagioli attributes this kind of reaction to "the structure, scale, and social robustness of the scientific community that makes some of its members read local critiques as general ones" (ibid.). Although sympathetic to this assessment, I believe that an effective way of addressing it is to adopt a more engaged and "informed" approach to the subject matter. As will be seen throughout this study, I have applied many ideas and insights from science studies here, but I sometimes find them inadequate because of their distance from formal and technical issues that are at the heart of AI. I have, therefore, conducted this work from a perspective that involves both the formal-technical and conceptual-critical aspects of AI. Following Agre (1997), I call this approach a technical-critical practice.

Technical-Critical Practice

Technical work of the kind pursued in AI often involves problems that are incrementally solved to improve performance. Having bugs, glitches, and problems, in other words, is an inherent part of technical practice, and should not be taken as an indication of failure. One cannot get into the water, as an old Persian adage says, without getting one's feet wet. What matters in assessing technical work, therefore, is the way the work confronts and solves such bugs, glitches, and problems. A project can do this by paying explicit attention to the underlying assumptions and biases that have generated a problem, or by sticking to those assumptions and trying to find quick and accessible "fixes"; it can be patient, starting from small and well-understood domains and slowly proceeding to more sophisticated ideas, as is normally the case in science, or it can impatiently leap from raw intuitions to complicated systems; it can remain committed to well-laid-out principles (of design, performance, or psychological realism) throughout its development, or it can violate those principles, if indeed it has any, in successive stages.

From this perspective, the importance of a project in AI does not so much depend on its size, scope, or sophistication as it does on the match between what it does, what it signifies, and what it claims to do and signify. Thus, a system that seems trivial in its ambitions may be more promising, by this measure, than a grand project with hidden disparities between word and deed. Fantasy and hype are found not only in a mismatch between claims and accomplishments, or in the emanation of unfounded predictions and undeliverable promises for the future, but also in the disparity between multiple practices (building, theorizing, and talking) and in the usage of a great deal of psychological language that often tends to make the gaps seem smaller than they are (McDermott 1976). This perspective also clarifies my notion of "dream," which plays a central role in this writing: by "dream" I do not mean to suggest illusion or mere fantasy, but something that motivates inquiry, drives action, and invites commitment.

Attribution Fallacy and Generalized Eliza Effect

My purpose, therefore, is not only to criticize the actual *programs*, but the misleading effect of the communication techniques used to talk about the programs – their discourses, to use one of the key notions of this writing. As we will see throughout this survey, there is a tendency in AI to exploit the *Eliza effect* (see later in this chapter) by smoothly conflating the real-world events being modeled with the tiny stripped-down versions that are in the models. When one reads reports, articles, and books written about various AI programs, it is often next to impossible to realize how stripped-down the world of the program really is, because of this insidious phenomenon that researchers and authors rarely try to discourage. This constant sliding back and forth between the reader's image of a real event and pieces of code that use variables whose names suggest a great deal of visual richness has the inevitable effect of contaminating an uncritical (or even a critical) reader's mind with a great deal of the imagery associated with the real event. Known in AI as the *Eliza effect*, this is a very common phenomenon that is manifested in diverse shapes and forms, many examples of which we will see in following chapters – for example, a visit to the zoo, a football game, a cooking session, a learning process, an eyeball-to-eyeball encounter between individuals, seeing a computer-generated painting, or listening to a computer-composed Chopin-style mazurka. The diversity of these manifestations points to a very broad phenomenon that I call the "Generalized Eliza Effect" (GEE). In short, GEE has to do with the often-exaggerated abilities of AI artifacts to delude the casual observer.

The flip side of this phenomenon is what I call the "Attribution Fallacy": the propensity of people to uncritically accept implicit suggestions that some

AI program or other is dealing with real-world situations. When a program supposedly explains why a shuttle launch failed, people take for granted that the program has an image or model of the situation roughly comparable to their own. The truth may be extremely remote from that – but few AI authors include in their articles a disclaimer that states: "Warning: Entities in models appear to be much more complex than they really are." And unfortunately, by not doing so, they implicitly encourage their readers to let their *own* concepts slide and glide fluidly back and forth between the real world and the model, so that in the end no clear notion is built up about how microscopic the worlds being dealt with really are.

The blame for this deception falls primarily on the researchers and authors who do nothing to try to stop the Eliza effect dead in its tracks. They may not want to do so, partly because they have too much invested in their projects, partly because, being human, they themselves fall to a certain degree for the same Eliza effect, and partly because, as the previous discussion suggests, they are under opposing pressures due to the scientific and engineering aspirations of AI. These pressures sometimes even result in a conflict of objectives within a single approach, as we will see later.

In brief, this book pursues a number of different goals – namely, to criticize AI approaches and systems in terms of the gap between their scientific claims and their engineering achievements, to expose the discourses that are used in covering the above gap, and to understand and explain the related phenomena of the Generalized Eliza Effect and the Attribution Fallacy. The last point obviously has more to do with human beings than with computers and AI systems, but that does not diminish its relevance to our purposes. As a matter of fact, to highlight the significance of this point, I sometimes have chosen to examine and critique AI systems that might otherwise be old, minor, or insignificant (even in the eyes of their originators). The advantage of such systems for our purposes here, however, is that they reveal the Eliza effect in its full scope and strength. Ironically, being "inferior" examples of AI, such systems can easily illustrate our human susceptibility to the Eliza effect, in ways that "superior" examples cannot. This, I believe, is one of the major "indirect" lessons of AI for cognitive science.

At any rate, my purpose is not to advocate certain AI approaches while debunking others. It is, rather, to contribute to a better understanding of the field of AI, to contribute to its progress and improvement, and, in so doing, to draw lessons for cognitive science. This constructive approach is inspired by, and, I believe, is in line with previous critiques that pursued a similar goal – most notably, McDermott (1976, 1987), Hofstadter (1985, 1995), Winograd and Flores (1986), Smith (1991, 1996, forthcoming), and

Agre (1997a,b, 2002) from within AI, and Dreyfus (1972, 1992), Suchman (1987, 2007) Collins (1990), Edwards (1996), Forsythe (2001), and Woolgar (1985, 1995) from outside the field.

THE CRITICAL SPECTRUM

Because of the character of its subject matter, research in AI could well come to have far-reaching implications for other disciplines such as anthropology, biology, philosophy, psychology, and sociology. Small wonder, then, that AI has been the subject of scrutiny and criticism since its early days. Such criticisms have come from a variety of quarters, with multifarious agendas and criteria, but one can broadly classify them as philosophical, social, or (as in the present case) reflexive.

Philosophical critiques fall across a wide spectrum – ranging from total embrace (e.g., Boden 1990, Dennett 1991) to somewhat supportive (Churchland 1989, Clark 1997, Dretske 1994, Haugeland 1981, 1985) to sharply critical (Dreyfus 1972, 1992, Putnam 1975, 1990) to totally dismissive (Searle 1984, 1992). The most controversial views have been those of Dreyfus and Searle. Dreyfus originally criticized AI for its failure to capture the essence of human experience, which he characterized as a set of skills for getting around in the world. This view was in sharp contrast with the common view in traditional AI that intelligence consists, by and large, in the manipulation of symbols by an isolated mind, and that it has little to do with bodily skills and with coping with the environment. Over the course of time, there has been some convergence between Dreyfus's views and those of AI community. Many AI researchers have come to agree with his point of view, and Dreyfus has shown a willingness to embrace parts of AI – for instance, connectionism. Searle, by contrast, has persistently dismissed a major strand of AI on the grounds that AI systems intrinsically lack "intentionality" (i.e., they are unconscious and the signs they manipulate are devoid of all meaning; see Chapter 2).

The overall response of the AI community to these critiques has usually been one of incomprehension or outrage but also, on occasion, cautious reflection. I would contend that these critiques have contributed to the vigor and disciplinary awareness of AI, although in rather different ways. The same could not be said about sociological critiques, which have been mostly disregarded, if at all recognized, by the AI community. This disregard doesn't mean, however, that such critiques have had no valuable points to contribute.

Social critiques of AI originate in various disciplines. Some anthropologists have tried to describe AI as a culture that projects its own values onto its systems Suchman (1987, 2007) has famously shown how the classical notion of planning in AI took plans as control structures that precede and determine actions. Forsythe (2001) has argued that AI people, because of the technical character of their field, greatly value technical prowess, and typically focus on the technical aspects of their systems at the expense of other (psychological, cultural) aspects. This overemphasis on techniques, Forsythe argues, often results in AI systems that might not be as effective and useful as one would hope in a real-world environment, as is illustrated, for instance, by the failure of most medical expert systems (see Chapter 4).

Sociologists, on the other hand, have variously focused on how AI metaphors and practices shape, and are shaped by, the social aspects of human experience (Collins 1990), on the institutional context that has given rise to AI, especially in relation to the U.S. military and its technical projects in the Cold War era (Edwards 1996), on the role of AI (as a part of computer technology) in shaping contemporary psyches (Turkle 1985), and on the broader social and cultural context of AI practices (Bloomfield 1987; Woolgar 1985, 1987).

Both the social and the philosophical critiques of AI can be characterized as "external," not only because they originate from outside the field, but also because their proponents question some of the core premises held within the AI community. Along with these critiques, there has also been dissent from inside AI by computer scientists and professionals, sometimes on ethical grounds (Weizenbaum 1976; Joy 2000; Lanier 2000), other times in terms of theoretical issues (McDermott 1976, 1987), and still other times with an explicit concern for the improvement of AI systems (Winograd and Flores 1986; Hofstadter et al. 1995; Smith 1996; Agre 1997).

ON DISCIPLINES AND METHODS

The present study has been informed by all of the above critiques, and, as the reader will notice, I have drawn on each where appropriate. This assertion might impart a pluralistic image on the study, far beyond its reality. Therefore, some clarification is in order here. The kinds of questions asked here have traditionally belonged to the realm of philosophy and philosophy of science, the topics and discussions are largely technical, and the conclusions arrived at are broadly sociological. However, the apparent eclectic character of the approach is not quite novel. Steven Shapin, in his sociohistorical study of the production of scientific knowledge in seventeenth-century England, faces a similar situation, following an approach comparable to the current one. Rather than being apologetic about this approach, Shapin asserts that he has "followed the questions, and the resources for addressing them, wherever they happened to be in the academic culture" (1994: xv). I follow a similar tack here.

At the same time, I am fully aware of the kinds of issues that this approach might raise. For instance, the current study apparently fails to deliver the type of "radical criticism" envisioned in certain schools of thought in science studies. Most importantly, by taking "cognition" as a prior concept and as happening in individuals, my approach may implicitly suggest a peripheral status for sociology. Or as Woolgar (1995: 177) argues, it may seem to take as resource what sociology takes as topic (namely, individual cognition). However, as I hope to show throughout this study, the direction of developments in AI has increasingly revealed the "leaking" of cognition from individual minds to situated practices. In fact, a major outcome of the current study, captured in the concept of Generalized Eliza Effect, is to corroborate the sociological insight that, "To appreciate how thinking happens, we need to see what kinds of actual social practice give rise to attributions of 'thinking'" (ibid.: 175).

With this caveat, there are a number of sources that have inspired this study in a more direct way, the influence of which I would like to recount here, not only to acknowledge my intellectual debt to them but also to position the present study with respect to some of these views. The sources come from both inside and outside of AI.

AN INSIDER'S VIEW

My thinking begins with Douglas Hofstadter, who originally proposed this study as part of an attempt to counter what he considers to be an intolerable amount of hype about the capabilities of AI systems propagated by their creators, their advocates, and the media. Hofstadter is an insider to AI in more than one way. Not only has he been an active researcher in the field, but his seminal book *Gödel, Escher, Bach: an Eternal Golden Braid* (first published in 1979 and reprinted many times since) has probably introduced and attracted more people to AI than any single work in the history of the field.[7] As someone who has greatly contributed to the popular interest in AI, therefore, Hofstadter considers vigilant criticism a crucial step toward the overall health and vigor of the field. In his own writings, he has frequently warned against "hype," "show versus substance," and "uncritical publicity."[8] However, these criticisms have been blithely ignored by the AI community, and the reason has to be sought in the difference between mainstream AI and Hofstadter's views.

Hofstadter has a special vision of AI, which I dub "Hofstadter's Romantic Dream" because of its deep conviction that there could be a discipline of AI devoid of self-promotion, grandstanding, and implausibly grandiose claims (see Chapter 9). The following passage, which outlines the kind of research done by Hofstadter's group FARG (Fluid Analogies Research Group), provides the general features of this vision:

From its very outset, the intellectual goals and activities of FARG have been characterized by two quite distinct strands, one of them concerned with developing detailed computer models of concepts and analogical thinking in carefully-designed, highly-restricted microdomains, and the other concerned with observing, classifying, and speculating about mental processes in their full, unrestricted glory. The latter has served as a constant stream of ideas and inspirations for the former. (Hofstadter 1995: Introduction)

This characterization of FARG's research strategy, construed as a general vision of how to do AI, involves the following main features:[9]

- the main objective of AI is to understand the intricate workings of the human mind and of intelligence in general.
- research in AI consists of a painstaking and patient process of discovery and understanding in "carefully-designed and highly-restricted microdomains."
- what guides this research is very careful and very persistent observation by the researcher of human beings and of their mental processes.

As in most AI, the implicit assumption in the above strategy is that the development of computer models allows good ideas to be winnowed from bad ideas. We might wonder why mainstream AI would not be receptive to these views, and Hofstadter, speaking of "the knotty problem of evaluating research" in AI, provides an answer:

Those people who are interested in *results* will begin with a standard technology, not even questioning it at all, and then build a big system that solves many complex problems and impresses a lot of people. (1995: 53)

This interest in "results," we should remember, is what I attribute to the engineering ethos of mainstream AI, and it accounts for the central tension between a desire for "working" systems, on the one hand, and the ambition of conducting scientific inquiry, on the other. Similarly, a major focus of our study throughout the coming chapters is the "questioning of standard technologies." In some serious sense, therefore, the present work should be seen as an attempt to portray the roots of AI's many defects and foibles, as Hofstadter had proposed earlier. It is also an attempt to help Hofstadter's Dream materialize (see Chapter 8), not only by making criticisms of AI systems but also by providing positive suggestions.

In addition to Hofstadter's views, there have also been other sources of inspiration from within AI that have guided this work. Most notable is the work of Brian Cantwell Smith on the foundations of computing, which is motivated by what he considers the inadequacies of the dominant theories of computing in dealing with the computing work carried out in the real world – the "one hundred billion lines of C^{++}" that Smith (1997) estimates are running on the computers around the world. In particular, for our purposes here, Smith finds two problems with such theories – namely, that they take computing to be:

i) too *abstract*, and therefore too far removed from the constraints of physical implementation; and consequently.
ii) too *detached*, and therefore too separated from computation's social, cultural, and historical surroundings.

AI is influenced by these conceptions of computing, and has influenced them, as is clear from the prevalence of symbolic views in, say, the Physical Symbol Systems Hypothesis (Newell and Simon 1976; see Chapter 1). These same conceptions have generated the grounds for misunderstanding among philosophers such as John Searle, who take very literally the in-principle claims of the dominant theories of computing (Chapter 2). Thus, not only would the examination of current theories of computing be necessary for a better appreciation of computers, it is also necessary for providing a more realistic picture of AI. What needs to be done, according to Smith, is to start over, by asking, "What is a computer?" This kind of metaphysical inquiry is a strategy that he has pursued for some twenty years in order to figure out what computation is.

The examination of computational theories also has led Smith to more fundamental observations about the character of work in areas like AI (Smith 1996). One of Smith's key ideas is what he calls "irreduction" (cf. Latour 1987). Framed in terms of a commercial metaphor, the idea is that, for any assumption one makes in advancing a viewpoint, one should be clear and explicit about: "i) Where one bought it; ii) How much one paid; and iii) How one got it from there to here" (Smith 1996: 78).[10] Failing to observe this principle often results in a tendency to inscribe one's concepts and categories onto an artifact, and then to read those same concepts back off the artifact, as if they were inherent to it.[11] This type of error, as we have seen, is very common in AI, and throughout the following chapters I try to show its occurrence in different places – for example, in the attribution of commonsense knowledge to Cyc (Chapter 3), in the attribution of human-like language capabilities to some connectionist networks (Chapter 5), or in the attribution of social development to Kismet (Chapter 7).

Finally, among the intellectual sources of this work from within the field, I should mention Phil Agre's critique of AI, which seems to be driven by intuitions and concerns very similar to my own.[12] Agre (1997) begins with the premise that AI is "a potentially valuable... [but presently] misguided enterprise," and draws attention to the role that metaphors have played in the formation and development of AI. Metaphors, because of their nature, tend to highlight certain aspects at the expense of others. For instance, the metaphor of the mind as a space with an inside and an outside, which is at the heart of traditional AI and cognitive science (see Chapter 1), takes mind to be "inside" and focuses our attention on the inner workings at the expense of other bodily functions or social surroundings. Translated into practice, this metaphor results in models and systems that try to solve everything within the boundaries of a detached compartment, be it a brain, or a computer.

The analyses of such models in terms of the same metaphorical ideas (of inside and outside), as has often happened in AI, may result in further refinements, but they do not bring about any substantive change within the existing framework. This kind of assimilation to the mainstream (or "issue recycling," as Agre calls it) is, for instance, what happened to both case-based reasoning and connectionism, which, remaining attached to the inside–outside metaphor of the mind, have been unable to bring about much change to the basic assumptions of classical AI, and have thus regenerated issues and problems similar in character to those of their predecessors.

One way to interrupt this process of issue recycling, according to Agre, is to conduct a critical and reflexive analysis that examines the original metaphors and ideas in order to discover their limits. This kind of reflexive analysis is part of what the present study has tried to accomplish. A major ambition of each chapter is to contribute positively to future research not only by highlighting the insightful aspects of each approach but also by tracing the sources of problems all the way back to the primordial assumptions and presuppositions of the given approach. As Agre points out, "critical analysis does not replace practical work; nor should it be viewed as a kibitzer invalidating this work from a comfortable seat in back" (305). This caveat has been respected throughout the writing of the present work. To be more specific, nowhere in my study have I attempted to invalidate a work by making criticisms of it. The purpose, rather, has always been to expose the assumptions that are often taken for granted in technical work, and that might therefore be at the root of problems.

Given all these valuable sources of insight from people within AI, whose explicit intention is to contribute to the improvement of the field, the question remains as to what has prevented them from being taken seriously, or, in other words, what stands in the way of the realization of an AI that is seriously committed to the original vision of its founders as a discipline that aims to understand the human mind and human cognition. This is, in some serious sense, the most central question of the present study, and in order to answer it I have had to draw upon sources outside of AI – for example, the history and philosophy and science, science and technology studies, anthropology, philosophy, and others.

AN OUTSIDER'S VIEW

Throughout the coming chapters, we will see the vast gulf that separates today's mainstream AI from the visions of its originators and from the views such as those discussed earlier. What generates this gulf? Put differently, what is the source of the confusion that has plagued AI over most of its history? I suggest that the tension between scientific and engineering practices is at the root of this development, and I will discuss the diverse manifestations of this tension in various schools. A tension on its own, however, cannot fully explain the situation, which is why I also suggest that we should look at the contextual conditions that allow, encourage, or intensify the tension. To do that, I argue, we have to broaden our view in order to see the bigger picture; we need, in other words, to study AI in the making (Latour 1987). That is, we need to study AI theories, models, and systems not only as the products of intuitions and ideas of the people who create them, but also as the products of the social, institutional, and cultural contexts in which those ideas are shaped and realized – for example, in the AI labs around the world. Such a study would provide a more comprehensive picture of AI than the traditional way of looking just at the final products, as they are usually presented in textbooks, journal articles, and conferences. This contextual approach is basically the one followed by most practitioners of science studies, and I have found it useful for my purpose here.

A CLOSE-UP VIEW

A reasonable way of studying AI in the making would be to conduct an ethnographical study – that is, for the person who does the study (this author, in our case) to be present in many AI labs for an extended period of time, and to closely observe the builders of systems in their multiple activities not only as researchers, but also as administrators, negotiators, fund-raisers, graduate assistants, and so on. Such presence was not possible in this project for a number of reasons, not the least of which was the multitude of systems under study and the geographical and temporal dispersion of the main labs or people behind them.[13] What made up for ethnography, however, was my position as a *participant observer* – that is, someone who for many years has interacted with the AI community on a continuous basis. This perspective made it possible for me to watch different projects as they were being developed, to listen to researchers giving talks and presentations, occasionally to visit them at the places of their work, and, of course, as someone deeply interested in the question of mind and intelligence, to be closely engaged in the intellectual discussions surrounding AI topics. Furthermore, I have drawn upon various other studies that have been conducted in a similar or different fashion. These multiple resources from inside and outside of AI have, I believe, have made it possible for this study to paint a quite realistic picture of the current situation in AI.

My guiding framework for this aspect of the study is the work of the late Rob Kling and his view of Social Informatics as "the interdisciplinary study of the design, uses, and consequences of information technologies that takes into account their interaction with institutional and cultural contexts" (Kling 1999). One of the contributions of Kling is the idea of computerizing as social movement:

[C]omputerization movements communicate key ideological beliefs about the favorable links between computerization and a preferred social order, which helps legitimate relatively high levels of computing investment for many potential adopters. These ideologies also set adopters' expectation about what they should use computing for and how they should organize access to it. (Kling and Iacono 1995)

These authors identify AI as one such computerization movement that has especially attracted a lot of business, media, and scientific attention in the United States. We will see various manifestations of these in the following chapters.

OUTLINE

People in AI use the notion of "approach" to refer to research programs with common conceptual frameworks – that is, with a common set of intuitions, metaphors, and philosophies together with their accompanying tools and formalisms. On this basis, they divide the field into different approaches –

Table P.2. The approaches and systems studied here.

Chapter	Approach	Main theme	The example systems
I	**Problem Solving**	Reasoning	General Problem Solver
II	**Supercomputing**	Computing power	Deep Blue
III	**Cybernetic**	Self-regulation	Cyborgs
IV	**Knowledge-Intensive**	Knowledge	**Cyc**
V	**Case-Based**	Experience	Coach/ Chef
VI	**Connectionist**	Neural-like architecture	Neural models of language learning
VII	**Dynamical**	Temporality	**HKB/DFT/ ...**
VIII	**Embodied**	Embodiment	Cog
IX	**Analogical**	Analogy-making	Copycat/Aaron/Emmy

mainly symbolic, connectionist, and situated (inter-actionist). I have devised a more fine-grained classification that respects this division, but that is more useful for my purposes. Within each of the approaches that I have singled out, then, I have selected one (or a few) major system(s) that, I believe, represent the particular approach and its main tenets. Table P.2 lists the approaches, together with their representative system(s).

Chapter 1 takes a historical look at AI, tracing its origins back to modern philosophers such as Descartes, logicians such as Boole, and more recently to the ideas of Alan Turing. It briefly examines the views of Newell and Simon, two major AI pioneers and their program called the *General Problem Solver* (GPS), as well as the cultural and institutional context of AI development.

Chapter 2 is on what I have called "supercomputing AI," a good example of which is the chess-playing program Deep Blue developed at IBM. For both historical and intellectual reasons, chess has been a favorite domain of AI since its beginning. Although it is a game and, for that reason, an "unrealistic" domain, chess provides the grounds for discussing some of the most basic intuitions, methods, and techniques of AI. I have followed tradition in using chess as an example, although I pursue a different goal and, at times, arrive at different conclusions from a typical AI account of chess.

Chapter 3 builds on the previous chapter to discuss a specific view of AI that is probably best described as "cybernetic AI." The main thrust of this view is its emphasis on computing power, but also on intelligence as a disembodied information construct. The engineer, inventor, and futurist Ray Kurzweil is one of the most outspoken proponents of this view, although he is not an official (academic) member of the AI community. However, this view also finds advocates among respected members of the community (e.g., Hans Moravec of Carnegie-Melon University), making it worthwhile to explore.

Chapter 4 is on knowledge-intensive AI, as best exemplified by the Cyc project. "Knowledge" is a fundamental term in AI (and elsewhere), with very many connotations. What I have called the knowledge-intensive approach is based on a rather broad meaning of the term that will be outlined in the chapter. Although there are other projects that fall within this category, Cyc stands out in terms of size, scope, and endurance.

Chapters 5 and 6 are on case-based and connectionist AI, both of which happen to be very prolific in terms of the number and diversity of models that they have produced. The diversity of topics makes the choice of any single project that represents them rather difficult. Therefore, I have chosen more than one project in these chapters. The models discussed in Chapter 4 deal with planning within the case-based framework, but also provide the opportunity to discuss planning more broadly. In Chapter 5, in which quite a few projects are discussed, the domain of language processing was selected as the common topic, not only because of its importance but also in order to bring coherence to the chapter.

Chapter 7 is on dynamicist AI, which, in a way, is not an approach in the same sense as the others. Historically speaking, dynamical systems theory is a formal and mathematical tool applied in areas as widespread as physics, psychology, economics, ecology, and sociology. The dynamical approach in AI and cognitive science is a broad set of models and techniques with rather undefined boundaries. Many connectionist and robotic modelers, for instance, express allegiance to dynamical principles. Still, a group of researchers insists on the identity of the dynamical framework as distinct and independent from any other approach. The reason I chose to discuss it, besides respecting the intuitions of this group, was to demonstrate how it is a good example of the strength of the formalist tradition.

Chapter 8 is on the neorobotic approach, which is the most recent and probably the most vigorous area in current AI research. Robots have been a part of AI from the beginning, but what makes the new robots distinct and worthy of particular attention is that they are built on new principles and ideas, totally distinct from those of traditional AI. Furthermore, an explicit effort is often made to make these robots more and more like human beings in their appearance and behavior. Many laboratories around the world are active in humanoid robotics, and many forums have been devoted to the same topic – for example, the International Symposium on Humanoid Robots (HURO). I selected the Cog/Kismet project at MIT for this chapter both because of its prominence and because of the diversity of the themes it pursues.

Chapter 9 is on AI models of creativity, in particular analogical models such as Copycat developed by Hofstadter and his students (1995). These models are built on a particular view of cognition and on an approach that emphasizes the importance of "micro-domains" in AI modeling. As such, they provide an interesting counterbalance to the current trend toward real-world domains. But in so doing they also raise questions about the engineering aspirations of AI.

Despite my intention to provide a realistic and unbiased picture of the current situation in AI, I should stress that this survey, like any other of its kind, is necessarily incomplete, partly subjective, and, consequently, bound to be controversial. To minimize misunderstanding, the Epilogue seeks to pull together the lessons drawn from the preceding chapters and to shed more light on the broader situation by providing a perspective mainly due to Social Informatics.

The chapters can be read independent of each other. They are ordered partly chronologically, according to the timing of approaches and models, but mainly thematically on the basis of how ideas have developed in AI and how one approach has succeeded the previous ones, seeking to fix their pitfalls and problems. I should emphasize that I do not have in mind an ideal Platonic model of AI and its practices towards which things are, or should be, moving; nor, I believe, does anyone else have privileged access to such a model. Rather, AI is the collection of the extant practices, discourses, artifacts, and institutions assembled around a common project (as vague and controversial as such a project might be). Far from being predetermined, the future path of AI will be created again and again by the interactions among this heterogeneous group of people, technologies, ideas, ideals, and activities. Critical analysis can play a pivotal role in this formative process, and I hope that this study can serve as a stimulant for more critical discussion, both within and outside the field of AI.

1   GPS: The Origins of AI

Turing's Computational Dream

We may hope that machines will eventually compete with men in all purely intellectual fields.

– Alan Turing (1950)

Computers are everywhere – on our desks, shelves, and laps; in our offices, factories, and labs; in grocery stores, gas stations, and hotels; and in our rockets, trains, and cabs. They are ubiquitous.

Computers are also talked about in all types of places and by all types of people. These discourses about computers usually invoke common themes such as their enormous speed of operation, their humongous capacity for storing data, their effectiveness as communication and coordination mediums, their promise for enhancing our mental capabilities, and their potential for undermining our selfhood, identity, and privacy. Outstanding among these, however, is the theme of computers as "thinking machines." It is to this theme that the field of Artificial Intelligence (AI) owes its emergence.

Computers are at the core of AI. In their current incarnation, almost all AI systems are built on the versatile silicon chip, the substrate of digital computers. An overall understanding of electronic computing is, therefore, a prerequisite for appreciating what AI is all about. To understand AI, however, one also must understand many other things that have contributed to its formation and development. These include intellectual history as well as the social, cultural, and institutional environment in which AI is practiced.

AI is, at some level, a philosophical project (Dennett 1990; Agre 1995; Smith 1996). Most approaches to AI have their origins in the philosophies of past and present, and can thus be construed as attempts to address the questions posed by those philosophies. I argue that among these, the views of two philosophers, Descartes and Hobbes, have had the most significant influence on AI thinking. For our purposes, these influences are best labeled as "mentalism" and "logicism"[1] – topics that have been extensively discussed elsewhere but that I now briefly describe myself.[2]

THE WORLD, THE MIND, AND THE WORLD INSIDE THE MIND

> [T]here is an important sense in which how the world is makes no difference to one's mental states.
>   – Jerry Fodor (1980), commenting on Descartes

The medieval worldview was based on two major Aristotelian dichotomies: one, in the nonliving world, between the heavenly realm of constantly moving specks of light and the earthly realm of natural elements; the other, in the living (especially human) world, between the body and the soul. Although there was no direct link between these two dichotomies, they somehow aligned and supported each other, with the body belonging to the ephemeral world of matter, and the soul to the eternal world of the heavens.[3]

Western thought since the seventeenth century has followed rather divergent paths in dealing with these dual dichotomies. It dissolved the first one, putting in its place a universal science of mechanics that applies equally to terrestrial and heavenly bodies, and that has been gradually integrated into a unified science of physics that encompasses not only the motion of visible, tangible objects but also such diverse phenomena as heat and electromagnetism. By contrast, with respect to the soul–body dichotomy, modern thought gave it a more rigorous form – that is, a sharp dualism between mind and body. It gave the mind the status of an *independent inner realm* that deserves to be studied on its own right, in complete isolation from the body (as Descartes insisted in reaction to theologians of the time). Descartes was so personally convinced of the autonomy of the mind as not to be able to "clearly distinguish wakefulness from sleep" (Descartes 1979).

By treating mind–body dualism in this manner, modern science established both a new discipline – the science of psychology – and a central question for it to tackle – the relation between the mind and the body. The history of psychology and its neighboring disciplines over the past three hundred years could, at some level, be understood as the attempt to solve the so-called mind–body problem and to penetrate the veil erected by Descartes and his contemporaries between the mental and the physical. AI is one of the latest instances of this collective attempt. In particular, early forms of AI pushed the mind-as-an-inner-world idea to its limits by regarding thought processes as taking place in the inner world of the mind, "independent of their environmental causes and effects" (Fodor 1980: 231).

Descartes' dualism posited two different worlds: one of primary qualities, such as size, shape, and weight, and one of secondary qualities, such as color, taste, and smell – an external world of "objective" reality, and a different world of "subjective" experience. A major concern of the scientific inheritors of this view was, therefore, to bridge these two worlds through physiology, especially the brain. Perception, for instance, was understood as the direct effect of sensory stimuli (such as light particles bouncing from objects) on the brain. Initial AI models adopted the main premises of this view – for instance, the dichotomy between primary and secondary qualities – and viewed perception as an inferential mechanism that reasons from internal sense impressions to the outside phenomena that must have produced them (Marr 1982).

Thinking as Logical Reasoning

While the mind–body separation provided psychology with an autonomous subject matter or content, logicism – the view that thinking mainly consists of making logical inferences – was arguably most influential in AI in terms of method and approach. One way to recognize this influence is to notice that despite more than fifty years of tumultuous history, strong assaults from different angles, and the emergence of viable alternatives, logic is still a core player in AI with respect to which other contenders position themselves.

Classical logic, originally formulated by Aristotle, was turned into logicism, an intellectual pillar of modern thought, by Thomas Hobbes, Gottfried Wilhelm Leibniz, Blaise Pascal, and others in the seventeenth century; was formalized and mathematized by George Boole, Augustus De Morgan, Gottlob Frege, Bertrand Russell, Alfred North Whitehead, and others in the nineteenth and early twentieth centuries; was adopted as the theoretical foundation of computer science by Alan Turing and others in the 1940s; was partly translated to computer architectures by mathematicians such as John von Neumann; and was taken up by AI pioneers John McCarthy, Allen Newell, and Herbert Simon as the governing framework for AI in the 1950s.

The breadth of logic makes it impossible to render a satisfactory synopsis in a space like this. The reader is referred to any standard text on first-order logic for a more formal treatment (e.g., DeLong 1970, Manna and Waldinger 1985; Hacking 1979). Here I will introduce two key ideas from the logicist tradition that, I believe, have had a lasting impact on AI: the focus on representations and the separation of meaning and form.

Representations at the Center of Thinking

At the crux of early AI was the idea that intelligent beings interact with the world through the mediation of (mental) representations. Although there is intense disagreement on the nature of representations (see, for instance, Clapin 2002 for a recent debate within cognitive science), the core intuition among most AI researchers (and philosophers) is that they are "about" other things. In planning a party, for example, one thinks *about* the date, the guests, food and drinks, the cost, and so on. Some of these might be present during the act of thinking (e.g., the drinks, if one happens to be making the plan at home or at the supermarket), some exist but are not present (e.g., the guests), some do not exist yet (e.g., the meal), and some might never come into existence (a joyful party for everyone) (Clapin 2002). The fact that we can have thoughts, plans, decisions, hopes, ideas, and so on about things and events so diverse in terms of their degree of reach and accessibility (temporal, spatial, and logical) is intuitively strong enough to justify the assumption that there are such things as mental representations that stand for things or events, whether real or potential.

This assumption about the centrality of representations is not unique to logic. What is unique is that, unlike early versions of mind-as-an-inner-world that took representations to be *image*-like replicas of what is represented, logic takes them to be *word*-like in their most basic form (Pylyshyn 1984: 41). Hence, thinking in the logicist picture crucially consists of reasoning – that is, the transformation of propositions (sentences expressed in a formal notation such as predicate calculus) according to the syntactical rules of logic (also known as "deductive rules of inference").

Meaning and Form: Isolated from Each Other

> [The mind] will be freed from having to think directly of things themselves, and yet everything will come out correctly.
>
> – Parkinson (1966), commenting on Leibniz

Not only does logic take thinking to be mainly deductive in nature, it also takes deductions to be formal. In the widest sense of the word, *formal* means that deductions are:[4]

syntactic – they proceed only by appeal to the shape and arrangement of symbols and not by appeal to the meanings (denotations or connotations) of those symbols.

algorithmic – the process of deduction is as explicitly and precisely rule-governed as is elementary arithmetic.

> **mechanical** – the rules can be carried out by a simple computing machine, with no originality or special insight into the nature of the problem being required.

Formal logic provides syntactic rules that work with no recourse to outside events (Fodor 1980; Pylyshyn 1984). A *logic machine* to carry out such rules was conceived, and partly built, by Leibniz more than two centuries ago: in principle, it is a fixed mechanism that runs indefinitely, and from valid inputs generates valid outputs. The driving force of this machine is a set of syntactic rules, its input a set of sentences, and its output formal derivations based on the input. Thus, given (1) and (2) (as statements of a falsely held view about computers), a mechanism equipped with the rule of *modus ponens* would produce (3):

(1)   All logic machines are formal systems.
(2)   Computers are logic machines.
(3)   Computers are formal systems.

And this follows, according to this rule, independently of what the specific terms such as *logic machine, computer,* or *formal system* mean in these sentences. The same rule, applied to (nonsensical) sentences (4) and (5), would lead to (6):

(4)   All yags are zags.
(5)   Zig is a yag.
(6)   Zig is a zag.

The appeal of logic is therefore in its dual character as the provider of an effective formal mechanism *and* as the vehicle of an expressive representational language (Pylyshyn 1984: 196; Smith 1999).

THE MIND AS A COMPUTER

The convergence of the foregoing views in the mid-twentieth century found a dramatic culmination in the idea of the mind as a computer: "the view that mental states and processes are *computational*" (Fodor 1980: 226). (The exact meaning of *computational* could be a bone of contention, but I will disregard that for the moment.)[5] Technically, this view is closely linked to modern digital computers, but it has much deeper historical roots, famously captured in Hobbes's dictum "Reasoning is reckoning" and instantiated in Leibniz's wheel, Babbage's Analytic Engine, and so on.

The development of digital computers followed a series of important findings in mathematical logic during the first half of the twentieth century. These historical lineages are accounted for in numerous studies, both as formal commentaries (e.g., Hayes 1973; Kowalski 1977; Davis 1988) and as broad studies of the modern intellectual scene (e.g., Hofstadter 1979; Bolter 1984). Taking these links for granted, I wish here to highlight (what seem to be) three major contributions of computational views to AI: the idea of a universal machine, the related notion of digital abstraction, and the idea of computers as instantiations of cognitive behavior.

Computers as Universal Machines

> It is possible to invent a single machine which can be used to compute any computable sequence.
>
> – Alan Turing (1936)

The idea of an all-purpose automatic calculating machine was conceived as early as the 1830s by Charles Babbage, who remarked glibly about his engine that "it could do everything but compose country dances" (Huskey and Huskey 1980: 300 – Babbage would have probably been gleefully surprised to learn that computers do, in fact, compose country dances nowadays; see Cope 2001 and Chapter 8 of this volume). The idea, however, was not realized concretely until the advent of electronic computers, about a hundred years later. Turing was arguably the first person to theorize about the idea, and he did so in roughly three major strokes. What was needed, according to Turing, was:

- to analyze, in an intuitive fashion, what *human* computers do when they calculate with paper and pencil.
- to propose an abstract model of this human activity by breaking it up into simple mechanical steps, based on other simplifying assumptions (e.g., the use of one- instead of two-dimensional paper, limiting the types and number of symbols that the computer observes at any given moment).
- to actually devise in detail a machine that implements this abstract model.

The first of these steps is straightforward, and falls in line with the atomistic tradition in science. The second step gave birth to the notion of a universal machine – a machine that could perform all conceivable computations. As this was a rather unexpected consequence, however – nothing in the prior history of technology had such a strong feature – the third step was taken as "a significant vindication" of the prior two (Davis 1988: 157).

This threefold scheme reveals a pattern that seems to have set a precedent for the later practice of AI – namely, the stages of observing and decomposing some aspect of human behavior into small, functional steps, of throwing away spurious aspects and maintaining only those that are deemed relevant, and of constructing an abstract model that can be implemented on an actual machine. Most important, it explains the prevalent belief among AI researchers in the idea of *explaining by building*. We will come across this standard pattern of activity, which, for ease of reference, I will call *the three As of AI* (analysis, abstraction, attainment) again and again throughout the following chapters.

Computers as Intelligent Artifacts

The cognitive approach – as opposed to, for instance, the behaviorist approach (Skinner 1985) – to the study of human psychology is based on the idea that people's behavior is determined by the (representational) content of their minds – namely, by their beliefs, goals, and desires. To think that Dullsburg is a boring town, according to the cognitive view, is to have a representation of it as boring and to be in a special relation – that is, belief – to that representation. To want to leave Dullsburg and reside in Joyville, similarly, is to have some representation of these places, of the desire to leave one, and of the intention to live in the other. This is the crux of the "belief-desire-intention" model of human psychology.

Intuitively, this might sound like a (if not the only) plausible viewpoint to us half a century after the rise of cognitivism, but it was not so appealing less than a hundred years ago, when behaviorism sanctioned only those theories of psychology that dealt with observable behaviors and rejected as unscientific those that invoked "nonobservable" mental processes. The shift of focus from directly observable behavior to mental phenomena that are not directly observable marks a serious change of attitude that has much to do with the emergence of digital computers and theories thereof. Pylyshyn articulates this link as follows:

What makes it possible for humans . . . to act on the basis of representations is that they instantiate such representations physically as cognitive codes and that their behavior is a causal consequence of operations carried out on these codes. Since this is precisely what computers do, [it] amounts to a claim that cognition *is* a type of computation. (1984: xiii)

Although it is unclear what is meant by "cognitive codes" in this passage, the basic idea is that the brain, like the computer, has distinct classes of physical states that *cause* behaviors that are meaningfully distinct. In this case, for instance, there is a physical state of your brain that represents your belief in the boringness of Dullsburg, there is another physical state that represents the excitement of Joyville. These states are not only physically distinct, they can cause distinct behaviors such as interest in one town and repulsion for another. In other words, physically distinct states can give rise to behaviors that are semantically distinct – that is, behaviors that bear different relations to the outside world. Since this physically driven and semantically distinct behavior is roughly what computers also manifest, the argument goes, then cognition is a type of computation.

On the basis of intuitions such as this, computers have acquired a central role in cognitive theorizing – not merely as tools and instruments for studying human behavior, but also, and more importantly, as *instantiations* of such behavior. Pylyshyn (1984: 74–75) highlights the role of the computer implementation of psychological theories in three major respects: the representation of cognitive states in terms of symbolic expressions that can be interpreted as describing aspects of the outside world; the representation of rules that apply to these symbols; and the mapping of this system of symbols and rules onto causal physical laws so as to preserve a coherent semantic relationship between the symbols and the outside world. These principles found explicit realization in some of the earliest models of AI, such as the General Problem Solver (Newell and Simon 1961).

INTELLIGENCE AS PROBLEM SOLVING

The idea of an *agent* trying to change its internal *state* in order to come up with a sequence of *actions* as a possible *solution to a problem* or as a means to achieve a *goal* is deeply rooted in traditional AI and in its view of the nature of intelligence. According to this view, an intelligent agent "moves" in a space of problems ("problem space") of varying difficulties and types that, most often, also makes the tools for solving those problems available, and the task of the agent is to discover those tools and to figure out the least costly or most efficient way to achieve its preset goals. In chess, for example, the problem is to find the best next move, and the tools are the legal moves of the game. This picture, as we shall see in the next chapter, accurately portrays a chess-playing machine whose preset, given goal is to win a game – or more precisely, to put the opponent's king in a checkmate position on the (virtual) board – by taking a finite number of discrete steps according to prescribed rules. The question is, does this picture also accurately portray how human beings behave and conduct their lives in real situations? In other words, do we also live in a world of problems where our task is to follow prescribed rules that would lead us to the solution of those problems (provided that we are intelligent enough)?

There are people who definitely answer yes to the last question. The philosopher Karl Popper, for instance, argued that all life situations can be framed as problem-solving activities. (A collection of his essays is entitled *All Life Is Problem-Solving*.) In AI, this view takes on various forms: logic systems, rational agents, general problem solvers, and so on, whose common premise is that search plays a central role in intelligent behavior. For the proponents of this view, search is not only a technique and method; it is the royal road to intelligence. An influential version of this view is the *physical symbol system hypothesis* proposed by AI pioneers Allen Newell and Herbert Simon (1976).

Taking AI as an empirical science, Newell and Simon (1976) seek to devise for it "laws of qualitative structure" on a par with the cell doctrine in biology, plate tectonics in geology, atomism in physical chemistry, and so forth. The physical symbol system hypothesis, according to these authors, is such a law. Symbols are, in their view, physical patterns (neural activity in the brain or electrical pulses in a computer), and many interrelated symbols taken together constitute a *symbol structure*; a physical symbol system is, therefore, "a machine that produces through time an evolving collection of symbol structures." The thesis is that a machine like this (whether a human being or a digital computer) "has the necessary and sufficient conditions for general intelligent action" (p. 116). How so?

To explain how a physical symbols system can be intelligent, Newell and Simon propose a second qualitative law, to be discussed next.

Heuristic-Search Hypothesis

The solutions to problems are represented as symbol structures. A physical symbol system exercises its intelligence in problem solving by search – that is, by generating and progressively modifying symbol structures until it produces a solution structure. (Newell and Simon 1976: 120)

In this way, Newell and Simon assigned search a central role that has been accepted in much of AI practice ever since. They themselves actually devised and built many models on this principle, one of the most influential of which was the General Problem Solver (GPS). Taking, among other things, chess as a typical example, GPS dealt exclusively with "objects" and "operators" that transform them. Proving mathematical theorems, for instance, is described as the transformation of axioms or theorems (objects) into other theorems using rules of inference (operators) (Newell, Shaw, and Simon 1960: 258). Similarly, the behavior of experimental subjects in solving abstract problems (usually in well-defined domains) is interpreted in identical terms and simulated on the computer.

Although this principled way of studying human thought offered certain advances with respect to previous methods of doing psychology, its the-world-in-the-mind character is evident on different dimensions: from the characterization of problems in an abstract mental space to the search for solutions in the same space (Agre 1997a: 54–56). This particular view of mind dominated AI for more than three decades and, as I will show in the following chapters, provides the backdrop against which much of later development in the field can be understood. This survey of modern Western intellectual history partly explains the dominance of this view. However, as we see next, the social, cultural, and institutional milieu in which AI is practiced has put its own stamp on the character of the field as well.

THE SOCIAL, CULTURAL, AND INSTITUTIONAL BACKGROUND

Technological systems are social constructions (Bijker, Hughes, and Pinch 1997). Computer technologies are social not only because of their ubiquitous use but also because society at large has become their defining locus (Smith forthcoming (a), Introduction: 25): that is, what phenomena and artifacts should be included in the realm of computing and computers is decided out-side academia, and "some of the most imaginative computer science research is being produced by artists, set designers, and movie producers, not just by technicians and people with PhDs" (ibid.). Similar observations can be made about AI as a social phenomenon, as a brief look at the popular culture would indicate.

The Popular Culture

For better or worse, AI has come to occupy a special place within the popu-lar culture, in ways that other computer-related areas have not. One of the reasons for this fascination is, of course, that people sense that the issues raised by AI are directly related to their self-image as human beings (see the Prologue). The flip side of this is that those issues are commonly considered fair game for lay philosophizing (Crevier 1993: 7). It is thus that AI finds a host of casual commentators among reporters, advertisers, moviemakers, and the general public – something that is not possible in physics, for example (although to some extent it happens nonetheless).

Each group of such commentators engages in discourses about comput-ers that are specific to their particular goals, strategies, and roles. Politicians, for instance, usually talk about computers as vehicles of progress and social well-being (the extensive discussion by high officials of the U.S. administration in the early 1990's of the so-called *information superhighway* was a prominent example). Businesspeople, Wall Street consultants, and the vendors of computer technology, on the other hand, typically highlight the impact of computer-related technologies (e.g., expert systems and "smart" products of all sorts) on efficiency and productivity. To advance their agenda, all of these groups usually depend on the claims of the AI community about the outcomes of their research (of the kind we will study in the following chapters). Although the relation between the research community and the outside commentators might often be indirect and mediated, its significance can hardly be overestimated. In fact, as Edwards (1996: Preface) has suggested, film and fiction have played a crucial role in dramatizing the goals of AI and in creating a connection in the popular culture between computational views of mind and what he calls the "closed world" of Cold War military strategies in the United States. Journalists, too, have played a major role in communicating AI claims to the public, partly because of their professional enthusiasm for provocative topics, but also because AI projects and ideas, as opposed to more esoteric disciplines such as theoretical physics, can be explained "in words understandable to anyone" (Crevier 1993: 7).

The Culture of AI

Popular culture and its engagement with AI have contributed much to the development of the discipline (Bloomfield 1987: 73). The high esteem enjoyed by AI practitioners as experts in a technical field, the jumping on the AI bandwagon by researchers from other disciplines, the strong popular following for work in AI, and the interest of artists, businesspeople, journalists, military planners, policy makers, and so on – all have shaped the embedding circumstances of the AI culture during its first three decades. Here I want to discuss the culture of AI as manifested in the views and social bonds of its circle of practitioners. The AI community is embedded in a broad cultural context that is partly continuous with other cultures and partly distinct from them. Significant among the broader context are the cultures of engineers and entrepreneurs, and the most recent example is the so-called hacker culture of computer enthusiasts.

The Engineering Culture: Technological Determinism
Although engineering is old as a profession, the engineering community as a distinct social group, as we know it today, is a rather new phenomenon.[6]

In the United States, for instance, the number of engineers grew from about one hundred in 1870 to forty-three hundred in 1914 (Noble 1977). This drastic increase was accompanied by a number of significant social and institutional changes – most notably, the separation between the conception and the execution of work, the automation of production, and the standardization of engineering practices. This quantitative change also was accompanied by what David Noble calls a "Darwinian view of technological development," which assumes that "the flow of creative invention passes progressively through three successive filters, each of which further guarantees that only the 'best' alternatives survive":

- an objective technical filter that selects the most scientifically sound solution to a given problem.
- the pecuniary rationality of the hard-nosed businessperson, who selects the most practical and most economical solutions.
- the self-correcting mechanism of the market that ensures that only the best innovations survive. (1984: 144–45).

Engineers, who play a major role in at least the first two stages, are usually among the believers and advocates of this view. As such, the typical engineer's self-image is one of "an objective referee" who purports to use the rigorous tools of mathematics to seek solutions for problems defined by some authority (Agre and Schuler 1997). This worldview is, therefore, attended by a strong professional sense of engineering practice as the creation of order from social chaos, and of engineers as the benefactors of society as a whole. It is also accompanied by a strong belief in a number of strict binary oppositions: order versus chaos, reason versus emotion, mathematics versus language, technology versus society (Noble 1984: 41; Agre and Schuler 1997).

Computer professionals, by and large, share the ideological outlook of engineers, with an enhanced view of technological development as "autonomous and uncontrollable when viewed from any given individual's perspective – something to be lived by rather than collectively chosen" (Agre and Schuler 1997). This sense of technological determinism can be explained by the magnitude, complexity, and relentlessly changing character of the computer industry, which puts the typical professional under constant pressure to catch up, inducing a strong perception of technology as the dominant actor (ibid.).

One outcome of this deterministic outlook is what Kling (1980, 1997) calls "utopian" and "dystopian" views of computer technology. Utopians, according to Kling, "enchant us with images of new technologies that offer exciting possibilities of manipulating large amounts of information rapidly with little effort, to enhance control, to create insights, to search for information, and to facilitate cooperative work between people" (1997: 41). Terms like "virtual," "smart," and "intelligent," Kling points out, are often sprinkled through these accounts and help give them a buoyant image (ibid.). Dystopians, by contrast, often portray a darker social vision in which any likely form of computerization will amplify human misery.

AI provides fertile ground for the proliferation of utopian and dystopian views, numerous traces and examples of which we will see throughout this survey.

The Entrepreneurial Culture: Commercialism

Closely related to the engineering outlook is the entrepreneurial perspective, which is quite common, especially among the more renowned of computer and AI professionals, and even more especially in the United States, where, according to Winner (1986), the equivalence of abundance and freedom is taken for granted in the popular culture.[7] The so-called Silicon Valley style of entrepreneurial spirit is based on the idea that computer entrepreneurs "make money out of ideas" either selling their ideas to venture capitalists or, if they have a big enough name, establishing their own business. "It is a culture where the amount of money to be made, and the speed at which the money is made, are the supreme values" (Castells 2001: 55–60; also 1996: 53–60).

Examples of money-making from ideas were abundant during the so-called dot-com bubble of the 1990s and its subsequent bursting, for which computer enthusiasts took both much credit and blame. The Silicon Valley value system is clearly manifested in AI, where a considerable number of the pioneers and big names are known to pursue a business life in parallel with, and sometimes directly linked to, their research and academic work (see the Epilogue). What justifies this attitude is the strong self-image of the entrepreneur as a generator of creative power and social well-being, an image that is especially in tune with the broader culture in the United States (and, as we shall see, partly explains the differences in the practice of AI between the United States and Europe). Its adverse implication, however, is the pervasive image of "greedy businessmen"[8] (Athanasiou 1985: 14), on the one hand, and the "intellectual hubris of AI," on the other, both of which have been the subject of commentary (Turkle 1984: 269). Whether the motivation is personal profit or institutional advantage, the intricate dynamics of entrepreneurial behavior is something that one should keep in mind when looking for sources of hype in a high-technology pursuit such as AI.

The Hacker Culture: Technocracy

While the engineering and entrepreneurial subcultures were direct or indirect contributions of professional lineages, the most distinctive feature of the computer profession is what has come to be known as "hacker culture" – the domain of those individuals variously characterized, with or without justification, as "compulsive programmers" (Weizenbaum 1976), or as "socially gauche to the point of being unworldly" and "adolescent mechanical geniuses capable of improvising brilliantly out of scraps and patches for the sheer love of solving sweet problems" (Roszak 1994: 137–38), or as "programmer-virtuosos who [are] interested in taking large, complex computer systems and pushing them to their limits" (Turkle 1995: 31). It is, indeed, hard to find a single commonly accepted characterization of the hacker culture, especially in light of the changes brought about by the Internet and the so-called virtual communities formed around it, of which hacker groups are a prime example (Castells 2001: 46–49).

The extensive networking of computers that picked up the pace in the 1990s, especially on the Internet, has had a great influence on the way computers are used. To many people today, being at a computer is synonymous with being connected to the Internet (Wellman 2001: 2031). Taking these developments into account, Castells considers the central aspects of the hacker culture to be technomeritocracy (which places much value on technical skill and knowledge), an obsession with autonomy and freedom (to create, appropriate, and redistribute knowledge), and a "gift culture" – that is, a culture that works on the basis of reciprocity in sharing computer code, but also, paradoxically, promotes commercialization.

Although the AI community could not have remained detached from these developments, work in AI still consists, by and large, of intensive programming in a rather isolated way. AI people are more of traditional hackers who tend to work alone. This is not to say that such work does not involve all kinds of institutional activities that are typically part and parcel of any technoscientific research (Latour 1987). The next discussion highlights some aspect of such activities.

The Institutional Milieu

> [The] fine fit between new theories and devices and the requirements of established power [is] hardly fortuitous.
>
> – David Noble (1984)

No account of scientific practice can be complete without taking note of the material resources that support it and the kinds of power relations that they incur. As David Noble (1984) has argued, the ability of scientists and engineers to theorize, invent, and experiment derives in large part from the power of their patrons. In the United States, where the government is the major source of funding for academic research, the Defense Department, especially DARPA (Defense Advanced Research Program Agency), has played a decisive role in the development of computer technologies and AI (Noble 1984: 55–56; Castells 1996: 60; Edwards 1996). Edwards portrays this relationship as part of a wider historical context, where the strategic plans of the Defense Department for a global command-and-control system have converged with the tools, metaphors, and theories of computers and of AI.

The generous support of the military at many stages during the history of AI is sometimes described in mythic proportions. McCorduck summarizes the philosophy of the Rand Corporation: "Here's a bag of money, go off and spend it in the best interests of the Air Force" (1979: 117). This, as Agre (1997b) has pointed out, has typically been intended to leave a large degree of latitude in research objectives and methods. Even if this were true in certain periods, the close tie between the military and AI, far from being pervasive and steady, was severely reduced at times, mainly because of the frequent failure of AI to deliver on its promises, about which we will have much to say in the remainder of this work.

Altogether, the implications of military ties for the overall direction of development in AI should not be underestimated. In fact, one can discern a close parallel between the development of military strategies after World War II and the shift of theoretical focus in AI from the centrally controlled, modularized symbolic systems of the 1950s through the 1970s, through the distributed connectionist networks of the 1980s and the 1990s, to the more recent Internet-based warfare and humanoid robots that are meant to act and look like human beings. To be sure, the parallels are far more complex than a unidirectional influence, let alone a simple cause–effect relationship, but they certainly attest to a confluence of interests, motivations, theories, technologies, and military strategies that have resonated with each other in intricate ways. In particular, they should serve as a reminder that the state, no less than the innovative entrepreneur in the garage, was a major contributor to the development of computer technology and AI (Castells 1996: 60; Edwards 1996). Based on considerations such as these, Kling and Iacono (1995) described AI as a computerization movement similar in character to office automation, personal computing, networking, and so on. We will examine the implications of this view of AI in more detail in the Epilogue.

WEAVING THINGS TOGETHER

> It is not so much our judgments as it is our prejudices that constitute
> our being. . . . Prejudices are biases of our openness to the world. They are
> simply conditions whereby we experience something – whereby what we
> encounter says something to us.
>
> – Hans G. Gadamer (1976)

The confluence of these intellectual, cultural, and material aspects provides
the background for understanding the history and practices of AI. Keeping
this background in mind throughout our survey will help us to understand
many aspects of AI that can hardly be explained otherwise. In particular, it
will shed light on those assumptions, convictions, and biases that are taken
for granted within the field, without explicit attention or acknowledgment.

The Fabric of AI

To sum up what we have discussed so far, I would like here to list the above
set of influences and their most common manifestations in AI.[9] I find the
word "thread" appropriate for the situation, based on the metaphor of AI as
a fabric made of various strands of ideas, cultures, and institutions (Latour
1999: 80, 106–07).

The Mentalist Thread
- giving explanatory priority to internal mental processes, as opposed to
  focusing on external behavior.
- taking the mind as a mirror of the world, and mental representations as
  surrogates of outside objects, properties, and events.
- taking perception as a kind of inverse optics: working backward from sense
  impressions to infer the outside phenomena that might have produced
  them (Hurlbert and Poggio 1988; see Agre 2002).
- taking actions as executions of mental constructs (plans).

The Formalist Thread
- separating form from meaning (syntax from semantics) and seeking to
  align them by some type of mapping (Fodor 1980).
- separating the mind from the body but seeking to bridge them by invoking
  "transducers" (Pylyshyn 1984).[10]

The Computationalist Thread
- a tendency to inscribe one's concepts and categories onto an artifact and
  then to read those same concepts back off the artifact, as if they were
  inherent in it.

- the idea that computer implementation is the best, if not the only, way of understanding human cognition, and that those aspects of human behavior that cannot be encoded in present-day computers are insignificant.

Professional Threads
- the engineer's view of the world as disorderly and of the human role as imposing order on it.
- the engineer's self-image as the implementer of a deterministic course of technological development.
- the entrepreneur's disposition toward money as the ultimate value and criterion of success.
- the hacker's view of computer and technical work as the most valued human activity.

Institutional Threads
- the pressure of seeking funding resources and its consequences in terms of research goals and claims.
- the implications of close ties with the military in terms of research priorities, metaphors, and frameworks of thought.

The idea behind this list is not to make up quick-and-easy labels to be attached to views and ideas, nor is it to present these threads as causes of prevalent problems faced in technical work. On the contrary, not only are such simplifications and generalizations wrong, they are impossible to make in any reasonable fashion. Each approach and project has its own unique path of development that can be discovered only through a close examination of conceptual and technical details. This will be our tack in the current writing.

Colors of Criticism

To put things on equal footing, a similar distanced scrutiny of some of the common critiques of AI is also needed. While some critiques raise justified points, others may derive from misunderstandings, prejudices, and flaws in grasping technologies in general and AI in particular. Let me thus mention the most common forms that such criticisms take.

The Skeptical Critique
- This involves adopting a business-as-usual attitude, and taking computers as just another technology that does not differ significantly from technologies of the past: "Computer romanticism is the latest version of the nineteenth and twentieth-century faith ... that has always expected to

generate freedom, democracy, and justice through sheer material abundance" (Winner 1986: 108).

The Exclusionist Critique

- This is a belief in the special place of the human species in the universe, based on the premise that computers are mere machines, and following a stereotyped argument – namely, that human intelligence is, or requires, X (intentions, emotions, social life, biology) and that computers lack X because they are mere machines, mechanisms, and so on (Searle 1980).

The Neo-Luddite Critique

- This is a general discontent with technology and its implications for human society (Roszak 1994).

With this background in mind, our task in the coming chapters would be to steer clear from utopian and dystopian views that pervade much of the discourse about AI, and to achieve a realistic understanding based on the close empirical study of particular AI systems.

2 Deep Blue: Supercomputing AI

Hobbes' Numerical Dream

Reasoning is reckoning.

– Thomas Hobbes

C hess might well be the most rigorous form of human thinking – the jewel in the crown of thought. Yet we have relinquished this most prized jewel to our own creation, the computing machine. This, of course, did not happen easily. It took more than four decades of intense effort. But in May 1997, in the second match between Garry Kasparov and Deep Blue, it finally took place.

This event was seen as a turning point not only in the history of chess but also, and more importantly, in the history of the relation between humans and machines. Various speculations about this event's implications have been put forth, which we briefly examine in this chapter, specifically in regard to the capabilities of the brute-force methods of AI. The Kasparov–Deep Blue match, however, could also be viewed as a scientific event. Deep Blue was, in a serious way, an *experiment* in AI and cognitive science. As such, it brings to light interesting facets of scientific practice that might not be easily discernible in paradigmatic "laboratory" experiments – for example, the role of metaphors in scientific thinking, the relationship between theory and practice in science, and the significance of the cultural and material conditions on the outcome of science.

To start out, I will discuss the standard techniques of computer chess and some aspects of human chess. Then taking chess as the prime example, I address the central questions, highlighting some of the differences in opinion among different commentators. At the end, I turn to the broader implications mentioned earlier.

39

BACKGROUND: HUMANS VERSUS MACHINES

I don't know how we can exist knowing that there exists something mentally
stronger than us.
                    – Garry Kasparov, on the eve of his match with Deep Thought

In August 1996, after a long series of preparatory steps, the chess-playing
program Deep Blue confronted Garry Kasparov in a six-game regulated and
timed match under the auspices of the International Computer Chess Association in Philadelphia. Deep Blue was the last link in a chain of programs
that started as a graduate-student project at Carnegie-Mellon University in
1985 and ended as a major project at International Business Machines (IBM).
Ironically, 1985 was also the year Kasparov became the undisputed chess
champion of the world.

IBM had allocated a prize fund of $500,000, to be split between the winner
(80 percent) and the loser (20 percent). However, having decisively defeated
many other computer chess programs during the previous ten years[1] and,
especially, having beaten Deep Thought – Deep Blue's immediate predecessor – in October 1989, Kasparov initially preferred a winner-take-all arrangement for the prize.

The match took place over eight days in a highly professional setting (in
terms of lighting, temperature, type of board and pieces,[2] silence, audience,
commentators, etc.), with the obvious twist that a human proxy made the
moves decided by Deep Blue on the physical board. The match also received
wide media coverage. *Newsweek* described Kasparov as "the brain's last stand"
and David Levy, a former chess master from Britain and a skeptic about computer chess programs, declared he would jump off a bridge if the computer
garnered a single point. After his victory, Kasparov was hailed as the savior
of the human race and of its dignity.

Kasparov won the match by a score of 4 to 2, but the outcome was partly
attributed to unfavorable circumstances for Deep Blue. Because of time constraints, among other things, the system that entered the contest was actually a
scaled-down version of what IBM had originally planned. The scaling-down
was both in the number of processors – 192 as opposed to 1,024 – and in
their speed. It was estimated that Deep Blue would have been more powerful
by a factor of ten (a phrase of dubious precision) if the target system had
been implemented. But even this "small" version was enough for Kasparov
to exclaim, "Here, for the first time, we are seeing something intelligent." But
was this really intelligence?

The Beginning or the End?

The question of Deep Blue's intelligence was seriously posed during the rematch that took place nine months later, in May 1997. This time Kasparov, having won the first game and lost the second, reached three consecutive draws with Deep Blue. The outcome of the match thus hinged on the sixth and final game. On May 11, in a shocking finale that lasted barely more than an hour, World Champion Garry Kasparov resigned after only nineteen moves, handing a historic match victory to Deep Blue. The Deep Blue development team took home the $700,000 first prize, while Kasparov received $400,000. The *New York Times* proclaimed, "IBM chess machine beats humanity's champ."[3]

Kasparov, who afterward attributed the defeat to his poor frame of mind entering the game, challenged Deep Blue to a new confrontation: "I think the competition has just started. This is just the beginning." Kasparov's challenge was, however, turned down by IBM, for reasons allegedly having to do with its ambivalence toward AI (Crevier 1993: 58, 221).[4] The leader of the Deep Blue development team merely pointed out that there was more to Deep Blue's battle with Garry Kasparov than a game of chess. "This will benefit everyone – from the audience to school children, to businesses everywhere, even to Garry Kasparov." What for Kasparov was the beginning was the end for IBM.

Style or Brute Force?

The IBM team attributed their success to three changes in their machine: more power, more chess knowledge, and the possibility of changing various parameters between successive games. These changes made it possible for Deep Blue to search twice as many positions per second as the year before, and to do this with enhanced chess knowledge. It could now examine two hundred million chess positions per second and could search to depths of fourteen plies (a ply being a single move by a single player).

On the other hand, according to chess experts, Kasparov had erred in not studying the games played the previous year. Experts pointed out that whereas all the games he had ever played were accessible to the Deep Blue team, he was essentially in the dark about Deep Blue. According to international grandmaster Yasser Seirawan, Kasparov had two options: to play like Kasparov or to play like "Mr. Anti–Deep Blue." For the human player, doing the former runs the risk of playing to the strengths of the machine, while doing the latter risks disorientation. Humans play more weakly in unfamiliar situations, and although they may often find their way around better than machines, machines can compensate for that with brute force. Kasparov had presumably chosen to play as Mr. Anti–Deep Blue. Unfortunately, as a result of all this, Seirawan speculates, we were never able to see the fabulous calculating abilities of Deep Blue. Not once did we see a spectacular example of brute force producing a solution that differed significantly from that suggested by intuition. Put differently, Seirawan seems to suggest, Deep Blue played chess like a human, taking us to the core question of this chapter.

This discussion, which relates but a small sample of the reactions to the Kasparov–Deep Blue match, shows how different people – from Kasparov and IBM's team leader to chess experts and public media – talked about the event. Although this event was not directly associated with AI (see note 4), people in AI also have taken it seriously from their own perspective. The central issue for them is whether computers can perform other tasks, normally thought of as solely human, in a way that does not "differ significantly from that suggested by intuition." We shall see that a clear answer to this question is not easily found. Judgments vary drastically, and to see how, we need to look at some of the basic premises of AI.

COMPUTER CHESS: AN OVERVIEW

> But are these new marvels of mankind, characterized by megabytes and megahertz, really playing chess?
>> Monroe Newborn, Former President of the International Computer Chess Association

With the advent of computers in the 1950s, chess became one of the first domains in which their capabilities could be tested. The interest in chess and other similar games on the part of computer scientists derives from various considerations, including their "formal" character – roughly, the discreteness and determinateness of the moves and pieces (Haugeland 1981). This jibes with the early AI notion of thinking as a purely mental activity, of planning in the head and executing in the outside world, and of problem solving as search in a problem space (see Chapter 1; cf. Agre 1997a: 55). In the case of chess, this interest is further enhanced by its manageable complexity and by a decomposability that allows techniques of parallel computing to be brought to bear.

Thus, soon after the appearance of von Neumann computers, Claude Shannon (1950) published a paper entitled "Programming a Computer for Playing Chess," and in 1953 Alan Turing proposed a chess-playing program

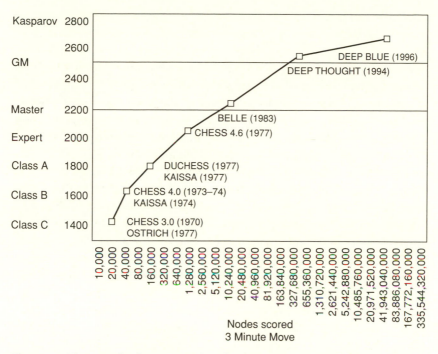

Figure 2.1. The growth of computer-chess level as a function of the size of the tree searched during a three-minute move (from Newborn 1997, with permission).

and hand-simulated it. The first running chess programs appeared in the late 1950s. Early optimism was buoyed by modest success. The challenge, however, proved to be much greater than original estimates had it. It is easy to locate the source of the optimism: a mere quantitative extrapolation of the prevailing trend at every point, even at the very outset (as plotted by Newborn; see Figure 2.1).

Competing Metaphors: Computers as Birds, Race Cars, and Fruit Flies

If the trends indicated in Figure 2.1 are reliable, the obvious conclusion is that computers will sooner or later pass master levels of chess performance. Such reasoning, which underwrote the optimistic view of computer chess, is a recurrent pattern in AI.

Kasparov had another kind of optimism; he maintained, "the best humans will improve when the day comes that a computer really challenges them" (Newborn 1997: 175). Newborn compares this viewpoint to that of birds who, for quite a while, "wore smiles on their fine feathered faces, watching mankind's efforts to fly."[5] Even after observing the first airplanes sharing their ultraterrestrial space, he says, "they remained in a state of denial, contending that although mankind was making some progress, what they were watching couldn't be called flying." Despite its appeal, Newborn admits, the metaphor does not carry over to the new domain in all respects. Although building flying machines was a goal unto itself, computers initially were programmed to play chess in order to understand how the human mind works – how it thinks, how it solves difficult problems, what intelligence is all about, how learning occurs. The corollary, of course, was that once these processes were understood, they could be replicated on a computer (ibid., 2).

It is this observation that prompts Newborn to say that chess serves the same purpose for AI scientists as fruit flies do for geneticists, or that it may serve the computer industry as auto racing has served the auto industry: "[M]any of the advances in the auto world were first tried on racing models and then after refinement incorporated into commercial vehicles."

These three metaphors – birds, racecars, and fruit flies – actually convey different views of AI, and, consequently, have different implications. While the racecar metaphor is accurate for engineering purposes, for instance, the analogy between chess and fruit flies would hold only if a number of other assumptions were in place – for example, if chess-playing were as typical an example of human thought processes as fruit flies are of genetic hereditary processes – or, to use Newborn's own expression, if we believed that computers are "really playing chess." In short, these metaphors highlight different aspects of AI practice.

Intelligence as Search in a Problem Space

Search is one of the most basic and common techniques in AI. Its origin is in computer science, where search algorithms are the bread and butter of the field – they range from searching for a list item, a table entry, or an alphanumeric string in a database, to searching for a word in a dictionary, a book in a digital library, or the maximum, minimum, or median in a set of numerical data. A myriad of data structures and clever techniques have been devised by computer scientists to make efficient search possible.

The most familiar data structure is a tree, where the data items are put together like branches splitting off of other branches. There are two very basic tree-search methods in such a structure. In *breadth-first search*, one first looks at all items at the same depth – that is, at the same distance from the root. In *depth-first search*, by contrast, one follows a branch all the way down to the leaves before going back to the root to begin a new path.[6] However, many variations and combinations of these methods have been proposed because each method has some drawbacks – mainly inefficiency or large memory requirement. One of the more important variations is *iterative deepening*, a depth-first search in which the depth by which branches are visited is increased in a stepwise, iterative manner – first all leaves at depth one from the root, during the second iteration all those at depth two, and so on. In this way, the nodes are visited in the same order as in a breadth-first search, except that some are visited multiple times. In return for this redundancy, this method is "complete" – that is, it is guaranteed to find the best choice (according to some evaluation function). The other advantage is that lower-depth solutions, if they exist, will be detected early on.

These search methods are *uninformed*, or blind, in that every branch or leaf has an equal chance of being looked at, irrespective of its promise. AI is, however, more interested in *informed* search methods, in which branches are explored to different levels of detail on the basis of an "educated guess" about their promise of success. As we shall see shortly, an informed version of iterative-deepening search is the mainstay of computer chess of the brute-force variety. What makes this variety of computer chess attractive is its potential for parallel processing, (partially credited by IBM's team leader for Deep Blue's success).

The conception of a chess game as a tree structure also makes it possible to break up the search space into separate parts (corresponding to the branches of the tree), each one of which can be evaluated by a separate processor. Although this is very different from the types of parallel processing attributed to the human brain (see Chapter 5), it is a technique that works well enough. A psychologically realistic model, by contrast, will not depend so heavily on search methods. The Dutch psychologist de Groot, for instance, showed that experts, unlike novices, perceive the chessboard not as an arrangement of individual pieces but in terms of groups or *chunks*. That there is a strong perceptual dimension to human chess-playing is also shown in the mistakes that are committed by human players but not by computers – for example, paying too much attention to the center of the board at the expense of the periphery (Newborn 1997: 85).

These considerations, in fact, gave rise to a project designed in the 1970s at Carnegie-Mellon University by Hans Berliner, a computer scientist and top-notch chess-player himself – a project that never achieved spectacular success in terms of victories, and that eventually petered out, leaving the domain wide open to its brute-force competitors. The tension in computer chess between brute-force methods and those that are psychologically more plausible but technically more challenging directly speaks to the main thesis of this writing. As we shall see again and again, the prevalence of brute-force methods is an example of a widespread trend in AI that would shape the direction of development of the field in favor of short-term outcomes. The central techniques of computer chess-playing that are discussed next, therefore, belong solely to the brute-force variety.

Common Techniques in Computer Chess

Search is the most basic technique used in computer chess, but it is not the only one. There are other methods that vary not only in their degree of emphasis on search but also in their dependence on state-of-the-art technology. All methods, however, share the following features:

- conception of the whole game as a *tree structure*, each alternate level of which represents the possible moves by a particular player (see Appendix A);
- division of the game into three main *phases*: opening, middlegame, and endgame (the number of possibilities explodes during the middlegame, and most of the effort in computer chess is focused on this stage);
- use of a *search method* to enumerate all legal moves at any given point in the game, and of a *pruning algorithm* to eliminate some of the (unpromising) moves early on;
- use of a *scoring function* (also known as "static evaluation") as a quick-and-dirty measure of the desirability of a position from the point of view of one of the players.

All of these were among the features of the very first chess program developed by Claude Shannon in 1950, and they are still present in almost any chess program today. Shannon proposed two search methods – one with a fixed depth and one with variable depth. The second method uses the notion of *quiescence*, or *stability*, to determine whether or not a search path shows promise for further exploration. At any point during the game, each player is faced with the question, "Given the present situation, what is the best thing that can be done with it?" What is, in other words, the "best" move? Part of the answer is to obtain an estimate of the desirability of a board situation by *static evaluation*.

For this purpose, Shannon introduced the notion of a scoring function – namely, a function that assigns a numerical value to a board situation according to a number of easily discernable (and, hence, easily computable) features. Shannon proposed three such features:

- *material*: assigns values to pieces as follows: queen $= 9$, rook $= 5$, bishop $= 3$, knight $= 3$, pawn $= 1$ and king $= 200$ (to make sure it is never traded off with any other piece);

- *pawn formation*: assigns a penalty of 0.5 for each doubled or isolated pawn – that is, for a pawn that is either blocked by another one or left useless on the board without any obvious role;
- *mobility*: assigns 0.1 for every different move available to the player in a given position.[7]

The crux of brute-force computer chess involves the combination of such a simple and shallow scoring function with what is called "backup." This notion allows static evaluation, which does not explicitly look ahead into the branching tree at all, to be the tool by which a deep look-ahead can be achieved. The idea is very simple, all coming from the fact that the answer to the central question – "What is the best move for me?" – is, by definition, that move that would leave one's opponent in the toughest situation.[8] At the same time, however, the answer depends on what your opponent does in the next move, which, in turn, depends on what you do afterward, and so on. Thus, in order to select the next move, you should try to imagine all possible moves and pretend, for each one, that you have made the move, and then evaluate the board from the point of view of the opponent. The opponent would use the same strategy. Both players, in other words, look ahead by putting themselves in the opponent's shoes for a few cycles in the future. This recursive process, obviously, cannot go on forever, and has to "bottom out" at some point; and it does so by using the *static* evaluation provided by the scoring function instead of *look-ahead* evaluation. In the case of human chess-players, as we shall see, explicit deep look-ahead of this sort does not play a major role. It is the strongest suit for machines, however, and it is here that backup comes into play.

Given enough computational power and speed, the rather simple and elegant algorithm that implements the above idea – referred to as *minimax* in AI literature – works amazingly well in most circumstances. For efficiency, it is further embellished with one or more "pruning" methods (see Appendix A). Other search enhancement techniques include: *transposition tables*, the main idea of which is to store, for later use, information about each state or position as it is reached and evaluated; *optimization techniques*, where, for instance, the value assigned to a piece, or to a position, can be adjusted by the program as it plays different games and gains experience; *the method of analogies*, based on the idea of the similarity between two positions (according to some crude fixed similarity criteria); *opening and endgame databases*, useful because the number of possibilities in the opening and endgame stages is relatively small.

Once software techniques have been thoroughly explored and exploited, the obvious next step is to look at hardware. Two main possibilities arise in this realm: the development of special-purpose hardware and the use of many processors at the same time. Both of these strategies are motivated by the idea that speed is a crucial component of intelligence. For decades, this observation has motivated a quest for achieving ever more efficient performance, and this holds true not only in computer chess but also elsewhere in AI. The idea of multiple processors, on the other hand, has turned out to work effectively only in special domains such as chess. For technical reasons that are not germane to our study, in other domains the ideal of attaining an N-fold speedup when using N processors is never reached. Problems of communication, coherence, consistency, and synchronization among processors are some of the main reasons (Hennessy and Patterson 1996). However, if the task is broken down in an optimal way, a good deal of improvement is attainable. Deep Blue, for instance, employed 192 processors in its 1996 match against Kasparov.

Brute Force: The Key to the Success of Computer Chess

The sketchy overview provided here reveals that many things have contributed to the continuous improvement of computer chess, which culminated in the victory of Deep Blue: expert chess knowledge, programming skill, and hardware technology, together with the organizational and financial support of institutions such as universities, IBM, and the International Computer Chess Association. Segregating the contribution of each of these is not only infeasible, it is also undesirable because it would lead to a noncontextual analysis that runs against the grain of the premises of this essay. However, for the purposes of this chapter, I am going to start with the intellectual aspects. This, as we shall see, will enable us to draw certain substantive conclusions from the chess domain, especially with regard to the idea of generalizing it to other areas of human activity. This is important in light of the fact that Deep Blue's victory has motivated many other speculations about the future of relations between humans and machines.

The first conclusion has to do with the chess knowledge built into Deep Blue (calling it "knowledge" may not be completely justified, but I will use it as a shorthand). The algorithmic skills and strategic knowledge of programmers have contributed greatly to the impressive current status of computer chess. Indeed, the style of play manifested by specific chess programs is so distinctive that one could comfortably speak of chess programs carrying the signatures of their creators (Newborn 1997: 281).[9] The constitution of IBM's Deep Blue team, which included a former grandmaster, an electrical engineer, a software engineer, and a programmer (who was also an expert player), reveals the emphasis placed on chess skill and informed methods of playing. This implies, among other things, that much of Deep Blue's chess skill could be described as "inherited" from its creators (more on this later).

Despite different machines' styles, however, the fact is that computers beat human beings not because of a better or stronger style; they win primarily because of the raw speed provided by hardware (Deep Blue was developed by IBM, after all, not by Microsoft). The importance of raw hardware speed is best demonstrated by looking at the history of computer chess. As history shows, despite occasional victories, computers offered little promise in the chess world until hardware was speeded up considerably (for an insider's view, see Newborn 1997). Deep Thought (version 0.02) was the first chess program to defeat a grandmaster in a regulation match, and it did so mostly because of its sophisticated custom-tailored hardware. The same could be said with even more cause about Deep Blue (remember that the enhancements to Deep Blue between the first match and the rematch, which improved its performance, were largely hardware related). In short, computers like Deep Blue can defeat human masters thanks primarily to their computational power. Brute force is the key to present-day computers' chess-playing capabilities.

To stop at this point, however, is to leave untold the other half of the story – that is, the part that deals with the interpretation of these results in terms of their significance for the AI project. It is over this interpretation that opinions begin to diverge, not only within AI but also among its critics and outside observers. To illustrate this, let me take note of two other conclusions. First, the minimax algorithm, which is at the heart of brute-force methods, is based on the assumption of *rational* behavior on the part of the opponent – that is, on the assumption that the opponent will always choose one of the moves that minimizes (or comes close to minimizing) the machine's score.[10] This is a safe and reasonable assumption that holds most of the time. In the unlikely event that it doesn't – for example, when the opponent makes a serious blunder – it is still the best strategy to follow; in fact, it is even more justified, because human blunders make the machine's search process all the easier and it can more quickly swoop down for the kill. A machine that follows this strategy, therefore, could be said to behave *rationally* in the chess domain.

The second point about the minimax algorithm is that the number assigned to a board at any level represents the degree of estimated "promise" of a specific node and the branches that emanate from it (this is because the opponent might not always play their best). This is part of the reason why chess is an "interesting" game. It is interesting because there are enough degrees of freedom at each point to make the opponent's move unpredictable. In computer chess, this unpredictability is manifested in the speculative nature of the board scores found through look-ahead and backup.

The significance of these points for our purposes here is that they demonstrate how very simple techniques such as minimax can capture in purely numerical terms, even in a crude sense – at least in a formalized domain such as chess – such intricate and subjective notions as *rationality* and *promise*. In a believer's eye, this is significant because it suggests implications beyond chess. If we can formalize the notion of *promise* (of a move in chess), the believer would speculate, we might also be able to formalize closely related notions such as *hunch, intuition,* and *insight,* which seem to lie at the heart of human intelligence. All these may be, at bottom, the outcome of unconscious processes that resemble brute-force search – or so would go the believer's hunch. The skeptic, by contrast, would attribute less, if any, credit to the machine, and no psychological significance to the victory of Deep Blue.

The Chess Dilemma

Before Deep Blue's victory over the human world champion, many people (e.g., Eliot Hearst, psychologist and former vice president of the U.S. Chess Federation and a member of the U.S. Olympic chess team)[11] believed that playing chess well is closely linked to other, more general human skills. To be a good chess-player, they contended, one needs intuitive skills for making subtle judgments, for making analogies, and for recalling memories associatively (Hofstadter 2001: 34). Therefore, they concluded, world-class chess would not succumb easily to machines. Others maintained that the characteristics of chess make it a suitable domain for machines. If anything, they argued, computers are better than human beings in complex, determinate, and discrete task domains that call for a great deal of computation – and chess, as we have seen, is precisely such a domain.

Deep Blue's victory apparently lends support to the position of the latter group – namely, those who do not link chess-playing capabilities with the deepest attributes of human intelligence. But it also leaves us with an apparent dilemma: if, as we often have assumed, playing chess requires intelligence of a certain quality, how could machines surpass us so soundly, and if it does not, then what is wrong with that perennial assumption about chess? A number of answers to this dilemma might be proposed:

- Computers don't really play chess; there is no similarity between chess-playing in machines and humans, or, for that matter, between machines' chess-playing and being intelligent – Deep Blue's victory is of no significance for either human or computer intelligence.
- Computers beat us in chess because chess is a formal domain, and so Deep Blue's victory reveals a fact solely about the domain of chess.
- Computers can mimic human skills in domains such as chess to the extent that we, as social beings, are willing and able to mechanize our behaviors

in those domains – hence, Deep Blue's victory signifies a fact about us human beings.

- Computers can be said to play chess as long as we ignore certain aspects of human chess-playing behavior – chess is formal only in retrospect and, as such, Deep Blue's victory signifies facts about our ways of looking at things or our theories.

- Chess is a typical domain of human mental behavior; thus, what we have seen happening in chess will, sooner or later, happen elsewhere – Deep Blue's victory signifies an in-principle equivalence between human and computer intelligence.

In this section, using the chess dilemma as an appetizer, I want to introduce different views about computer intelligence, presenting questions that these views raise as well as issues they need to address. Current supercomputers play chess in ways that might have little in common with the ways humans play it – for example, in the *calculative* method of computers, as opposed to the *perceptual* skills of chess masters (de Groot 1946; Hofstadter 1979: 286; Haugeland 1981: 16; Dennett 1991). This observation, however, does not diminish the significance of chess, and of Deep Blue's victory over the human champion, for understanding the human mind, if we believe that there are general principles of intelligence.

The Skeptical View: "Computers Are Not Intelligent because They Are Not Original"

The skeptical view usually begins with the premise that computers are not original. The philosopher John Searle, for instance, sees a major difference between Kasparov's "consciously looking at a chessboard, studying the position, and trying to figure out his next move" and Deep Blue, which "has a bunch of meaningless symbols that the programmers use to represent the positions of the pieces on the board . . . [and] a bunch of equally meaningless symbols that the programmers use to represent options for possible moves" (2002: 61). "The real competition," Searle suggests, "was not between Kasparov and the machine, but between Kasparov and a team of engineers and programmers" (ibid.: 63). From this assertion, he concludes that despite its "wonderful hardware and software" (which are also achievements of the engineers and the programmers), Deep Blue has no psychological relevance at all.

This sounds like a substantive objection, and we need to analyze it carefully. A clarification, however, is needed at this point. To be sure, as the now-famous maxim attributed to Lady Lovelace put, the machine "does only what it has been told to do" – hence, the argument for lack of originality.[12] There is a difference, however, between following instructions and being totally predictable, between one's telling the machine what to do and one's knowing exactly what it will do, between the machine doing what it has been told and doing it in ways that are totally transparent to a human being. In other words – and this is a subtlety that some AI skeptics fail to appreciate – from the observation that programmers are behind something it does not follow that the machine's behavior is totally transparent to, and predictable by, its builders. To see how this might be possible, think of paper airplanes.[13] A paper airplane (or a dart, for that matter) goes *exactly* where you throw it – it is just that you yourself *do not know* exactly where you threw it, and hence you simply have to watch where it goes and realize, a posteriori, that *that* is where you threw it!

A simple explanation is that there are many parameters involved in determining the precise path of the paper airplane (or dart): Gravity is just one (about whose effect we presumably know enough); other parameters include the shape of the plane, the angle and thrust with which it is thrown, and the position of the fingers; add air pressure, air movement (wind), temperature gradient – in short, the aerodynamics of flight – and it all becomes quite complicated. Had we known all these parameters and their values and correlations, and had we known how to use this knowledge, and how to do so in split-second amounts of time, then we would have been able to predict the precise path. Attaining such detailed knowledge, however, is virtually impossible; and therefore so is the prediction of the path.

A similar thing could be said about complex computer programs. Although programs might show traces of the techniques and styles built into them by programmers and chess masters, their behavior is in no way predictable by those same developers. More often than not, the creators of complex programs of any kind are surprised by the behavior exhibited by their programs, and in fact humans are often soundly defeated by their mechanical creations.

Instead of paper airplanes, we could, of course, as Newborn has suggested and as Searle would probably agree, liken computers to real airplanes – or to rockets, for that matter – that, like computers, are complex technological artifacts, and that, as we all know, can be accurately guided and made to land on remote locations such as distant planets. This is an interesting proposal that touches on crucial aspects of the nature of computing (discussed in Chapter 1). Essential to this nature is that computers work by virtue of the purely physical properties of machines – and this makes them similar to airplanes. Equally essential, however, is that, unlike airplanes, computers are *representational* artifacts.

But how, Searle would object, could a machine that doesn't know what chess is, or even how a pawn or a bishop looks, be representational, be *about* chess, or be taken as playing the game of chess? "The computer does not know that the symbols represent chess pieces and chess moves, because it does not know anything. As far as the computer is concerned, the symbols could be used to represent baseball plays or dance steps or numbers or nothing at all" (2002: 61).

In short, Searle's main objection, as in his previous criticisms of AI, has to do with the source of meaning and originality in computers. This, as Hofstadter (1985: 650) points out, is one of the subtlest issues that AI should be able to shed light on – namely, the question of "What is meaning?" The problem with Searle's objection is that he turns an observation – "Current computers do not have semantics" – to an in-principle argument – "Computers cannot have semantics" (ibid.).

The Social Constructivist View: "Computers Can Act Intelligently to the Extent that Humans Act Mechanically"

The constructivist view, held by a group of sociologists, suggests that the boundary between humans and machines is permeable at least insofar as humans are willing to act like machines. Humans determine where the boundary is, and they can even erase it by choosing to act in certain ways. Collins and Kusch (1998) have developed an elaborate theory of the *shape of actions* with the purpose of establishing new boundaries between humans and machines. According to this theory, human actions fall into two general categories. In *polimorphic* (from "polis" and "morph," roughly meaning "socially shaped") actions such as voting, greeting, praying, shopping, or writing a love letter, humans draw upon their understanding of society to perform the action. These are *formative* actions in the sense that they each constitute a form of life. Praying, for instance, is different in the Islamic and Catholic forms of life, partly making them distinguishable from each other. The variable, intentional, or institutional character of polimorphic actions makes them essentially nonmimicable for things like machines that are not part of the pertinent society or form of life. By contrast, in *mimeomorphic* (or machine-like) actions such as blinking or swinging a golf club, there is a one-to-one mapping between the action and observable behaviors, making them mimicable by machines. In other words, machines can act intelligently to the extent that humans, as social beings, are willing and able to act mechanically.

During the last few centuries, chess has transformed from a courting activity of aristocracy to a regulated championship match in public spectacle. This can be partly understood as a shift from a polimorphic action to a mimeomorphic one where humans are made to act, to a certain degree, in a machine-like fashion.[14] Unfortunately, Collins and Kusch do not discuss chess directly, making it difficult to understand their view on the questions raised here.[15] However, one can make inferences about chess from their discussions of other topics. Collins and Kusch (1998: 119–120) classify machines in two ways: first, according to what they do, and, second, according to how they work. In respect to what they do, the authors suggest that machines are of three types: as *tools* they amplify our ability to do what we can already do; as *proxies* they replace us by doing what we already do (perhaps better than we do it); and as *novelties* they do types of things that we could never do without them. According to this typology, hammers and word processors are tools, thermostat and medical expert systems count as proxies (see Chapter 3), and fridge-freezers and rockets are novelties, as is a laser and a virtual-reality headset. Asserting that the boundaries between these categories are relative to our standpoint and to the level of analysis – "we can always turn a tool into a proxy by taking a lower vantage point," and vice versa (ibid.) – the main thrust of their argument is that "what have been taken to be proxies should really be thought of as tools" (p. 121). Pocket calculators, according to Collins and Kusch, do not do arithmetic; they do only a tiny part of arithmetic.

The main argument behind this assertion is what Collins and Kusch call "Repair, Attribution, and all That" or "RAT": "We think a pocket calculator does arithmetic after the fashion of a proxy, or even an agent, because we continually repair its errors and attribute high-level arithmetical agency to it" – for instance, when we interpret the answer 6.9999996 of a calculator to the product "7/11 × 11" as 7. This is what the authors mean by "repair" – a common phenomenon when we deal with machines and pets, but also in our interactions with fellow human beings. What makes the human case different is that the pattern of skill and repair work is roughly symmetrical between the parties. By the same token, the attribution of agency to machines would make sense if the RAT is balanced between us and them, a condition that is hardly attained with present-day computers – unless, of course, we either "put social knowledge into computers" or we eliminate the need for it by acting in a machine-like fashion. In short, according Collins and Kusch

(1998: 125), "machines can only be proxies where whatever we want to bring about can be brought about through mimeomorphic actions."

The notion of RAT provides a useful way of understanding human and computer interaction.[16] We saw explicit examples of repair work by the IBM team on Deep Blue between and throughout the games – for example, when the team fine-tuned the machine's strategy according to opponent's play. To be sure, there have been many other such "repair" works that are not discussed here. All of this seems to lend support to the idea that Deep Blue might indeed be a tool, rather than a proxy, according to Collins and Kusch's categories. But there are two caveats. First, the balance between Deep Blue and humans in terms of their respective repair work is far beyond what we can say of pocket calculators. In fact, in an interesting twist, it was the humans who played as *proxies* of Deep Blue (e.g., when they physically performed the move decided by the machine). Second, even human beings when they interact with each other do not have the proclaimed balance and symmetry in the repair work. Rather, their contribution seems to follow the contours of authority, status, and expertise – think of the interactions between a nurse and a patient in a hospital, a manager and an employee, a mechanic and a car owner, a parent and a child, and so on.

The Existential View: "Computers Can Be Intelligent, but Only in Formal Domains"

A third view, attributed to Hubert Dreyfus, describes the difference between the chess-playing skills of humans and machines as one of "zeroing in" versus "counting out" (Dreyfus 1992: 102). This is basically the distinction between the perceptual skills of chess masters versus the brute-force method of current machines. That brute-force methods can give rise to world-class computer chess is attributable, according to this view, to the specific character of chess. Dreyfus divides the world into *formal* and *informal* knowledge domains. "The important distinction between those domains where symbolic information-processing machines can behave intelligently and those where they cannot is a function of the kinds of domains themselves and the correlative kinds of knowledge we can have of them" (1991: 717). Dreyfus would therefore interpret Deep Blue's victory as showing that chess is a formal domain.

Haugeland (1985) develops a formal account of chess that supports the existential view. He describes chess as a "formal system" – finite, discrete, repeatable, medium-independent, and so on. In this view, all that ultimately matters about chess pieces is the set of legal moves that they can make at any given position on the board. A knight, for example, is nothing but a token of the game that can make L-shaped jumps to any position on the board as long as it does not land on another piece of the same color and does not leave the board's boundaries. The knight is defined by this abstract pattern or rule, and not by the physical shape of the object that instantiates it, let alone the material of which that object is made. The same could be said of any other piece and of a chess game in general – which, at that same level of abstraction, is the combination of tokens, positions, and legal moves.

Dreyfus and Haugeland see the success of computer chess as revealing nothing but some previously unsuspected facts about the nature of the game of chess. The interesting question for their existential view, then, is to figure out which domains of human activity are formal and which are not.

The Humanist View: "Deep Blue Does Indeed Play Chess but Only in a Formal Manner"

A closely related view grants that chess is formal in the sense described above, but argues that it is so only in *retrospect*. Human actions that exhibit some kind of logic after the fact are often not produced through a logical process. However, if we prune all the so-called superfluous, or "extralogical," facets from the behavior, a logical core might remain, which makes a retrospective formal analysis of the behavior possible. But this is likely to be deceptive. Hofstadter, for example, taking note of the commonality between chess and music composition, observes that every chess-player or every composer "has idiosyncratic nuances that seem logical a posteriori but that are not easy to anticipate a priori" (1985: 208).

What Hofstadter focuses on is not "the kind of logical analysis that occurs *after* the game" but the ability to play good chess in the first place: "Good chess moves spring from the organization of a good chess mind: a set of perceptions arranged in such a way that certain kinds of ideas leap to mind when certain subtle patterns or cues are present" (ibid.; emphasis Hofstadter's). As someone interested in the workings of the mind, Hofstadter wants to know how a "good chess mind" works.

The Believer's View: "Computers Can become Intelligent, Unconditionally"

Finally, there are believers who take chess-playing as a typical example of human thinking. Having observed the steady rise of computers' capabilities in the face of the stationary level of human intelligence, they conclude that sooner or later computers will surpass us in other domains as well. This argument, therefore, hinges crucially on computers' speed of operation or, more generally, on "computational power."

Speed in processing, performance, and response – for example, speed in doing a math calculation, in playing basketball, or in an unpredictable driving situation – is a crucial component of intelligent behavior, both in machines and in human beings. Given the same task at comparable levels of competence, the person who performs it more swiftly is usually considered more intelligent, agile, alert, and so on. In common perception, an animal that in an instant figures out how to escape from a predator is considered intelligent, but not one that does not respond as quickly – speed determines if the animal lives or dies. Similarly, a person who instantaneously comes up with a witty response to a putdown is considered more intelligent than someone who only thinks of a clever comeback the next day. Agility and responsiveness, in other words, are taken as a sign of intelligence. (Lay parlance, of course, also distinguishes wisdom, as opposed to intelligence, as an attribute that has much to do with life experience but not necessarily much with speed.) The common denominator linking all of this is *speed of processing* – a term that has become current because of computational metaphors.

A more general, but related, term is *computational power* of the brain, which is a metaphorical notion construed literally. Comparing the putative computational power and capacity of the human brain with that of computers is fairly commonplace in certain AI circles, as well as in the popular media. Despite its intuitive appeal, however, it is not clear how to determine the "computational power" of the human brain.

Is it given by the number of neurons in the brain, the total number of connections (synapses) among neurons, or the number of cells that are part of the total nervous system (including the peripheral senses of vision, hearing, touch, and smell, and internal senses that bring signals to and from organs such as the heart, the stomach, and the lungs)? Is it the number of operations per second, the quantity of data stored in bits within the brain (if that is a meaningful notion), the number of objects or people that one can recognize, the number of input words the brain can process in one minute, or some other mathematical measure? None of these answers can lay claim to correctness because neuroscience has yet to establish the fundamental building block of computation in the brain.

Even if neuroscience had managed to do this, however, it would not necessarily translate into a precise mathematical notion of the brain's computational power.[17] The brain is not a homogeneous aggregate of units whose overall computational capacity could be obtained by the summation of the

capacities of its units. From what we know, it is a complex hierarchical organization with different levels and modes of processing. Furthermore, the
brain functions in close collaboration with other bodily organs, and is heavily dependent on them. It may well be that one cannot isolate the brain and
assign a specific computational capacity to it without taking these ancillary
organs into account. To all this, add the increasingly validated idea that the
human brain is a constructive learning system – that is, one whose computational resources alter as the system learns (Quartz and Sejnowski 1997).
This suggests that the computational power of the brain, rather than being
fixed and constant, changes with the problems, resources, and opportunities
presented to it by the environment.

Nevertheless, having made these caveats, let us make a very rough calculation of what is usually considered the computational capacity of the brain,
just to have a point of reference. The total number of neurons in the brain is
on the order of a hundred billion (10^{11}), each one having roughly one thousand (10^3) synapses. With a processing time of about ten milliseconds for each
neural signal, this would give our brains a computing capacity of about ten
million billion (10^{16}) bits per second.[18] By contrast, a typical desktop personal
computer runs at 10 GHz (10^{10} operations per second) or roughly 10^{11} bits
per second.[19] Mainframe computers have a computing capacity at least two
orders of magnitude higher (10^{13} bps). This estimate suggests that even today
we are not all that far away from having computers with the computational
capacity of the human brain (as calculated in the earlier sense).

There are indeed people within the AI community, as we shall see in
Chapter 4, who believe, based on estimates like the one just made, that computational power is not the main bottleneck in our quest to achieve the level
of human intelligence in machines. They blame other fundamental obstacles, such as insufficient knowledge inside the computer or lack of physical
interaction with the world, and they therefore prescribe routes to this goal.
Others, however, argue that augmenting the power of computers by a few
orders of magnitude is all that is needed. The latter group bases its arguments
on a number of scientific premises and technological findings to which we
shall turn in the next chapter. Before doing that, however, let us draw some
conclusions from the study of chess.

DEEP BLUE AS AN EXPERIMENT IN TECHNOSCIENCE

The fact that Deep Blue beat the world chess champion is certainly of special
historic significance, if not for its own sake, as a turning point in human–
machine relations. Insisting that computers cannot be original, as skeptics do,

does not do justice to this event – it basically amounts to a head-in-the-sand strategy. Taking chess, on the other hand, as the ultimate manifestation of human intelligence and the victory of Deep Blue as a telling sign of machine superiority, as believers do, does not do justice to the rich and multifaceted character of human intelligence – it is reading too much into one incident and putting too much emphasis on one isolated aspect of intelligence.

What We Have Learned *about* Chess

Hofstadter (1999) has pointed out that "Deep Blue taught us that chess is more mechanical than we had realized." It did not show us that all thought is brute-force search, nor did it even prove that human chess thinking is purely brute-force search. All it showed us is that chess is *amenable* to brute-force techniques. Our discussion has revealed that present-day chess-playing systems play chess *rationally*, although they may not play it perceptually or emotionally, and they do this because "chess is more mechanical than we had realized."

AI succeeded in chess partly because the formal aspects of chess are easily amenable to algorithmic methods and partly because computer technology relatively rapidly reached such speed and sophistication as to be able to handle chess more effectively than human beings can. Both steps were required for the success that computer chess has had. Achievements in speed and technology enabled engineers to design and build special hardware dedicated exclusively to chess. On the other hands, the formal character of chess enabled computer programmers to ignore all the "extraneous" aspects of the game and to get at its purely logical core – this is the origin of static evaluation, backup, pruning, and other computer chess techniques discussed earlier.

Our study of chess also reveals how assumptions lead to specific mechanisms and become reified in them. Recall, for instance, that backup was based on the assumption that both players behave rationally in any given situation. The rationality assumption leads naturally to minimax search, and hence lies at the core of computer chess. This assumption – that rationality is essential to chess, but the direct visual perception of the board, for instance, is not – was a small first step toward the success of the whole endeavor, because it gave a definite answer to a basic question about the constitution of chess: What is chess? The mechanisms of static evaluation and backup, by contrast, provided a definite answer to a very different basic question about the domain: How should one play chess? Although there is no clear borderline between the *what* and the *how* aspects of a domain, making the distinction and getting a grip on both were crucial to the success of computer chess.

What We Have Learned *from* Chess

In reviewing the debate over chess, we discover that different views tend to focus on different issues while marginalizing others, asking different questions and, of course, getting different answers. Each view is usually driven by an overarching metaphor about chess and how it relates to human cognition.

What Is the Relationship between Chess and Intelligence? Margins and Metaphors

Given that search is one of the most crucial components in chess programs, much of what one concludes from computer chess hinges on how one views search. The engineering-minded might find the racecar metaphor tellingly useful. Machines play chess, they would argue, with enough intensity to beat human beings. We can thus marvel at the beauty of chess programs and the elegance of techniques such as backup and pruning in the same way that we admire the technology behind racecars and their magnificent performance. In so doing, this group concludes, we might learn useful things about the human mind.

By contrast, the scientific-minded who consider search itself a close simulacrum of intelligence would lean toward the fruit-fly analogy. On the face of it, fruit flies are of extreme interest to geneticists because of their short generation span (on the order of three weeks), which allows many natural phenomena – gene expression, cell division, even behavior – to be observed at a pace not otherwise possible. And, despite their short life span, fruit flies manifest many of the traits of larger organisms. A similar claim could be made, according to believers in the fruit-fly analogy, about chess-playing and intelligence: Chess-playing is a typical thinking behavior. Thus, machines that play good chess, they conclude, are not only indisputably intelligent, they provide good examples of what human intelligence is all about and how it can be achieved in AI.

The racecar and fruit-fly metaphors reveal the tension between the scientific and engineering aspects of AI in a rather straightforward manner. Mainstream AI seeks to resolve this tension by focusing on the third – flight – metaphor, which directs our attention to the so-called general mechanisms of intelligent behavior. Chrisley (2002), for instance, has argued that early attempts to achieve artificial flight and to understand natural flight failed because scientists tried to mimic nature too closely. "It wasn't until scientists looked at simple, synthetic systems (such as Bernoulli's aerofoil), which could arbitrarily manipulated and studied, that the general aerodynamic principles that underlie both artificial and natural flight could be identified." AI can similarly uncover the general principles of intelligence, Chrisley suggests, through its simple (but increasingly complex) systems. This argument, we notice, is based on the assumption that there are *general principles* of intelligence, similar to aerodynamic principles. As we have seen, one group of such principles derives from the idea of search in a problem space.

Each of these metaphors represents a certain view of AI and its basic goals, and each one is meaningful in its own right. Applying them is perfectly fine as long as one keeps in mind the limits of their efficacy and the fact that, like all metaphors, they inevitably highlight certain aspects and marginalize others. In AI, furthermore, due to its dual scientific and engineering aspirations and the tension that results from this, paying attention to the margins of metaphors is imperative in both research and presentation of research findings. Inattentiveness to this imperative often results in overblown claims about a certain finding, the underestimation of alternatives, or both. In fact, significant issues are sometimes lost by a whole set of metaphors. In the case of chess, as I argue next, all of these metaphors underplay an important facet of the scientific enterprise – namely, the significance of the cultural and material conditions that enable scientific practice.

Who Beat Kasparov? Science as Normative Practice

What is lost in these metaphors are the material culture and practices that give rise to particular theories and understandings of "intelligence." In his study of early research on *Drosophila*, for instance, Robert Kohler explains how the mode of genetic practice that started around 1910 by Thomas Morgan at Columbia University was made possible by the invention of a novel kind of scientific instrument, the "standard" organism – namely, the fruit fly, *Drosophila melanogaster* (1999: 244). Lloyd demonstrates how this "instrument," by providing an abundance of data and opportunities for research, played an autocatalytic effect in genetic research of the time. As he observes, this is a clear illustration of "the power of material culture and practices radically to reshape experimenters' aims and concepts. We like to think that ideas and theories precede the nitty-gritty of lab practice, but in fact practice more usually precedes theory" (ibid.: 247).

A similar observation can be made about chess and its intended role in AI research. Deep Blue and the culture that gave rise to it played a defining role in how we think and theorize about human intelligence. The technical, financial, and organizational power mobilized by IBM was an influential factor in the development of chess-playing machines. To a great extent, IBM determined what goals were followed, what types of questions were sanctioned, what techniques and technologies were considered, what time frames were allowed, and so on. It was within this context that chess came to be *about* a general concept of intelligence, and a professional match between a human and a machine turned into a historical experiment.

The philosopher Joseph Rouse echoes these points when he argues for the *normative* character of scientific practice. Arguing that science depends on its context not only for funding and material resources "but also for much of what is ultimately at issue or at stake in scientific practices," Rouse suggests, "What a practice is, including what counts as an instance of the practice, is bound up with its *significance*, i.e., with what is at issue and at stake in the practice, to whom or what it *matters*, and hence with how the practice is *appropriately* or *perspicuously* described (Rouse 1999: 445, 449; original emphasis). We have seen all of these facets at work in the case of Kasparov–Deep Blue match as an instance of an intelligence contest.

In a serious sense, therefore, it was IBM that beat Kasparov, not Deep Blue. The Kasparov–Deep Blue match was a battle between the technical, financial, and organizational might of a big corporation (situated in the bigger techno-scientific culture of the late twentieth century) and the cognitive, emotional, and intellectual resources of a master chess-player and all of the "optimists" who rallied behind him. Like Kasparov, Deep Blue was an important part of this battle, and should take due credit for its accomplishment, but certainly not full credit.

But, Finally, Do Computers Play Chess? Language, Knowledge, and Power

Many interesting implications follow from Rouse's account, especially with regard to the notions of language, knowledge, and power. Newborn began his report by asking whether computers *really* play chess. Perhaps the point of Newborn's question is to highlight the metaphorical character of words such as "play" when applied to computers, or the fact that the meaning of words is largely stretched in such contexts. But much more, I want to suggest, is going on, and I want to use the example of "play" to draw some conclusions about the capabilities of computers, and about the broader significance of these in our understanding of AI.

Unpacking the innocuously simple concept of "play" in the context of chess, reveals a rather complex inner structure with various dimensions:

- knowing the rules of chess;
- following the rules of chess (including those of professional matches – e.g., timing);
- making "rational" decisions in most, if not all, situations in the game;

- favoring winning situations over others;
- caring about the outcome.

As we move down this list, the dimensions become more and more nuanced, making it difficult to draw a border between machine and human behavior. One would be hard-pressed to talk about Deep Blue "caring about the outcome," for instance, than it "knowing the rules." But overall it would be safe to say that a good deal of what constitutes the concept of "playing" is obtained by the machine. In a serious sense, therefore, computers do play chess. Saying this, however, does not necessarily imply that computers have anything like a goal (winning), an emotional investment, or an expectation of social reward. Thus, if *play* connotes all these qualities, as it probably does, we might be better off using another term for what computers do – *computer-play*, *com-play*, or, most economically, *c-play*. Unfortunately, though, this would lead to our having to say *c-plan, c-act, c-execute, c-talk, c-see, c-think, c-understand*, even *c-compute*!

No one, needless to say, explicitly advocates such a proposal, mainly thanks to the flexibility of human language. If airplanes can be said to fly, engines to run, batteries to die, and lamps to burn, computers also can be said to play. In a sense, saying of a three-year-old that they "play" baseball also relies on the same plasticity of our concepts. This much is almost always agreed on. However, there is much more going on, as issues of language and power are closely tied in together: "Whether an unfamiliar way of speaking about or dealing with a situation is taken as an innovation, a mistake, a curiosity, an irony, or a humdrum variation on the familiar depends crucially upon asymmetries of power among those who encounter it" (Rouse 1999: 449). At the end of the day, in other words, whether we interpret Deep Blue's moves as "playing" chess and the outcome as "victory" of machines over human beings largely depends on who has the final word – IBM and its team or Kasparov and his supporters. This, as we saw, remains largely unsettled by the facts; Kasparov and the IBM team leader were yet to agree as to whether this was the beginning or the end of the story.

"Do computers really play chess?" might not be a useful question to ask, because of the dynamic and variable character of interpretations. A more useful question would be to ask what we learn about intelligence in general by studying chess. The flight analogy might turn out to be the most productive in thinking about this question. Chess, as I suggested in the beginning, might well be the most rigorous form of human thinking, but machines do not need to mimic human behavior in all details in order to help us uncover the general principles and mechanisms of intelligent behavior.

3   Cyborgs: Cybernetic AI

Haraway's Hybrid Dream

> By the late twentieth century, we are all chimeras, theorized and fabricated hybrids
> of machine and organism; in short, we are cyborgs.
>
> – Donna Haraway: A Cyborg Manifesto

Cyborgs are organism-machine hybrids. In science fiction, as in reality, cyborgs are the product of the merging of carbon and silicon, flesh and electronic circuitry, organic and inorganic, and even the physical and the virtual. As such, they can be biological organisms (such as humans) augmented with machinery, machines (such as humanoid robots) made to look like natural organisms, or fanciful creatures that fuse the realms of the physical and the digital in extraordinary ways. In all these shapes, the image of a cyborg appeals to our techno-utopian dreams, while challenging our deepest human sensibilities at the same time. The image is indeed an "an ironic dream of a common language" (Haraway 1991: 149).

This multiple crossbreeding has given rise to a whole family of cyborgs that are proliferating rapidly, turning our globe literally into a cyborg planet. The casual observer might find it increasingly onerous to tell science from science fiction, real from imaginary, physical from virtual, as the borders between these realms are becoming more and more permeable. This might lead to a certain degree of confusion about what is possible and what is impossible.[1] My goal in this chapter is to shed some light on these distinctions, especially as they relate to debates in AI. The tree in Figure 3.1 represents a tentative attempt to capture the current state of affairs on the cyborg planet. At the time of this writing, many of the cyborg categories shown on this tree have been realized in one form or another using existing technologies (examples of which are shown at the bottom of the tree): digital implants that allow the user to "see" or "hear" frequencies such as infrared or ultrasound that are beyond our natural reach; spinal implants that trigger orgasm at the push

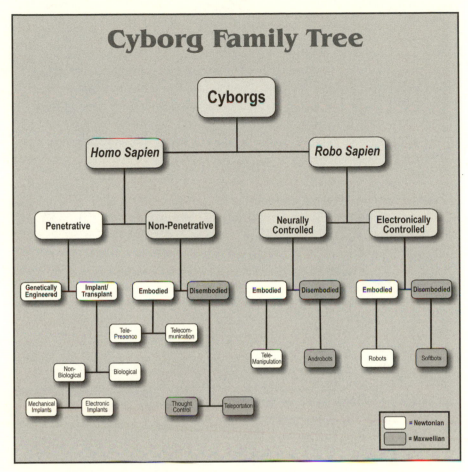

Figure 3.1. The Cyborg family tree, circa MMVII.

of a button; cell phones that can monitor your vital signs and call for help in case of emergency; telerobotic arms that can be directly controlled in the manner of a biological arm from hundreds of miles away; physical robots (or virtual chat bots) representing (or impersonating) a person at a distant site; frontal lobe implants that allow paraplegic patients to move a cursor on the screen at will; visual cortex implants that give a sense of vision to the blind; and so on and so forth – the list goes on indefinitely.[2]

The tree in Figure 3.1 also illustrates a major split in AI between those who believe that the future development of AI rests mostly with disembodied cyborgs (e.g., virtual software agents) versus those who advocate an embodied approach. For sake of brevity, I am going to call these views, respectively,

Newtonian and Maxwellian. Our focus in this chapter is on Maxwellians, who occupy the right branch on most of the subtrees in the figure, leaving Newtonians alone until Chapter 8. In particular, we examine those technologies that, according to certain views, epitomize natural evolution by other means. These have been the centerpiece in a series of debates among reputable AI practitioners and entrepreneurs, with speculations ranging from utopian dreams of a silicon-based disease-free eternal life for human beings (in the shape of software) to dystopian nightmares of a despotic society ruled or consumed by robots.

EVOLUTION BY OTHER MEANS

Space travel challenges mankind not only technologically, but also spiritually, in that it invites man to take an active part in his own biological evolution.

– Clynes and Kline

The term "cyborg" was first introduced in 1960 by Manfred Clynes and Nathan Kline in their paper titled "Cyborgs and Space," published in the journal *Aeronautics*. Addressed to an aviation audience, the paper proposed an imaginative solution to the problem of human survival in outer space. Rather than providing artificial, earth-like environments, the authors suggested, let us alter humans to cope with the unfamiliar conditions. They opined that the right response to the calling of space travel for humans might be "to take active part in [their] biological evolution." They believed that the combination of computational and cybernetic techniques would allow the creation of human-machine hybrids in which physiological functions such as metabolism, respiration, and sleep are regulated by electronic devices. They called these self-regulating cybernetic organisms cyborgs. The canonical image of a cyborg is that of *Robo sapiens* which constitute, we are told, "a new evolutionary phylum that will occupy the same niche as *Homo sapiens*" (Hayles 2005; cf. Menzel and D'Aluisio 2000)

The philosopher Andy Clark, who has narrated the story of the genesis of "cyborg" in more detail, intimates that Clynes and Kline "were not dreamers, just creative scientists engaged in matters of national (and international) importance" (Clark 2003: 13). In fact, following their footsteps and flipping the canonical image of a cyborg over, Clark builds a fascinating theory of humans as (disguised) *natural-born* cyborgs. "For what is special about human brains, and what best explains the distinctive features of human intelligence," he argues, "is precisely their ability to enter into deep and complex relationships with nonbiological constructs, props, and aids" (ibid.: 5). More importantly, he continues, "This ability [...] does not depend on physical wire-and-implant mergers, so much as on our *openness to information-processing mergers*" (ibid.; emphasis added). This vision of self-regulating human-machine systems that allow seamless information flow without necessarily involving physical intrusion is central to what I call cybernetic AI.

Nonpenetrative Technologies: Beyond the Human Skin

The lowly wire, it might be said, provides electrical circuits with a distinctive feature that is absent from mechanical structures: (what seems to be) *action at a distance*. More accurately, however, this is a property of electromagnetic waves, not wires, for as Clark Maxwell discovered in the nineteenth century, these waves can travel over long distances through different mediums (metal, air, vacuum, etc.) without significant attenuation. This very property of electromagnetic waves allows the sun to warm the earth, an electric potential generated at a hydroelectric plant in, say, the Amazons to illuminate the streets of Atlanta, and the image broadcast from CNN (the Cable News Network) in Atlanta to be seen on television screens in Addis Ababa. This basic property of the physical universe also has direct implications for cyborg technologies called "nonpenetrative modes of personal augmentation" by Kevin Warwick, a professor at the Department of Cybernetics at the University of Reading in England (cf. Clark 2003: 24).

Aspiring to be one of the first human beings to sense the world using more than the natural human abilities, Warwick has embarked on a long-term experiment that involves digital implants hooked up directly to his nervous system, allowing him to directly communicate with the environment (and other similarly wired people) from remote locations. Thrilled by the image of "all those wires, chips, and transmitters grafted into pulsating organic matter," Clark (2003: 21–24) contends that, "the most potent near-future technologies will be those that offer integration and transformation *without* implants or surgery: human-machine mergers that simply bypass, rather than penetrate, the old biological borders of skin and skull." Based on this vision, he argues that the effective boundary of the human body is much beyond the biological boundary (the skin). Taken to extremes, Clark's vision seems to render the human body irrelevant to the workings of the mind. Or so imply the Maxwellians, who form the major camp in cybernetic AI.

The major themes in cybernetic approaches are self-regulation, pattern recognition, and control. These approaches exploit the computational power that was at the basis of supercomputing AI, and augment it with a number of techniques and technologies, some old and others in the making, that share the brute character of natural evolution. One group of such techniques has come to be known as genetic algorithms.

Genetic Algorithms: Natural Evolution on a Silicon Chip

Many approaches in AI are inspired by ideas and theories from biology. These biologically motivated attempts have led to different brands of AI – neural networks (modeling the brain; see Chapter 6), machine learning (mimicking human learning), and genetic algorithms (simulating biological evolution).

Genetic algorithms were first proposed by John Holland (1975). As their name implies, these techniques were inspired by certain mechanisms of evolutionary biology – mutation, crossover, and inversion – which are universally utilized by organisms to alter or shuffle segments of their DNA. The key idea of genetic algorithms is to think of strings of bits (ones and zeros) as genes, and to apply the above operators to transform the gene pool from generation to generation. Long bit-strings consisting of many genes are thus analogous to individual genomes in a population. In nature, evolutionary (or natural) selection accounts for the survival of the fittest genomes. In genetic algorithms, this role of selector is played by the programmer, who devises both the selection criteria and the mechanism by which such selection takes place. As Mitchell (1996) points out, for this technique to work, what is often needed is both computational parallelism – many processors evaluating many bit-strings at the same time – and an intelligent strategy for choosing which bit-strings should survive and which should die. The first is a matter of computational hardware, and the second is matter of programming skill. Together, the two give rise to a highly effective parallelism for searching for solutions through a large number of possibilities at the same time.

Carrying out genetic algorithms normally involves a huge amount of computation. In order to be carried out efficiently, therefore, the process requires increasingly cheap and fast machinery. This is what an empirical observation known as "Moore's Law" suggests will be the case for the foreseeable future.

Moore's Law: Keeping Up with a Promise

One of the earliest electronic general-purpose computers, ENIAC (Electronic Numerical Integrator and Calculator), was built at the University of Pennsylvania during World War II (but was not publicized until 1946). This machine was enormous – a hundred feet long, eight-and-a-half feet high, and several feet wide, three orders of magnitude bigger than the largest machines built today – and, yet, it was five orders of magnitude slower than a typical personal computer of today. For the next half-century, even to the present day, computer technology has maintained a steady rate of improvement in terms of memory, speed, and cost. In 1945, stored-program computers did not exist. Today, one can purchase, for a few hundred dollars, a personal computer that has far more main memory and peripheral storage, as well as a much higher speed, than a $1 million computer in 1965. This rate of improvement is due both to advances in transistor technology and to innovations in computer architecture. With the emergence of microprocessors in the late 1970s, for instance, the technology maintained a 35 percent growth per year in performance. Since the mid-1980s, however, thanks in large part to architectural innovations, annual growth has exceeded 50 percent (Hennessy and Patterson 1996).

Much of this improvement derives from the invention of integrated circuits, which allowed the placement of ever more electronic components on ever smaller silicon chips. The number of transistors on an Intel chip, for example, increased from 3,500 in 1972 to 7,500,000 in 1997 – a growth of roughly 30 percent per year. Since the bottleneck for execution speed is the transmission time between components, which of course shrinks as the distance between components shrinks, this miniaturization implies a proportional increase in speed as well. On the other hand, the cost of manufacturing a chip has remained nearly constant, independent of its number of components. In other words, for a fixed cost, both the number of components on a chip and the speed have roughly doubled every two years for the past few decades.

In 1965, Gordon Moore, a former chair of Intel Corp. and one of the inventors of the integrated circuit, captured this trend in what has come to be known as Moore's Law of Integrated Circuits. According to this empirical law, the surface area of a state-of-the-art transistor gets reduced by approximately 50 percent every twenty-four months. Over the last four decades, this rate has largely been maintained within the computer industry. The industry has even expressed confidence that the rate will be maintained for another decade or so by using techniques such as high-resolution optical lithography. Of course, there is a limit to the degree of compaction of components on a chip: we cannot shrink beyond the size of an atom.

This, in turn, implies a limit to the degree of progress that can be achieved through sheer computing power (except for making ever bigger machines, which is not a realistic alternative for most applications). Although the limit is impressively large, its mere existence seems to imply that purely computational approaches can go only so far, and no further. The obvious question is, what would happen at this point? It turns out that science and technology already have a number of potential solutions up their sleeve.

Quantum Computing: A New Frontier

Present-day digital computer technology works on the basis of the modulation of electron flow through miniature devices such as a MOSFET (metal-oxide-semiconductor field effect transistor). The modulation of the flow works on principles that are quantum-mechanical in nature, but thanks to their "large" physical dimensions, the large number of constituent particles, and interactions with the environment, quantum effects do not show up in these devices – they operate in the so-called classical realm. Further reduction in dimensions is not possible because, at a certain point, nondeterministic quantum-mechanical effects begin to prevail.[3]

Quantum computing, as its name suggests, is rooted in quantum mechanics, and works on the basis of quantum logic.[4] Instead of *bits*, it deals with *qubits* (quantum bits). Like a bit, a qubit can be in one of two states; but unlike bits, qubits can also exist in *superpositions* of those states. Furthermore, they also can be *entangled* with other qubits. Roughly speaking, entanglement is the result of nonlocal correlations among the parts of a quantum system. What this means is that we cannot fully understand the state of the system by dividing it up into parts and studying the separate states of the parts. Information can be encoded in nonlocal correlations among the parts of the system. In fact, as Preskill (1997) points out, much of the art of designing quantum algorithms involves finding ways to make efficient use of the nonlocal correlations. Superposition and entanglement are the sources of power of quantum computing because, unlike the classical case, a qubit is equivalent to a vector in a two-dimensional space of real numbers. The state of a system with N qubits would thus involve 2^N such vectors (each of which is equivalent to one complex number). A system with a mere 100 qubits, for instance, is equivalent to $2^{100} = 10^{30}$ complex numbers – a magnitude far too big for any classical computer to handle.[5]

Despite the enormous potential that might in theory be opened up by quantum computing, there are serious limitations inherent in the idea, the most important of which are:

- Quantum information cannot be copied with perfect fidelity.
- Quantum information can be transferred with almost perfect fidelity, but in the process the original must be destroyed.
- Any measurement performed on a quantum system destroys most of the information contained in the system.

- Generally, the state in which a quantum system ends up can be determined only probabilistically.
- Certain parameters cannot simultaneously have precisely defined values (Meglicki 2000).

Difficulties associated with these limitations make the design and manufacturing of real quantum computers a daunting task. At the present state of the art, researchers would be content if they managed to build a quantum computer with as many as just two or three qubits. Meglicki speculates that "quantum computing is at the point where classical computing was 70 years ago" (2000). Many questions about how a practical quantum computer could be built or what might be done with it are still completely open.[6]

Furthermore, despite possible breakthroughs of quantum computing in terms of speed, many of the complexity results of computer science would still hold, especially the absolute results about intractable problems. There is also much to be done about simpler (tractable) problems – those that require computing times that do not drastically increase with the size of the input.[7] Searching a database is one such problem. Assume that you are given a phone number and want to find the name that corresponds to it in the phone book. The amount of time required for this task is bounded by (i.e., it is at worst proportional to) the number of entries in the phone book. This is the limit of classical algorithms. Grover (1996) has proposed a quantum algorithm that is quadratically faster than classical algorithms – a huge improvement but still not exponential (what is needed to tackle intractable problems). This algorithm has been proved to be optimal – that is, it is the best that could be in principle done within the realm of quantum computing.

Finally, as in classical computing, there are enormous sources of error for which error-detection and error-rectification mechanisms are needed if quantum computing is ever to have real-world applications. The sources of quantum error – ranging from the impact of cosmic rays to the isolation of the quantum computer from its immediate environment – are of far greater complexity than in the classical case. Some error-detection schemes are presently under study, but, as a result of the ubiquitous presence of environmental interactions, most of them are only at the stage of theoretical development.

In short, quantum computing is still extremely speculative. No one yet has a clear idea as to how quantum computers could be constructed.

Nanotechnology: Science Fiction in the Lab

The other major technology that should be mentioned is nanotechnology. Broadly speaking, this term refers to the use of materials with dimensions from one nanometer (one billionth of a meter) to one hundred nanometers. This scale includes collections of a few atoms, semiconductor wafers (as small as twenty nanometers), and protein-based "motors." For this reason, the enterprise has engaged physicists and chemists as much as it has attracted biologists and computer engineers. One intriguing idea that originated in science fiction but that has nonetheless attracted serious attention is that of miniature "assemblers" that can presumably build anything atom by atom from the ground up (this idea has gained enough momentum to trigger great concern as to its long-term threat to humanity[8]). One possibility for such assemblers might lie in self-replicating molecules, such as peptides. Generally speaking, however, nanotechnology is no less embryonic than quantum computing.[9]

This was just a small sample of burgeoning technologies currently under investigation in AI and related fields. There are many other technologies such as Augmented Reality, Wearable Computers, and Tangible User Interfaces that have direct relevance to AI and cognitive science. Clark (2003, especially Chapter 2) provides some sites and sources where they are discussed or investigated. For our purposes here, this sample is enough to give an idea of where the technology is heading. We turn now to various interpretations of these developments from figures both within and outside the AI community.

CYBORG PLANET: THE CLASH OF UTOPIAN AND DYSTOPIAN VIEWS

Despite the embryonic state of quantum computing and nanotechnology, there are still enough alternatives on the horizon to maintain, even to increase, the current rate of progress in "computational power." And, thus, the vision of AI as the execution of lots of brute-force computation augmented by techniques such as genetic algorithms – namely, what I have dubbed "cybernetic AI" – may still be viable for quite a while. As in the case of chess, the interesting question, however, is the cognitive and philosophical significance of this engineering fact. Cybernetic AI, by its very nature, has of late provided a breeding ground for various utopian and dystopian views and narratives, leading to a heated debate among their proponents.

What follows is a reconstruction of this debate, at one polar extreme of which stand AI researchers such as Hans Moravec (of the Robotics Laboratory at Carnegie-Mellon University) and entrepreneurs such as Ray Kurzweil (the author of two controversial books on AI and the inventor of a number of commercially popular devices), as opposed to computer experts such as Bill Joy (cofounder of Sun Microsystems) and Jaron Lanier (a major contributor to the development of virtual reality) and the philosopher John Searle. In between these poles, and in close parallel with the chess debate, are other commentators who take their insights from within or without AI. The discussion begins with the views expressed in Kurzweil (1999), which, as we shall see, is mainly responsible for triggering a rather sustained wave of debate in the last few years.

Smart Cyborgs: From Microchips to the Grand Universe

All that is needed to solve a surprisingly wide range of intelligent problems is exactly this: simple methods combined with heavy doses of computation.... Ultimately, with sufficient computational brute force (which will be ample in the twenty-first century) and the right formulas in the right combination, there are few definable problems that will fail to yield.

– Ray Kurzweil, *The Age of Spiritual Machines*

This statement is basically the manifesto of cybernetic AI. The observed trends in microprocessor technology, together with the alluring promise of new quantum-mechanical and biological computation, have provided Kurzweil with evidence that he presumably considers strong enough to make a quantitative extrapolation to the future. We already saw one example of such extrapolation in the discussion of computer chess (Figure 2.1). Figures 3.2 and 3.3, from Kurzweil, give a similar picture for the broader phenomenon of computational power.

The first of these summarizes what, according to Kurzweil, has happened so far; the second purports to be a logical extension of past trends into the new century. Taking a practical stance, he has presented the data in terms of the amount of computing capacity that $1,000 could, can, and will be able to buy at the given times. The images on the right side of Figure 3.3 are iconic representations of the following claims: "human capacity in a $1,000 personal computer is achieved around the year 2020,... the brain power of a small village by the year 2030, [that of] the entire population of the United States by 2048, and a trillion human brains by 2060." The upshot of all this is the futuristic prediction: if we estimate the human Earth population at 10 billion persons, one penny's worth of computing circa 2099 will have a billion times greater computing capacity than all humans on Earth" (1999: 105).

Kurzweil begins his survey with some general observations about time and evolution. He suggests, for instance, that DNA-based genetics is fundamentally based on digital computation and that technology is "evolution by other means" – a theme that, as we saw, is central to cybernetic AI and to the

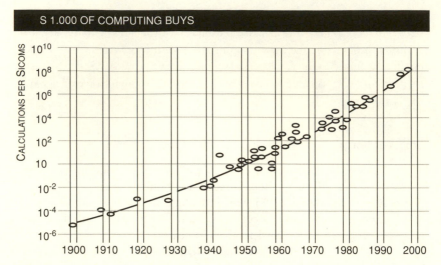

Figure 3.2. The growth of computing in the twentieth century (from Kurzweil 1999, with permission).

original notion of a cyborg. Computation, which he defines as "the ability to remember and to solve problems," is thus inevitable, he says, because it has "constituted the cutting edge in the evolution of multicellular organisms." His central point is that evolution, both in biology and in technology, has

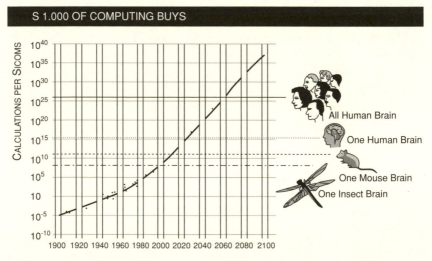

Figure 3.3. The growth of computing in the twentieth and twenty-first centuries (from Kurzweil 1999, with permission).

"an exponentially quickening pace" – it begins slowly and picks up speed with the passage of time (ibid.: 13–18).

Kurzweil's technical discussion starts when he invokes Moore's Law and the data represented in Figure 3.2 in order to conclude, together with Hans Moravec and David Waltz (of Nippon Electric Company), that during the last hundred years, "computers have been growing exponentially in power, long before the invention of the integrated circuit in 1958 or even the transistor in 1947" (ibid.: 24). In other words, according to this view, Moore's Law (involving solely solid-state transistor technology) "was not the first, but the fifth paradigm to continue the now one-century-long exponential growth of computing."[10] A pattern, then, emerges: "Each new paradigm came along just when needed" (ibid.); and "another computational technology will pick up where Moore's Law will have left off, without missing a beat" (33). Coupled with his definition of intelligence as "the ability to use optimally limited resources," Kurzweil's conclusion falls out almost immediately – namely, that computers are rapidly catching up with humans in terms of intelligence, and will soon surpass human intelligence.

The technological determinism conveyed in this last statement is too evident to need elaboration – a clear sense of "inevitability" of technological progress as a response to a putative need and in a rather linear fashion is claimed (*laws*, after all, are supposed to capture the inevitable). First came evolution, then technology, and later, as we will see, computers, and it is they that allegedly will henceforth determine the fate of nature as well as that of human beings. I note in passing that a similar deterministic worldview underlies all the claims that Kurzweil makes throughout his book. We should keep this in mind in order to be able to understand the mode of thought of which Kurzweil is but one representative.

In the same deterministic spirit, Kurzweil proceeds to make a leap from Moore's Law to his own "laws," which he claims are more fundamental, in that they allegedly express enduring attributes of nature, having nothing intrinsically to do with engineering, technology, or even humanity. The Law of Time and Chaos, the Law of Increasing Chaos, and the Law of Accelerating Returns, as he calls them, all reiterate the same deterministic theme on cosmological scales. The upshot of these laws is that computation is "the essence of order" (ibid.: 33).

These speculations about the possibilities arising from the exponential increase of computational power allow Kurzweil to make futuristic predictions about "uploading" a piece of classic literature into a computer-enhanced brain in a matter of seconds (c. 2009); about relationships between people and automated personalities as companions, teachers, caretakers, and lovers, with "virtual sex" being on the rise (c. 2019); about the widespread use of nanoproduced food, which has the correct nutritional composition and the same taste and texture as organically produced food and is unaffected by limited resources, bad weather, or spoilage (c. 2049); and the disappearance of any clear distinction between humans and computers, and of immortality for conscious entities (c. 2099). These predictions are the outcome of a tangled web of fact and fantasy, the untangling of which constitutes our goal in the remainder of this chapter.

CYBORGS: THE GOOD, THE BAD, AND EVERYTHING IN BETWEEN

If there is any merit to the idea that computers are growing in capability in what seems to be a relentless march forward, then sooner or later we should expect their entry into all domains of human activity – and not only domains like chess, but also activities that since time immemorial have been thought of as uniquely human. Today, we have computer versions of medical diagnosis, musical composition, translation, poetry, movies, and painting; tomorrow we may have similar versions of teaching, writing (e.g., novels), driving, and all sorts of creative activities. The next step would be computer friends, mates, mentors, and rulers. The line of thought that takes seriously quantitative extrapolations like those shown in the graphs of Figures 3.2 and 3.3, is, in a way, a reflection on what seems to be an inevitable trend manifested by these examples.

One of the possible ways to understand the view behind predictions of this sort is to think of it as merely a quantitative view of intelligence, of the kind that lurks behind the idea of IQ ratings and the various tests devised for their measurement. If one sees, as Kurzweil does, a direct correlation between computational power and intelligence, then some of his conclusions follow rather easily. It does not matter whether the correlation is seen in IQ or in some other number; what matters, according to this view, is that quantification is possible. We should merely wait, the proponents of the quantitative view suggest, for the new technologies to arrive; then history, they hope, will once again be on our side.

This quantitative view is further backed up by premises like these:

- Intelligence is a kind of pattern manipulation, and computers can do that. Hence, computers have the potential to be intelligent. (This is the basic premise of AI.)[11]
- We now have all the proper ideas in place to allow computers themselves to discover the proper kinds of pattern manipulation for intelligence, which

will automatically emerge from intense competition for survival in virtual environments.

- All we need is to have hardware fast enough to allow the evolution enough time to find the winners in the intelligence competition.

These assumptions are, more or less, explicitly acknowledged by Kurzweil and people who share his views. Indeed, Kurzweil proposes, in his book, a specific recipe for "How to build an intelligent machine in three easy paradigms" – namely, recursion, neural nets, and simulated evolution (genetic algorithms).[12] These views have triggered hope and enthusiasm, on the one hand, and concern and opposition, on the other, from within the ranks of the technological elite itself.

Good Cyborgs: Future Friends

For many people, the scenario of increasingly close relationships with computers is not only plausible, it is desirable. The picture of a world where machines happily coexist with human beings, sharing their work and contributing to their lives is appealing, after all. Examples of this picture are abundant in popular culture, especially movies and science fiction. The movie *Bicentennial Man*, for instance, portrays a domestic humanoid robot that gradually transforms into a full-blooded human being, marries a flesh-and-skin female, and eventually dies hand-in-hand with his human partner.

Within AI itself, there are those who are willing to *expand* the "circle of empathy" of the human species to be able to embrace potential nonbiological cousins. This inclusionist view considers potentially sentient machines not as exploitable laborers but as our companions and partners. There is nothing, according to this picture, intrinsically superior about carbon-based biological intelligence relative to its silicon-based counterpart. Hofstadter, for instance, wonders:

Why can we humans not open our little minds to the potential idea that if, in some wild and far-off day, we finally succeeded in collectively creating nonbiological creatures that perceived, that enjoyed, that suffered, that joked, that loved, that hated, that even created, the very word "we" would at that very moment have opened up its semantic field to embrace these, the products of our hearts' deepest yearnings? (1997: 492)

An optimistic outlook lies behind these statements – namely, that "genuine artificial intelligence," if and when it becomes a reality, would come as a "package" – a rich blend of thoughts, feelings, emotions, and so on – that is, of all that we consider human.

What would happen if robots do not turn out as friendly as we expect them to be? Not to worry, argues Jerone Lanier, who believes that computers are never going to be smarter than human beings.

Silly Cyborgs: Command and Control

Lanier (2000) challenges Kurzweil on the technical grounds of what he calls the "Great Shame of computer science" – namely, "that we don't seem to be able to write software much better as computers get much faster." He uses this argument against the "fetishizing of Moore's Law that seduces researchers into complacency." Lanier observes that, despite improvements in hardware speed, computer interfaces tend to respond more slowly because of a worse-than-linear rate of increase in computational overhead and the effect of so-called legacy code – that is, the original program that usually forms the core of each software package and on which everything else is built. According to Lanier, this bottleneck, resulting from software brittleness, nullifies all enhancements due to Moore's Law. The bottom line is that, despite the "eschatological" dreams and promises of people like Kurzweil, Lanier argues, no computer-initiated doomsday for the human race will take place.[13] Or will it?

Although it always involves some subjective number-fiddling (especially before 1950 or so), one can argue with some persuasiveness that Moore's Law held for the full duration of the twentieth century. However, as to its extension to the twenty-first century, things are far murkier. As much evidence as there is in its favor, two arguments work against it. First, as Lanier argues, technological growth has not brought along with it a proportional growth in software development. In fact, if Lanier is correct, the speedup of hardware is more than offset by the slowing down of software. Whether we fully agree or not (and as an empirical claim it must be supported by real data), there is certainly some merit to Lanier's claims of a serious bottleneck. This becomes more obvious if we notice that breaking out of the bottleneck calls for serious human involvement, implying that, in the foreseeable future, computer technology will still be dependent on human intervention for improvement. None of the proposed software techniques, including the genetic-algorithm techniques that play a crucial role in Kurzweil's arguments, have yet endowed computers with the necessary self-programming capabilities. As is reported in Hofstadter (1999), John Holland and John Koza – the originators of and central figures behind genetic algorithms and genetic programming – believe that the idea that "intelligence would simply grow automatically out of genetic algorithms, much as a tomato plant automatically grows from a seed in a garden, [is rooted in] ungrounded fantasies." In other words, they do not foresee "any kind of rapid, exponential progress toward the goal of human-level intelligence."

Second, as Kurzweil himself notes, "there will inevitably be technological discontinuities in the twenty-first century," by which he means that any specific technology, such as chip manufacturing, will eventually run up against a brick wall – whence his projection that novel technologies, such as quantum computing, will reliably and regularly take over (Kurzweil 1999: 110). At present, however, quantum computing and nanotechnology are extremely rudimentary and so speculative that basing arguments on their "certain" emergence and success are very dubious. In short, we have no guarantee of the continuing prevalence of Moore's Law or its analogues even in the near future, let alone one hundred years from now, or further.

This argument might not sit well with people like Bill Joy, who are convinced that "we should be able to meet or exceed the Moore's law rate of progress for another 30 years, [by which time] we are likely to be able to build machines, in quantity, a million times as powerful as the personal computers of today – sufficient to implement the dreams of Kurzweil and Moravec" (Joy 2000: 7). What would happen, then?

Dangerous Cyborgs: Robots in Rebellion

Our most powerful 21st-century technologies – robotics, genetic engineering, and nanotech – are threatening to make humans an endangered species.

– Bill Joy

In an article titled "Why the Future Doesn't Need Us," published by *Wired* magazine, Joy (2000) provides a sincere report of how he was taken aback when he encountered Kurzweil's ideas, and how these ideas led him to see "some merit in the reasoning" outlined by Theodore Kaczynski, the Unabomber. The reasoning details the doomsday scenario in which either robots or a tiny elite of humans will take control of the human race, reducing it to "the status of domestic animals." As a cofounder of Sun Microsystems and a key player behind influential technologies such as the Unix operating system and the Java programming language, Bill Joy is well placed within the inner circle of the technological elite. Therefore, his ideas should be taken with the same seriousness that he affords to Kurzweil's futuristic predictions, especially that they are expressed from what seems to be a deeply human concern. Let us see if we can seek any comfort for Bill Joy in what historians of technology have to say. History matters here because that is how Kurzweil tries to make his case: a supposedly historical perspective, but a simplistic and linear view of history, I would like to argue.

Kurzweil provides data to show the trend that computation followed over the twentieth century. He mentions a good number of mechanical calculating devices, starting with Babbage's Analytical Engine and ending with the electromechanical Zuse 3 in 1941. (For reasons that are not clear, he transports the Analytical Engine from the 1860s to 1900 in his discussion.) But his data constitute more of a report than an analysis or an explanation. He does not tell us how or why this trend prevailed in that century; which scientific and technological tools were needed; how much the developments in physics and chemistry at the turn of the century contributed to this trend's gaining momentum; which technologies in which areas preceded the invention of each new computing machine; which social forces joined together in order for this to be possible; what economic and political mechanisms were at work that made such a trend favorable; which historical barriers had to be surpassed before this could happen; and so on.

A genuinely historical analysis would need to take all of the above into account. Historian of technology Paul Edwards (1996) has argued at length how, in the context of what he calls the "closed-world view" of America during the Cold War, the social, cultural, and institutional specificities of the era contributed to the emergence of computer technology in general, and AI in particular. Langdon Winner, another historian of technology, has described "computer romanticism" as "the latest version of the nineteenth- and twentieth-century faith . . . that have always expected to generate freedom, democracy and justice through sheer material abundance" (1986: 108). He argues that this faith is based on a number of key assumptions about the equivalence of information, knowledge, power, and democracy. Kling and Iacono (1995: 129–130) explain how AI was institutionalized as part of mainstream computer science (through curricular integration, dedicated journals and venues, a "special interest group" within the Association of Computing Machinery), and how funding support, commercial interest, and exaggerated accounts by media transformed AI into a major computerization movement of the late twentieth century (see the Prologue).

Arguments of this nature, I suspect, might do little to put to rest Joy's deep concerns about the future of the human race. But at least they present a different view of history from what technologists are typically attuned to. What these arguments imply is that it is not possible to understand the development of technology in isolation from its sociohistorical context. This perspective is in sharp contrast to Kurzweil's Darwinian view of technological development, which portrays technological development in abstract isolation from the context of its use, promotion, and acceptance. As David Noble has shown, this view considers the flow of creative invention to follow its own inner logic with successively filtered processes that guarantee the survival of "best" alternatives (see Chapter 1).

Cold Cyborgs: Zealous Zombies

There is a common intuition among people to the effect that computers and robots lack an essential aspect of what makes us human. As Sherry Turkle (1995) reports from her interviews with different groups, people's normal response to the claims of AI is to agree with "the premise that human minds are some kind of computer" but, at the same time, to find ways "to think of themselves as something more than that." Turkle continues:

Their sense of personal identity often focused on whatever they defined as "not cognition" or "beyond information." People commonly referred to spontaneity, feelings, intentionality, and sensuality in describing what made them special. They conceded to the rule-based computer some power of reason and then turned their attention to the soul and spirit in the human machine. (Turkle 1997: 129)

These lay intuitions about the nature of human intelligence on the part of people have their parallels in serious intellectual debates, especially among philosophers. There is a wide spectrum of such "exclusionist" views that, while granting the possibility of machine intelligence growing in capabilities to an unlimited extent, associate human intelligence with some other human attribute that is allegedly inaccessible to machines – for example, consciousness, embodiment, biology. The philosopher Thomas Nagel, for instance, has written of "robots and automata that behaved like people though they experienced nothing" (1974). He singles out "subjective experience" as the key fact of human life that cannot be captured by "reductive analysis" and artificial simulation.

The most outspoken advocate of the exclusionist view, however, is John Searle. As we saw in the case of chess, Searle's main argument is based on the putative lack of original meaning in computers. Like Nagel, however, he is also concerned with consciousness, which he takes to be a direct product of "the causal powers of the brain" (2002: 67). Thus, although he poses "no objection in principle to constructing an artificial hardware system that would duplicate the powers of the brain to cause consciousness using some chemistry different from neurons," he argues that "computation by itself is insufficient to guarantee any such causal powers" (ibid.). Searle's main argument relies on his famous thought experiment of the Chinese room, against which much has been written, with essentially no impact on Searle himself, however. Thus, I do not need to repeat those arguments here. Instead, I want to try to clarify his arguments a bit further. Searle disagrees particularly vehemently with claims like the following, which is presumably based on the ideas of J. Storrs Hall, a computer scientist at Rutgers University:

There are a variety of proposals for nanotechnology swarms, in which the real environment is constructed from interacting multitudes of nanomachines. In all of the swarm conceptions, physical reality becomes a lot like virtual reality. You can be sleeping in your bed one moment, and have the room transform into your kitchen as you awake. Actually, change that to a dining room as there's no need for a kitchen. Related nanotechnology will instantly create whatever meal you desire. When you finish eating, the room can transform into a study, or a game room, or a swimming pool, or a redwood forest, or the Taj Mahal. You get the idea. (Kurzweil 1999: 145)

As we see, physical and material reality becomes totally malleable in this picture, which is based on the notion that "consciousness and identity are not a function of the specific particles at all, because our own particles are constantly changing" (Kurzweil 1999: 54). In other words, in the spirit of the "beam me up" teleportation technology of *Star Trek* and other science fiction stories, it assumes that consciousness is not a function of the actual particles, but solely of their pattern and organization (ibid.). Searle strongly disagrees with this position and attributes it to the confusion between "simulation" and "duplication," which he takes to be a symptom of a deeper confusion – namely, that between what he calls "observer-independent" and "observer-relative" features of the world. Examples of the first category, according to Searle, are molecules, mountains, and tectonic plates; examples of the second, money, marriage, and government.

Searle includes computation in the second category, arguing that "the machine knows nothing about computation.... The computation is observer-relative, or ... 'in the eye of the beholder'" (2002: 69). This argument is, in fact, a variation on a distinction that is usually made between "original meaning" and "derivative meaning," one example of which we saw in discussing chess in the previous chapter. The common theme in both arguments is that computations performed by a machine, regardless of their complexity, are meaningless, and that we are the ones who attribute meaning to them. We have seen the limits of this argument in the discussion of chess. The interesting point, however, is how Searle's objection is itself based on a radically brain-in-the-vat conception of intelligence, which attributes consciousness to alleged "causal properties of the brain." Searle's clash with Kurzweil, therefore, is not over the latter's mentalistic attitude; it is over his claim that "We will be software, not hardware" and can inhabit whatever hardware we like best (Searle 2002: 59). Let us examine this claim more closely.

Bad Cyborgs: Soulful Swarms

Our discussion earlier in this chapter about the irrelevance of the biological skin in delineating the effective boundary of the human body might lead to the conclusion that the body itself is also irrelevant to cognition, that the body is "mere jelly" as Hans Moravec muses, and that we will soon be mere "software," as Kurzweil claims. Moravec, for instance, has suggested that the self is a kind of persisting higher-order pattern that can be abstracted from the body as an information-based construct (1998). As we saw earlier, Andy Clark also seems to see great promise in nonpenetrative technologies that allow us to transcend our biological skins. However, in discussing "bad borgs," he scorns what he calls a "popular caricature" of Moravec's vision that takes the idea quite literally.[14] A champion of embodied cognition himself, Clark "roundly reject[s] the vision of the self as a kind of ethereal, information-based construct," arguing that, "There is no informationally constituted *user* relative to whom all the rest is just *tools*. It is . . . *tools all the way down*" (2003: 192; emphasis is Clark's). By Clark's measures, therefore, "it would be crazy to identify the physical basis of oneself solely with the machinery of the conscious goings-on" (ibid.). Where do Kurzweil's views fall in this picture?

Kurzweil, as we saw, bases his claims on two key conjectures about the nature of consciousness and intelligence: (1) that intelligence is nothing but the capability to search and manipulate patterns that lie in a very large but well-defined "problem space"; and (2) that consciousness is a pattern that is independent of and separable from the material substrate on which it is implemented. The first is part of his "easy recipe" for building intelligent machines – namely, the combination of three ideas: neural networks, recursion, and genetic algorithms; the second is articulated by Kurzweil in discussing consciousness. The second conjecture is of such a character that it could only be decided empirically; it is one of several competing views about the nature of consciousness. While some philosophers argue that human consciousness is *qualitatively* different from the type of consciousness that any other entity might conceivably have, the view represented by Kurzweil maintains that the difference is only *quantitative* and that we just have to wait for the right technology to arrive in order to establish this.

The first conjecture about intelligence, as we saw at the outset, is one of the most commonplace ideas in AI, and it has given rise to the centrality of search among AI methods. Many of the methods I have discussed in this and the previous chapter – from game trees to genetic algorithms – are varieties of search. As the complexity of problems increases, however, the space in which the search is performed explodes to very large dimensions. The domain of chess, with roughly 10^{120} possible games, provides only the most modest of examples of such problem spaces. Speculative technologies such as quantum computing are supposed to help in addressing this problem – the problem of search in ever-enlarging spaces. Despite the potentially impressive capabilities these technologies may provide, however, they have their own limitations, as we observed already.

These difficulties, however, do not keep Kurzweil from making shakily grounded speculations about other realms. For instance, to the question "How about creating art?," Kurzweil replies:

Here a quantum computer would have considerable value. Creating a work of art involves solving a series, possibly an extensive series, of problems. A quantum computer could consider every possible combination of elements – words, notes, strokes – for each such decision. We still need a way to test each answer to the sequence of aesthetic problems, but the quantum computer would be ideal for instantly searching through a universe of possibilities. (Kurzweil 1999)

This view of art and artistic creation is simply a logical extension of the extreme view of intelligence as merely search in a vast but predetermined space of possibilities. It should not surprise us, therefore, to see Kurzweil call the following a "haiku poem" produced by his "Cybernetic Poet after reading poems by Wendy Dennis" (ibid.):

PAGE

Sashay down the page
through the lioness
nestled in my soul.

I leave it to the reader to decide whether or not this is a haiku – it might well be. But I cannot help wondering whose "soul" is being referred to by the machine. The language of "souls" and "spirits" is, of course, no longer scientifically respectable, and the poem should be judged according to the canons of its appropriate genre. The example, however, points to a problem that runs deep into Kurzweil's way of thinking, which, I want to argue, represents old ideas in modern dress.

Take the idea of uploading all of French literature into our brains via a memory implant, which Kurzweil discusses with ecstatic fervor. According to this idea, at some point in the near future, we should be able to learn and enjoy French literature instantly, avoiding the boredom of listening to shabby professors, studying at night, taking exams, and so on. To understand the thinking behind this idea, let us look at a more familiar technology: the wristwatch. David Landes (2000) has chronicled the history of the development of timekeeping technologies in modern times and how they have enabled us to factor time constantly into our social and individual activities; how we have become time-disciplined and time-conscious, in other words. As Clark (2003: 41) notes, however, "what counts here is not always *consciously knowing* the time.... Rather, the crucial factor is the constant and easy availability of the time, *should we desire to know it*" (original emphasis). The poise for easy use and deployment is the characteristic of what are called "transparent technologies," of which the wristwatch is a homely example. It is this transparency that makes us unhesitatingly reply "yes," even before consulting our wristwatches, when somebody asks us about the time on the street. What this suggests, according to Clark, is that "the line between that which is *easily and readily accessible* and that which should be counted as *part of the knowledge base* of an active intelligent system is slim and unstable indeed" (ibid.: 42; emphasis is Clark's). In other words, your "yes" answer to the question "Do you know the time" amounts to the literal truth, for you do know the time. "It is just that the 'you' that knows the time is no longer the bare biological organism but the hybrid biotechnological system that now includes wristwatch as a proper part" (ibid.).

Clark compares this with the case of an Oxford dictionary, an equally ubiquitous technology available in most households. The difference here is that, unlike the case of the wristwatch, if someone asks the meaning of a word which we do not know, we won't say "Yes, I know what that word means" and then proceed to consult the dictionary. How can we explain this difference? The difference is in the distinct histories of wristwatches and dictionaries, which has turned the former, but not the latter, into a transparent technology. The passage to transparency involves a process of *coevolution*, in which the technology becomes increasingly easy to use and access while humans learn to use technology through social, cultural, and educational change – a process that, according to Landes, took over a hundred years in the case of wristwatches. Both sides of the coevolution are fascinating in their own right but, as Clark points out, the technological story pales beside the human-centered story.

The example of timing technologies is but one example in a series of old and new technologies – pen, paper, written words, numerical notations, and so on – that allow what Clark, following Vygotsky (1986), calls "scaffolded thinking." The unusual degree of cortical plasticity together with the

unusually extended period of learning and development allows us to assimilate a whole range of nonbiological props, scaffoldings, tools, and resources,
making humans (but not dogs, cats, or dolphins) natural-born cyborgs. What
makes us distinct, therefore, is the capability of our minds to break out of the
skin and skull boundaries, and to leak into the external world. Rather than
locate the individual thinking system within the metabolic frontiers of skin
and skull, Clark argues, "A thoroughgoing physicalism should allow mind to
determine – by its actions, capacities, and effects – its own place and location
in the natural order" (2003: 43). Failing to appreciate this point, according
to Clark, amounts to the old idea of special spirit-stuff in modern dress.

It should be now clear why Kurzweil's French-literature-on-a-chip scenario is one such old idea disguised in modern dress. Technically speaking,
we know that a present-day thumb drive has enough memory space to easily store all of French literature. What makes it different from an implanted
chip, therefore, is only that one is inside the skin and the other is not. If Clark
is correct, however, this doesn't matter. Actually, he makes a more radical
point, almost erasing the distinction between biological and nonbiological
memory:

It just *doesn't matter* whether the data are stored somewhere inside the biological
organism or stored in the external world. What matters is how information is
poised for retrieval and for immediate use as and when required. Often, of course,
information stored outside the skull is not efficiently poised for access and use as
information stored in the head. And often, the biological brain is insufficiently
aware of exactly *what* information is stored outside to make maximum use of
it. . . . But the more these drawbacks are overcome, the less it seems to matter
(scientifically and philosophically) exactly *where* various processes and data
stores are physically located, and whether they are neurally or technologically
realized. The opportunistic biological brain doesn't care. Nor – for most purposes – should we." (Clark 2003: 69; emphasis in the original)

The fact that Kurzweil cares about *where* the information is leaves little room
for misinterpreting his views. In the spirit of the old mentalistic tradition,
Kurzweil wants to import mind into matter, rather than allowing the mind
to determine its own place in the natural order. The closer one looks, the
more Kurzweil's cyborgs look as "bad borgs." They are bad not in the sense
that Joy fears, Lanier deplores, or Searle excludes, and not even because they
violate our basic commonsensical intuitions, which are also supported by the
latest research in neuroscience, but because they are based on shaky scientific
claims, nascent laboratory technologies, unwarranted historical generalizations, and simplistic philosophical assumptions.

Conclusion: An Ongoing Story

> Children, AI computer programs, and nonhuman primates: all here
> embody 'almost minds.' Who or what has fully human status?... What
> is the end, or telos, of this discourse of approximation, reproduction, and
> communication, in which the boundaries among machines, animals, and
> humans are exceedingly permeable? Where will this evolutionary, devel-
> opmental, and historical communicative commerce take us in the techno-
> bio-politics of difference?
>
> — Donna Haraway: Primate Visions

The story of cyborgs as natural-artificial hybrids does not end here. It will
go on, physically and virtually, in our extended bodies and minds, with the
cyborg family tree spreading out in various directions. Whatever our ethical
and philosophical position, we cannot help but be impressed by the capabilities that cybernetic technologies provide to biological human beings and
the vast horizon that they open up for cognitive and cultural development.
Even the most hardheaded critics of modern technology have their place in
the cyborg lineage, as they rarely hesitate to take advantage of technology
when push comes to shove – in matters of life and death, for example. The
question, therefore, is not whether we are cyborgs or not; "*Tools Are Us*," as
Clark does not tire of reminding us, and *homo faber* – tool-makers – we are
as Karl Marx determined more than a century ago. The question is how we
confront the fact that we are cyborgs, practically and ethically.

What We Have Learned *about* Cybernetic AI:
Cyborg Horizons

Cybernetic AI has a lot to offer to the future of AI. The technologies listed in
Figure 3.1 are just a small sample of what is out there, and although some of
them are not the direct products of AI research and practice, ideas from AI
have had an indisputable impact on their inception and implementation. The
fact that there is disagreement among AI practitioners and engineers as to
the potentials of these technologies illustrates the degree of uncertainty that
is still involved in our understanding of these technologies. The difference
of opinion between Kurzwel and Lanier, for instance, reflects the tension
between the views of a practically minded engineer and the speculations of
a futurist who seeks to push the boundaries of AI into the realm of science
fiction. Although Lanier stops at the technical threshold and highlights the
practical challenges facing AI (and computer science, in general), Kurzweil
begins with an engineering thesis – that intelligence is the optimal utilization

of resources – but generalizes that idea into a universal characterization of intelligence. These generalizations are problematic in many ways.

First, Kurzweil's extrapolations are simplistically linear (Haraway 1991). His views present a clear case of technological determinism – the idea that the development of technology follows its own inner logic, driving history and society forward with the compelling force of that logic. Kurzweil might indeed have a valid point about the accelerating pace of technological development during the last century or so. Like other technologists of his guild, however, he tries to make his case by simplifying the story. In this story, human motivations, alliances, conflicts, and so on do not play a role. It is mainly machines and technologies marching forward in a linear progression, taking humans along like thoughtless slaves. Students of science and technology studies have for many years challenged this type of deterministic view by attracting our attention to *cultural imaginaries* and the material practices that they animate (Castañeda and Suchman 2005). By showing that claims about universals always come from particularly positioned persons, they question the assumed innocence of technological tales and their "rigorous exclusion of contextualizing politics" (Haraway 1989: 156; cf. Castañeda and Suchman 2005). At stake, as Katherine Hayles has argued, "is not so much the risky game of long-term predictions as contending for how we now understand ... what it means to be human" (2005: 131).

Kurzweil's futuristic predictions also can be seen in a similar light. Many people, including this author, share his excitement about the horizons that new technologies can open to future generations. However, I am skeptical of his attempts to erase the boundary between science and science fiction. Cybernetic technologies might have rendered many boundaries increasingly porous, pushing the perceived perimeter of possibility outward, but the physical structure of our world, as well as the cultural and economic realities of human societies, still impose their dictum, presenting insurmountable resistance to our most sought-out fantasies.[15] There is, in other words, a limit to what *can* be done in reality.

What We Have Learned *from* Cybernetic AI: Cyborg Ethics

> We must recognize that, in a very deep sense, we were always hybrid beings, joint products of our biological nature and mutilayered linguistic, cultural, and technological webs. Only then can we confront, without fear or prejudice, the specific demons in our cyborg closets. Only then can we actively structure the kinds of world, technology, and culture that will build the kinds of *people* we choose to be.
>
> – Clark (2003: 195)

Artifacts embody social, political, and ethical values (Winner 1986). AI creations do this more pungently, and cybernetic AI, as a result of its malleable character, brings ethical issues to the forefront.[16] The celebrated science fiction writer Isaac Asimov addressed these issues in his three laws of robotics.[17] The alleged purpose of these laws is to protect the human species from potential harms by its own creations. The ethical issues raised by computer technologies, however, are far greater in scope and deeper in implication than can be afforded by Asimov's laws of fifty years ago. The concerns voiced by Bill Joy provide a small sample of such issues, and, despite their dystopian semblance, they cannot be taken lightly. Even if we rule out the doomsday scenario, there are other concerns that are real and pressing at the moment – from issues of privacy, surveillance, and freedom of speech to the more enduring questions of social justice, equitable access, and environmental degradation. The urgency of these issues is such that even an optimist such as Andy Clark is heedful, discussing them in a separate chapter of his book (Clark 2003). However, we need a much more serious and systematic approach.

One of the reasons why these issues have become critical is the ubiquitous, but invisible, presence of computer technologies in our daily lives. Ironically, as new technologies become incorporated into our daily practice, we tend to notice them less, not more. Soon, we cease thinking of them as technologies at all (Bruce 1999). Henry Petroski (1989) in his book, *The Pencil*, refers to the meticulous list Henry David Thoreau made prior to his adventure in the woods:

But there is one object that Thoreau neglected to mention, one that he most certainly carried himself. For without this object Thoreau could not . . . [sketch] the fleeting fauna, . . . label his blotting paper pressing leaves . . . record the measurements he made . . . write home . . . [or] make his list. Without a pencil Thoreau would have been lost in the Maine woods. (pp. 3–4)

This is a striking example of the invisibility of technologies. The Thoreaus of our times probably also would take their laptops, GPS tracking devices, and maybe cell phones when they take similar adventures in the wild. Any one of these devices, however, would turn the desired seclusion into an illusion, because of the monitoring capability that they offer to anyone who might take interest in "watching" the adventurer, especially to the government and private companies such as Google and Yahoo whose services have become an indispensable part of contemporary life. People are more exposed nowadays than they think.

AI research cannot remain indifferent to these social and ethical questions. AI methods and technologies are increasingly used in areas as varied as web searching, video games, educational software, data mining, and financial forecasting, and a brief look at the impact of these areas on the broader culture, economy, and individual psyches should alert AI practitioners to the significance of what they contribute, but also to the concomitant moral duties and social responsibilities. The right approach to these issues is what Kling (1997: 2) called a "heads-up" view of computer technologies, "one that examines the social choices of whether and how to computerize an activity, and the relationships between computerized activity and other parts of our social world," as opposed to heads-in view of technophiles and the heads-back view of technophobes.

4   Cyc: Knowledge-Intensive AI

Boole's Logical Dream

Cyc is one of the most ambitious projects in the history of AI. Launched in 1984, it was originally envisioned as a three-decade research program that would proceed in three distinct stages (see Figure 4.1):

1. slow hand-coding of a large knowledge base;
2. fast and self-initiated acquisition of more knowledge through reading and assimilation of databases by the machine, leading to a point at which the system, according to its creators, having gone "beyond the frontiers of human knowledge," would be capable of:
3. conducting its own research-and-development projects through learning by discovery, in order to continue ever expanding its knowledge base.

The first stage was envisaged as ending in 1994, the second by the late 1990s, and, as Doug Lenat, the main figure behind the project, put it, "Soon after, say by 2001, we planned to have it learning on its own, by automated discovery methods" (Lenat 1997b). By going through these stages, Cyc was intended to break out of AI's so-called knowledge acquisition bottleneck. According to initial estimates, the critical mass for passing through the first stage of hand-coding was on the order of one million facts. Putting such a large number of facts together with the heuristics necessary to apply them under the right circumstances was a daunting task that called for a "large, high-risk, high-payoff, decade-sized project" (Lenat and Guha 1990: Preface). Cyc was supposed to be exactly such a system – a $50 million project that in its first decade would require two person-centuries for data entry.

In this chapter, after a brief introduction to Cyc and to the conceptual and historical motivations behind it, especially expert systems and their problems, I review some of the perceived remedies to such problems in AI and elsewhere, of which Cyc is a prominent example. We then examine Cyc in theory and

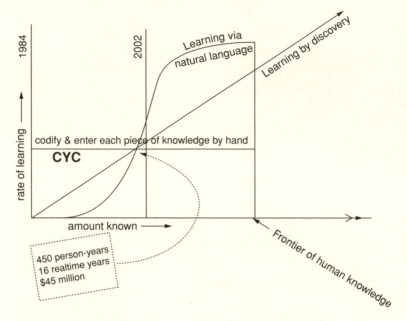

Figure 4.1. The growth of Cyc as envisaged by its creators (from Lenat 2002, with permission).

in practice, and analyze the problems that challenge Cyc in achieving its proclaimed goals. Finally, I discuss some of the lessons this project can bring to AI.

BACKGROUND: MACHINES *WITHOUT* COMMON SENSE

As was suggested earlier, the Cyc project was motivated by the idea that a vast amount of knowledge is the key to intelligence. What we need to achieve human-level intelligence, the creators of Cyc believed, is to provide a machine with enough *commonsense knowledge* for it to be able to continue the process of knowledge acquisition on its own. Explicitly, after a decade Cyc was meant to achieve the following:

As a broad "driving force" or "forcing function," we chose to encode the knowledge [necessary] to understand a one-volume desk encyclopedia and a newspaper – including editorials, advertisements, advice columns, and so on. This does *not* mean the contents of such works (though, frankly, we often add some of that as well!); rather, it means ferreting out and representing the underlying common-sense knowledge that the writers of those articles assumed that their readers already possessed. (Lenat and Guha 1990: 29; emphasis Lenat and Guha's)

Cyc was designed using principles derived from classical symbolic logic, although, as we shall see, this does not necessarily position its developers in the logicist camp introduced in Chapter 1.[1] By and large, it consists of explicit representations of knowledge linked together by logical rules of inference. In this chapter, I will use the term *formal* to mean any system that is based on this type of explicit, logic-based representations.[2] Using Cyc as a prominent example, my purpose is to explicate the motivations, assumptions, and tensions built into formal systems, so conceived.

The Search Engine that Mistakes "Politics" for "Science"

The emphasis on commonsense knowledge in Cyc derives from the fact that computer systems often perform scandalously poorly in domains where human beings feel most comfortable. To give an example of such performance, let me begin with an anecdotal report.

Anyone who has ever used the search engines available on the World Wide Web has probably noticed that, despite considerable improvements in recent years, they still perform poorly in certain occasions. For instance, in response to my query to an online bookstore for the title *The Crisis of European Sciences and Transcendental Phenomenology* (by Edmund Husserl), the search engine returned more than ten "matching titles," none of which was the title in question. Given that the title is long, I tried again, this time providing only the first three substantive words (i.e., *Crisis, European, Sciences*) only to get, to my surprise, twenty matching titles, one of which was the original one. The other nineteen ranged over a number of different topics. I have listed five of them here in the order they appeared:

The Crisis of European Sciences and Transcendental Phenomenology	3+
Limits of Persuasion: Germany and the Yugoslav Crisis	1
Crisis and Choice in European Social Democracy	2
The Crisis in Representation in Europe	2−
The Death of Britain? The UK's Continental Crisis	1(?)
Security, Identity, and Nation Building: Cyprus and the EU in Comparative Perspective	0(?)

Although these might be quite intriguing titles in their own right, their conceptual distance from the object of my inquiry reveals the ignorance behind the response on the part of the search engine. Obviously, like any other search engine, this one had first tried to match as many words as possible in order to respond. Result 1 (in complete match with the three words), Result 2 (with one match), and Result 3 (with two matches) are outcomes of this attempt. The pattern of the outputs shows, further, that the matching has been performed in the order of the input string. That is, first the word *crisis* is matched, then *European*, and finally *sciences*. the target title was the first on the output list, it also implies that titles with the maximum matching have priority. Furthermore, this means that the search is not a linear search in which the matches are simply listed in the order they are encountered.

Result 4 reveals even more flexibility because it shows that the search engine doesn't stop at exact matches – *Europe* is also considered as a possible match for *European*. And because of its rank in the ordering, Result 5 cannot be only a match for *crisis*. (The position of the word *crisis* within the string could not be the reason, because in Result 2 it was also in final position.) Should we, then, say that the search engine knew that Britain is part of Europe and used that knowledge to come up with this response (in the given position)? Or maybe it knew that Europe is a continent? If this sounds dubious, then Result 6 should certainly convince us that, in addition to simple string matching, something else is going on here. For there is precisely *no* match, in the literal sense, for the words occurring in Result 6. The only way to justify this response is to conclude that the machine "knows" that the *E* in *EU* – not just any *E* as, for example, in *EZ* – stands for Europe, and this is what has prompted it to give this response. If this is the case, how much "knowledge" – and consequently, in light of Cyc's philosophy, "intelligence" – are we willing to attribute to this search engine? The question becomes more complicated if we notice that no attempt was made by the search engine at *understanding* any of the titles involved, because my query was about science and all the titles returned were about politics.

This short anecdote clearly illustrates why having commonsense knowledge might be useful for computer systems. What originally motivated the Cyc project, however, was not the poor performance of search engines (the World Wide Web did not exist in 1984), but the problems faced by "expert systems." Before we attempt to answer the above question about the search engine's intelligence, therefore, a brief sketch of these systems may prove helpful.

Expert Systems: Knowledge Engineers at Work

In the late 1960s and early 1970s, a decline of interest in AI research on the part of funding agencies led practitioners to look for practical problems to solve. As knowledge was conceived to be the key to such endeavor, a new class of artifacts ("expert systems") and a new group of practitioners ("knowledge engineers") appeared on the scene. The task of a knowledge engineer is threefold (Hayes 1990: 201):

- To elicit from an expert – that is, "a human being whose head contains knowledge" – the knowledge (they intuit) they deploy in dealing with their area of expertise.[3]
- To formalize this knowledge, using a suitable representational language, in a knowledge base.
- To compare the performance of this formalization with that of the expert for the purpose of "correcting" machine behavior – that is, bringing it closer to the expert's introspective account.

Dendral and Mycin were among the first expert systems. Developed by Edward Feigenbaum and his colleagues over a period of ten years, Dendral was an expert system for the analysis of the molecular structure of chemical compounds – a tedious task traditionally performed by chemists taking educated guesses on the data obtained from mass spectroscopy.[4] Dendral consisted of a set of IF–THEN rules like the following, together with the logic required to combine them (Feigenbaum and Barr 1982; in Crevier 1993: 149):

IF
    the spectrum for the molecule has two peaks at masses x_1 and x_2 such
      that
        $x_1 + x_2 =$ Molecular Weight $+ 28$, AND
        $x_1 - 28$ is a high peak, AND
        $x_2 - 28$ is a high peak, AND
      at least one of x_1 or x_2 is high,
THEN
    the molecule contains a ketone group.

In this way, Dendral drastically reduced the effort needed to determine the structure of a chemical substance, narrowing the search down in some cases better than chemists could, and demonstrating the possibility of capturing expert knowledge as a set of rules in a machine. The integration of the rules and meta-rules (i.e., the rules that determine which rules to apply) was, however, a major weakness of Dendral and prevented its expansion beyond a certain point.

Mycin, an expert system for the diagnosis of infectious blood diseases, could overcome this limitation by using "production systems" – again a set of IF–THEN rules like the following – but with the mechanisms for deciding

when and how to apply the rules separated from the set of rules themselves
(ibid: 151):

IF
>   the site of the culture is blood, AND the gram strain is positive, AND
>   the portal of entry is gastrointestinal tract, AND
>   the abdomen is the locus of infection, OR
>   the pelvis is the locus of infection

THEN
>   there is strongly suggestive evidence that Enterobacteriaceae is the
>   class of organisms for which therapy should cover.

Mycin used a tree structure for searching through the rules. The mechanism (or "control structure") for exploring the tree was, however, separated
from the tree description, giving rise to a modular, two-part construction
and making it possible to conceive of representation and control as comprising distinct issues. Expert systems were, as such, considered to be not
about "reasoning" but about "knowing" (Crevier 1993: 156). The accompanying shift from the expression and control of knowledge (as in heuristic search; see Chapter 2) to the manipulation of massive amounts of it,
as Herbert Simon pointed out, took place not so much because of new
insights about the importance of knowledge as because of advancements in
hardware technology, especially in computer storage capacity (Crevier 1993:
146–47).

This separation between description and knowledge, on the one hand,
and control and reasoning, on the other, as we shall see later, turned into a
dictum in projects such as Cyc, where most of the emphasis is put on the
former at the expense of the latter.

The Expert System that Mistakes Cars for People

The early success of expert systems bestowed on AI the respect it was longing
for, not only in academia, but also in business, where, according to some
accounts, billions of dollars were invested in expert systems for manufacturing, financial services, machinery diagnosis, and so on. But this success was
very limited because the competence of such systems was restricted to very
narrow domains. Two of the most notorious examples of such limitations
come from a medical diagnosis program that, given the data for the case of a
1969 Chevrolet – reddish-brown spots on the body – diagnosed it as suffering
from measles, and a car loan authorization program that approved a loan
to a teenager who had claimed to have worked at the same job for twenty

years. The problem, of course, was that the builders of the system had failed to include the fact in the knowledge base: that the given Chevrolet is not a human being, and that one cannot have work experience that is longer than one's age. Another program, given the case of a patient with kidney infection, prescribed boiling the kidney in hot water – a good remedy against infection, but a terrible failure to understand the basics of what was going on.

To state the obvious, these programs seemed to lack an important feature of intelligence: Despite apparent sophistication and expertise in specialized areas like medicine, they demonstrated a clear lack of understanding of very basic facts that a human being takes for granted. They either had to be given the minutest details, as in the first two cases, or else they seemed to be missing very basic knowledge (e.g., about living organisms), as in the third. What was it that was missing, though?

PERCEIVED REMEDIES

Many answers are conceivable – that machines are hopelessly unreliable whatever we put into them; that the knowledge engineers had not done their job properly; that our notion of expert knowledge might be totally misguided; that we know what expert knowledge consists of but we need to equip machines with a more basic substrate (common sense) before they can successfully use their expert knowledge; and so on. This last view found the strongest support in AI, and was pursued in two directions whose respective objectives were: (i) to formalize commonsense knowledge in a principled way; (ii) to engineer commonsense knowledge in an ad hoc manner. I will examine these and other alternatives in what follows.

The Formalization of Commonsense Knowledge

John McCarthy and Patrick Hayes pioneered work on the formalization of commonsense knowledge by proposing "to use all of our knowledge to construct a computer program that knows" (1969: 466–67). McCarthy pursued this path by enhancing classical logic with new mechanisms. Circumscription, for instance, allows one to neglect certain categories unless their existence explicitly follows from the statement of the problem and commonsense knowledge. McCarthy (1986: 91) gives a simple example. Suppose that I hire you to build me a birdcage and you don't put a top on it. I can get out of paying for it even if you tell the judge that I never said my bird could fly. In other words, in any situation involving a bird, if the bird cannot fly, and this is relevant, then I must say so. Whereas if the bird can fly, McCarthy argues, there is no requirement to mention the fact – the category of "non-flying birds" can, therefore, be neglected by default.

Hayes proposed to formalize our knowledge of naïve physics (as exemplified in his *Naïve Physics Manifesto*), naïve psychology, and naïve epistemology (1990: 197). Based on this proposal, he laid out a comprehensive research program for AI, according to which AI should "deliberately postpone detailed consideration of implementation" – that is, of computational issues having to do with search, control, and so on. In its place, he suggested, we should develop a formalism that is *thorough* (it must cover the whole range of everyday phenomena), reasonably *detailed, dense* (the ratio of facts to concepts needs to be fairly high), and *uniform* (there should be a common formal language) (172).

Hayes's proposal was intended to mark a reversal in emphasis in AI research, from "working programs" to "correct representations" (173, 198). The prevailing attitude in AI – "that research which does not result fairly quickly in a working program of some kind is somehow useless, or at least highly suspicious" (173) – he argued, has resulted in weak and unfaithful representations of the world. Thus, "even accepting the criterion [of working programs] as an ultimate test of an AI theory," "applying it too rigorously too soon (typically, after three years' work) is self-defeating. *We are never going to get an adequate formalization of common sense by making short forays into small areas, no matter how many of them we make*" (199–200; emphasis Hayes's).

To achieve this adequate formalization, Hayes suggested, we need to follow the practice of knowledge engineers, who "formalize, criticize, and correct" to the point of satisfactory performance (see earlier). The ideal way is therefore to have a committee, each member of which is assigned a "cluster" to formalize – scales of measurement (e.g., size, extent, amount), shapes and orientation, substances, and so on. What makes this feasible, Hayes believed, is that common sense is a domain "in which we are all experts, in the required sense" (202). The major problem – "who is to say that where one has got to is not far enough?" – could also be addressed by depending on intuition: "people's common intuition is the guide" (ibid.).

I will examine the theoretical underpinnings of this view more closely in the next chapter. Here I want to show how it influenced the Cyc approach.

The Engineering of Commonsense Knowledge

The Cyc group followed Hayes's research program in all respects but one. They agreed that "knowledge must be extracted" from people and other sources, but disagreed that one needs to develop a "deep theory" of things for the purpose of formalizing the knowledge thus extracted. Their self-described "scruffy" methodology, as opposed to McCarthy and Hayes's "neat" approach, was to "collect, e.g., all the facts and heuristics about 'Water' that newspaper articles assume their readers already know ... [rather than] aim to somehow capture a deeper theory of 'Water' in all its various forms" (Lenat and Feigenbaum 1991: 219). They aimed to collect, in other words, "the millions of facts that we all know and that we assume everyone else knows" (Lenat and Guha 1990: 4). The Cyc group's approach was motivated by the belief that the problem with expert systems was one of *brittleness*[5] – that is, the inability of these systems to handle novel and unexpected situations. They believed that expert systems had fallen into what they called "the representation trap," which they defined as:

choosing a set of long, complex primitives (predicate names) that have a lot of knowledge compiled within them, and writing rules that are also tailored to the program's domain (omitting premises that needn't be worried about in that particular task). The bait in the trap is the fact that it works – at least within the narrow domain for which that particular program was designed. The catch is that the resultant system is isolated and brittle. (Lenat and Guha 1990: 17)

Or, as Lenat and Feigenbaum more concisely put it, the system uses "variable names pregnant with meaning – pregnant to the user, but barren to the system" (1991: 240). The remedy, according to them, was to provide AI systems with commonsense knowledge consisting of both general facts and methods (heuristics) for applying those facts. Lenat and Feigenbaum's assumption agreed with one of the main premises of expert systems – namely, that knowledge can be elicited from human beings and encoded in a format suitable for computer consumption. What they considered to be missing was "one immense knowledge base spanning human consensus reality, to serve as scaffolding for specific clusters of expert knowledge" (188). What made them optimistic about the task of creating this immense knowledge base in a comparatively short time – hence the claim "artificial intelligence is within our grasp" (ibid.) – was, rather ironically, the success, albeit limited, of expert systems: "intelligent artifacts that perform well, using knowledge, on specialized tasks within narrowly defined domains" (189).

Cyc, in sum, was intended to overcome brittleness and to break through the knowledge acquisition bottleneck by acquiring the commonsense knowledge that presumably underlies intelligence by means of an accurate model of the world in the form of explicitly encoded representations (i.e., sentences); and it was meant to achieve this goal over the course of about a decade. But there were views, both within and without AI, that were dubious about such an approach. Most of these views agreed on notions such as the experiential, tacit, and distributed character of human knowledge.

The Boolean Dream

Douglas Hofstadter was one of those within AI who found the idea of logically formalizing thought and common sense an elegant chimera, which he called the "Boolean dream," in honor of George Boole, the nineteenth-century logician, who believed that "the laws of thought" amounted to formal rules for manipulating propositions (Hofstadter 1985b: 654). He argued that there is a sharp contrast between expert systems' approach and how people, using their common sense, "perceive patterns anywhere and everywhere, without knowing in advance where to look" (640). But, unlike Hayes, he suggested, "Common sense is not an 'area of expertise', but a general – that is, domain-independent – capacity that has to do with fluidity in representation of concepts, an ability to sift what is important from what is not, an ability to find unanticipated similarities between totally different concepts" (ibid.). "We have a long way to go," he stated, "before our programs exhibit this cognitive style."

Brian Smith was another figure within AI who disagreed with Lenat and Feigenbaum on both accounts: their method and their theory. Smith warned against "conceptual tunneling" – the leap from broad intuitions, which "often have the superficial air of the obvious," to detailed proposals, "with essentially no need for intermediate conceptual results" (1991: 252). He pointed out that Cyc, with its first stage costing roughly $50 million, is a project with very high ambitions – the encoding of all of consensus reality, the substrate for all other knowledge-based systems, the groundwork for all future AI, and so forth. And "untutored pragmatism," as has been claimed for Cyc, he argues, "loses force in the face of a task of this magnitude (you can bridge a creek without a theory, but you won't put a satellite into orbit around Neptune)" (258).

Smith also opposed many of the assumptions put forth by Lenat and Feigenbaum (and built into Cyc) – for example, that all human knowledge is either explicitly represented or could be logically inferred from explicit knowledge, that meaning is independent of context and use, that there is only one mode of representation of human knowledge (sentences). "Knowledge and intelligence," Smith argued, "require participation in the world" (286).

Diana Forsythe, who spent many years closely studying the development of expert systems in AI, criticized the view, common to the philosophy both of

Cyc and of expert systems, that human knowledge is "something concrete . . . a 'thing' that can be extracted, like a mineral or a diseased tooth." She described the knowledge-engineering method of knowledge elicitation as "a sort of surgical or engineering task, in which the substance to be mined or operated upon is a human brain," and she suggested that the proponents of expert-system building view their task merely "as a matter of information transfer, not of the construction or translation of knowledge" (2001: 46–47).

In sum, in confronting the problems of expert systems, critics like those mentioned earlier seek explanations of these problems in points like the following (Forsythe 2001):

- knowledge is socially and culturally constituted;
- knowledge is not self-evident but must be interpreted;
- people are not aware of everything they know and a good deal of knowledge is tacit;
- much knowledge is not in people's heads at all but, rather, is distributed in their bodily skills and social know-how;
- the relation between what people think, say, and are observed to do is highly complex;
- because of all this, complete and unambiguous knowledge about expert procedures is unlikely to be transmitted through elicitation.

Committed to a different view, however, the Cyc group decided to overcome the limits of expert systems by creating a broad platform to support all future work in AI. They were determined to bring Boole's dream to realization.

CYC IN THEORY: ANCIENT IDEAS, MODERN TECHNOLOGIES

> Our purpose was not to understand more about how the human mind works, nor to test some particular theory of intelligence. Instead, we built nothing more nor less than an artifact, taking a very nuts-and-bolts engineering approach to the whole project.
> – Lenat, *From 2001 to 2001: Common Sense and the Mind of HAL*

A tradition of dividing research strategies into the "neat" and the "scruffy" has prevailed in AI, the reasons for which are not only methodical but also geographical, institutional, and even personal (Crevier, 1993; cf. Lenat & and Feigenbaum 1991; Schank 1995). Although there is no clear characterization of either one, the distinction is basically between those who follow a formal or "scientific" strategy and those who adopt an informal or engineering stance. AI workers often tend to associate themselves with one of these two camps. Lenat and Feigenbaum, for instance, call themselves "pragmatists and engineers; tradesmen, not philosophers" (1991: 237), denying interest, as this excerpt indicates, both in theory and in human intelligence. In so doing, they presumably intend to avoid theoretical questions and to protect themselves from theoreticians, who "can sit around for decades and bemoan the impenetrable mystique of the human intellect" (1991: 236). This doesn't mean that there is no theory behind Cyc; quite the contrary.

In terms of method, the theory behind Cyc has its roots not in modern computer or cognitive theories but in ancient Greek tradition and the value that it put on axiomatic-deductive reasoning. In this method, certain indemonstrable starting points, axioms, definitions, or postulates are first set out, allowing the mathematician to proceed to the strict deductive proof of a series of theorems (Lloyd 1999: 304). Best exemplified by Euclid's *Elements*, this method also was applied in other areas such as hydrostatics and astronomy. Archimedes, for instance, used it in his work *On Floating Bodies*, and Aristarchus in his *On the Sizes and Distances of the Sun and the Moon* (ibid.). However, as Lloyd demonstrates, not all deductive reasoning is based on a limited number of "explicit indemonstrable starting points" (ibid.). For example, classical Chinese mathematics, despite its sophistication, did not use axioms. Rather, it was based on a kind of algorithmic demonstration more akin to *proof by construction* of modern theories of computing (Cohen 1997: 16).

In terms of content, the theory behind Cyc is based on two main claims (Lenat and Feigenbaum 1991). One, as we saw, is the total denial of any relevance to the Cyc project of aspects of human intelligence. The other is the theoretical claim that knowledge, especially of the commonsense variety, is all we need for intelligence, and that formal systems like Cyc can acquire this knowledge first by spoon-feeding and eventually on their own. The important point is that the second claim is made despite the first one; that is, commonsense knowledge (which is a deeply human phenomenon) is being asserted as the project's target, and yet no overt attempt is being made to incorporate mechanisms of human cognition.

Cyc and Human Cognition

In the context of a discussion about explicit representations, Lenat and Feigenbaum, calling themselves "AI scientists, not cognitive psychologists," say that they "don't care whether that [the way Cyc works]'s 'really' how people solve problems or get around in the real world" (1991: 235). I want to argue that assertions like this are not sensible for a delicate reason.

The objective of Cyc is to capture commonsense knowledge, which falls in the domain of human activity. Human knowledge, as these authors themselves have made clear in several places (e.g., 192), is not limited to facts, but also encompasses heuristics and rules for applying those facts. In discussing this, they even go as far as saying, "Raw perception and low-level muscle coordination are not part of what we are calling knowledge, though of course propositions about what you have perceived, about the act of your perceiving it, etc., are knowledge" (1991: 235). Heuristics and procedures, however, are species-dependent – bees, dogs, mice, and humans all have heuristics for doing things, but the ways they do it are probably as different as their body sizes or skin textures. In navigation, for instance, different species use different heuristics: bees use a combination of dancing and wiggling to communicate the distance and angle of a food source with their peers; ants use chemical traces, wasps use another mechanism, and so on (Gallistel 1998). If heuristics are part of what Lenat and Feigenbaum call knowledge, then commonsense knowledge is species-specific.[6] It follows that one cannot capture human commonsense knowledge without paying attention to the idiosyncrasies of human behavior.[7]

In short, the question is whether Lenat and Feigenbaum can get away with the bravado of "not caring" about whether Cyc bears any resemblance to human cognition. The answer would seem to be no, because the goals and ambitions of their project commit them otherwise. This tension between Cyc's goals, on the one hand, and its proclaimed engineering approach, on the other, is one of the clearest manifestations of what I have dubbed the main tension of AI. Despite this, in what follows, I will no longer worry about the project's psychological plausibility, and I will simply look at Cyc in terms of what its authors claim for it – namely, its high degree of commonsense knowledge.

Cyc and Human Knowledge

As we saw at the outset, Cyc is founded on one key intuition: that human-level intelligence is attainable by providing a machine with explicitly represented commonsense knowledge. According to this view, knowledge – vast amounts of it – is the key to intelligence, and so little else is required that the Cyc group considers the current generation of personal computers as possible candidates for the realization of human-level intelligence race – as long as they are provided with sufficient amounts of knowledge: "[P]ersonal computers are already so powerful that they are not the bottleneck problem at all [in achieving human-level machine intelligence]" (Lenat 1997). A similar claim has been made about our present state of understanding of reasoning methods and control structures. In supporting the idea that "knowledge is all there is," Lenat and Feigenbaum go so far as to say, "No sophisticated, as-yet-unknown control structure is required for intelligent behavior" (1991: 192). They believe that "we already understand induction, deduction, analogy, specialization, generalization, and so on, well enough" – although not fully – to be able to focus our efforts on knowledge almost exclusively, the hope being that we will complete our understanding of the rest in the process. This belief in what they call the *knowledge-as-power hypothesis* is held so strongly that they are prepared to "bet their professional lives" on it (ibid.: 212).

This intuition, when dissected, consists of two main theses. One is that knowledge is sufficient for intelligence; the other is that systems such as Cyc can acquire this knowledge and hence can be intelligent. The first thesis is too wide a topic to be covered fully here. A brief look at the literature in and around cognitive science and AI reveals that an agreed-on definition of knowledge is far from available. Serious challenges from different perspectives have been raised during the last couple of decades against the possibility of explaining intelligent behavior solely in terms of knowledge. Prominent among them are views from sense experience and embodiment (Brooks 1991; Clark 1997), emergence (Churchland 1989; Hofstadter 1985), existential experience (Dreyfus 1972; Haugeland 1998), social experience (Hutchins 1995; Suchman 1987), intentionality (Searle 1980), and metaphysics (Smith 1996). These views may diverge among themselves, but their common bottom line is that knowledge alone is not enough for human intelligence. However, this leads to an open-ended philosophical debate. Hence, I shall not dwell any further on the issue of sufficiency of knowledge.

What Is Commonsense Knowledge?

A similar observation could be made about "common sense" with the caveat that, to the best of my knowledge, no one in AI and cognitive science has tried to provide an account of the term *common sense*, even though it is widespread. After the eighteenth-century Scottish school of commonsense philosophy (Reid [1785] 1969), the closest accounts we have of common sense belong to American pragmatists such as John Dewey (1950), William James ([1907] 1998), and Charles S. Peirce ([1905] 1940), and to Karl Popper (1972), all of which are philosophical speculations rather than scientific accounts of the kind AI research seeks to implement. Because of this lack, it would be worthwhile to develop a clearer notion of common sense, but we have yet to see such an attempt in AI.[8]

The ambiguity of this term is greatly consequential for a project like Cyc. In fact, the meaning of the term *common sense* has changed drastically for the Cyc group since they launched the project in 1984. Originally, they deemed commonsense knowledge to be "real world factual knowledge, the sort found in an encyclopedia" – hence the project's name (Lenat et al. 1986). Later, as we saw, the term's meaning changed to "the knowledge that an encyclopedia would assume the reader knows without being told (e.g., an object can't be in two places at once)" (ibid.). Even with this new conception in mind, Lenat and Guha admit that they include "some of that [encyclopedic knowledge] as well" (1990: 29). Given the central role that this notion plays in their project, this uncertainty and ambiguity might be one of the reasons for the difficulties that Cyc has faced in practice.

To get a picture of such difficulties, I will now move on to Lenat and Feigenbaum's second major thesis – namely, that a system such as Cyc can acquire common sense. We will see that there are many barriers that stand in the way of Cyc, or any other formal system, acquiring commonsense knowledge. It would follow, then, that even if knowledge were sufficient for intelligence, Cyc would not be in the running because it would be unable to obtain sufficient knowledge.

CYC IN PRACTICE

In the absence of any demonstrations or protocols allowing the general public to interact with Cyc, it is difficult to obtain a clear sense of its performance and capabilities on a continuous basis. Previously, the only sources were the scattered reports in the Cyc literature itself (especially its Web site, which features an up-to-date report on its stage of development), occasional interviews or news releases in the media, or a unique report by Vaughan Pratt of Stanford University's Computer Science Department, also available on the Web.[9] This report was the result of a prearranged visit paid in 1994 by Pratt to Cyc's site in Austin, during which he was allowed to interact directly with Cyc in a question-and-answer session. Recently, Cycorp (the corporation that has owned Cyc since 1994) has made a portion of the system, called OpenCyc, available to the public. This version does not represent Cyc's full range of capabilities because, according to Cycorp, it includes only 5 percent of the whole knowledge base. Finally, there is the possibility of taking part in training courses conducted to familiarize interested parties with Cyc. This author took part in one such course in October of 2002. The visits by Pratt and myself will be the main sources of information for the review in this section. However, to afford readers an understanding of Cycorp's view, I would like first to briefly introduce the current applications of Cyc.

Cyc in the Eyes of Its Creators

> An investment in knowledge pays the best interest.
> – Benjamin Franklin, *Poor Richard's Almanac*

Since its initial design, Cyc has gone through a metamorphosis: it began in the mid-1980s as the biggest-ever AI experiment and was publicized as such, but wound up in the mid-1990s as a proprietary business enterprise (Cycorp). Later, Cyc was introduced as a "multi-contextual knowledge base and inference engine ... that will enable a variety of knowledge-intensive products and services," a system "with applications to many real-world business problems."[10] This shift of focus and purpose makes it difficult to judge Cyc on purely theoretical grounds. However, it still leaves some room for judging it in terms of performance – what it is claimed to accomplish.

The shared sentiment among "Cyclists," as the managers and employees of Cyc call themselves, seems to be that these real-world applications serve two purposes. One is to provide the money for the survival of the project and its march toward the goal of becoming the ubiquitous substrate of any future computer system. The other is to demonstrate the current capabilities of Cyc, which, in their view, distinguishes it from any other AI system, past or present. For instance, the bar graph in Figure 4.2, according to Cycorp, shows how Cyc rated in a contest conducted by DARPA: it far surpassed the sum total of performance of many other similar projects (from CMU, MIT, Stanford, and elsewhere) according to various performance indices. The nature of these indices is not known to us, but the transcript shown in Figure 4.3 illustrates the type of questions used to evaluate the competing systems. Judged by the example, it seems that expert knowledge of, say, Anthrax was crucial. The distinctive character of Cyc is its ability to combine and integrate information from different sources, as manifested in its question about whether "anthrax" meant the heavy metal band or the bacteria.

This example illustrates one of the major touted applications of Cyc, which, according to Cycorp's Web site, are divided into five categories:

- integration of heterogeneous databases;
- knowledge-enhanced retrieval of captioned information;
- guided integration of structured terminology (GIST);

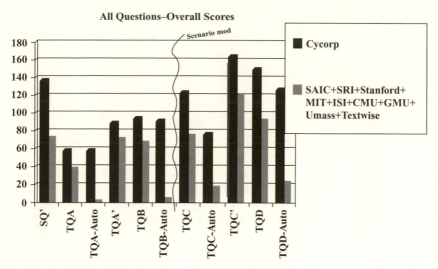

Figure 4.2. The performance of Cyc compared to other systems. (*Source:* Cycorp workshop documents).

- distributed AI;
- retrieval of information from the World Wide Web.

Our interest in this chapter, as I already mentioned, is in the so-called grand vision behind Cyc – that is, the acquisition of human commonsense knowledge. Rather than going into the details of these applications, therefore,

---

System: Ready for input.
User: what do you know about anthrax?
System: By anthrax do you mean
        (1) the heavy metal band or (2) bacteria?
User: 2
System: Here is what I know about it:
Anthrax is a species of organism.
All anthrax is a bacterium.
All anthrax can lethally infect mammals.
Anthrax is extremely toxic for people to inhale.
Iraq has biological weapons that deliver anthrax.
Anthrax is opaque, tangible, microscopic.
Anthrax can be dried into spores stored indefinitely.

Figure 4.3. A transcript of a query session with Cyc. (*Source:* Cycorp workshop documents).

I want to outline the fundamental claim that lies behind all of them – namely, the distinction between information and knowledge.

Information versus Knowledge

In criticizing the performance of databases such as the one described earlier, the Cyc group makes the following distinction between information and knowledge:

> Current database systems are information-rich but knowledge-poor. They have a very flat structure that incorporates little or no semantic-level knowledge. A personnel database may know that "Fred Utz" is a "professor" who works for "Harvard University," but it does not know what these strings mean, what a person is, what a professor is, or what a university is. Cyc, however, does know.

The claim, in other words, is that, unlike other database systems, Cyc *knows* what each of theses strings means. Later in the same document, an example is provided that is supposed to test Cyc's ability along these lines. The example involves two imaginary tables. One of them is a table of people that has three fields: name, job title, and employer's name. The other, a table of employers, has two fields: the employer's name and the state where the employer is located. Now, imagine that the following query is posed: "Show me people who hold an advanced degree and live in New England." Presumably, the tables do not have any data that answer this query in a literal manner. "But Cyc knows that doctors, lawyers, and professors hold advanced degrees, that people generally live near their place of work, and that New England is comprised of six specific states. So Cyc converts this query into a query for doctors, lawyers, and professors whose employer is located in one of those six states ... "

Although this example does not prove the claim that Cyc knows what a person, a professor, or a lawyer is, it does give some clue as to what is intended by the distinction made by the Cyc group between knowledge and information. Now we can ask a similar question to the one we asked about the Web search engine: How much knowledge and intelligence are we willing to attribute to Cyc because of this? More specifically, how different is the "knowledge," attributed to Cyc, that New England is comprised of six specific states from the mere "information," possessed by the plain-vanilla search engine, that England is part of Europe? Or, for that matter, how different is the "knowledge" that doctors and lawyers hold advanced degrees from the mere "information" that Europe is a continent?

As far as one can tell from the example, the single advantage that Cyc has over the competing knowledge bases is that it can *infer*, or derive, the required data (about people with advanced degrees, about the states comprising New England, etc.) from what it already has at its disposal. But is this enough to make Cyc *qualitatively* different from its competitors? The answer to this question, obviously, depends on what we mean by "qualitative difference." The main distinction, according to the Cyc group, is that ordinary search engines basically do a lookup in their tables, whereas Cyc may retrieve the data from different "microtheories" or frames.[11] For instance, in order for it to be able to answer this query in the described manner, Cyc would need a microtheory for Advanced Degree with assertions about education, universities, the degrees they offer, . . . and professions whose holders are supposed to have received higher education. The assertions (or the fillers of the slots) will be lists that include further assertions about (or pointers to the slots for) doctors, lawyers, professors, and so on. In short, rather than looking up the answer directly, Cyc arrives at it by following a chain of inferences or by looking up the fillers for the slots (which are themselves, by the way, logical assertions using strings of the "FredUtz" sort).

Similar observations could be made about another of Cyc's applications – namely, the retrieval of captioned information. To use an example from Cyc, think of the photo of "a soldier holding a gun to a woman's head," which could be captioned as such for purposes of retrieval. this works, it is not ideal because the caption is too specific. One would like the photo to be retrievable by any number of queries, including "someone in danger," "a frightened person," or "a man threatening a woman." As the Cycorp document points out, however, this is "beyond the abilities of even the most sophisticated of traditional text-searching tools, all of which are based on simple string matching and synonyms." Such tools lack either the natural-language interface or the commonsense knowledge required to match the more general queries. Cyc, however, "is not crippled by such a liability," so the claim goes, because it "knows that guns shoot bullets and are designed to kill people; that having a gun to one's head therefore threatens one's life; that those whose lives are threatened feel fear; and that the image in question is, in all likelihood, a good match for each of the queries above."

So, once again, we are faced with the claim that Cyc *knows* such and such in a way that is fundamentally different from "simple string matching and synonyms." To be sure, Cyc does not perform "simple" string-matching in order to figure out, for instance, that a *threat* to one's life generates *fear*, and it probably does not do a dictionary type of lookup either.[12] The point is, however, that it has to do some sort of string-matching at some point in its processing. How so? Presumably, Cyc has a frame or, equivalently, a number of assertions to the effect that guns are thus and so; that having a gun to one's head implies this and that; . . . and so on and so forth. At some level, these assertions will be represented as sets of alphanumeric strings of IF–THEN statements like the following (simplified here to sentences in predicate logic for ease of legibility):

IF Gun(X), THEN Shoot (X, Bullet)
IF Point (Gun, Person), THEN Threat (Life (Person))
IF Threat (Life (Person)), THEN Has-Emotions (Fear, Person)

This is obviously a simplification of what happens in Cyc, but it captures what is being done in its knowledge base at some level.[13] The point is, for Cyc to retrieve this specific photo in reply to all of the cited queries, it needs to have been given all the above facts (along with many others) *explicitly* at some point. There is no other way that Cyc could answer the questions, or succeed at the match, because explicit representation is inherent to Cyc's philosophy.

Whether these differences by themselves suggest a qualitative advantage for Cyc – in the sense that, unlike its competitors, it "knows" what those other assertions or frames are – is a question that needs careful analysis, and that I will address later.

Cyc in the Eyes of a Visitor Circa 1994

As was stated earlier, Vaughan Pratt's report of his visit to Cyc is unique in that it is the only report of a direct interaction between Cyc and someone from outside the team. The visit took place in 1994, ten years into the project. Incidentally, 1994 was the milestone originally set forth for the completion of the first stage of the project, after which Cyc was supposed to be able to carry out self-initiated assimilation of texts and databases. It was also the year by the end of which "the Cyc program was mature enough to spin off from MCC[14] as a new company – Cycorp – to commercialize the technology and begin its widespread deployment" (Lenat 1997). Pratt's visit was arranged in advance and consisted of a number of demos and miscellaneous questions. I will focus on one of the demos and a couple of questions posed to Cyc by Pratt.

Demo 2 in Pratt's report is about the retrieval of online images by caption. This demo consisted of twenty images, each one described by half a dozen axioms in CycL.[15]

- The request "Someone relaxing" yields an image of three men in swimsuits, holding surfboards.

- The request "Find someone at risk of skin cancer" yields both the above image and a photo of a girl lying on a beach.
- Pratt tries a couple of other requests that work, but then he asks for "A tree" and Cyc fails to retrieve a picture captioned "A girl with presents in front of a Christmas tree." The same happens with the request "A Christmas tree."

Pratt asserts that Cyc finds the first image by "making a connection between relaxing and previously entered attributes of the image" – attributes like "being on a beach" or "reclining." In the second case, according to Pratt, the logic used is that "reclining at the beach implies sun-tanning and sun-tanning promotes risk of skin cancer." The axioms used in the inference made by Cyc for the first case is:

1. (➔ (logAnd (allInstanceOf RA RecreationalActivity)
   (allInstanceOf X SentientAnimal)
   (DoneBy RA X)
   (holdsIn RA (feelsEmotion X RelaxedEmotion Positive))))
2. (➔ (performedBy X Y)(doneBy X Y))
3. (allInstanceOf G1 AdultMalePerson)
4. (allGenls Vertebrate SentientAnimal)
5. (allGenls Mammal Vertebrate)
6. (allGenls Primate Mammal)
7. (allGenls Person Primate)
8. (allGenls HumanAdult Person)
9. (allGenls AdultMalePerson HumanAdult)

Given that "allGenls" means that its first argument is a subset of its second argument, and "allInstanceOf" means that its first argument is an instance of its second argument, what this says is that G1 (one of the three surfers), who is an adult-male-person (which is a subset of all human-adults, which is a subset of all-people, which is a subset of all-primates, ... which is a subset of all-sentient-animals), has a relaxed-emotion when doing a recreational-activity. Pratt adds, "These axioms plus certain of the half dozen or so properties typed in for that photo permitted the inference that G1 ... was surfing." Lest we not fall into the representation trap, as Cyclists usually point out, one can replace each of these strings with any other alphanumeric string – e.g., a, b, c, ... – and still get the same response from Cyc. Is it not possible, then, that we are dealing with another case of brittleness where, in Lenat and Guha's own words, the human user is 'using variable names pregnant with meaning – pregnant to the user, but barren to the system' (1990: 240)? Put differently, does this not suggest that all Cyc is doing is manipulating alphanumeric strings, which is also what the search engines that it is claimed to surpass did, except maybe in a more sophisticated manner?

The report goes on to give a few examples of questions asked by Pratt (P.Q.), put into the proper format by the Cyc team (C.Q.), and given by the machine as responses (C.R.). Some are listed here, together with an explanation (EX) by Cyc's team as to the reason for the observed behavior.

P.Q.: Does Cyc know that bread is food?
C.Q.: (evaluate-term '(#%allGenls #%Bread #%Food)
C.R.: True

P.Q: Does Cyc consider bread to be a drink?
C.Q: (evaluate-term '(#%allGenls #%Bread #%Drink)
C.R.: NIL
EX: This is an indication of no knowledge. So, the following axiom is added: (#%MutuallyDisjointWith #%Bread #%Drink)

P.Q.: Does Cyc know that people need food?
C.Q.: Show all axioms having "Dying" as a consequence.
C.R.: None
(Cyc found hang-gliding and touching toxic substances to be potential causes of death, but not starvation or anything related to food.)

EX: Cyc knows that lack of food causes hunger. And it knows that starvation is one way to cause death. The reason it does not respond is, in effect, it is missing the definition of starvation.

Finally, Pratt reports that observing the performance so far "discouraged me from continuing." He had prepared a list of questions that he meant to pose to Cyc, but he came to the conclusion that "the bulk of my questions were going to be well beyond Cyc's present grasp."[16] Pratt's own judgment of the level of the questions is that his "expectations had been set way too high." (This, he says, in addition to the fact that a natural-language interface was available only in the case of image retrieval.) Nevertheless, simply lowering one's expectations does not seem to him to be a way of coaxing better behavior out of Cyc. He sums up his visit in this way:

After looking at the axioms it is clear to me that merely lowering expectations is not sufficient in order to come up with a suite of questions that Cyc is likely to be able to answer say 20% of. The distribution of Cyc's half-million axioms in "knowledge space" showed no discernible pattern that would allow me to construct such a suite, short of simply picking particular axioms out of Cyc's databases and carefully phrasing questions around those axioms. And even then our experiences with "Is bread a drink" and the Christmas tree indicated that Cyc would still have difficulty with a sizable percentage of the questions of a suite constructed this way.

In other words, according to Pratt, the problem with Cyc is not only the level of one's expectations, nor is it the lack of a discernible pattern or coherence among the axioms, for, as the examples show, help given to Cyc to compensate for its lack still did not enable it to answer the simplest of queries. There must thus be something else lacking.

Although Pratt does not speculate on what this crucial missing ingredient might be, the set of questions he had originally intended to ask suggests two things. First, he intuitively knew where to look for that something else. There is a minimal set of things that any normal adult in modern Western culture is supposed to know, and Pratt's intended questions would have done a good job of checking for the presence of this minimum basis. Second, and at the same time, his intended questions reveal that he took a great deal for granted concerning Cyc's knowledge. For instance, basic concepts such as time, position, size, material, color; physical properties such a hard and soft, wet and dry, external and internal; activities such as living, moving, walking, running, flying; social concepts such as people, society, country, government, party, election, candidate, vote, winning and losing, lobbying, money, bank, stealing, borrowing, and buying,... and a host of other basic notions were all assumed to lie solidly within the grasp of Cyc. Unfortunately, such assumptions proved to be overly generous and far from realistic.

Cyc in the Eyes of a Visitor Circa 2002

In October 2002, an opportunity came up for me to take part in a workshop and to closely interact with Cyc.[17] During the workshop, the participants were introduced to the past and potential applications of Cyc, mostly as a database integration medium – an application that is in high demand by business and government in light of the growing number of heterogeneous databases and the challenge that this poses for any attempt at integrating them interoperably.[18] Such applications, of course, are of such magnitude that their feasibility can hardly be tested in a workshop environment, so we had to depend on the reports of Cyc managers and employees about these. But, as part of the hands-on training, we also had the opportunity to interact with Cyc directly. One such opportunity was to give a short story to the knowledge base, and to ask questions about it afterward.

The story was very short and simple, but the encoding process was very long and tedious, and I will not go into it here. It was the story of a family's visit to the zoo, and we needed to create a "microtheory" for the whole event and for its individual parts and places (see the section on contexts later in this chapter). After this, we had the chance to pose questions. One of the questions that my teammate and I asked was: (olderThan #$Bill #$Bobby), to which Cyc returned "No Answer" (after checking seventy-seven subproofs). Being surprised, we tried to find the inference rule that deals with such a question:

(implies (AND (age ?X ?AgeX) (age ?Y ?AgeY) (greaterThan ?AgeX ?AgeY)(older Than ?X ?Y)))

Then, having noticed that the system should be explicitly told that ?X and ?Y are alive in order for it to compare their ages, we added the following to the knowledge base, repeated the original question, and still got "No Answer" (Bill, Martha, Bobby, and Karen were, respectively, the father, the mother, the son, and the daughter of the Boyd family):

(#$OrganismExistentialState #$BillBoyd #$alive)
(#$OrganismExistentialState #$BobbyBoyd #$alive)

Next, we thought maybe we should explicitly tell Cyc that Bill is the father of Bobby (although we had earlier told it that Bill is a *parent* of Bobby), but this still did not bring about an answer. Finally, by following the inference chain and finding the following axiom, we discovered that we also need to tell Cyc that Bill is the biological father of Bobby:

(implies (OrganismExistential ?X #$Alive) (OrganismExistential ?Y #$Alive) (biologicalFather ?X ?Y) (olderThan ?X ?Y))

So we added this piece of information, and finally (after about two hours of fiddling with the system) got a positive answer to the original question.

This experiment shows one simple example of the kinds of problems that Cyc is still facing. Although it might be possible for someone to make a feeble case for the idea that it makes sense for the system to be uncertain about the age relation of the two individuals until it learns about their biological kinship, it also shows the extremely cumbersome and unrealistically torturous process of making Cyc do anything useful at this point. This became more obvious when it similarly gave "No Answer" to the following questions:

- Does Bill love Bobby?
- Is Bobby the sibling of Karen?
- Is Bill the spouse of Bill?
- Is Bill the spouse of Karen?

Taken at face value, this means that Cyc does not know that:

- people usually love their children;
- children of the same parents are siblings;
- people cannot marry themselves;
- parents do not marry their children.[19]

Notice that the main point is not whether Cyc does or does not have such "knowledge" stored somewhere in its knowledge base – it might well. The point is that, even if existent, this "knowledge" is buried under an extremely tangled and cluttered pile of propositions, axioms, and inference rules, to the extent that its practical usability becomes a matter of serious doubt.

Cyc, in my observation, is crumbling under its own weight. If for no other reason (and, as we shall see shortly, there is no shortage of other reasons), this seems to be jeopardizing the project. The original decision to largely neglect control structures and their crucial role has come back to haunt Cyc in disturbing ways (more on this later).

Incompatible Views: Alphanumeric Strings or Sites of Meaning

It seems that we are faced with two opposite views of the capabilities of Cyc: one belonging to its creators and the other to two visitors who, judging by their reports, walked in as unbiased observers. The two views are incompatible and, at times, severely contradictory. There is, for instance, a vast gulf between Pratt's report on Cyc's knowledge of "food" as of 1994 and Lenat and Feigenbaum's claim, back in 1991, that Cyc has this much understanding of human needs and habits: "The knowledge in KB [knowledge base] about people – such as eating and sleeping – is used to help guess why a user isn't responding at 12:30 pm or 12:30 am" (1991: 240).

The question is, thus, how we are to judge between these opposing views, if not on practical grounds. Should we believe, with the Cyc group, that Cyc has meaningful *knowledge*, as opposed to mere *information*, in its database? Or should we conclude that it does not even have many of the most basic commonsense notions needed for knowing? Clearly, part of the discrepancy results from different presuppositions and expectations that each side has. At some level, though, the answer to the question depends largely on what one means by terms such as "knowledge," "information," and "meaning."

As these examples have probably revealed, however, making a distinction between information and knowledge seems to be a hopeless, if not pointless, task. The borderline between the two notions is too fuzzy to permit such a distinction. We might have our own intuitions about what either term means, but there is no guarantee that, as with many other intuitions, this one is not also built on shaky foundations. Our best bet, therefore, would be to try to develop these intuitions by facing the questions and challenges that they raise.

WHAT IS THIS THING CALLED KNOWLEDGE?

> Retain, I pray you, this suspicion about common sense.
>   – William James, *Pragmatism*

Recall that the ambition driving Cyc is "to break the 'software brittleness bottleneck' once and for all" – that is, to break away from dependence on specific and limited domain knowledge by resorting to common sense. In order for this to happen, a number of assumptions and premises have to be correct – namely, that:

- there exists a *universal* body of commonsense knowledge shared across cultures, societies, times, and places (what Lenat and Feigenbaum call "consensus reality");
- this body of knowledge can be *fully explicated*, effectively communicated, and consistently encoded in a computer, which, in turn, requires that
- there is a machine-accessible formalism (language) for encoding it.

These are significant assumptions, a full analysis of which is beyond our scope. In what follows, I am going to examine them to the extent allowable here.

What Is Consensus Reality?

There is a body of knowledge that most adult human beings share. Lenat and Feigenbaum call this "consensus reality," and give the following as examples:

- Water flows downhill.
- Living things get diseases.
- Doing work requires energy.
- People live for a single, contiguous, finite interval of time.
- Most cars today are riding on four tires.
- Each tire a car is riding on is mounted on a wheel.
- If you fall asleep while driving, your car will start to head out of your lane pretty soon.
- If something big is between you and the thing you want, you probably will have to go around it. (1991: 197)

Consensus Reality Is Indefinite and Indeterminate

Judged by the examples, this list could, in principle, be extended indefinitely, and the problem is that we do not precisely know which subset of that extended list to consider as consensus reality. The problem is not only the magnitude of the knowledge – although that could be a huge problem by itself. It is also that there is no criterion for judging whether some knowledge is shared or not. Could we go by statistics, for instance, and count as consensus reality whatever knowledge is shared by more than 70 percent (or 85 percent or 99 percent) of people, and exclude the rest? This is obviously impossible, if not absurd. It is absurd because some fact may not be explicitly known to people as individuals, but *taken for granted* by them in the sense of them behaving *as if* they know it.

Consensus Reality Is Socially Distributed Knowledge

The example of expert knowledge is a case in point. Not many of us are meteorologists, but most of us take our umbrellas along when we hear showers forecast on the radio. In such cases, knowing whom to listen to is as important as knowing that one needs an umbrella in rainy weather. We know whom to turn to for professional knowledge of particular sorts – a mechanic for cars, a doctor for illness, a meteorologist for weather. We take their word for what they are supposed to know, but we also have a sense for when to become skeptical of them. Do these types of knowledge belong to consensus reality? They do, I suggest, but in a social sense.

This social character of consensus reality is crucial, as the name that Lenat and Feigenbaum have given it implies. AI researchers, having long ignored this social aspect, now hope to capture it in an isolated knowledge base. But then they must face the question of how much knowledge to include. Take the game of Twenty Questions. In order for this game to be playable, a lot is presumed as common between the players – most important, a shared, discretized ontology (and language). This shared carving-up of the world is so crucial that, one could claim, two people from different cultures would not be able to play the game unless the scope were tremendously limited. By the same token, if expert knowledge were allowed, the game could not even be played between individuals with the same culture and language. It is because of such limitations that twenty turns out to be a reasonable upper limit for the number of questions that can be asked. Otherwise, the whole point of the game would be undermined.[20] When it comes to real-life situations, however, it is not so obvious how one could put any limits on the shared knowledge of a society. For this reason, Cyc's developers have had to ponder long and hard on what to include and what to exclude from the knowledge base. This is one

major source of their trouble, but there is another closely related problem –
namely, that consensus reality is not universal.

Consensus Reality Is Variable

There is a difference between "public" and "universal." Not everything shared
by members of a culture is universal. Knowledge and beliefs vary across
cultures and within the same culture in time. Our routine knowledge of
cars, of the kind mentioned in the above examples, was totally unimagined
by people a hundred years ago. Much the same could be said about basic
computer knowledge until about two decades ago (and it still applies to
many individuals in this society and many non-Western societies).

In short, as Lenat and Guha point out throughout their book (1990), the
questions of what to include, how to keep track of it, and how to change it
are among the most serious problems faced by the Cyc group in practice. No
wonder that at some point (around 1991) the number of encoded assertions
of Cyc had reached two million, only to be cut back later to half a million, as
a result of redundancy and consistency considerations.[21]

HOW TO DEAL WITH TACIT KNOWLEDGE

A major premise in Cyc's approach is that most, if not all, human knowledge is
explicit or could be made explicit by elicitation, introspection, or some other
method. Many facets of human knowledge and experience, however, seem to
be tacit, in the sense that a judgment is often made without the judger being
able to articulate the reasons for it – for example, when one judges that two
people look alike, that a specific utterance sounds dangerous, that a situation
seems critical, or that the trick to do something lies in this or that. Every
language is full of idioms devised for exactly such instances; "looks like,"
"sounds like," (an idea) "being in the air," "to have a hunch," "to sense,"
"to have an inkling," and "to feel like" are but a few such instances in English.

Although there is no comprehensive account of what tacit knowledge is
and what role it plays in cognition, examples like this support the claim that
it is prevalent in daily life. This lack of theory might encourage some people
to take the belief in tacit knowledge as mystical and nonscientific talk. Such
a position is unfounded, however. In fact, science has not been mute with
respect to the challenges posed by tacit judgments. The problem of face recognition is one such challenge. For more than three decades, psychologists have
worked on elucidating the mechanisms used by human beings for recogniz-
ing familiar faces (Farah et al. 1998), for judging the affect in facial expressions
(happy, sad, angry, surprised, embarrassed, etc.) (Townsend 2000), and even
for telling the difference between male and female faces (Brucell et al. 1993).

The commercial systems built for face recognition in some security applica-tions, despite their relative success, are built on principles that do not show any similarity with human performance and hence cannot contribute much to our understanding of face recognition in humans (Cottrell et al. 2000). None of this, however, means that face recognition is a mysterious or mystical phenomenon that will remain forever incomprehensible. All it means is that there are important mechanisms behind many of our judgments that we do not yet clearly understand.

Sociologists have written widely about tacit knowledge. Collins (1990) uses the failure of a fictional spy trained to impersonate a permanent resident of a city to argue that "the space of our knowledge is larger than the space of our concepts" (which is, in turn, larger than the space of our language). Michael Polanyi (1958) used the example of learning the skill of riding a bicycle without having any explicit knowledge of the law of gravity, the concept of center of mass, and so on. One's knowledge of the height of a doorway or of the risers of the steps in a standard staircase is another such example. Most of us do not have an explicit knowledge of what these dimensions precisely are (e.g., to the quarter inch), but, if solicited, we might be able to provide roughly correct estimates. Architects, as professional experts, do have precise ideas about such dimensions, but that is achieved through special training, not by personal experience (an example that speaks for the role of formal education in filling in the gaps in commonsense knowledge).

Some philosophers use the term *nonconceptual content* to refer to those detailed and local aspects of our experience (Smith 1999), where even a rough articulation is not possible – for example, riding a motorcycle and knowing, but being unable to tell, how fast one is traveling (Cussins 1998). A simi-lar thing happens in the case of expert knowledge, where one can hope to make explicit a piece of expertise that is otherwise implicit. Experts, however, usually find it very difficult to articulate things that they know by heart. Orga-nizations have discovered how difficult it is to illicit expert knowledge and capture in computer systems. The managerial reform that started in the mid-1990s under the rubric of Knowledge Management is largely undermined for this reasons (Day 2005, Ekbia and Hara 2005).

The tacitness of knowledge could, therefore, have different reasons:

- the innate (biological) origin of the knowledge (the sense of gravity in bicycling);
- the sensual or perceptual nature of the knowledge (as in taste);
- the individual (private) character of the experience that has given rise to knowledge (the case of motorcycle speed);
- the habitual nature of knowledge (the height of the steps in a staircase);

- the vastness of knowledge (the case of the spy);
- the complexity of knowledge (the case of experts).

In short, the tacit side of knowledge is too important in human intelligence to be taken lightly. Its significance diminishes the prospects of Cyc's success because "the vast majority of [its] content," according to Lenat and Feigenbaum, "is declarative" (1991: 237). It also works against the bold claim, postulated as a principle by the same authors, that "[M]uch of the knowledge in an intelligent system needs to be represented explicitly, declaratively, although compiled forms of it may also be present" (Lenat and Feigenbaum 1991: 191).[22] Regrettably, the authors do not tell us what they mean by "vast majority" – whether it is 80, 90, 99, or 99.99 percent. This matters, because we could then decide whether or not, in their view, the explicit portion is large enough for one to ignore the remaining parts, and whether tacit knowledge is so negligible that we can ignore it.[23]

HOW TO DEAL WITH MEANING

An original tenet in Cyc's approach was that logical assertions, unlike linguistic utterances, have a universal meaning independent of their context of use – hence the claim that "our sentences in logic have been 'universalized' to the extent humanly possible" (Lenat and Feigenbaum 1991: 243). This last qualification is meant to communicate that universalizing meaning is "indeed very very hard," but not impossible (ibid.).

With Lenat and Feigenbaum (1991) as his point of departure, Smith (1991) addresses, among other things, the dependence of meaning on context. He argues, on the basis of about a dozen criteria, that Cyc shares many of the tenets of what he calls the logicist approach (roughly equivalent to what in this chapter I have called "formal"). One of the problems of this approach, Smith argues, is that it cannot embrace use-dependent meaning because it fixes the meanings of words explicitly and independently of context, once and for all. Cyc, as we have seen, was claimed to have overcome this problem by using its vast store of commonsense "knowledge" – an aspect that presumably made it superior to similar systems that only have "information." In discussing some of the examples provided by the Cyc group, however, we have already found reasons to be skeptical of this claim. To clarify the point further, let me elaborate on one of the examples.

Even in a clear-cut query such as the one about New Englanders with advanced degrees, where the whole point is to provide a list of people, it is not all that clear what type of commonsense knowledge is needed for a useful answer. Here, as elsewhere, there are many ambiguities: What is meant by "hold a degree" – is the holding literal (in a hand), or metaphorical, as in "holding a belief," or neither? What does it mean to have an "advanced degree"? In what sense is a degree advanced? Does Cyc really know what "advance" means in all different contexts – in military maneuvers, in social progress, as a suggestive (sexual) gesture, in a car engine (when the timing is off), or finally in having a higher degree? Are postdocs earning an advanced degree? What about a Ph.D. holder who does not have a job (and in all likelihood is the target of this query in an applied situation) or who works at home? Do people who work at home live "near" their work? What distances are considered "near" in this context – one yard, one hundred yards, one mile, ten miles? What is the place of work of a pilot or a taxi driver? Does Cyc really know about all these cases? Does it know that *live* has subtly different meanings in the following sentences?

- Fred lives in an apartment.
- Mary lives in Boston.
- John lives with his parents.
- They live on a meager income.
- Most organisms can't live without air.
- Fish live in the sea, but amphibians live both in water and on land.

The dynamic, unstable, and contextual character of meaning is extensively discussed and demonstrated by linguists (e.g., Gee 1999). The developers of Cyc originally agreed that there is variability of meaning in natural language but, true to their logicist stance, they attempted to confront this by making the context explicit – by "including explicit clauses that refer to the sorts of contextual information that would be omitted in natural language utterances" (Lenat and Feigenbaum 1991). The problems generated by this attitude, as I shall discuss next, have engaged the Cyc group throughout the project.

CONTEXT, CHANGE, AND THE FRAME PROBLEM

That context is a problematic issue for formal systems such as Cyc and cannot be handled within a logical framework can best be shown by looking at the history of Cyc's treatment of context. This history includes three main stages, which I will discuss in turn.

Infancy: "Context Doesn't Matter"

During the first stage of the project, as we just saw, the Cyc group basically ignored context, downplaying its role as much as possible in their writings. Thus, while they agreed that "the kinds of uses of a proposition may be

limited and biased by the way we choose to represent it," they were quick
to add, "Use-dependent meaning does not imply that we have to abandon
the computational framework of logic" (Lenat and Feigenbaum 1991: 245). It
turned out, however, that context is not as superfluous as the Cyc group had
hoped. Hence the following flashback, some years later:

The...most important lesson we have learned along the way was that it was
foolhardy to try to maintain consistency in one huge flat Cyc knowledge base.
We eventually carved it up into hundreds of contexts or microtheories. Each one
of those is consistent with itself, but there can be contradictions among them.
Thus, in the context of working in an office it's socially unacceptable to jump up
screaming whenever good things happen, while in the context of a football game
it's socially unacceptable *not* to. (Lenat 1997; emphasis Lenat's)

Growth Years: "Microtheories"

On the basis of observations like this, the remedy seemed to the Cyc group to
lie in breaking up the knowledge base into smaller pieces, in such a way that
in place of a single monolithic store of knowledge they now "had hundreds of
'microtheories,' each of which is essentially a bundle of assertions that share
a common set of assumptions" (Lenat and Guha 1990). Initially, this "explicit
context mechanism" seemed a step forward to the Cyc group. Without it, there
was no hope for Cyc's huge knowledge base ever to be pulled together in any
meaningful way. As Jack Copeland has argued, however, from a strictly logical
point of view, this still "looks like quicksand," for "Cyc is not a collection
of expert-system KBs working independently of one another but a single,
integrated whole." Thus, he says, "There is no a priori reason to think that
the effects of inconsistency will not spread from butte to butte, poisoning the
entire KB" (1997).

To illustrate this problem of consistency among microtheories, consider
an example coming from Lenat himself:

Before we let robotic chauffeurs drive around our streets, I'd want the automated
driver to have a general common sense about the value of a cat versus a child
versus a car bumper, about children chasing balls into streets, about young dogs
being more likely to dart in front of cars than old dogs (which, in turn, are more
likely to bolt than elm trees are), about death being a very undesirable thing.
(Lenat 1997)

Lenat's point is well taken. But what would happen if Cyc, with its hundreds of microtheories and its tedious inference mechanism (of the kind I
reported from my experience), were allowed to be the brains for a robotic

chauffeur? The knowledge that children play (sometimes on the street) would be in one microtheory (say, the microtheory of children or of games); the knowledge that dogs may dart in front of cars in another microtheory (say, the microtheory of pets); and the knowledge that living things might die because of a car crash, together with the knowledge that this is undesirable, in yet another microtheory (say, of death); and so on. Given all this knowledge, if confronted with a situation in which both a child and a dog appeared in front of the car, the Cyc-driven robot could not make the right decision, because these pieces of knowledge belong to different contexts, which might provide contradictory guidelines. Putting all these facts into the same microtheory is not an option because one would be back at the old flat-knowledge-base Cyc.

Fortunately, Lenat and the Cyc group did not plan for a Cyc chauffeur as early as 1994. Despite all the hope invested in microtheories, Lenat (1997a: 3) admits that this first foray into contexts had many inadequacies, one of which was the problem of inconsistency. But there were other problems, such as the issues of "lifting," or "importing," across contexts – that is, "asserting $P \rightarrow Q$ [P implies Q] in one context C_1 and, then, context C_2, and failing to have Q concluded in some asking context C_3" (because the original assertion was not importable into C_3) (ibid.).

Despite these problems, microtheories, as I reported from my visit, constituted the dominant framework in Cyc for dealing with context. In analogy with our experience of Earth's curvature, issues of consistency are docked by maintaining consistency locally (within a microtheory) and disregarding it globally (across microtheories). Inconsistency notwithstanding, however, as we saw in the example of the zoo visit, the mere task of pulling assertions from different microtheories still seems to be a major challenge for Cyc. The most serious problem, however, is that of "relevance" – that is, in what context an assertion belongs.

Adulthood: Context Dissected

The most recent stage in the development of context in Cyc involves "the theory of context spaces," intended to correct what Lenat (1998) calls the *black box* approach to contexts in AI. As opposed to alternative views that, according to Lenat, take contexts as two-tier reified (named) objects, consisting of assumptions and content, the new approach in Cyc takes contexts as consisting of multiple dimensions, precisely twelve in number: Absolute Time, Type of Time, Absolute Place, Type of Place, Culture, Sophistication/Security, Granularity, Epistemology, Argument-Preference, Topic, Justification, and

Anthropology. By breaking up the set of contexts in this manner, the Cyc group, according to Lenat, achieves a number of goals simultaneously – faster knowledge entry, faster automated inference, and, of course, getting at the fine structure of contexts for the sake of a better understanding and a more effective implementation.

Since I have not observed the implementation of this scheme in Cyc and, furthermore, it is not possible to go into details of all these dimensions here, I will focus on one dimension (Time) that is of specific interest to AI research.

How to Deal with Change

Consider the sentence "Bill Clinton is the president of the United States." This is true in some contexts (e.g., the year 1997) and false in other contexts (e.g., the year 1900).[24] Now consider the sentence "Bill Clinton is the president of the United States in 1997." According to the logicist view advocated by the Cyc group, this statement is true for all time, not just during 1997. In the year 9999 it will still be true. In 1900 no one knew this fact, but, according to Lenat, it was nonetheless true. It was largely irrelevant in 1900, in the sense that no one then acted differently because of it (since no one knew it). Thus, many assertions are, strictly speaking, *true* at all times, or for a wide swath of the timeline, but are only *relevant* to some small sliver(s) of time (Lenat 1997b: 28).

This reasoning persuaded Lenat to assign two dimensions to time, one for *truth* and one for *relevance*. Furthermore, by (classical) logic we know that for any proposition P, at any moment, P is not true if and only if not-P is true. But it might often be the case that both P and not-P are irrelevant, at the same moment. This suggests that each context should be divided into four subcontexts, which contain assertions with the following properties:

- The content is only true.
- The content is both true and relevant.
- The content is true throughout a whole time-interval.
- The content is true sometime during that interval.

In comparison to time-independent classical logic, this scheme constitutes a step toward a more realistic account. It introduces time and change, thus making it possible to understand inference as a *process* – which it really is – rather than a static phenomenon – which it fundamentally is not.[25] For that reason, this scheme fits assertions about facts such as the presidency of Bill Clinton that "are only true" after a certain point in time (i.e., facts with temporal endurance). This, of course, depends on the granularity of time that one has in mind. Since we (and Cyc) are talking about common sense, a time stretch of the order of daily activities is what matters. Such activities, however, are not as enduring and permanent as presidencies and geologic eras; they are rapidly fluctuating and sometimes hold only during short intervals. That is, statements about such activities fall mostly into the fourth category.

Think of driving again. In a typical situation, the facts that are relevant to driving behavior are things like: a car is in front of me; its right-turn signal is on; the traffic light ahead is green; there is enough distance between us (so that when I arrive at the intersection, it will have made its right turn); I can thus proceed at my same speed; and so on. I don't mean to suggest that we *consciously* go through such chains of inference at each moment during driving. Actually, as in the case of tacit judgments, there are good reasons to believe that we do not. The point is to notice how, at any given moment, any one of these facts can instantly change, thus disturbing the above chain of inference – for instance, if the car in front of me makes a sudden stop or if a pedestrian starts crossing the street. Notice how this single new fact overshadows everything else, and in the blink of an eye becomes more relevant than all previous ones.

In case driving sounds atypical of our thought processes, Dennett (1990) provides the example of a few fictitious robots, each of which is meant to be an improved version of the previous one (see Chapter 8). Nevertheless, they all fail because of the same underlying difficulty – namely, the *frame problem*: roughly, the problem of determining which things in the world change as a result of an action.[26] Dennett muses, "A walking encyclopedia will walk over a cliff, for all its knowledge of cliffs and the effects of gravity, unless it is designed in such a fashion that it can find the right bits of knowledge at the right times, so it can plan its engagements with the real world" (159). As things stand now, Cyc is not destined to become a walking encyclopedia, but this will not protect it from committing "fatal" errors similar in nature to walking over a cliff.

Various attempts have been made within the AI community to tackle the problem by enhancing logic (McCarthy 1980), by creating new variations on it (McDermott 1982), or by reconceptualizing the whole approach from the ground up (Hayes 1979). The Cyc project, thanks to its affiliation with classical logic, provides a testbed for many such ideas. For instance, nonmonotonic logic has been applied in Cyc to resolve some of the problems posed by the entry of new pieces of information that contradict previous ones (see Pratt's report for an example). This is done in nonmonotonic logic by making conclusions *defeasible* – that is, "subject to withdrawal given more premises" (McDermott 1987: 216). As McDermott has argued, however, this approach does not seem to solve the problem of intractability that is at the root of the frame problem (218). Therefore, he concludes, "there is no appeal to non-monotonicity as a way out of some of the problems of deduction" (222).

The "problems of deduction," as McDermott calls them, are numerous, and they directly affect the prospects of success of a project like Cyc. I will next examine one such problem.

The Limits of Deductive Inference

On a very basic level, an assumption of the logicist approach is that a significant amount of thought is deductive. Hofstadter (1985, 2000), Dennett (1990), and McDermott (1987), among others, have argued that this assumption does not bear out in cases that constitute typical thinking behavior – for example, when one decides to prepare a late-night snack (planning), when one finds a cup emptied and concludes that someone else drank its contents, or those cases in which one makes a hypothesis and examines it for contradictions (abduction), not to speak of perceptual behaviors such as the recognition of a face, a letter form, or a musical style. As these examples show, there appears to be much more going on in thinking than pure deductive inference: "no matter how many axioms you write, most of the inferences you want will not follow from them" (McDermott 1987: 222). Let me highlight here a couple of implications of the assumption of purely deductive inference for Cyc.

First, this assumption was taken as a justification for the claim that knowledge, not the processes (or "control structures") that use it, is crucial for intelligence. This is manifested in Cyc in the relatively small importance that was originally accorded to inference methods and control structures. Lenat and Feigenbaum, for instance, claimed, "No sophisticated, as-yet-unknown control structure is required for intelligent behavior" (1991: 192). The claim, in other words, was that we already know enough about thinking processes and need not worry about them any more. This, I think, is the flip side of the view behind the knowledge hypothesis, which, more recently, was bluntly phrased by Lenat as follows:

This view is best likened to priming a pump. Visualize your brain as a knowledge pump. Knowledge goes in, gets stored, combined, copied, or whatever; from time to time, you say or write or do things that are, in effect, ways for your brain to emit knowledge. On a good day, the knowledge you give out may be as good or better than the knowledge you put in. (1997)

Lenat's pump metaphor has the pump "emitting" knowledge just as it takes it in. According to reliable reports, one such emission took place when

Cyc came up with the idea that "All people are famous." This blunder had a simple explanation: Having been given information only about famous people, the machine made a reasonable generalization, by strictly following the inductive rules of inference. Such is the consequence of giving too much weight to knowledge at the cost of neglecting other aspects of thinking, such as inference mechanisms and control structures. But the more serious consequence is that, in my judgment (from my short visit), nowadays a lot of effort and energy is spent in Cyc in providing the huge knowledge base the necessary procedures and mechanisms to coordinate the various pieces of its information already encoded in it.

Another consequence of the above assumption (about the dominantly deductive character of thinking) for Cyc is ambivalence about the kinds of representational formats that can be suitably used in Cyc. Although the Cyc group has tried not to limit the knowledge base to a specific representational format, they have failed to be consistent in this regard. Originally, the dominant forms of representation were frames and assertions. CycL, a "superficially frame-based language," was used for frame representations, and in addition there was the CycL *constraint language*, which is essentially the language of first-order predicate calculus. Currently, Cyc uses CycL as its main declarative language, in combination with "a grab-bag," to use Lenat's term, "of dozens of special-purpose inference procedures and data structures" (see Figure 4.3). This hybrid approach has its merits. The most obvious advantage is the favorable trade-off it provides between expressiveness and efficiency. At the same time, it has resulted in many contradictory remarks:

- "CycL is frame-based." (Lenat and Guha 1990: 35)
- "CYC® is not a frame-based system; the CYC® team thinks of the KB instead as a sea of assertions being no more 'about' one of the terms involved than another." (Cycorp Web page)
- "CycL . . . is essentially an augmentation of first-order predicate calculus." (ibid.)

Because this chapter focuses on issues of commonsense knowledge, I have not here taken issue with the capabilities of Cyc's representation scheme, and have assumed that it is reasonably good. As these examples show, however, issues of representation are extremely crucial and complicated.

FOREVER ON THE THRESHOLD

Cyc is a huge, time-consuming, expensive project, unique in the history of AI so far. In light of what we have seen in this study, it would be worthwhile to ask whether the lessons we have learned about it or from it are as big.

What We Have Learned *about* Cyc

As I noted in the beginning of the chapter, the vision behind both Hayes's view and Cyc's approach, despite their differences, was to build a broad platform on which all future AI systems could draw. Cyc was considered by some to be a crucial experiment in AI, the performance of which would determine the fate of a whole class of knowledge-driven models and, even more significantly, of the whole field of AI (Lenat and Feigenbaum 1990: 187). Furthermore, the outcome of this experiment was expected to be clear somewhere around the turn of the century. The question for us now is therefore, "How do we assess whether Cyc has succeeded in achieving its goal?" Or, as McDermott wonders, "How are we supposed to know when we have made progress in formalizing knowledge? . . . How will we know when we've written down most of what people know about the subject? . . . How will we know we're really getting there?" (McDermott 1990: 208).

These are, of course, important questions because of their implications for the whole knowledge-intensive program. Since most arguments are advanced in terms of properties of formal systems in general, any result about Cyc may apply to all systems that fall into this category because of the formality of their approach – that is, their adherence to the logicist framework, their limitation to explicit forms of knowledge, and their incapability of dealing with context- and use-dependent meaning.

In the absence of agreed-on criteria, these are difficult questions to answer. Hayes anticipated this problem when he outlined his proposed research program, but his answer – "that people's common intuition is the guide" – is hardly a solution, given the overwhelming variability among such intuitions. Hayes assumed that the project would be done "when all the straightforward inferences follow from the axioms that have been written down," and this is based on the conviction that, "If something is obvious to people, then it must have a short proof" (McDermott 1990). As McDermott points out, however, this would make sense only if a substantial portion of the inferences people make were deductive.

Unfortunately, the only other reasonable way to judge if Cyc has reached its goals – namely, interacting directly with Cyc over a long period of time – is not a real option either, mainly because of the secretive character of the project (thanks to its business orientation). To the best of my knowledge, OpenCyc, that portion of Cyc that has recently been made public, does not provide much chance for direct interaction. Even if it did, it could always be claimed not to be representative of the full scope of the project in terms of its capabilities.

Occasional public pronouncements about the project are another potential source of information. In interviews with the *Los Angeles Times* (June 21, 2001) and the Associated Press (*Hoosier Times*, June 9, 2002), for instance, Lenat announced that "Cyc has goals, long- and short-range.... It has an awareness of itself. It doesn't 'care' about things in the same sense that we do, but on the other hand, we ourselves are only a small number of generations away from creatures who operated solely on instinct." These are far-ranging claims whose imprecise nature – what is self-awareness or caring, for instance? – makes them impossible to judge. When it comes to concrete examples, however, the same old ones that Pratt had found problematic are released to the media – for example, "Cyc knows that people have to be a certain age before they're hired for a job," or that, in response to an image of people relaxing, it turned up "a photo of some men holding surfboards." If we take these examples as representative of Cyc's abilities, then we face the same kinds of questions Pratt faced during his visit about a decade ago – basic questions like, "Does Cyc really know what an animal or a person is?" "Does it know why people work?" Or why they obtain advanced degrees, for that matter? Does it truly know what a school, an education, a job, an income, and making a living are? How many of these detailed facts should Cyc have in its knowledge base before it can legitimately be said to "know" that people have to be a certain age in order to have a job? What kinds of queries would Cyc have to answer in order to allow an outside observer to conclude that Cyc truly has a sense, in ways that other knowledge bases don't, of what it is for a person to have a job?

The nonexhaustible nature of such questions, as well as the variability, uncertainty, and specificity involved in answering them, the main reasons for which we discussed in this chapter, strongly suggest that Cyc will never reach "the frontiers of human knowledge" that its creators had envisioned; it will always be stuck on the threshold.

WHAT WE HAVE LEARNED *FROM* CYC

The substantive lesson to be learned from Cyc is that the brittleness of AI systems may not be due to a lack of knowledge. Knowledge in whatever quantity and form, as many critics of logicist AI have pointed out, is not the key component of intelligence, and human beings are not walking encyclopedias. There is much more to human cognition, in other words, than pure factual knowledge. Intelligence is *not* knowledge.

To some, this last assertion is so obvious that they might wonder why a project such as Cyc might get underway to begin with. They ask, What

intuitions drive smart people such as the creators of Cyc or their financial supporters to embark on a project such as this? There are, to be sure,
economic and institutional reasons behind the project the discussion of
which would take us into the realm of guesswork and speculation that I
would rather avoid. But there are also intellectual and historical reasons that
interest us more compellingly. These have mainly to do with the axiomatic-
deductive approach adopted by the Cyc group. This approach, as we noted
earlier, is a culturally specific viewpoint with its origins in the ancient Greek
tradition.

In his study of the relation between culture and cognition, Lloyd (1999) has
demonstrated the contrast between the Greek and Chinese traditions in the
areas of mathematics, astronomy, and medicine. In mathematics, for example, the dominant Greek viewpoint valued proof in the axiomatic-deductive
mode, whereas the Chinese attached importance to constructive proofs that
show that an algorithm preserves truth.[27] The significance of this difference
is *not* that these views lead to different mathematical truths — $2 + 2 = 4$
in both China and Greece, and the square of the hypotenuse of a triangle is
the sum of squares of its sides in both traditions. As Lloyd asserts, "mathematical truths do not vary across cultures, but the status of those truths and
what they are truths about, the nature of mathematical subject matter, *are*
questions to which different answers have been given, and not just in modern
times" (1999: 304). By demonstrating similar contrasts between Greek and
Chinese medicine, Lloyd argues that there is nothing preordained about the
dominance of axiomatic-deductive method in the practice of science (ibid.:
306). More relevantly, he takes issue with those cognitive scientists who "tend
to adopt as their working assumption that there are basic uniformities in all
humans," and also with those historians and philosophers who "argue similarly that basic human conceptions of space, time, causality, number, even
natural kinds, are cross-culturally invariant" (ibid.: 312). This list constitutes
an important part of what philosophers call universal ontologies, and what
Cyc people call consensus reality. The disputed working assumption is cor-
roborated, Lloyd reminds us, by the fact that "an infant aged one year or a
child aged three or six will perform very similarly in experimental situations
to others of the same age, whatever their background." Yet this reasoning
comes under considerable strain, he argues, "from the apparent diversities
in the *explicit* theories and concepts actually developed in cultures worldwide, including ancient cultures" (ibid.). Wherever we might have started
as infants, we seem to end with quite different sets of beliefs about stars,
the human body, and diseases, as well as space, time, causality, number, and
nature – almost everything under (and above) the blue sky, in short.

This cultural specificity of particular modes of thinking and the way they shape our views about the nature of things is an important point in the study of systems such as Cyc and what they purport to accomplish. Cyc is driven by a universalist view that operates both at the meta-theoretical level that informs the method, and at the theoretical level where content is developed. The unspoken intuition, as Lloyd (ibid.) has succinctly articulated, is basically that "whatever views may be expressed by the actors [people from different backgrounds] themselves, at a deeper level there are implicit cross-cultural universals that can be elicited by questioning, provided you ask the right questions." This, I believe, is the thinking behind Cyc.

Equally important are the lessons that could be learned from the Cyc group's attitude toward the problems they have faced throughout the project. Two examples are revealing in this respect. One is the approach that Pratt witnessed during his interaction with Cyc. In discovering that Cyc does not know about starvation, the reaction by the developers was to just add another axiom (i.e., that lack of food can be a cause of death). This incident is a good example of McDermott's point that we can never know when enough axioms are put in, but it also reveals a not-seeing-the-forest-for-the-tree mentality. This mentality of paying great attention to the insertion of minuscule facts but little attention to their overall pattern (e.g., the control structure) was revealed also in the numerous redundancies discovered in Cyc after about a decade.

The other example comes from Cyc's treatment of context – the "biggest lesson," in Lenat's own words, for the group itself. From the initial neglect of context to microtheories and, most recently, the multidimensional context space discussed by Lenat (1997b), Cyc has apparently come a long way in grappling with this key issue. This most recent account displays a set of useful insights that point to serious theoretical engagement with the issues. A close look at some of the proposed dimensions, however, reveals that what is presented might, in fact, simply be slightly more sophisticated versions of the same old intuitions. I already discussed the inadequacy of the Time dimension in capturing typical commonsensical behaviors. For the sake of illustration, let me introduce (using Lenat's own words) another dimension – Topic: "Given a context C, what is it 'about'? It could be *about* a person, a group of people, a field of study, a type of event, a particular event, an occupation, an academic discipline, a novel or mythos, preparing for a certain event or kind of event, etc." (ibid.: 45).

Lenat uses this question and answer to motivate the dimension of Topic in his theory of context space. As the answer suggests, the idea behind the Topic dimension is to think of each assertion in context C to be "by default, relevant to and helping to talk about and explain and interrelate the things that C is *about*" (ibid.). The point is to narrow down the space of possibilities to a limited number of topics, thereby making things manageable. Lenat gives the following example:

Consider a context whose topic is "shipwrecks and people and fish." Each assertion in the context will probably refer to one or more of those three terms, or
to elements of one or more of those three collections; moreover, the assertions
will likely interrelate (an element of) one of those three terms to (an element of)
another of those three terms. (ibid.)

At first glance, this makes intuitive sense. Lenat suggests that this might be the best way for breaking up Cyc's gigantic knowledge base into smaller, more manageable clumps. To expand the possibilities even more, he advises, this dimension can be further broken down to subdimensions, in the nature of "Dewey's decimal system, newspaper ads, encyclopedia topics, around goals of agents, or on the basis of academic disciplines, etc." (ibid.). Lenat also introduces the notion of subtopic, as something that interrelates two contexts in ways that the subset relation doesn't. "Freshwater algae" and "Dam-building," for instance, are subtopics of "rivers," but they are not subsets or elements of the same notion.

One could obviously push this line of thought in any direction and come up with a myriad possible dividing schemes. The question naturally arises, "What criteria are used for breaking up contexts into different topics?" This question, which was posed by Smith (1991) about Cyc's old scheme of parti-tioning its knowledge base into microtheories, seems to raise even thornier issues here than it did there. Furthermore, even if we assume that the question about criteria is resolved, the crucial issue is how this scheme would benefit Cyc. For instance, how much help can it offer when one faces an assertion like the following?

*A growing number of children in underdeveloped countries suffer from
hunger and disease.*

When it comes to pinpointing Topic, this sentence could be *about* numer-ous different topics, from children, population, food, medicine, and drugs, to agriculture, geopolitics, pharmaceutical companies, military spending, humanitarian aid, philanthropic causes, third-world debt, and so on. The choice of the topic, it seems, depends on context. In other words, in order to fix the topic, we need to resort to context in the first place. But Topic was deemed one of the dimensions of context space. In short, according to

Cyc's new theory, we need Topic to determine context and we need context to determine Topic. Vicious circularity seems inevitable.

These examples, I believe, illustrate the tension between the scientific and engineering aspirations of AI. Going over the history of Cyc, one observes a recurring pattern of making intuitive assumptions, facing problems, and attempting to fix those problems by creating increasingly subtle and disguised versions of the original intuitions. The recurring pattern would regenerate itself so long as basic assumptions (here, of the logicist kind) are adhered to. And the way out of it is not to relinquish one's intuitions (an impossible dictum to follow anyhow) but to be willing, as Smith (1991) proposed, to flesh out the middle ground between intuitions and technical proposals with painstaking conceptual work, and to be ready to bend to the implications of such work if they do not match the original intuitions. This might be the most effective way to deal with the tension.

5   Coach and Chef: Case-Based AI

Wittgenstein's Scruffy Dream

We do talk of artificial feet, but not of artificial pain in the foot.

— Ludwig Wittgenstein

C ase-based reasoning (CBR) is a prolific research program in AI and cognitive science. Originally motivated by the study of natural-language processing, it has been applied to computer models of story-understanding, learning, and planning, as well as a host of commercial, manufacturing, legal, and educational areas such as multimedia instruction and design.

As its name implies, case-based reasoning involves the interplay of two major themes: a (positive) theme about "cases" and a (negative) theme about "reasoning." The core intuition in CBR is that people reason and learn from experience, and that the knowledge acquired from experience, captured in *cases*, is central to their understanding of the world. In the domain of language, this intuition gives primacy to meaning and "semantics," as opposed to form and "syntax," which were of prime concern in the logicist approach.[1] As a negative claim, therefore, CBR presents a challenge to (formal) logic. It promotes a different kind of reasoning than deductive inference, and emphasizes the role of memory in human cognition.

This chapter is structured to reflect these two themes. Starting with a brief overview of classical models and the treatment of meaning in the logicist tradition, it provides the background conditions for the later discussion of linguistic approaches to meaning, which sets the stage for CBR. It then introduces Coach and Chef, two CBR models of planning in the domains of, respectively, (American) football and cooking, and examines issues of memory and adaptation, which are central to CBR, and concludes by surveying the prevailing trends within the CBR approach.

BACKGROUND: FORM AND CONTENT

> Real thinking has nothing to do with logic at all. Real thinking means
> retrieval of the right information at the right time.
> — Riesbeck and Schank (1989: 5)

CBR, as this statement indicates, can be partly understood as a project coun-
tering the logicist tradition, as exemplified in AI by Cyc. However, Cyc, as
its creators like to say, represents a *scruffy* version of the logicist approach –
scruffy in the sense that it does not commit itself exclusively to the particular
formalism of predicate logic, but also takes advantage of other formalisms,
such as frames, that fit its goals (as we saw in Chapter 4).[2] A more principled version of the logicist approach, which does make such a commitment,
is embodied in the views of Fodor and Pylyshyn and the so-called *classical
models* of cognition that they advocate.

Classical Models

> What makes syntactic operations a species of formal operations is that
> being syntactic is a way of *not* being semantic. Formal operations are the
> ones that are specified without reference to such semantic properties of
> representation as, for example, truth, reference, and meaning.
> — Jerry Fodor (1980)

Formal logic, as we saw in Chapter 1, takes deduction to be *formal* – that
is, syntactic, algorithmic, and mechanical. A corollary of this view is that
syntactic operations can be carried out independently of semantics – but,
at the same time, this view maintains that "the syntax of a formula encodes
its meaning" (Fodor and Pylyshyn 1997: 324). Brought into the context of
computer and cognitive science, this view gives rise to classical models of
thought, which, according to these authors, are (ibid.):

1. **Atomistic:** meaning-carrying structures are built from meaning-
   carrying atoms that are linked together in a structurally complex
   manner.
2. **Systematic:** there are syntactic transformation rules that carry truth-
   bearing structures into other truth-bearing structures, yet without
   exploiting the meanings of the structures involved, but only their external form.

This picture of the nature of mind resembles that of a solid (e.g., a dia-
mond crystal) in which all the familiar macroscopic properties derive solely

from the properties of the constituent atoms (symbols, words) and molecules (phrases, sentences), and from the way these are connected and structured together in a lattice. Just as diamonds are clear, hard, and glittery, thanks to the particular arrangement of carbon atoms in them, minds are cognitive, intentional (directed toward the world), and intelligent, thanks to the structural properties of their symbols and representations. The central thesis in this picture is that, by simply following formal rules, a logic-based cognitive system can maintain its semantic coherence and thereby make valid inferences about the world. What matters, therefore, according to this picture, is the application of the right rules to the right structures.

Assume, for instance, that we want to build a system that understands the domain of football, in the sense that it could take a text (e.g., a newspaper report of a football game) and answer questions such as, "Which team was the winner?" "What was their strategy and what plays did they use?" "Did they try a bootleg?" "Did they succeed in this play?" "If not, what was the cause of the failure?" "How could this type of failure be avoided?" All the system needs, according to the classical model, in order to be able to answer such questions, is to be given the right pool of primitive concepts – "winner," "quarterback," "cornerback," "down," "play," "pass," "blitz," "bootleg," "sweep," ... etc. – and the right set of rules that operate on formulas (sentences) made out of those concepts. Assume, for the sake of a trivial example, that the following short text is given to the system ("QB," "HB," and "CB" symbolize, respectively, the offensive quarterback, the halfback, and the defensive cornerback):

The QB and the HB ran toward the CB.

If asked "Who ran toward the CB?," the system could apply the syntactic rules of logic (or, in this case, English grammar) to find the answer. The applicable rule here involves a *predicate* relation between a syntactic structure of the form "$(S_1$ and S_2 predicate)." In this case,

$$\text{``}S_1 \text{ and } S_2 \text{ [predicate]''} \rightarrow \text{1. ``}S_1 \text{ [predicate]''}$$
$$\text{2. ``}S_2 \text{ [predicate]''}$$

Given that the predicate here is "ran toward the CB," the application of this syntactic rule makes it possible for the system to infer both that the QB ran toward the CB and that the HB ran toward the CB – an inference (actually, two) that has semantic value in the sense that it reports a truth about the world. If the sentence were instead about John and Mary running toward Sam, or X and Y toward Z, the system would perform a similar analysis, since the referent of the atoms are irrelevant. The syntactic rule works independently of what is being referred to.

TWO VIEWS OF MEANING

In classical models, syntactic rules come in many varieties – from purely *grammatical* rules of language as in augmented transition networks (Woods 1975), to *heuristic* rules of inference in GPS (Newell and Simon 1961), to the *domain-specific* rules of expert systems in DENDRAL (Buchanan et al. 1969; see Chapter 4). The common premise in all these formalisms is that the system (a mind) operates on the basis of a set of rules, and the task of AI modeling is to discover and implement these rules in computer systems. This common premise is rooted in a logico-philosophical theory of objective meaning (formulated by Frege, Tarski, Carnap, and others), which is concerned with specifying the nature of truth and reference. According to this theory, sentences are true or false independently of whether we recognize them as true or false, even of whether anybody has ever thought of them (Santambrogio and Violi 1988: 4). In the world in which the QB and HB *really* ran toward the CB, in other words, S is true (as are S_1 and S_2), irrespective of whether anyone has ever thought about or reported on this event.

The "objective" theory of meaning was motivated by a mistrust of psychologism – that is, a mistrust of anything that has to do with the processes going on in an individual mind. That this view should have had such a great influence on AI, whose main focus should presumably be the understanding of mental processes, seems, in retrospect, an ironic fact that can be explained only by taking note of the intellectual origins of AI in the logicist tradition (see Chapter 1). A psychologically driven reaction to this trend can be seen in a close intellectual relative of AI and of the cognitive view of mind – namely, psycholinguistics. The psycholinguistic tradition sees meaning not in terms of "truth conditions," but as "what is converted into speech by a speaker and conveyed to a hearer" (Santambrogio and Violi 1988: 10):

> Cognitive semantics is first of all a theory of understanding and of language use, as opposed to a theory of abstract entities called "meanings." As such, it is clearly sensitive to empirical constraints of various kinds; it must depict what actually "goes on in our mind" (psychological realism), and it must explain how language can be so efficiently learned by human beings.

As far as issues of meaning are concerned, CBR belongs to the cognitive-semantics tradition. The striving for psychological realism, as we shall see, has been a strong guiding force in the development of CBR, and is motivated by the belief that "the best way to approach the problem of building an intelligent machine is to emulate human cognition" (Schank and Kass 1988: 181). Human intelligence has to do with getting "the right information at the right time," according to the proponents of CBR, and information, in their view, has mainly to do with world knowledge. Therefore, the main challenges to those who would design and implement a computational model of mind are "what data structures are useful for representing knowledge and what algorithms operate on those knowledge structures to produce intelligent behavior" (ibid.).

The three-decade development of ideas in CBR could be generally understood as attempts to meet these challenges. "Scripts," "plans," "memory organization patterns," "explanation patterns," and all other theoretical constructs that we will come to know in this chapter are, in fact, attempts at realizing such data structures and algorithms in a psychologically plausible manner.

The philosopher Ludwig Wittgenstein also challenged the idea that human language derives its meaning from an objective world, and argued that the meaning of any utterance depends on the human and cultural context of its use. In contemporary AI terminology, this amounts to the claim that language is "scruffy" and not "neat." CBR could perhaps be thought of as an attempt to realize Wittgenstein's view in computer systems (through the use of "scripts" and other data structures), but it fails, as we shall see, to take into account the other side of this view – namely, the difficulty, if not the impossibility, of capturing life forms in fixed, rule-based structures (Neumaier 1987; Woolgar 1995).

FROM ATOMS OF MEANING TO CASES OF EXPERIENCE

The origins of CBR lie in the early work of Roger Schank and his students on natural language processing. What differentiated their work from most other work on natural language processing in those days was the "integrated knowledge hypothesis" – namely, "that meaning and processing knowledge are often crucial at even the earliest points in the process of understanding language" (Schank and Birnbaum 1984: 212; cf. Schank and Leake 2001).[3] Schank's first step in modeling this view of language was his development of the theory of *conceptual dependency*.

Conceptual Dependency: A Theory of Content

The theory of conceptual dependency (henceforth "CD") assumes and seeks to formulate "a conceptual base into which utterances in natural language are mapped during understanding" (Schank 1972:188). It assumes, in other words, that underneath any linguistic utterance (sentence) there are non-linguistic representations. These representations are "image-like in nature, in that each concept is processed with respect to the whole picture that is created" (ibid.: 241) and they are governed by a set of rules that map the inputs into a "predefined representation scheme" (Schank and Leake 2001). CD seeks to find these rules and representations.

In the mid-1960s, Schank introduced a number of *primitives* out of which all meaning could presumably be constructed in an unambiguous and language-independent way, "in much the way that atoms combine to make molecules" (Schank and Riesbeck 1981: 14). The primitives are Lisp atoms (i.e., alphanumeric strings) that represent about a dozen acts that involve "simply the moving about of ideas or physical objects" (ibid.) – for example:

- PTRANS: to change the location of an object ("physical transfer")
- MTRANS: to transfer information, either within memory or between people ("mental transfer")
- ATTEND: to focus a sense organ on a stimulus
- INGEST: to absorb something inside an animate object (eat, drink, inject)

More complex or esoteric acts were thought of either as representing relationships between primitives (e.g., "prevent," "instigate"), as describing unknown actions that result in a given state (e.g., "frighten," "comfort," "hurt"), or as the results of other conceptualizations (e.g., "love," "hate") (ibid.). It is difficult to understand how this could be reasonably done. Even more difficult is to understand how the CD primitives can be the bearers of meaning in any serious sense of the word. Two types of elemental concepts in CD, for example, are "nominals" and "modifiers," which are (at least in theory) image-like representations of objects and predicates. Thus, "a word that is a realization of a nominal concept tends to produce a picture of that real world item [e.g., a 'ball,' 'broccoli,' or 'block'] in the mind of the hearer" (ibid.: 192). It is not clear how alphanumeric strings, which are claimed not to belong to any specific natural language, can be "image-like representations of objects and predicates."

These ambiguities notwithstanding, the next step in the formulation of CD was to put the above primitive concepts together in a type of structure called a "conceptual dependency network." In computer models, these take the form of a list-like data structure.[4] For instance, sentences (1), (2), and (3) are represented by (1)*, (2)*, and (3)*, respectively:[5]

(1)   The quarterback passed the ball to the halfback.
(1)* [PTRANS (ACTOR quarterback)(OBJ ball)
          (TO halfback)(FROM quarterback)(TIME past)]

(2)   The cornerback saw the halfback.
(2)* [ATTEND (ACTOR cornerback)(OBJ (PART-OF cornerback))
                (TO halfback)(FROM?)(TIME past)]

(3)   John ate the broccoli with the fork.
(3)* [INGEST (ACTOR John)(OBJ broccoli)
                (TO mouth-of-John)(FROM fork)

The creators of CD considered it to be a first fundamental step towards the integration of world knowledge and language, but a close look at CD reveals the kind of wishful thinking that lurks behind it. Although the encoding of actions such as passing a ball might look simple at first glance, problems start to emerge in representing even the most trivial of ideas. How does one represent the following sentences in CD notation, for example?

- John fell.
- John likes to drink.
- John amazed Mary.

In the first sentence, it would seem at first that John is the filler of the ACTOR slot, but an equally plausible understanding of it would have John being the OBJECT, with the actor being the force of gravity. In the second sentence, one can fill in the slots by taking note of facts such as that the ACTOR for "drink" and "like" should be the same in English, but representing "like" is not straightforward at all – for example, one needs to express it as a state of mind and assign a positive number to it (Similarly, the state of being "dead" is represented as (HEALTH-VAL –10). Finally, in the third sentence, to say that John did the ACTION "amaze" disregards the fact that "amaze" does not refer to any particular action. Rather it refers to a state of Mary that was caused by John's action, and this could be anywhere from John hitting a ball a long distance, his being very generous, or perhaps his saying that he was sorry. Thus, the ACTION, OBJECT, and DIRECTION of the CD are all unknown for this sentence.

The creators of CD were aware of these problems and challenges – in fact, all of the above examples come from Schank and Riesbeck (1981) – but the solution that they offered was rather awkward. In discussing the sentence "John likes to drink," for example, they observe that, "a person hearing this sentence knows a lot of information about John derived from the inference that alcoholic beverages are ingested by John frequently and from other inferences about the effects of such repeated actions" (ibid.: 13). Therefore, they suggest:

To get a computer to understand English, it is necessary to get the computer to make the same inferences. This can only be done by forcing the machine to seek to fill in missing slots in a CD and by giving it some methods of doing that. Without the rigid format of CD, an understanding mechanism would not know what it did not know. Knowing what information you need is a crucial part of understanding. (ibid.)

The wishful thinking behind this proposal is evident not only in the assertion that "the rigid format of CD" could help an understanding mechanism find out the right information at the right time but also in the supposition that CD primitives are laden with rich semantics. Despite the desire for psychological plausibility of their models, writers on CD are not clear about its relation to human cognition – for example, about the origins of CD primitives in human beings (whether they are outcomes of an evolutionary process or of learning). In CBR computer models, these primitives are simply taken for granted, making these models vulnerable to the objection that their scheme does nothing but relate words to other words, or translate from one language to another. Johnson-Laird (1988), for instance, charges these schemes with the "symbolic fallacy" – namely, that they entirely skip the key question of how words relate to the world.

Having faced issues such as this, CBR workers tried to enrich their models by introducing new structures to the original CD scheme. The main function of these is to bring world knowledge to bear in processing and understanding language, as formulated in the integrated knowledge hypothesis. Once they observed that "extracting the meaning of individual sentences is only part of understanding," Schank and his group realized that "understanding their connections and ramifications is crucial as well" (Schank and Leake 2001). Indeed, the formulation of these connections engaged Schank and his students for some three decades. Scripts and plans (Schank and Abelson 1977), memory organization packets (Schank 1982), and explanation patterns (Schank 1986), to be discussed in the next section, are the most important of their proposals for mechanizing the process of understanding.

Before we discuss these topics, however, a clarification of the differences between the Cyc and CBR approaches is needed. Despite the fact that they both emphasize the importance of knowledge in (language) understanding, these two approaches are based on totally different notions of "meaning." CD begins with primitives – atoms of meaning – and builds up from there. These primitives also constitute the basic level of CBR models. In analyzing the sentence "Mary ate a Macintosh," for instance, the analysis proceeds by mapping the word "ate" to INGEST, which provides the expectation that its object should be some kind of food. This would presumably rule out "Macintosh" as designating a type of computer or raincoat in favor of a type of apple (Schank and Leake 2001).[6]

Therefore, CD shares with Cyc an emphasis on world knowledge, but differs from it in two major respects. First, unlike Cyc and classical models, CD's basic representations do not encode propositions (they encode more primitive concepts such as actions) Second, and more importantly, the two approaches follow opposite paths in dealing with meaning. Roughly speaking, CD's approach, taking the meaning of certain primitives for granted, begins (supposedly) with semantic objects and builds structures out of them, whereas the logicist belief is that meaning is attached to objects (i.e., symbols) thanks to an isomorphism between syntactically manipulated structures and the external world. The similarity of CD and classical models because they both involve some sort of atomism is, therefore, misleading.

Schank and his colleagues sometimes highlight their differences with the logicist approach by asserting that, "It is the meaning of an input structure that is needed, not its syntactic structure" (Schank and Riesbeck 1981: 189). Many repudiations of any interest in syntax have, over the years, led to the frequent impression that CBR does not involve syntax in any manner – a conclusion that, as we have seen, is utterly contradicted by the formal nature of CD notation and its highly structured networks. Although Schank repeatedly denied any interest in *linguistic* syntax (i.e., grammar), he nonetheless could not avoid the use of syntax in his programs and data structures, since computers do nothing but follow syntactic rules and syntactically manipulate data structures! Therefore, although the CBR approach tries to focus solely on content and to marginalize form, it certainly does not dispense with syntax altogether.

Integrating Knowledge and Language

> Scripts are *frozen* inference chains, stored in memory. Scripts don't make thinking easier – they make thinking unnecessary. . . . An Explanation Pattern is a *fossilized* explanation. It functions in much the same way as a script does.
>
> – Schank, Kass, and Riesbeck (1994: 59/77)

Scripts, like frames, are data structures for representing stereotyped sequences of events, such as a football play (come to the line of scrimmage in a given formation, hike the ball, hand the ball off, run towards the goal, etc.).

The idea behind scripts is to provide automatic contexts by generating stereo-typed sets of expectations. According to this idea, in hearing a story such as the following, for instance, expectations help us fill in the gaps – for example, that the quarterback has the ball and that a tackle takes place:

The quarterback received the hike, ran toward the line of scrimmage, and was stopped five seconds later.

But we do not seem to keep every detail of every event in memory. In football, for example, there are different types of run – a run to the line of scrimmage, a run toward a specific player, a run towards the goal, and so on. While each of these may constitute a distinct concept, the common features among them can all be captured in a single higher-level (i.e., abstract) memory structure for "run." In other words, the theory is that memories are organized in hierarchies of stereotyped structures that vary in their degree of detail. The theory of memory organization packets (MOPs) was devised to implement this vision in a computational fashion.

Giving Flexibility and Structure to Memory

A MOP contains knowledge about an abstract class of events, especially complex events. "They involve standard AI notions such as frames, abstrac-tion, inheritance, and so on, but applied to dynamically changing knowledge bases, i.e., systems that learn new knowledge in the process of understanding and problem solving" (Riesbeck and Schank 1989). A MOP can represent an *instance* – a particular occurrence of an event as well as a generic event (like a template). To represent events in football, for instance, there could be a MOP behind the scenes of each of the terms RUN, PASS, TACKLE, and SHORT-PASS, and so on. Each of these terms, in turn, might have *specializations* – for example, one MOP apiece for RUN-TO-GOAL, RUN-TO-PLAYER, RUN-TO-SCRIMMAGE, and so on.[7] They also can be "packaged" to create bigger chunks (Schank 1982), such as a play composed of a sequence of events (hiking the ball, running to scrimmage, running toward the goal on the offensive side, seeing an offensive player, running to him, and tackling him). Here are some examples of MOPs (of these events) being compounded into larger MOPs.[8]

```
(DEFMOP I-M-BOOTLEG-RUN (M-OFFENSIVE-PLAY)
    (1  M-HIKE (ACTOR I-M-C)(TO I-M-QB))
    (2  M-RUN-TO-SCRIMMAGE (ACTOR I-M-QB))
    (2  M-RUN-TO-GOAL (ACTOR I-M-QB)))
```

```
(DEFMOP M-CB-DEFEND (M-DEFENSIVE-PLAY)
    (1  M-DETECT (ACTOR I-M-CB) (INFO M-PASS))
    (2  M-RUN (ACTOR I-M-CB) (TO M-OFFENSIVE-PLAYER))
    (3  M-TACKLE  (ACTOR  I-M-CB)  (OBJECT  M-OFFENSIVE-
       PLAYER)))
```

MOPs were explicitly designed to address an issue that scripts were too rigid to solve – namely, that events do not always follow a stereotyped sequence, but instead often involve novelties and anomalies. Under such circumstances, people's expectations are violated, leading them to seek an explanation. This gave rise to a notion called "explanation patterns" (XPs). The sequence of events in these two MOPs, for instance, counts as a failure for the offensive team because one of its players – the ball carrier – is tackled by the defense's cornerback. To learn from this failure, and to allegedly avoid a similar result later on, an XP (itself a certain type of MOP) is generated, saying in effect that this is a failure for the offense because the tackle occurs in the same time cycle (i.e., BAD-CYCLE) as the run for the goal:

```
(DEFMOP I-M-BOOTLEG-XP (M-EXPLANATION) INSTANCE
    (FAILURE M-FAILURE
        (STATE M-BAD-CYCLE
            (1  M-RUN-TO-GOAL (ACTOR I-M-QB))
            (2  M-TACKLE (ACTOR I-M-CB)(OBJECT I-M-QB))))
```

To recap, Schank and his colleagues, unsatisfied with the logicist approach and committed to a psychologically motivated view of meaning, originally devised the CD idea, which involved ignoring, as much as possible, the grammar of the input passage. This strategy, however, proved to be too restrictive for any interesting account of language understanding. This led to the introduction of increasingly complex and abstract structures in order to enhance the CD scheme. These modifications were, in effect, the price that had to be paid for the initial sidestepping of grammatical syntax and structure. Unfortunately, scripts, MOPs, and so on, were found, despite the attempt to make them flexible, to be *still* too rigid ("frozen" and "fossilized"), and their shortcomings eventually precipitated the development of case-based reasoning.

Over the years, case-based reasoning has been put to test in numerous models, two of which will be the subject of our study for the rest of this chapter.

COACH: A MODEL OF PLANNING

Coach is a model of how novel offensive plays are devised by a football coach.[9] This model was devised by Schank's doctoral student Gregg Collins in the 1980s and is included in *Inside Case-based Reasoning* – an edited volume that discusses a number of CBR models (Riesbeck and Schank 1989).

Plan creation in Coach is conceived of as a modification process pursued by a goal-driven system that learns from experiencing failures.[10] Therefore, explanations for failures (XPs) play a crucial role in Coach. For example, there is an XP for the offensive failure in a "sweep" play, where the halfback, running with the ball, is unexpectedly tackled by the defense cornerback. Equipped with explanations, the model is meant to devise a novel plan that would avoid such failures. Such a plan, known as the *option* play, was in fact introduced in football many decades ago. A computer model that could on its own devise this plan by learning from failures of other types of play could be claimed to have invented a truly novel plan in principle. In short, the ideal behavior for Coach would be the detection of a potential hitch in a previous plan and the analysis of that defect for the purpose of creating a new plan, but without going through a process of trial and error in the real (or simulated) world. Collins (1989) discusses a general strategy called "Fork" to capture this.

Briefly, the idea behind Fork is that when one has a choice between two alternative plans (that might involve shared steps) in a competitive situation and the opponent is keen on discovering one's plan before a deadline, then one should try to keep the opponent in the dark as long as possible and should be prepared to change plans midway.[11] To implement this model, Collins catalogued a number of plan-adjustment strategies that he considered to be *domain-independent* in the sense that "the problem situation associated with the strategy is independent of the physics of the world" (1989: 255). The usefulness of such strategies (or, alternatively, *transformation rules*) resides, according to Collins, in the fact that "there is a knowledge level of description that deals with agents and rational goal-plan behavior" (256; cf. Newell 1981). One such strategy is "Fork," which, in Collins's view, is applied in many competitive environments, from games such as tic-tac-toe to real-life situations such as business and political negotiations. The core idea in Fork is to force an adversary into making a committed choice before you yourself are committed one way or the other. Collins (1989: 285) has formulated Fork in the general way shown in Table 5.1.

The important point to notice in this strategy is that once one has started executing a plan, one is committed to carrying that plan through – "to stay the course," in the political language used by the Bush administration in

Table 5.1. The Fork strategy (from Collins 1989)

Fork:
   If:
      We are competing;
      I have to decide between two plans;
      You pick a counterplan by detecting what my choice is;
      There is a deadline on when you have to choose;
   Then:
      I should create a new plan which has these steps:
      The steps shared by the alternatives, if any;
      A modified form of one of the alternatives, which can be executed until your
         deadline forces you to make a decision;
      A step to detect which choice you made;
      A step to decide whether to keep doing the current alternative or not;
      A step to cross over to the second alternative, if necessary;
      A modified form of the second alternative, which can pick up from the crossover
         point.

---

dealing with Iraq. The option play can thus be understood as an instance of Fork (see Figure 5.1).

In his article, Collins also included the diagram in Figure 5.1, which shows that the crucial point in the play is for QB and HB to run in unison and in parallel in order to keep the defensive CB in a state of uncertainty as to who will be the final carrier of the ball (i.e., to deceive him), until the CB winds up selecting between one of the two options – either tackle the QB or tackle the HB – in which case the ball will be transferred to the other player, who can then hopefully run with it to the goal. Collins describes this process in the following manner:

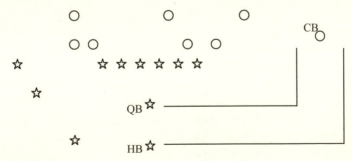

Figure 5.1. A schematic of the option play.

MicroCoach's plan repair is guided by considering both failing plays together [that is, the plays where, respectively, the halfback and the quarterback carry the ball and are tackled by the defensive team]. Both cases involve a corner-back tackle. Since he cannot tackle both the quarterback and the halfback, one possibility is to create a new play that has elements from both plays. The real Coach generates the option play, a kind of fork, where the decision as to who will carry the ball to the goal is delayed until the cornerback moves in one direction or the other. MicroCoach generates a simpler alternative, where the ball is not passed from the quarterback to the halfback until the cor-nerback has committed himself to pursuing the quarterback (Collins 1989: 291).

The main idea behind a model like Coach, then, is to account for the invention of the option play "by saying that the planner recognized a cir-cumstance in football where the Fork strategy would reasonably apply, and created the option as an implementation of the Fork strategy for football" (283). More generally, such a model would illustrate the utility of domain-independent plan-modification strategies. Construed in this fashion, the model also presents a very clear success criterion – namely, its capability to apply a domain-independent rule to a specific domain.

To get some perspective on this view of planning, we need to step back for a moment and look at the notion of planning as it was originally conceived in AI.

STRIPS: PLANNING IN THE ABSTRACT

The classical idea of planning in AI was originally motivated by the intu-ition that actions are unproblematic executions of predetermined plans. This simplistic conception, however, was shown to be insufficient for uncertain environments that change in ways that may undermine a fixed plan. A sim-ple shopping plan, for instance, could be undercut in a number of ways: the car might break down, the traffic might be jammed, an item might be sold out, and so on. Furthermore, keeping explicit track of all conceivable things that might possibly change will obviously be prohibitively costly. The classic notion, therefore, failed on two counts: *correctness* and *efficiency* (Agre and Horswill 1992: 363).

As a remedy, this early scheme for planning was improved by the idea of interleaving plans and actions, so that plans could be revised in real time. In the early 1970s, Fikes, Hart, and Nilsson (1972) took this idea and com-bined it with GPS methods of problem solving (see Chapter 1), to devise a scheme called STRIPS.[12] This scheme, which was originally designed for a robot called Shakey, provides a good example to be compared with Coach's approach.

Shakey, built at Stanford Research Institute, moved in a small world of seven rooms and eight doors, pushing and stacking square boxes according to typed instructions given to it in simplified English (Fikes et al. 1972).[13] Shakey's control algorithm STRIPS used an enhanced version of GPS. Unlike GPS, which operated on the basis of observing explicitly differences between the current state and its goal, STRIPS used differences more implicitly. The way this worked was to use rules made up of three parts – "preconditions," a "delete list," and an "add formula" – all defined as lists of predicates such as ON(a, b), CLEAR(c), HOLDING(a), and so on. A rule for picking up block b, for instance, might look like this:

Preconditions:	ONTABLE (b), CLEAR (b), HANDEMPTY
Delete list:	ONTABLE (b), HANDEMPTY
Add formula:	HOLDING (b)

In English, the first line means: "b" is on the table, has nothing on top of it, and Shakey's hand is empty. The other lines are straightforward, given this. The differences between the goal state and the current state are, therefore, the predicates of the goal state that are unmatched by the current state. As a result, the applicable rule, being one that contains in its add formula at least one of the desired predicates, need not be figured out by explicit calculation of the difference. This scheme provides a significant improvement over the classical scheme in terms of both correctness and efficiency, especially for the simplified world of Shakey. But it still suffers from the problem of requiring the explicit enumeration in advance of all the preconditions and outcomes of an action – a problem that can become serious in a swift game such as football but not in a domain like chess, making the latter, as opposed to the former, amenable to planning schemes such as that mentioned earlier. Collins, however, sees the difference between football and chess in a different light:

> Like chess, football is a game, and hence highly constrains the set of situations we have to worry about. Unlike chess, however, football requires reasoning about time and space, and, most importantly, about *opponents* and how they *reason about your strategies*. Planning and counter-planning [Carbonell, 1981] are fundamental to football. One major problem with football is that it is not an easy domain to experiment in. Novices and fledging AI programs don't get to coach football teams. (1989, 261–62; emphasis Collins's)

In other words, Collins seems to see two fundamental differences between chess and football: (i) football involves reasoning about time and space; and (ii) strategic planning is fundamental to football. However, in light of what we know about these games, the second point sounds counterintuitive, for, if anything, chess seems to be more about reasoning and strategy than football, not the other way around. Ignoring what Collins says about chess (because it is flawed), we can interpret his statements as follows:

i) *acting* in time and space is essentially equivalent to *reasoning* about time and space;

ii) such reasoning, performed in the abstract, always intervenes between plans and actions; and hence

iii) what matters in football is reasoning about strategy or, more specifically, the adaptation of an abstract plan to a physical situation.

I wish to examine these assumptions next.

Reasoning about Time and Space

The Fork strategy outlined here involves a time component that would presumably apply to all domains where the strategy is followed. This is captured in the term "deadline" that shows up in both the preconditions and the consequent of Fork (Table 5.1). What this term signifies is that, irrespective of the domain, there is a key point in time beyond which the plan would be ineffective and meaningless. What is crucial in the implementation of the plan is to take into account the specific nature of the domain. The world of diplomacy, for example, involves politics, logistics, geography, and so on. The world of football, however, is largely physical. This is best manifested in Collins' own description of the option play:

The threshold must be far enough from the target to allow enough time to take whatever action depends on the detection [e.g., of the CB seeing the offender]. The physics of football says that a lateral pass takes about half a second, so the threshold distance between the cornerback and the quarterback must be such that the cornerback will not be able to cross it in less than half a second. More football physics determines that a player can cover about 2 yards in half a second. Hence, our plan says that the crossover plan will need to be executed when the cornerback approaches within 2 yards of the quarterback. The lateral pass is reliable at 5 yards, so we pick that value as a safe place to put the halfback. (Collins 1989: 288)

To apply the Fork strategy to football, therefore, would involve a close consideration of the physics of the domain. Rather than dealing directly with the physics, however, Collins seems to believe that this should take the form of *reasoning* about the physics, as evident from his assertion that: "*the physics of the domain is important only insofar as it is needed to carry out domain-independent strategies*" (269; Collins's emphasis). This premise, as we shall see next, has come under serious question within AI.

Does Acting Always Involve Reasoning?

> Nine-tenths of a swift game is as far as possible from the exploitation of a definite thought-out plan, hatched beforehand, and carried out exactly as was intended. The members of the team go rapidly into positions which they did not foresee, plan, or even immediately envisage ...
> — Frederic C. Bartlett, *Remembering* (1932)

Football certainly involves strategic planning – this is what a football coach does, after all. The question is, how closely followed are preplanned strategies in the real progress of the game? How does abstract planning (by the coach) get translated into concrete actions (by the players)? To what extent, in other words, are the details of a game thought out and hatched beforehand? Bartlett, as this passage shows, argued that the extent is very small. In the broader context of human activity, Bartlett was among psychologists who emphasize that choice of behavior is often possible, and even necessary, without advance planning. In a similar vein, some AI researchers have advanced the hypothesis that human behavior often consists of improvisations that are evoked by physical interaction with the environment, and does not involve continuous consultation with a stored plan of behavior (cf. Clancey 1997: 124). This conception of human behavior affects, in turn, other features of AI models such as representations.

Agre and Chapman (1987), for instance, developed a cognitive model of planning for a simulated robot that plays a commercial arcade videogame called Pengo, and their model utilized a notion of representation different from both the STRIPS and CBR models. Pengo is played on a two-dimensional "field" made of unit-sized "ice blocks." The goal of the human player is to navigate a "penguin" in this field, protecting it from "killer bees." Both the penguin and the bees can rearrange the field by kicking and sliding ice blocks, any of which would kill the opponent if it were to hit the opponent. The cognitive model, called Pengi, is a simulated robot that replaces the human player. The main feature of Pengi is that instead of keeping track of all the pieces (bees and blocks) from a bird's-eye view, it dynamically names things it encounters with descriptions such as "the ice cube that the ice cube I just kicked will collide with."

Agre and Chapman call this sort of representation "indexical" or "deictic" (these are technical terms borrowed from the philosophy of language and reference, and they simply mean that such a phrase can only be understood by reference to the robot's current location and its most recent actions). They claim that their scheme is computationally more efficient than a classical alternative (such as STRIPS), which would require the simulator to keep an updated model of the whole field at all moments.

By focusing on the here-and-now of the world, deictic representations promote a view of planning and activity that puts emphasis on improvisation rather than planning (we will see other aspects of this view in Chapter 8). If Agre and Chapman are correct about the efficiency of their scheme, the representational model of Coach might be problematic even in a simulated football environment, because Coach, as the diagram in Figure 5.1 illustrates, needs a bird's-eye view of the field in order to carry out a play. But there is, in fact, much more going on in that diagram than merely an overall representation of the football field, as I shall show next.

WHEN A PICTURE IS WORTH TEN THOUSAND WORDS

The old adage "A picture is worth a thousand words" has recently been the subject of interesting research in AI, logic, and psychology, mostly under the rubric of *diagrammatic reasoning*.[14] Jon Barwise and John Etchemendy (1994), for instance, have shown how a single change in a diagram can "generate a lot of information," saving a substantial number of inferences that in a purely linguistic medium would have to be carried out explicitly.

A Free Ride from Diagrams

Take the diagram in Figure 5.2(a), for example.[15] The features of the objects in this diagram are interpreted as in ordinary pictures – for example, their size, shape, location, and so on. So the large cube on the far left represents a large cube on the corresponding position on the board, and the small icon labeled "c" represents a small dodecahedron, and so on. The cylinder with a triangle symbol in front, on the other hand, represents an indeterminate object. Changing the cylinder to tetrahedron "a," as in Figure 5.2(b), however, provides a good deal of information that was missing from the previous picture – for example, that "a" is large, that "a" is larger than "c" but of the same size as the cube on the leftmost column, that every object in front of "c" is a large tetrahedron, that there are exactly two large tetrahedra and no small or medium ones, and so on. In short, a single change in the visual scene generates, at once, many other pieces of information, and obviates the need for a large number of inferences. This inherent efficacy of diagrams also

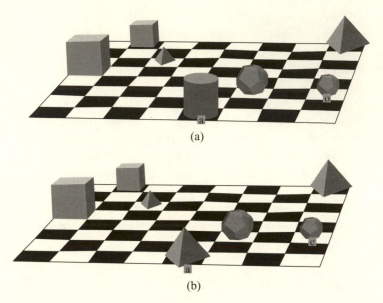

(a)

(b)

Figure 5.2. The efficacy of diagrams in making inferences (from Shimojima 1996, with permission).

explains their commonplace use in geometry as well as other branches of science (Larkin and Simon 1987).

Inspired by studies and observations such as this, Shimojima (1996) suggested that a common feature of a wide range of representation systems, especially visual representations, is their ability to manifest a phenomenon that he calls the "free ride."[16] Furthermore, following Larkin and Simon (1987), Shimojima argues that there are actually two kinds of free ride: (i) *static efficacy*, which has to do with the use of a representation as a record of information; and (ii) *dynamic efficacy*, which refers to the use of a representation as a site for updating information (1996: 19). To see what this means, let us take a look at an early AI program called Whisper (Funt 1980).

Whisper is a program that solves certain problems about the motions of collapsing objects by using diagrams. Given the diagram of a block structure that is about to collapse, for instance, the program should predict the sequence of events that would occur subsequently (see Figure 5.3; the blocks are assumed to have uniform density and thickness). Whisper does this by producing a series of diagrams that depict the sequence of events during the collapse. To do so, it uses a trial-and-error method, making successive estimates of values such as the angle that block B has to rotate around point k before it touches block D (roughly 28 degrees in Figure 5.3[b]). The diagram, however, also provides the additional information that there is a gap

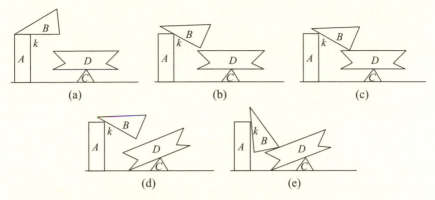

Figure 5.3. The diagrams used by Whisper for making inferences (from Funt 1980, with permission).

between the lowest surface of B and the top surface of D. This information helps Whisper correct its computation of B's rotation to finally arrive at the situation depicted in Figure 5.3(c). A similar process of trial and error produces the diagrams in Figures 5.3(d) and (e). The additional information, which becomes available as the result of changing the original diagram to reflect a rotation of 28 degrees, is what Funt calls "experimental feedback" to the program:

Usually feedback is thought of in terms of a robot immersed in a real world environment. In Whisper's case, however, the feedback is from a situation analogous to that in the real world – the diagram and diagram transformations – rather than from observation of actual falling objects. . . . Using this feedback Whisper is able to find when and where discontinuous changes in an object's motion occur without being forced to use sophisticated, "number-crunching" algorithms for touch tests for arbitrary shapes. (1980: 51)

In short, these examples seem to confirm Shimojima's claim that the use of visual representations does, in fact, provide new information that saves us from having to derive this information from the original data. The diagram in Figure 5.1, I suggest, also serves the same function in our understanding of the option play. At first glance, one might think that the purpose of the diagram in Collins (1989) is to help the reader visualize the arrangement of players in the option play, but it does much more than that. The reader effortlessly realizes that:

- most of the players in the two teams are facing each other;
- most of the players are too far away to play a direct role in the option play;
- most of the players are relatively stationary, compared to QB and HB;

- the QB and HB are on one side of the field, and are quite close to each other;
- the QB and HB have started to run together on parallel paths;
- the path followed by QB and HB is boot-shaped, and leads them toward the CB;
- the CB is in a position such that he can see the QB and HB throughout their run.

This partial list illustrates both the static efficacy of the diagram (in providing an overall bird's-eye view of the field) and its dynamic efficacy (in providing a *running* display of the game). Notice particularly that the parallel lines representing the QB and HB paths do not depict a snapshot of the scene; they show a trace that represents a whole sequence of motions taking place in time. In short, by looking at this diagram, a reader who is uninitiated in football does indeed get a free ride in visualizing the option play.

How about the program (Coach)? Does the program also get the free ride? It does not, because the diagram is not available to it. The question, then, arises as to how it gets the information required to understand (and devise) the option play. The question, in other words, is, "How does the computer model, without the benefit of representational efficacy of a diagram, apply the Fork strategy to football?" This, we should recall, is a central question the answer to which, according to Collins, determines the degree of success of Coach.

A Free Lunch for Coach

As it turns out, Collins (1989) does not address this question directly. Part of the reason, to venture a guess, might be that he does not see a serious difference between linguistic and imagistic representations, or between verbal and diagrammatic reasoning. What lends support to this speculation is the original intuition in the theory of conceptual dependency that there is such a thing as a nonlinguistic representation that is claimed to be "image-like in nature" (Schank 1982). It was probably based on this intuition that the creators of CD did not find it necessary to explain how language translated into CD notation is supposedly imbued with "image-like" qualities. Collins seems to depend on a similar intuition when he liberally throws in diagram 5.1 without drawing attention to its crucial role in helping humans understand the option play.

A brief look at the code, in fact, indicates how feebly time and space are dealt with. Instead of being treated as physical constraints that need to be dealt with in the implementation of the strategy, time and space are built into the program as arguments of logical functions. For example, the high-level function for the option play is DECEIVE, and one of the critical functions is MUTUAL-EXCLUSION, which encodes the commonsensical fact that CB cannot be in two locations at the same time. The main parameter in this function is TIME-CYCLE, which is defined as an integer-valued variable that stands in for instants of time – a common practice in AI, which is strongly diluted in Coach, because the whole duration of a play, as we saw in the earlier piece of code (page xxx), is broken up into two or three cycles, not into tenths of a second or so). Similarly, the decision of CB crucially depends on the parameter DISTANCE, as described in the earlier excerpt from Collins (1989) but DISTANCE is also broken, not into small increments, but into two conditions of LONG and SHORT.

In brief, the code reveals that the most crucial aspect of football – namely, the incorporation of the physics of the domain – is merely built into the program in coarse-grained parameters such as CYCLE and DISTANCE and in functions such as DECEIVE and MUTUAL-EXCLUSION. The computer model does not have access to the free ride provided by a diagram (and the visual apparatus that supports it), but it receives all the crucial ingredients as a free lunch.

What happens in Coach is the application of Fork to football *at an abstract level* that sets all the concrete issues of planning aside. This separation of planning and execution, built into the classical view of planning in AI, is therefore maintained in Coach. Planning is envisioned as a three-tiered process where we have a domain-independent strategy, domain-specific plans in the abstract, and executions of those plans in the concrete. A typical AI model of this sort, then, at best transforms the domain-independent strategy to abstract plans, while the treatment of crucial physical constraints of the world is done by the programmer, if dealt with at all. In Coach, as we saw, DISTANCE is just a variable with a couple of discrete values (rather than an essentially continuously changing number); time during a down involves just a handful of discrete "stills" with nothing comparable to players *moving* or moving *towards* or *away from* anything – it just has a few variables possibly clicking from one discrete value to another – and so on.

Indeed, the presence in Collins's text of the two-dimensional schematic diagram (Figure 5.1) cannot help suggesting to readers that *this* is the level of stripped-downness that Coach is dealing with – a two-dimensional world with genuine motion, with dots on a screen approaching each other and then separating, an entity called "BALL" attached to the property list of one of the dots and transferable under certain sets of conditions involving rapidly changing distances and times and so forth. In fact, though, no such continuously changing two-dimensional world exists in the model. But people *want* to believe that the program is "seeing" a football game at some plausible level of abstraction. The words that Coach manipulates are so full of associations for readers that they CANNOT be stripped of all their imagery.

Collins of course knew that his program didn't deal with anything resembling a two-dimensional world of smoothly moving dots (let alone simplified human bodies), and presumably he thought that his readers, too, would realize this. He couldn't have suspected, however, how powerful the Eliza effect is. This power was pointed out to me by Douglas Hofstadter in a personal communication some years ago (1999):

While teaching my 'Hype versus Hope in AI' seminar in 1995, somewhere in the middle of the semester, I myself read the two chapters on Coach in Riesbeck and Schank (1989), and I discovered all sorts of serious lacks in the program's representation of the game of football. I therefore gave as an assignment to my class to read those chapters and to look as hard as possible for the program's hidden weaknesses, of which I assured them there were many.

The next time my fifteen or so students came to class, I asked them what they had found. The most serious objections leveled against Coach were of the following sorts: 'It doesn't take into account the weather conditions'; 'It doesn't seem to have any representation of penalties'; 'It doesn't include home-team bias'; and other mild reproaches that took for granted an incredibly detailed and accurate model of genuine football played in a three-dimensional stadium before a large audience.

I was flabbergasted by this, for after all, these were all AI-oriented graduate students in computer science or cognitive science who had elected to take my seminar presumably because they were already somewhat inclined to believe that there is a lot of confusion in the field of AI, and they wanted to develop some skill at the art of separating the wheat from the chaff. Moreover, they had been exposed to my own very harsh criticism of various other projects for at least six weeks already, so they knew very well how weak an AI project can be, despite having a strong superficial façade.

Given their weak performance, I asked my students to go home and try again, and I renewed my insistence that there were far more serious lacks of football understanding to be found in Coach's code. The next time they came to class, although their criticisms were slightly more on target, they still had all completely missed the key fact that there really is nothing comparable in Coach to a two-dimensional field, or to players moving around in space, or even to motion or space or time at all. This was a revelation to me, because it made me realize that something in the pages of the chapters, or in the code, had induced a kind of stupor in my students.

These fifteen serious and presumably skeptical graduate students were essentially unable to divorce the English words that appeared throughout the computer code from their standard associations, even though they were all experienced programmers who knew full well that calling a variable "CHEESE" does not mean that it smells. But in a context where nearly every word in the code subliminally suggested familiar associations, and where the surrounding text repeatedly stated that the program was being "creative" and "original" and implied indirectly that the program had a mastery of ideas such as running and tackling and passing and blocking and so forth, it was impossible to prevent an avalanche of incorrect assumptions from taking place.

This avalanche was further accelerated, I speculated, by the presence in the chapter of the type of diagram that people who know football very well standardly use to sketch out the central ideas of various plays. Such a schematic sketch falls roughly halfway between people's imagery of football in its full, ferocious, real-time complexity and their vision of computers as being mathematical, precise, and rigid. This diagram looks like a halfway house that a computer could plausibly deal with – not too complex but not too simplified, either. Although Collins probably didn't intend to blur people's minds by including that sketch, I strongly suspect that virtually all of my students unconsciously took the sketch for a representation that the program could easily handle.

This was not rigorous thinking on the part of the students, obviously, but such sloppy thinking is par for the course when one reads, even when one reads critically. Although partly the fault of the author, it was a foible typical of most human readers. Indeed, it would have required many hours of intensely careful, critical, and also self-confident analysis to see through the code to the barren-ness of the program's representation of football, and even then, having found that barrenness, my students might well have doubted their own reasoning, for the simple reason that this AI program was being reported very seriously in a published book that was edited by two well-established researchers, whereas they were merely graduate students. It is very hard to trust one's own skeptical intuitions in the face of impressive claims, even if the claims seem at some level implausible.

Hofstadter mentioned to me that even he – a professor of computer science and a seasoned AI researcher – found himself questioning his own judgments about the program, and so he carefully examined the code a number of times, just to be sure that he wasn't missing some crucial aspect of the program.

These anecdotes illustrate the intricate ways that the Eliza effect can man-ifest itself. They reveal not only our susceptibility to commit the Attribution Fallacy, but also the intimidating effect that superficially sophisticated tech-nological products can have on us. This latter effect becomes more striking if we notice that Coach, compared to typical AI systems of today, was a relatively simple program, and even in CBR circles, it never evoked much interest, as is testified to by the absence of any citation or discussion of this model in CBR research literature and elsewhere. However, this very fact, rather than making Coach an inappropriate object for our critical study, makes it a fascinating and very appropriate one. Why?

Why Criticize Poor Old Coach?

Some people might wonder why on earth I chose Coach as a target of criticism if, as I have attempted to show, its model of its domain is so impoverished. Why attack such an easy target? There are two principal answers. One is that this program was accorded two chapters in the book *Inside Case-Based Reasoning*, edited by the two most prominent figures in the CBR school, and one has to assume that if those experts included this program in a book intended to showcase their ideas, then they thought it was meritorious and not insignificant. Coach may not be the flagship of all CBR projects, but it was certainly one of CBR's flagship projects at one point, and hence critiquing it is by no means hitting below the belt.

It is true that to have criticized the program (written in the 1980s) in the mid-1990s was one thing, whereas to do so nearly ten years later is another thing. To be more specific, a critical analysis of Coach's weaknesses written in 2005 may seem irrelevant or outmoded, since the state of the art of CBR may have changed considerably in the meantime. On the other hand, even if CBR has changed, much at its core has not changed, and therefore the close examination of Coach just given provides a model for how to critique CBR models in general; in other words, the criticism given here of Coach (in tandem with that of Chef, to come soon) constitutes something of a generic "recipe" for how to think about what any given CBR program really is, behind the scenes of its English-language façade (or "front end," as natural-language façades are often called in AI). Technologies change – albeit not as abruptly as many tend to believe – but ideas and intuitions behind them, as I mentioned in the Prologue, are often more durable.

The second answer to "Why rake poor old Coach over the coals?" is as follows. When the presumably AI-savvy participants in Douglas Hofstadter's "Hype versus Hope" seminar turned out to be unable to spot any of the main chinks in Coach's armor (even when told in advance that there were significant ones, and even when harsh criticism was the order of the day), this unsuspected gap in their perception stunningly reveals the undiminished power of the Eliza Effect on intelligent and well-prepared adults, three full decades after Joseph Weizenbaum had made the term and the notion "Eliza Effect" world-famous, particularly in the world of AI practitioners and students.

The irony is that the weaker the program that pulls the wool over people's eyes, the more deeply people are shown to be susceptible to the Eliza Effect. Put another way, the weaker the program that exerts an Eliza Effect over (presumed) sophisticates, the stronger and the more valuable is the lesson that the encounter teaches. Therefore, and paradoxically, the weaker a program

Coach is, the more powerfully this encounter with it reveals a serious problem concerning how AI programs in general are received by members of the AI community (not to mention how they are received by less informed people, such as scientists in other disciplines, journalists, and interested lay people). This is why it was not just fair but in fact very crucial for me to critique Coach in this work.

However, to make sure that more than one base is covered in the CBR camp, I shall now turn my attention to Chef, another model discussed in the same book (Riesbeck and Schank 1989), and perhaps one that possesses a greater mastery over its domain of discourse. That, at least, is the issue that we shall examine.

LEARNING FROM EXPERIENCE

> Case-based reasoning is the essence of how human reasoning works. People reason from experience. They use their own experiences if they have a relevant one, or they make use of the experience of others to the extent that they can obtain information about such experiences. An individual's knowledge is the collection of experiences that he has had or that he has heard about.
>
> – Riesbeck and Schank (1989: 7)

CBR, as we saw at the outset, is founded on two major themes: reasoning and experience. Thus far, we have focused on the first theme, which is mainly about reasoning, as it applies to meaning, planning, and so on. The second theme – that people reason from experience – is the topic of discussion for the rest of the chapter. I shall introduce this theme with Chef, a program that uses CBR techniques to invent new recipes, based on known ones.

Chef: Recipes versus Algorithms

> Chef is a case-based planner whose primary domain is Szechwan cooking. Chef creates new recipes, i.e., cooking plans, from old ones, in response to requests for dishes with particular ingredients and tastes. Chef has to build one plan that satisfies a number of goals simultaneously. In this, Chef's job is much harder than many other planners, which can create a simple sequence of plans to satisfy several goals.
>
> – Kristian Hammond (1989: 184)

This is a brief description of the computer model Chef in the words of its creator, Kristian Hammond. The idea in this model, as we see, is very clear.

Computers are notorious for being algorithmic beasts – and "algorithm" seems to be just a fancy word for "recipe." So what would be a better place for challenging these beasts than the limited domain of specialized recipes in, say, Szechwan cooking?

In fact, this statement about recipes being algorithms is not quite correct (Boden 1970; Knuth 1983: 6). Knuth, for example, argues that of the five important features of algorithms – finiteness, definiteness, input, output, and effectiveness – recipes notoriously lack definiteness: "Add a dash of salt," "toss lightly until the mixture is crumbly," "stir until it is crunchy" are anything but definite descriptions of things to do. This discrepancy between recipes and algorithms, therefore, invites a more sophisticated scheme, such as is sought in Chef. Of course, Chef is not meant to follow recipes; it creates them by making use of previous recipes and their failures.

Learning from Failure

Central to Chef's technique is its access to cases of past *experience* stored in its memory. Thus, for example, if it already has a plan for stir-fried chicken and green beans, it can use it to make a recipe for stir-fried chicken and broccoli, or stirred-fried beef and green beans. Not only can this technique generate a desired new recipe, it provides a great savings in computation because, according to Hammond, it saves the program from going over all "the seventeen steps performed on a dozen ingredients" involved, for instance, in the preparation of the above recipe (1989: 184).

The technique works in the following way: The program stores previous plans together with an explanation for their success or failure. In so doing, it becomes competent at anticipating and avoiding future failures. What underwrites this competence, according to Hammond, is "a strong model of the causality of the domain in which it operates," together with "a powerful memory organization" (ibid.). This enables Chef not to have to start from scratch every time it is asked to make a new recipe. So Chef would first find an old plan that satisfies as many of its goals as possible, and then would alter the plan to satisfy the remaining goals. In order to do this, it uses its knowledge to *simulate* the execution of the plan as "the program's equivalent of real world execution" (ibid.). For instance, in applying a failed beef-and-green-beans case to create a new beef-and-broccoli recipe, Chef simulates the execution of the former in order to find an explanation for its failure – for example, excessive water as the cause of the sogginess of the beans – and uses this explanation to create a recipe for the latter.

Explaining Failure

A plan failure, therefore, means two things to Chef. "First, it must repair the plan. Second, it has to repair its understanding of the world" (ibid.). This is where explanation comes in: "An explanation describes the failure, the step that caused it, and the conditions that had to be true for it to come about." Thus, by simulating the new recipe, which was created by simply substituting broccoli for green beans in the original one, Chef figures out, in advance, that something would go wrong. The simulation, according to Hammond, takes the form of a series of questions and answers (both provided by the program) such as the one in Figure 5.4. Hammond (1989: 188) explains the simulation process in the following way:

The simulation does not just report that "the broccoli is soggy"; it also reports that "water in the pan made the broccoli soggy," "cooking the meat left water in the pan," and so on. In other words, the real-world simulator and Chef's causal model of the world are one and the same.

Reading through a passage like this, one cannot help asking questions such as these: Does Chef really know if anything "tastes savory" or not? Does it really understand the English words it is manipulating? Does it have an image of sugar as powdery and sweet, of broccoli as a complicated plant shape, of a wok as the lower quarter of a metallic sphere, and so forth and so on? Does Chef have a sense of "sogginess" or "crispness," a sense of what wetness is or of how water flows, or for that matter, does it even have an understanding of gravity? These are the sorts of questions the reader should ponder in trying to make a judgment about Chef and indeed about CBR programs in general, because CBR programs tend to claim expertise in matters involving the familiar physical world. Do these programs know what they are talking about? Does a recipe-invention program need to know anything at all about gravity or wetness or how food looks or tastes, or would such knowledge just be icing on the cake?

One conceivable answer to all of these questions is "No! Chef does not have any sense of those things, and it does not need to because they are irrelevant." Similarly, for Coach, a proponent of CBR could argue, "that kind of detailed physics knowledge is irrelevant to developing new plays in football, in much the same way as the detailed biology of the blades of grass growing on the field is irrelevant." In other words, the level at which Chef (and Coach, and any model that works in this manner) works is abstract enough to spare it from such physical details. It is an advantage of these programs,

Explaining the following failures:
It is not the case that: The broccoli is now crisp.
In that: The broccoli is now soggy.
The broccoli is now a bad texture.
In that: The broccoli is now soggy.
In: BAD-BEEF-AND-BROCCOLI
ASKING THE QUESTION: 'What is the failure?'
ANSWER → The failure is: It is not the case that: The broccoli is now crisp.
ASKING THE QUESTION: 'What is the preferred state?'
ANSWER → The preferred state is: The broccoli is now crisp.
ASKING THE QUESTION: 'What was the plan to achieve
the preferred state?'
ANSWER → The plan was: Stir fry the sugar, soy sauce, rice, wine,
garlic, corn starch, broccoli and beef for three minutes.
ASKING THE QUESTION: 'What were the conditions that led
to the failure?'
ANSWER → The condition was: There is thin liquid in the pan from the
beef equaling 4.8 teaspoons.
ASKING THE QUESTION: 'What caused the conditions that led
to the failure?'
ANSWER → There is thin liquid in the pan from the beef equaling
4.8 teaspoons was caused by: Stir fry the sugar, soy sauce, rice wine,
garlic, corn starch, broccoli and beef for three minutes.
ASKING THE QUESTION: 'Do the conditions that caused the failure
satisfy any goals?'
ANSWER → The condition: There is thin liquid in the pan from the
beef equaling 4.8 teaspoons is a side-effect only and meets no goals.
ASKING THE QUESTION: 'What goals does the step which caused
the condition enabling the failure satisfy?'
ANSWER → The step: Stir fry the sugar, soy sauce, rice wine, garlic,
corn starch, broccoli and beef for three minutes.
Enables the satisfaction of the following goals:
The dish now tastes savory.
The beef is now tender.
CHEF explains the failures that it encounters through a causal description
of why they have occurred.

Figure 5.4. Chef's style of reasoning (from Hammond 1989, with permission).

the proponent might argue, that they can plan at this abstract level, which is removed from the physical details of the world – that is, in a "domain-independent" manner, to use the term suggested by Collins. So the editors of *Inside Case-Based Reasoning* would retort, "Congratulations – you've hit the nail on the head! Just as we advertised, we've shown how simple thinking and creativity really are. All you need to do is throw away the irrelevancies!"

Such a gleeful return thrust, if it were ever made, would be surprising, but it is worth considering how to reply to it.

First of all, such a position would amount to a retreat to the old days of classical planning strategies (as in Shakey), in which only the most abstract levels of the world were skimmed off in advance by humans, and logical reasoning in that rarefied domain yielded a fully anticipatory plan allowing no improvisation or modification in real time. In that case, how would Coach-style planning mark any kind of advance relative to classical logic-based planners? How could one even maintain that Coach involves the core of CBR (i.e., involves retrieving and adapting concrete real-world cases), when its "mental processes" are floating at such a high level of abstraction above the nitty-gritty details of real cases in the real world?

Second, how would celebrating Chef's ignorance about the physical world (and for that matter Coach's ignorance about space and time) jibe with the fact that the creator of the program felt it necessary to pay a great deal of attention to the physics of the domain in order to translate this abstract schema (or the Fork strategy) into the domain of Chef (Coach), so that the program could exploit it? On the one hand, in order to give Chef (Coach) sufficient understanding to use the schema, the programmers had to think carefully about the physics of the domain (and time and space as applied to runners, blockers, and laterals), but, on the other hand, in our hypothetical world of the gleeful retort, they would be proud to have developed a program in which those features of the domain are not present. But when one puts these two facts together, it all boils down to this: Hammond (Collins) spoon-fed Chef (Coach) with just exactly those features of the domain that he knew would allow it to make the right inference (or "invent" the option play) "on its own." Unfortunately, when this kind of in-advance filtering and spoon-feeding is seen to have taken place in an AI project, it strains credibility to hear any claim that creativity was realistically modeled in that project.

THE WORLD IS REGULAR, BUT . . .

With this introduction to Chef, we can now examine the theme of "learning from experience" closely. This theme is based on two tenets about the character of the world we live in:

The first tenet is that the world is regular; similar problems have similar solutions. . . . The second tenet is that the types of problems an agent encounters tend to recur. Consequently, future problems are likely to be similar to current problems. (Leake 1996: 3–4)

The interpretation of these tenets depends, of course, on what is intended by terms such as "regular," "similar," "experience," and so on. Let us begin our examination of Chef's method by looking at Hammond's statement that "the real-world simulator and Chef's causal model of the world are one and the same."

We Intervene in the World

The General Problem Solver view of early AI took the world as a set of problems, human thinking as consisting mainly of problem solving, and human activity as carrying out plans that are mentally worked out in every detail prior to execution. An alternative worldview would take the world as a benign place that largely can be dealt with through a set of routine everyday activities: taking showers, going to work, eating, driving, and so on. Failures are also a sort of routine activity, and there are routine methods (allowing the bypassing of thinking) for fixing failures.

CBR embraces this alternative view: it takes the world to be a regular setting for human activity. The development of ideas in CBR, in fact, illustrates how this view has unfolded in different phases; this is particularly clear in the introduction to Riesbeck and Schank (1989). Given that the world is regular, as these authors suggest, then human thought might be simpler than what many scientists have imagined. People use and adapt their prior experience when they face new situations, and thinking consists mainly in this process of remembering and adaptation.

The significance of *scripts*, therefore, is that they provide efficient ways of structuring experiences and of generating explanations. If one takes understanding to be explaining, as do Riesbeck and Schank, then the centrality of scripts in human thought becomes obvious at once, as does the role of memory, reminding, adaptation, and so on. A *case*, for instance, is defined as "a contextualized piece of knowledge representing an experience that teaches a lesson fundamental to achieving the goals of the reasoner" (Kolodner and Leake 1996). Cases are, in other words, central in CBR because they provide a cumulative scheme for *storing* prior knowledge. To make this scheme efficient, according to this view, what one needs is an effective method for indexing and retrieval in order to be able to access the relevant items from the "library of cases."

The strength of AI systems such as Chef, I suggest, is best judged in terms of their capability to capture "experience." By this measure, as I shall show, Chef unfortunately has very limited capabilities.

Causes, Explanations, and Adaptations

According to the scheme in Figure 5.4, Chef's task is to come up with a recipe that results in crispy, rather than soggy, broccoli. In order to do so, Chef seeks a "causal explanation" for its failure to produce crisp green beans – namely, the existence of "thin liquid in the pan from the beef" caused by the stir-frying of all ingredients for three minutes. It figures out that the extra liquid did not serve any purpose but was merely a side effect. It therefore decides to repair that step in the new recipe, in order to assure the crispness of the ingredients in the new recipe. It *adapts*, in other words, a previous case to the new situation. The first step in this process, as we see in Figure 5.4, is to seek an explanation for the failure of the previous case.

Such a pattern of reasoning – seeking explanations by going back from consequences to antecedents – is known as "abduction." As others have shown (e.g., McDermott 1990: 213), abduction has serious limitations – most importantly, it provides neither a necessary nor a sufficient link between the explaining and explained facts. In the Chef example, for instance, the sogginess of the broccoli is not *necessarily* the result of the "4.8 spoons" of beef water. It could be the result of many other things: the water from the sugar or the sauce, the quality of the broccoli or the wine, the temperature of the burner, the residual water from washing the ingredients, the humidity of the air, and so on. And in the opposite direction, the water from the beef is not *sufficient* to explain sogginess. Many other factors might have simultaneously contributed to the effect of water in changing the quality. And a burner with higher temperature, for instance, might have prevented the problem altogether.

In short, no single cause is necessary and sufficient to explain a phenomenon, and the multiplicity of causes may be too complex for any simple explanation to be satisfactory. This is a lesson that scientists, including psychologists, have learned the hard way (Roberts and Pashler 2000), and there is every reason to believe that its implications carry over to typical real-life situations. This is partly why cooking, as Knuth (1983) and others have noted, is underspecified by recipes. There is a gap, in other words, between a recipe and the act of cooking that needs to be filled by an expert's "skill," "experience," "judgment," and the like. As these are murky terms, however, CBR seeks to make them precise through the working of systems such as Chef. The important challenge for Chef, therefore, is to fill the earlier-mentioned gap. Since the idea is that Chef does this by the adaptation of a previous case, the central questions would consist in how the adaptation proceeds – for example, how Chef comes up with a three-and-a-half-minute time for stir-frying the ingredients; or, given that oil and wine are also liquids, how it singles out the water from the meat as the cause of sogginess.

The information in Figure 5.4 shows that the main elements of the explanation and adaptation mechanisms are given to Chef by the system builder. Chef, therefore, should not be attributed too much credit in this respect. A good part of the reason why not, I argue, has to do with how memory is viewed by the CBR community.

Memory as a Storehouse of Cases

Roughly speaking, the CBR approach to memory and reminding can be summarized as follows:

1. Experience, as a replay or adaptation of daily routines, is captured in discrete representations such as cases and scripts.
2. Memory is a storehouse or library of cases, indexed so as to make appropriate subsequent retrieval possible.
3. Understanding a situation, text, or story is achieved by explaining it, which in turn involves calling upon the right script.

These principles have greatly influenced the technical work in CBR, as is evident in the following passage:

Human memory depends upon good methods of labeling cases so that they can be retrieved when needed. Human experts are not systems of rules, they are libraries of experiences. (Riesbeck and Schank 1989: 7/15)

It is in this "storage" view of memory that CBR comes closest to the computer metaphor of mind. In particular, the emphasis on cases or scripts in CBR has turned the problem of remembering into a search paradigm based on efficient *indexing* – in other words, the strategy is to label and index cases as they occur so that, much later, they can be remembered and efficiently retrieved in "similar" situations. Chef, for instance, labels its recipes by "the goals they satisfy and the problems they avoid" (Hammond 1989: 267). That is, in searching for a plan similar to a stir-fried beef-and-broccoli dish, first it looks for a recipe that matches as many goals as possible, and next it tries to avoid possible problems (sogginess) by simulation, as was explained earlier. The beef-and-green-beans recipe has two complete matches (stir-fried and beef) and one partial match (green beans and broccoli) – the latter because green beans and broccoli are both vegetables. The property of "being a vegetable" is a clear enough similarity metric for this case, and justifies the priority given to it as a label for the case.

This scheme, however, has one major problem: it often employs surface similarities that are rarely useful in classifying interesting situations. For instance, while being a vegetable might be a good index in this case, the fact that broccoli is a rich source of calcium might be more relevant to someone with a family history of osteoporosis, making it more similar to cauliflower than green beans; hair color is not important if an applicant applies for a computer job, but it might be central if it is a modeling job (Kolodner 1996: 356). The question, then, is, "How do the relevant features emerge and come to light when one is dealing with a situation?"

Taking note of this problem, Kolodner (1996: 355) suggested that "indexing" might have been the wrong term, and that a more appropriate term might be "accessibility." An alternative solution that partly solves the problem is, in fact, pointed out by Wills and Kolodner (1996: 83–85). This consists of "a flexible and highly opportunistic manner" of redescribing new situations in terms of old ones. Rather than first saving (a description of) an experience in memory with the "right" labels and then using those labels to assess other situations, this alternative view lumps the two stages together, trying to make sense of a new situation by *seeing it as* a previous one, ideally somewhat in the manner of models of analogy-making such as Copycat and Metacat (Hofstadter and FARG 1995; see Chapter 9). This way of looking at similarity and remembering is in agreement with recent neurophysiological theories of memory such as Edelman's (1987) theory of neural group selection (see Clancey 1997: Chapter 7 for a good review of such theories).

The standard CBR "library of cases" metaphor for memory is not only a barrier to Wills's and Kolodner's conceptualization of remembering, but it also reinforces the view that essentially equates thinking with the mindless retrieval of well-indexed memories.

CONCLUSION: DIVERGENT ROADS

What we will not present in this book is a general apparatus for attempting to represent any or all knowledge . . . [A]nyone wondering, for example, whether we could get a computer to play squash or roll pasta dough should not wait with bated breath. The geometry of bouncing balls, the "feel" of dough texture, and many other aspects of human activities involve knowledge falling outside of present boundaries. This is because (among other reasons) visual and kinesthetic processes cannot readily be represented in verbal form. However, a great deal of the human scene can be represented verbally, and we have no lack of things to work on.

– Schank and Abelson (1977: 5)

This excerpt from the foreword to Schank and Abelson (1977) amounts to a position statement about the kinds of topics that, some years later, became the core issues of CBR research. It would seem, then, that football and cooking would not make good candidates "of things to work on." And yet, as we have seen, CBR fearlessly tackled such domains anyway, as projects such as Chef and Coach clearly demonstrate. This shift in perspective, I believe, has contributed a great deal to the development of ideas in CBR.

What We Have Learned *about* CBR? Potemkin Villages in AI

Case-based reasoning, as we have seen, began with a set of ideas and intuitions that, on first glance, are quite plausible:

- People learn from experience.
- There is more to thinking than rule-based inference or problem solving.
- Intelligence is more likely to be a continuum than a "now you have it, now you don't" affair (Riesbeck and Schank 1989: 373).
- We learn as much from our failures as we do from our successes (ibid.: 10).

Ideas like these abound in the CBR literature from the past to the present. One also can discern a healthy willingness to revise ideas when they prove to be inadequate. Despite this, however, the initial intuitions were developed under strong pressure from an engineering ethos in the practice of research. Schank (2001) states this explicitly: "I'm still interested in AI as a theoretical enterprise ... but since I'm a computer scientist, I like to build things that work." This engineering perspective is best shown in CBR's theory of human memory, which is considered the linchpin of CBR research and yet is described in very psychological terms: "My most important work is the attempt to get computers to be reminded the way people are reminded" (ibid.). Despite the explicitly stated interest in psychological realism, a parallel commitment to fixed, deterministic, and rigid modes of computer operation as models of human thought processes has stayed with CBR (Schank et al. 1994: 7).[17]

These engineering commitments, together with a narrow view of human experience that overlooks its strongly flexible character and its purposeful interaction with the material, social, and cultural environment (as we saw in the case of Chef), has resulted in biases that limit the efficacy of the original intuitions. My goal in this chapter was to show the discrepancies not only between CBR models and those intuitions, but also between what the models do and what it is claimed they do – for example, how Coach is claimed to be dealing with the domain of football (with all the rich physical features involved in it) or even merely with a two-dimensional world (with genuine motion, time, distance, etc.), whereas what it really does is rudimentary manipulation of Lisp atoms in the absence of any model of space, time, or motion; or how Chef is claimed to be creating recipes (that produce crisp, and not soggy, ingredients), whereas what it does is to go through a very rudimentary IF–THEN chain of reasoning (against the likes of which CBR was allegedly a revolt) in which the outcome is essentially spoon-fed to the program.

In short, despite all the trappings of real-world situations, the domains dealt with by Chef and Coach are nothing more than microworlds where the words denote paper-thin concepts. These worlds are Potemkin villages in the empire of AI.

I have suggested that part of the reason for this situation is the pressure imposed by dual (scientific and engineering) aspirations of AI. The uneasy coexistence, in CBR, of opposing tendencies generated by insightful and creative intuitions, on the one hand, and technology-induced pressures, on the other, is clearly manifest in the contributions to the anthology compiled by Leake (1996). First, there are chapters that emphasize, among other things, flexibility (82), stochastic processing (88), situation assessment as a key to remembering (35, 86), and the role of generalization and abstraction in thought processes (38).[18] These authors and their projects are still motivated by the conviction that cognitivist CBR "has the potential to change a lot in the way we look at intelligence and cognition" (Kolodner 1996: 370).

On the other hand, in the same book, there are chapters that adopt a much more pragmatic view with an emphasis on the notion of "intelligent components." Being wary of "rule-based reasoning with very big rules," this view finds the solution in "old-fashioned true CBR":

Artificial intelligence is the search for answers to the eternal question: *Why are computers so stupid?* That is, AI is a repair process. Cognitive science has, among others, the goal of understanding "what is intelligence?" AI has the goal of understanding "what is7 computer stupidity, and how can we get rid of it?" ... the problem of AI is to describe and build components that reduce the stupidity of the systems in which they function. That is, the goal should not be intelligent systems. The goal should be the improvement of how systems function through the development of intelligent parts to those systems. (Riesbeck 1996: 374–77)

An example of such a system, suggested as an alternative to an automated librarian, would be a library search program "that knows concepts, not keywords, that won't find James Cook when I'm searching great chefs in history." The goal, according to this view, "is not 'smart' appliances and cars that talk to us. The goal is street lamps that don't waste electricity on totally deserted sidewalks, and traffic lights that don't turn green for streets closed for construction" (ibid.). The explicit engineering spirit of this view would have the advantage of advancing a clear agenda not stressed by concerns of psychological realism, but, on the other hand it would lose contact with the lively and interesting intuitions that sparked the invention of CBR.

In brief, as we have seen throughout the chapter, CBR practitioners tend to present their views as expressions of defiance against the orthodoxy of the time, namely logic. And, as both Dennett (1995) and Minsky (1995) have pointed out, they tend to do this with shocks.[19] Some CBR practitioners take pride in this outlook, portraying themselves as "scruffy" researchers of AI who "believe that the mind is a hodge-podge of a range of oddball things that cause us to be intelligent" (Schank 1995: 175). They seem to forget that the more "oddball things" in an object of study, the more systematic, persistent, and patient should be the effort to make sense of them. A hodge-podge of oddball things cannot be dealt with by a hodge-podge of oddball theories.

What We Have Learned *From* CBR? Variations on A Theme

> To say that we expect future cases to be like past ones is, on its face, to say nothing... The sober fact is that we cannot expect every trait shared by past cases to carry forward to future cases.
>
>   – Quine and Ullian (1978: 86)

Experience matters: This might be the most consensual assertion about human life, which (the late) Wittgenstein reasserted most cogently. Any approach to AI that takes this seriously, therefore, is onto a good start. Experiences, furthermore, take place in repetitive patterns, and CBR seeks to capture the patterns in its various schemes such as scripts and cases. The schemes would, of course, work best when the same cases tend to recur frequently, and when life is orderly enough that a reasonable-sized repertoire of cases covers the vast majority of possible experiences (Agre 1997a: 311). Actually, human beings themselves often adopt an active role in minimizing diversity in situations – for example, when they put their tools in the same place at the end of a job, when they keep cutlery and plates clean so as not to run out of dishes, when they drive to work at the same time every day, and so on (Hammond, Converse, and Grass 1995). These "stabilization processes," as Hammond et al. have called them, play an important role in our regular interaction with the world, and human beings play an active role in them.

Our dealing with the world, as Dewey suggested, "is comparable to the operations of the bee who, like the ant, collects material from the external world, but unlike that industrious creature attacks and modifies the collected stuff in order to make it yield its hidden treasure" (1920/1948: 32). Knowing that one will return to the same job later, for instance, one is well advised to leave the tools on site rather than storing them in their usual place in the workshop; or hearing of a traffic jam on one's regular route, one should try to take a detour, if possible; or in the act of preparing a meal, one may well try out a new seasoning simply as a matter of change of routine, if for no other reason; and so on.

In short, while taking advantage of the regularities of the world, human beings also contribute to the creation of new regularities and, in so doing, exhibit different degrees of on-the-fly planning or improvisation. Planning as such is itself a kind of situated activity that results in interesting relationships between projections and actions (Suchman 2007). The interesting question, therefore, is to ask how the enduring aspects and the novel aspects are combined and managed together. That is, how does human activity reflect the regularities of situations and, at the same time, take into account the boundless variety of large and small contingencies that affect our everyday lives (Agre 1997a)? To repose the question posed by Hofstadter, how do we constantly, but creatively, make variations on a theme? (1985: 232; 1995: 55).

6   Language Learning: Connectionist AI

Hebb's Neural Dream

The first object of this book is to present a theory of behavior for psychologists; but another is to seek a common ground with the anatomist, physiologist, and neurologist, ... to make it possible for them to contribute to [psychological] theory.

– Donald Hebb: *The Organization of Behavior*

Connectionism is rooted in long-standing views about the human mind.[1] As a philosophy, it goes back to Hume's view that mental activity mainly consists in associations among ideas. As a scientific theory, it originates in the works of McCulloch and Pitts (1943), Hebb (1949), and Rosenblatt (1958), who developed theories of neural circuitry based on mutual activations and inhibitions among neurons. And as an approach in AI and cognitive science, it was instigated by a number of independent researchers during the 1970s and 1980s – for example, Dell (1986), Grossberg (1976), and McClelland and Rumelhart (1986). Most notably, the publication of *Parallel Distributed Processing* by the PDP Research Group in 1986 marks a resurgence of interest in connectionist approaches, which has persisted until now.

One of the active areas of connectionist modeling is language processing, which is an intriguing topic of research in AI and cognitive science. Probably no other topic has as immensely fascinated researchers in these fields, and none has been as challenging, elusive, and thwarting as natural language. Historically speaking, the beginnings of both AI and cognitive psychology have well-known linguistic facets – the former in Turing's idea of an intelligence test based on purely linguistic interaction between humans and a contested machine (Turing 1950), the latter in the assault by the linguist Noam Chomsky on behaviorism (Chomsky 1957). A survey of AI would, therefore, not be complete without dealing with models of language processing.

This chapter investigates connectionist models of language learning. Language is, admittedly, not the domain where connectionist models fare best, but it provides a good arena for discussing both their capabilities and their limitations. The chapter begins with a spotty sketch of previous attempts in AI to deal with language, followed by a brief survey of how connectionists are tackling this challenge.[2] The rest of the chapter is devoted to an outline of the main intuitions behind the connectionist approach and to the clarification of these intuitions through a close study of a number of connectionist models of language processing.

BACKGROUND: THE STORY OF LANGUAGE LEARNING IN AI

Because natural language has always exerted a powerful lure on the AI community, a very large number of models of language processing have been devised over the last few decades. In view of the enormous complexity of language, almost all of these models have tackled one or another limited aspect of language, and have broken it up into subsets, subtasks, or subdomains that have been attacked separately. A review that samples a few of these endeavors will offer some perspective.

The First Approach: Language in Microworlds

Limiting language to specific domains, which presumably involve a closed subset of the given natural language, is one of the avenues AI has pursued in language research to this date. The following are examples of this approach.

1967: STUDENT solved algebraic story problems such as this:

If the number of customers Tom gets is twice the square of 20 percent of the number of advertisements he runs, and the number of advertisements he runs is 45, what is the number of customers Tom gets? (Bobrow 1967)

STUDENT looked for cues such as "number," "twice," "square," and so on to break the above sentence into chunks, assigned variables to these chunks, formed equations, and solved them. A typical stumbling block of its approach to language was that it interpreted the phrase "the number of times I went to the movies" as the product of the two variables "the number of" and "I went to the movies" (Russell and Norvig 1995: 11)

1972: SHRDLU was a simulation of a robotic hand that moved colored blocks around in a virtual world shown on a monitor, following instructions given to it in natural language. It could precisely follow instructions as complicated as: "Find a block which is taller than the one you are holding and put it into the box" (Winograd 1972). For all its linguistic virtuosity, though, SHRDLU was very brittle, and was rigidly restricted to the blocks domain.

1997–foreseeable future: Jupiter is a conversational system that provides up-to-date weather information over the phone. It "knows" about more than five hundred cities worldwide, and gets its data from four different Web-based sources. Between May 1997 and May 2003, according to its developers, Jupiter handled over one hundred thousand calls, achieving word accuracy about 89 percent of the time on in-domain queries for novice users (over 98 percent for experienced users), and correct understanding of about 80 percent of in-domain queries for novice users (over 95 percent for experienced users). The system has a vocabulary of nearly two thousand words, and, according to its designers, can answer questions such as the following:

- What cities do you know about in California?
- How about in France?
- What will the temperature be in Boston tomorrow?
- What about the humidity?
- Are there any flood warnings in the United States?
- What is the wind speed in Chicago?
- How about London?
- Can you give me the forecast for Seattle?
- Will it rain tomorrow in Detroit?

Jupiter has even acquired a place at MIT's Museum in Cambridge. Unfortunately, it gives the same answer – namely, "In Boston Thursday, mostly cloudy in the morning, turning to sunny in the afternoon, . . . " – to all of the following questions:[3]

- What was the weather like in Boston today?
- What was the weather like in Boston and Chicago today?
- Was Boston colder than Detroit today?
- Is Boston colder in the winter than in the summer?

It would appear that Jupiter picks up the name of the first city mentioned in the question together with a familiar word (such as temperature, weather, etc.) and then simply produces an answer mechanically.

The Second Approach: Language as a Canned Product

Another approach, which is in some ways more attractive (and for that reason more deceptive), is to engage a machine in "natural" conversation by building in a limited repertoire of words that on the surface does not appear limited.

1965: Eliza played the role of a psychiatrist that conversed with human beings, and it did so in a deceptively convincing way. It managed to engage the "patient" in conversation by making suggestions such as: "Tell me more about your parents." The problem was that these were canned sentences drawn from a very small repertoire and emanated from a program that was as far from the mentality of a human psychiatrist, according to its own creator, as one could imagine (Weizenbaum 1976). Eliza had a great revelatory role in people's understanding of AI systems, and gave rise to the infamous "Eliza Effect" (see the Epilogue).

2002: Claire is a "virtual service representative" for the telephone company Sprint PCS. When you call in, first you need to make a few pushbutton selections about language (English or Spanish), phone number, and so on. Then you are directed to Claire, which greets you in a natural-sounding language. "She" then guides you through a menu of options, asking you to speak "naturally," and, if you speak clearly enough, puts you through to an artificial-sounding automated voice system. If you are not clear, however, she responds, "Hmmm . . . let me get more information"; and if you still continue to be unclear – by saying "Thanks," for instance, to her offer of help – she gracefully gives up: "We seem to be having trouble. Let me get someone to help you!"

Like its more primitive predecessors, Claire allegedly saves its company millions of dollars each year. The problem is, not only does it offer many irrelevant "options" to callers, taking much valuable time, it is also helpless in responding to even the most frequent customer inquiries, such as: "What is item x on my bill?," where the caller reads aloud a line on the bill.

1960s–Present: Language in Translation. Machine translation has for decades been an attractive goal to funding agencies such as the National Research Council in the United States, which sought to speed up the translation of scientific papers from Russian to English in the wake of the Sputnik launch in 1957 (Russell and Norvig 1995: 21).

1960s: The famous translation from the English "The spirit is willing but the flesh is weak" to Russian and then back to English, resulting in "The vodka is good but the meat is rotten" and others similar to it prompted an advisory committee to report in 1966 that "there has been no machine translation of general scientific text, and none is in immediate prospect" (ibid.).

2003: One of the numerous online translation engines (Prompt-Reverso) translated the same sentence to German as "Der Geist ist bereit, aber das Fleisch ist schwach," which when translated back to English by the same engine gives: "The spirit is ready, but the meat is weak."

In short, judging by performance, from Eliza to Claire, from STUDENT to Jupiter, and from the 1960s to 2003, AI seems to have had a hard time grappling with very basic issues in language processing. To be sure, there has been progress, but in light of both the investments and expectations, the state of the art is not nearly as impressive as, say, that of computer chess-playing.

The Third Approach: Language as a Set of Subtasks

The level of accomplishment illustrated by the above examples might suggest the adoption of a third approach – namely, breaking the problem of language into subtasks, and seeking to achieve good performance in isolated subtasks (or, to use the term suggested by Andy Clark (1997), "vertical microworlds") such as speech processing, text reading, grammar acquisition, and so on. This is roughly the tack that connectionists have followed.[4] In particular, as is outlined in Appendix C, they have further formulated these subtasks as a set of problems (e.g., segmentation, mapping, binding, grounding), or as operational dysfunctions of various types (e.g., inflectional errors, aphasia, dyslexia), each of which presumably calls for distinct solutions. The connectionist approach to language is also closely related to a statistical view of language. An overarching intuition within connectionism is to view language as a "bag of words" where the occurrence of words in certain places with certain frequencies provides the language learner with enough information to pick up the grammatical, phonetic, and even semantic regularities of the language. The main goal of this chapter is to show what connectionism has accomplished along these lines, and in so doing, to provide a perspective on connectionism in general.

NEURAL NETWORKS: A SYNOPSIS

What is usually referred to as the "symbolic approach" deals with cognitive phenomena at the *psychological level* – that is, at the level of beliefs, goals, plans, and so on, which are encoded as language-like sentences, and related to each other by inference rules. A model of language processing in that tradition would typically involve modules that deal with high-level language phenomena, such as a *grammar* (a set of syntactic and semantic rules), a *parsing algorithm* (specifying the order of application of grammatical rules, regulating the amounts of top-down or bottom-up processing, dynamically allocating memory resources), and an *oracle* (a procedure for deciding among rival interpretations of a phrase) (Steedman 1999). Research within this type of framework would involve designing the modules (often independent of

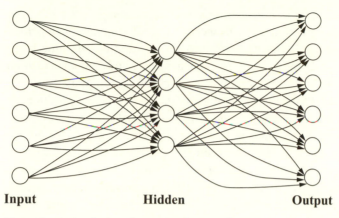

Input   **Hidden**   **Output**

Figure 6.1. A simple three-layer neural network.

each other), creating an interactive interface, selecting a vocabulary, and debugging the routines until predictable behavior is obtained.

Because of the rule-based character of the routines, debugging usually involves explicit tweaking of instructions, program flow, subroutines, and so on. Known among programmers as "hacking," this process usually calls for a transparent, "open-hood" mode of work (Turkle 1995: 42). A connectionist, to the contrary, suggests Turkle, works in a rather different mode of "playful exploration", sometimes called "tinkering" (ibid.: 61). Although hacking largely involves the manipulation of instructions for "how to think," tinkering mainly consists of adjusting mere numbers. To convey a sense for such tinkering, let me briefly describe how a connectionist model works.

How a Connectionist Model Works

Unlike the symbolic approach, the connectionist approach is motivated by the low-level architecture of the brain – whence the term "artificial neural networks" applied to connectionist models. Like the brain, which is a network consisting of a huge number of tightly connected neurons, artificial networks are composed of a large number of interconnected "nodes" (usually indicated by circles in diagrams), some of which serve as "input" nodes, some as "output" nodes, and others as "hidden" nodes (without direct connection to the outside world; the simplest models do not have hidden nodes; see Figure 6.1).

The nodes of a neural network are interconnected in ways that depend on the specific architecture. The *strength* of the connection between any two nodes is indicated by a numerical value, its *weight*, and the set of all connection values constitutes a pattern of connectivity. The *training* of the network, which takes place in discrete steps, proceeds by presenting the system with a set of input values and letting it modify and adjust its pattern of connectivity until it produces a desired output. At each step, each node has an *activation* level, also indicated by a numerical value. The activation is computed by using the *activation rule* (a function that combines the inputs), and it produces an output according to the *output function*. In most models, the activation rule is linear (the input values are simply added algebraically), and the output function is quasi-linear (the output is linearly proportional to the input up to a certain threshold where it is cut off). For training, the network follows a prespecified *learning rule* – for example, *backpropagation of error*, in which the output of the network is compared, at each step, with reference values delivered by a "teacher," and the error, if any, is fed back to the network in order to adjust the connection weights (Rumelhart, Hinton, and William 1986).

Tinkering: A Connectionist at Work

With this brief introduction, we can now look at a particular connectionist model – namely, one that learns the past tense of English verbs. Children start learning past-tense forms around the age of three, and certain patterns of error usually start to arise soon thereafter. One of these is the *overregularization* type of error manifested, for example, in children's creation of past tenses such as "goed" (instead of "went"), "eated" (instead of "ate"), and so on. At first glance, this is surprising because children usually manifest it at the age of four, after they have learned and used the correct irregular form of the same verbs early in their third year. This constitutes what has become known as a *U-shaped profile* of learning in developmental psychology (because the number of errors, having fallen around the age of three, starts to go up again at the age of four). The simulation of this activity is a difficult challenge (Plunkett and Juola 1999).

Nativists (the advocates of innate universal grammars; see Appendix C for a brief discussion of this view and the debates surrounding it) usually propose a prewired model that explains the learning of regular past tenses via a set of *rules* and that of irregular past tenses by an *associative memory*. The associative memory possesses a blocking mechanism that allows it to override the rule-based mechanism when dealing with irregular verbs (Pinker and Prince 1988). Connectionists, on the other hand, have proposed architectures whose behavior mimics the U-shaped curves exhibited by children's learning. One such model was proposed by Plunkett and Marchman (1991; see Figure 6.2: the U-shaped profile is manifest between the ages of thirty-six and forty-eight

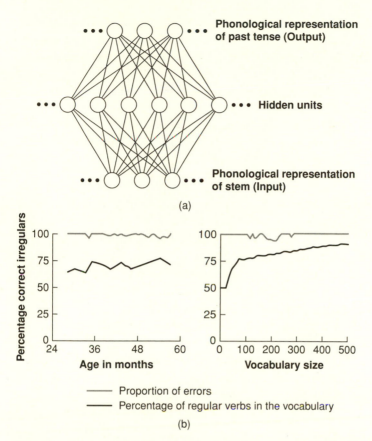

(a)

(b)

Figure 6.2. (a) A model for learning the English past tense; (b) The U-shaped profile of learning by the model and by children (from Plunkett and Marchman 1991, with permission).

months). The graphs, one from the real-life performance of a child and the other from the network performance, indicate the degree to which a simple connectionist model can simulate human behavior.

How did these researchers achieve this level of accuracy in the performance of their model? In rough outline, they had to do all of the following (see also Appendix B):

- decide on the manner of breaking up the domain into objects, features, and so on – in this case, into verb stems, suffixes, and inflections;
- decide on the encoding and presentation of the above to the network;
- design the architecture – that is, the number of layers, nodes, connections, and so on;

- decide on the activation rule, the output function, the learning regimen, and so on;
- select an appropriate corpus of data – in this case, an effective combination of regular and irregular verbs;
- carefully control the order and frequency of the presentation of the verbs to the network;
- train the network on a sample of five hundred verbs;
- decide on the number of times ("epochs") a set of input data should be presented to the network.

This list is incomplete, but it gives a feel for the painstaking process of trial and error involved at each step of connectionist model creation. What guides this process, as in most other work in AI, are the intuitions, skills, and experience of the researchers. What is distinctive about it (in comparison to the work of knowledge engineers, for instance) is that it takes place in a relatively opaque environment where there is no possibility to play around with explicit rules or instructions; instead, all one can do is tweak numerical values of various features and parameters. Of course, such tweaking can be repeated indefinitely often in pursuit of ever-better simulation of human behavior.[5] This is indicative less of a discrepancy in goals between symbolic and connectionist approaches than of a discrepancy in method and style of work. In the hands of a connectionist, the computer is, as Turkle (1995: 61) has suggested, "still a tool but less like a hammer and more like a harpsichord" (ibid.)

BASIC INTUITIONS: A FIRST PASS ON CONNECTIONISM

The idea behind connectionism is to study mind and cognition at a level that is much closer to the neural substrate than classical AI allowed. Built into the connectionist approach are, therefore, a number of assumptions that can be summarized as follows.[6]

1. **Architecture-over-function**: The proper level for understanding (and formalizing) cognitive behavior lies below the symbolic level, and the proper methodology for formalizing it is the construction of neural-like architectures. In short, architecture is primary and function is secondary (Rumelhart 1997).
2. **Decoupling**: With sufficient training, a neural network becomes so attuned to the regularities of the outside world as to be able to operate autonomously and represent those regularities faithfully (Rumelhart 1997).
3. **Learning**: Neural networks are designed to be able to learn (Churchland 1997; Hinton and Sejnowski 1986).[7]

4. **Prewiring:** Learning results from the modification of interneuronal connection strengths with experience, and is supported by innate learning rules and architectural features (Smolensky 1999).

5. **Adequacy:** For any cognitive task, there is, in principle, at least one connectionist network with a suitable architecture and learning rules that can be trained to carry out that task satisfactorily (Churchand 1997).[8]

6. **Neural reductionism:** Cognitive science is an empirical inquiry into the neural substrate of cognition (Churchland 1997).

The intuitive appeal of these assumptions was so great that early connectionists perceived their approach as finally laying "Real Foundations" as opposed to the "False Starts" of traditional AI (Graubard 1988) – they perceived their approach as a full-blown revolution, in other words. I will now comment on these six tenets underlying connectionism, although because the first three assumptions are widely discussed elsewhere, I will not go into them in great detail. The rest of the chapter is mostly devoted to the remaining three points, through a close study of a few connectionist models of language learning. I want to show that there are hidden presuppositions lurking behind these assumptions, and that these presuppositions give rise to tensions in connectionist research, as elsewhere in AI.

Architecture Over Function

Biological realism was one of the original motivations behind the connectionist movement. The idea was that connectionist models, by modeling cognition at the neural level, mimic the workings of the human brain as architectural analogues, not functional simulators. However, as the English-past-tense model shows, the independence of architecture from function is not as genuine as one might hope; indeed, behavioral outcome (i.e., function) plays a major motivating role in the design of connectionist models. The model developed by Plunkett and Marchman provides a good example of how hard connectionists try to make their models mimic human behavior, whatever tinkering is called for in the process, albeit within the architectural constraints of neural networks.

Decoupling: Connected Inside, Disconnected from Outside

The idea behind what I call "decoupling" is that, through training, a network becomes *attuned* to certain regularities of the outside world in such a way that it can operate more or less autonomously, even when it is *decoupled from the environment.* Thanks to the mapping established between "inside" and "outside", in other words, the internal connections and weights of a network collectively constitute a faithful representation of certain aspects of the world, making it possible for the network to interact appropriately with the environment. Inner connections, in other words, take over when the link to the outside world is severed. The past-tense model, for instance, learns certain regularities in the inflectional patterns of English over the course of a few thousand training cycles, after which it can correctly produce the past tense of many novel verbs in isolation. How does this happen?

This happens because the network encodes within its pattern of connectivity the right set of representations of its little world. Connectionist models are, thus, similar to classical AI models in this important respect – that is, in being representational. What makes them different is the character of their representations, which are *distributed* and *emergent.*

Distributed Representations
Probably the most important aspect of connectionist models (of PDP type) is the *distributed* character of their representations. These networks are quasi-democratic systems, where all nodes participate in all stages of processing and for all input combinations, so that no single node has a decisive role in the performance of the model. Instead, the pattern of activity of the nodes constitutes an implicit encoding of the input features, which the network sometimes even breaks up into a set of *microfeatures* (in nonlocalist encoding schemes, where an input such as a word, for instance, is represented not as one unit, but as a collection of phonemes).[9] Eventually, in an unpreprogrammed way, certain nodes may become so closely associated with certain features that they can be thought of as *encoding* those features. However, given the typically large number of hidden units in a system, it is not realistic to hope to determine how this takes place, and which nodes encode which features (or microfeatures). However, a successful implementation of the division of labor among nodes is the key to the success of neural networks.

Emergent Behavior
To see why this division of labor is important, think of the hidden-unit activities as the dimensions of a space in which the network navigates (see Figure 6.3; in the extreme case, where a maximum division of labor is created, the number of dimensions of the space will be equal to the number of hidden units). Notice that, unlike classical models, a connectionist network does not have explicit rules (similar to rules of logic) to follow, or an explicit goal to

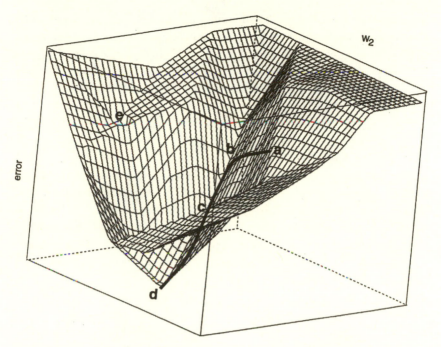

Figure 6.3. An error landscape (from Elman 1990, with permission).

achieve (as in models of planning). Tasks, as in the past-tense model, are better thought of as the satisfaction of a number of constraints (e.g., the inflectional patterns of the past tense in English) – whence the oft-heard characterization of neural networks as "constraint-satisfaction" models as opposed to the "goal-satisfaction" models of traditional AI. The main difference between the two styles of models is that in connectionist models, "soft" constraints can be satisfied to different degrees.[10] Connectionist researchers do their best to make their models find a point of maximal satisfaction of the constraints (or the minimal manifestation of errors). However, there can be traps, in that a network may wind up at a *local* minimum (e.g., point e in Figure 6.3), but mistake it for the global minimum (point d).

The most striking outcome of this type of processing is the capability of the networks to tackle cases in which black-and-white answers are not available. In the past-tense learning model, for example, if the input features are so vague as to make a decision impossible, none of the output nodes will reach the threshold of firing and of arriving at a reasonable output – that is, we get an undecided response. This is one (rather trivial) manifestation of what is normally called "graceful degradation" in connectionist systems. Other manifestations of the same phenomenon, as we shall later see, occur when the network is *lesioned* (damaged) by removing a number of its nodes or connections subsequent to the training phase. While a logic-based system is virtually certain to break down if pieces are cut out of it (imagine removing a deductive step from a logical inference chain), connectionist networks often survive such "attacks" very well.[11]

Learning

Connectionist models exhibit a considerable capability for detecting similarities, for generalizing and completing patterns, and, as is often stressed, for learning. One prerequisite for a cognitive system to generalize is for it to be able to disregard noise and to recognize what really matters in the impinging flux of stimuli from the environment. Connectionist models are in some ways very good at this, but they also have significant limitations, as we shall now see.

Built-in Primitives

The first limitation regarding the generalization capabilities of neural nets is that they often generalize only according to specific input/output representations or primitives decided on by the system builder.[12] As we shall see later, for instance, in networks dealing with morphology, words are often represented in consonant–vowel–consonant form, with these constituents clearly separated from each other by the modeler. Given that spoken words do not come with clearly indicated and separated constituents, this amounts in some cases to a trivialization, where a good part of the task has been *a priori* solved for the network. This is in sharp contrast to the way organisms parse the features of the objects of the outside world – namely, in accordance with the kinds of "affordances" that those objects provide in specific circumstances (Gibson 1978). The flat surface of a rock, for instance, may afford "climbability" for a deer, "sittability" for a human being on a mountain hike, or "steppability" for the same human being while crossing a creek. Similarly, the parsing of a chair into a seat, a back, and four legs is a categorization skill that needs to be learned in the right cultural context (where chairs are common objects of daily life), as does the parsing of words into building blocks such as vowels and consonants. Israel Rosenfield once said, "Real generalization creates *new* categories of information ... from the organism's point of view" (1988: 72). And William Clancey, building on this observation, contrasts the connectionist fashion of encoding input with the way human beings learn language. He suggests that the process of creating useful distinctions is "species-specific," and concludes that for human beings, in contrast to neural networks, "the primitive units [categories] are not input, nor are they built in as primitives" (Clancey 1997: 73).

In short, what these authors point out is that living organisms do not simply filter the world into a set of objective categories. Rather, they play an active role in generating and manipulating those categories – a capability well above that of simple neural networks.

Inflexibility

A more significant limitation of neural nets has to do with the decisive role that the training regimen plays in learning. As Paul Churchland, a strong advocate of connectionism, says, "nothing guarantees successful generalization: a network is always hostage to the quality of its training set relative to the total population" (1997: 280). One would tend to assume that learning from environmental data is an advantage, especially if we notice that for adaptation, living species depend heavily on what they pick up from their environment. And yet, learning from the environment could be problematical if it is not carried out with a flexibility that makes generalizations susceptible to adjustment, revision, or even reversal. A deer that manages to escape an approaching predator a number of times would be dead wrong to leap to the generalization that it is safe to get close to predators. Similarly, as Hofstadter points out, the capability for generalization in human beings crucially involves the ability to reperceive and rearrange things in novel ways, to reconfigure an idea, and to revise one's theory when it doesn't work in a new situation or is not appealing any more (Hofstadter 1995: 77). This type of flexibility, according to Hofstadter, requires the introduction of a hierarchy of ever more abstract concepts and the ability to make analogies at many levels of abstraction, which are beyond current connectionist models (ibid.: 466). As we shall see, slightly enhanced versions of connectionist models (such as the ART model discussed later in this chapter) that are built with this very issue in mind still need to go a long way before they could be claimed to be flexible while retaining meaningful connections with the outside world.

These caveats, in and of themselves, do not negate the ability of connectionist models to generalize significantly. After all, any model has to be built upon certain assumptions about the basic categories in its world, and as long as those categories do not trivialize the task by encoding the solution directly, the model deserves credit for its generalizations. Similarly, explicit training is often a part of the learning process, whether we are talking about living organisms or artificial networks. But, as recent research has started to show, flexibility calls for models that are much more structured than current networks, which try to simulate many highly diverse behaviors within a single fixed architecture (Regier 2000).

Some connectionists are of course aware of this shortcoming. In fact, the first attempt in this direction – that is, in the direction of giving more structure to neural networks (i.e., breaking up the homogeneity, adding new layers, and adding specialized modules) – was made in the early 1990s by adding a *context layer* to simple feedforward networks. Let us, therefore, step back and consider these so-called *recurrent networks*.

The Second Generation: Recurrent Networks

Most linguistic behavior happens in time – for example, speaking, hearing, reading, and so on. Therefore, a realistic model of these behaviors should incorporate time in one way or another. One of the problems with models such as Plunkett and Marchman's is that they receive their input all at once. In such models, a temporal sequence is stored in a buffer and represented as a pattern vector, the successive elements of which correspond to successive temporal events in the behavior (e.g., phonemes or words). This way of dealing with time is inherent to such architectures, and so, even their more advanced versions – for example, the one discussed in Plunkett and Juola (1999), which learns both English past-tense and plural morphology with a single architecture – also suffer from this unnatural defect.

To correct this problem, a number of connectionist researchers devised architectures that incorporated time in a more direct manner (Jordan 1986; Elman 1990). They did this by including *recurrent* connections that, in each step of processing, take the internal state (the activation pattern of hidden units) of the system, and copy it to the input layer, thereby endowing the system with a sort of "memory" of its own past. When you have a feedback loop of this sort, some phenomena can persist over time because they are fed back into the system (like audio feedback loops with screaming microphones whose sound persists), generating reverberations that last for a while and slowly decay over time. This is how recurrent connections give rise to a primitive kind of memory. One such architecture, known as a Simple Recurrent Network (SRN), includes as many additional units in the input layer as the number of hidden units (Elman 1990). These additional units are usually called "context units" because they augment the system's input with the context of its previous state (see Figure 6.4).

This type of modification resulted in significant improvement in terms of both the performance of the models and the task domains they can tackle. Grammar acquisition is one such domain. By using simple recurrent

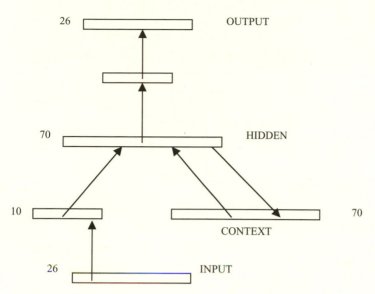

Figure 6.4. A simple recurrent network (from Elman 1990, with permission).

networks, Elman and his colleagues (Elman 1990, 1993; Morris, Cottrell, and Elman 1999), among others, have embarked on a comprehensive research program on grammar acquisition within the connectionist framework.

Learning to Dissect Language

One of the issues facing a nonnativist account of language acquisition is to explain how a language learner acquires primitive constructs such as words, morphemes, phonemes, and so on. That is, how do people discover that language is made of such primitives? This, we should notice, is different from the segmentation problem of speech perception (see Appendix C). In fact, arriving at notions such as "word" is a metalinguistic task, in the sense that it deals with language and linguistic concepts, rather than with the objects and events in the outside world to which language refers.

In any case, although it is commonplace to talk about the "atoms" of language as if they were givens, the discovery that they exist is an achievement on the part of a language learner (e.g., a child), and cannot be taken for granted. That it is an achievement becomes clearer if we notice that these atoms do not have sharp, objective boundaries. In English, for instance, the distinction between simple words (e.g., "book," "picture," "sky") and compound words (e.g., "bookshelf", "picture frame," "anyway," "notwithstanding," "skyscraper") and stock phrases (e.g., "Library of Congress," "state of the art," "graduate student," "play it by ear") is often murky and unclear. Indeed, the component words are very often not "heard" in a compound – consider the English words "understand," "because," "welcome," "cupboard," "wardrobe," and so on – or a compound will have meanings and connotations very different from its components – "crackpot," "hotbed," "highjack," "earwig," and so on (see Hofstadter 1993 for a careful analysis and a large set of examples).

Discovering the Notion of "Word"

Elman (1990) reports a connectionist network that discovered the notion of "word," where by "word" he simply means chunks or clusters of letters. The idea behind the design of this network, according to Elman, is that "the notion of 'word' (or something which maps on to this concept) could emerge as a consequence of learning the sequential structure of letter sequences that form words and sentences (but in which word boundaries are not marked)" (1990: 192). The recurrent network that performed this task is similar to the one in Figure 6.4, with five input units, twenty hidden units, five output units, and twenty context units. The input to the network consisted of sequences of letters, with each letter represented as a bit vector of length 5 (i.e., as a sequence of five 'o's or '1's). A sentence-generating program produced two hundred sentences of varying lengths (out of a lexicon of fifteen words) – for example, "Many years ago a boy and a girl lived together." The sentences were then concatenated, forming a stream of 1,270 words or 4,963 letters, and fed to the network. In total, the input was a stream of 4,963 separate 5-bit vectors, presented one at a time. The task of the network, given a sequence of such bit vectors, was to predict the next letter in the sequence.

During training, after ten presentations of the input, the network started to make predictions with more errors at word boundaries than within words. The explanation, according to Elman, is that "as more words are received the error rate declines, since the sequence is increasingly predictable" (ibid.). Although the errors simply reflect statistics of co-occurrence, the high-error regions could be taken as word boundaries. Of course, the regions are ambiguous at times (as in the case of "y" in "they," where the network could be undecided between, for instance, "the year" and "they earn"), but by and large the pattern of errors is a good indicator of word boundaries.

This, as Elman points out, is not a model of word acquisition yet, both because "prediction is not the major goal of the language learner," and because "the co-occurrence of sounds is only part of what identifies a word as such" (ibid.). What the network's performance shows, in fact, is that "there is information in the signal that could serve as a cue to the boundaries of linguistic units which must be learned, and it demonstrates the ability of simple recurrent networks to extract this information" (ibid.). In other words, the network performs a task that could be roughly considered to be the first step toward the discovery of the notion of word: the detection of distinct chunks separated by recognizable boundaries in the input stream.[13]

Discovering Lexical Classes from Word Order

To assign the network a more realistic task, Elman considered the problem of discovering lexical classes (nouns, verbs, etc.) from a given sequence of words, or, to be more concrete, the problem of predicting the order of successive words in a sequence (we will shortly see why these are descriptions of the same task). The input consisted of bit vectors, thirty-one bits in length, which represented twenty-nine words (two bits unused), with each word having a different 'on' bit assigned to it (all the other thirty bits set to 'o'). Ten thousand random two- and three-word sentences were generated, giving rise to a huge number (27,534) of word vectors that were concatenated and presented to the network. After this input was fed to the network six successive times, the connection weights were frozen (i.e., kept constant). The verbs used in the sentences were a combination of different types – transitive ("see," "chase"), intransitive ("think," "sleep"), perception ("smell," "see"), and so on – and there were likewise different types of nouns – human ("man," "woman"), animate ("cat," "mouse"), inanimate ("book," "rock"), and so on. The network was similar in structure to the previous one, except that there were thirty-one nodes in the input and output layers, and 150 hidden and context units. One difference between this and the previous task is that predictions turn out to be more uncertain, because many different words can be put together to make meaningful sentences.

This network learned to carry out the task to the desired level of accuracy. That is, although it was not able to predict the precise order of words, "it recognizes that (in this corpus) there is a class of inputs (namely, verbs) that typically follow other inputs (namely, nouns)" (Elman 1990: 199). Since the input representations did not provide such information, Elman argued, the network must have learned some generalization from the co-occurrence statistics (that is, from the way words occur together).

In order to see how this was accomplished, Elman suggests, one must look at the activation patterns of hidden units generated in response to each word and its context. A close examination of the patterns, using hierarchical clustering analysis, reveals that lexical items that have similar properties are grouped together in a hierarchical fashion. For instance, words denoting animals and words denoting humans each form a separate first-level cluster, the combination of which creates a second-level cluster for words denoting *animate* objects, which, in turn, in grouping with the second-level cluster of words denoting *inanimate* objects, produces the third-level cluster for *nouns*, and so on.

PREWIRING: A SECOND PASS ON CONNECTIONISM

We have seen that recurrent networks can use their (implicit) memory to discover different word classes by finding regularities within a word sequence. Recall, however, that the input sequence to these networks consists of a very small lexicon formed into a limited number of sentences. Notice further that the encoding of the input is very localized (bit vectors with one "on" bit for every word). This simplified representation of words was made in order to facilitate the goal of the experiment, which was to concentrate on how boundaries could be discovered in the first place. In real language, however, there is far more variability and complexity both in the linguistic and the nonlinguistic environments – for example, in terms of the number and diversity of words. These aspects were deliberately ignored in the model in order to focus on the question of whether there is enough regularity within the language input for learners to pick up. swanion

Finding plausible answers within the connectionist framework to these questions would constitute a major challenge to nativist views and a significant contribution to our understanding of language learning by children (see Appendix C). Elman (1993) sets about this undertaking by bringing learning and development together. His argument hinges on the fact that children go through significant developmental changes while learning language. The critical period for language learning, although known for a long time, was usually neglected in models of language acquisition, but Elman took it seriously and made a number of simulations in order to demonstrate the interdependence of learning and development. His goal in this study was to see if connectionist networks could "use distributed representations to encode complex, hierarchically organized information" (ibid.).

Advanced Tinkering

For this purpose, Elman experimented with embedded sentence structures such as "Boys who chase dogs see girls", which were randomly generated and then presented as bit vectors to a recurrent network. The task of the network this time was to predict the *next word* in the sequence; his previous simulations had failed on this task. Work by others had shown that learning would be facilitated if the input increased gradually in size (Plunkett and Marchman 1991), or if the network changed dynamically during learning – for example, acquiring additional nodes during processing (Shultz and Schmidt 1991). These findings suggested a different approach to Elman.

Tinkering with the Input

The new approach consisted of an input regimen that increased incrementally in complexity: first, five exposures to ten thousand simple sentences (e.g., "Cats chase dogs"); second, five exposures to a mixture of seventy-five hundred simple and twenty-five hundred complex sentences (e.g., "Dogs see boys who cats who Mary feeds chase"), and so on, until an epoch in which every sentence in the corpus is complex. Elman, in accord with his expectation, found that the network performed satisfactorily in terms of certain statistical measures, and this led him to conclude that "the behavior of the network partially resembles that of children . . . [in that] they begin with the simplest of structures, and build incrementally until they achieve the adult language" (ibid.).

As I mentioned earlier, however, there is also a discrepancy with the behavior of children, in that children are not exposed to carefully organized linguistic training sequences. This observation suggested to Elman a more realistic model, where, instead of the input changing, the network itself would change incrementally, as do children during development. Previous research had suggested that children's memory and attention span increase gradually as they mature (Kail 1984), and so it made sense to simulate this process. This is what Elman did next.

Tinkering with the Network

In this simulation, the whole body of sentences was presented to the network at once, but the network itself underwent change either by eliminating (and reintroducing) the recurrent connections every so often, or by increasing the memory "window" incrementally to cover a longer span of words.[14] The network completed this task, leading Elman to conclude that, "If the learning mechanism itself was allowed to undergo 'maturational changes' (in this case, increasing its memory capacity) during learning, then the outcome was just as good as if the environment itself had been gradually complicated" (ibid.). This idea of Elman has since come to be known as "starting small."

The idea of starting small has born more recent fruits. Morris, Cottrell, and Elman (1999), for example, have built a connectionist model of the "empirical acquisition of grammatical relations." Using a recurrent network, they demonstrated how grammatical relations such as *subject, object, patient,* and so on can be learned in a purely bottom-up fashion, without the need for an innate syntax. At the same time, however, this idea has been challenged by, among others, another group of connectionists who have arrived at opposite conclusions from Elman's. A close examination of this debate brings up interesting issues about the significance of connectionist models in our understanding of language learning. We begin with Elman's explanation of how these networks learn grammar.

The Idea of "Starting Small"

There is a surface paradox, captured in the phrase "less is more" (Newport 1990), in the idea that a network that begins with fewer nodes (or a smaller window) should be able to master a task better than a network that has all of the nodes and a large window of processing from the beginning. Elman (1993) sought to resolve this paradox by observing that starting small (or simple) helps constrain the "solution space" in ways that make further learning easier. According to Elman, at every stage of learning, a language learner deals with limited variance – for example, variance in number (singular versus plural), in grammatical category (subject, object, etc.), in verb type (transitive, intransitive, etc.), and in the degree of syntactic embedding. The problem is, however, that these variables may interact in complex ways, as is the case with long-distance dependencies.

In the sentence "The girl who the dogs that I chased down the block frightened ran away,"[15] for example, the evidence that the verb "frightened" is transitive is obscured because the direct object ("the girl") occurs ten words earlier (rather than in the default position, which is right after the verb) (Elman 1993). Therefore, if the network is given complex as well as simple sentences from the beginning, it will have a hard time figuring out these long-distance dependencies. If, on the other hand, we begin with a simple sample (or limit the network's window of processing), Elman argues, the network sees only a subset of the data. This subset, which contains only three of the four sources of variance (all except embedding) makes it possible, according to Elman, for the network to develop internal representations that successfully encode the variance. Later stages of learning, such as those resulting from long-distance interactions, are then constrained by the network's early decisions. In sum, Elman concludes:

The effect of early learning, thus, is to constrain the solution space to a much smaller region. The solution space is initially very large, and contains many false solutions (in network parlance, local error minima). The chances of stumbling on the correct solution are small. However, by selectively focusing on the simpler set of facts, the network appears to learn the basic distinctions – noun/verb/relative pronoun, singular/plural, etc. – which form the necessary basis for learning the more difficult set of facts which arise with complex sentences. (Elman 1993)

The Idea of "Starting Large"

Rhode and Plaut (1999) reported on work that was very similar to Elman's in terms of task, input, and architecture, but that led them to opposite conclusions: they trained a recurrent network on a set of embedded sentences, and the task for the network, as in Elman's experiment, was to predict the next word in a sentence. The main difference was that Rhode and Plaut's corpus constituted "a more naturalistic language . . . through the addition of semantic constraints" (Rhode and Plaut 1999: 74). One such constraint was the co-occurrence of certain verbs and nouns. Since dogs often chase cats, for instance, the verb "chase" gets associated with "dog," facilitating the task of the network in predicting that a sentence that begins with "The dog who . . . " is more likely to continue as "chased the cat" than with other alternatives. Another semantic constraint is that transitive verbs act only on certain objects. For example, all animals walk (intransitive sense), but only humans walk something else (transitive sense), and it is usually a dog (ibid.).

By incorporating such constraints in their training examples, Rhode and Plaut reported, they were able to train their network successfully without resorting to the idea of starting small in either of its forms – that is, without gradually increasing either the complexity of the sentences or the processing capacity of the network. The authors explain this sharp contrast with Elman's findings in terms of the contribution of the aforementioned semantic constraints. "A salient feature of the grammar used by Elman," they argue, "is that it is purely syntactic, in the sense that all words of a particular class, such as the singular nouns, were identical in usage" (Rhode and Plaut 1999: 72). As a consequence of this, they argue, the head noun of a long sentence in Elman's experiments would provide little information about the corresponding verb (ibid.). They conclude:

In summary, starting with simple training proved to be of no benefit and was actually a significant hindrance when semantic constraints applied across clauses. (Rhode and Plaut 1999: 85)

One of the implications of their study, Rhode and Plaut claim, is to call into question whether development plays any role in the acquisition of language (ibid.: 73). The more important implication for our purposes here is the significance of this debate in understanding the tensions within connectionist research.

Starting Small or Large?

This in-house debate between two groups of connectionist researchers raises important questions about the nature of language learning in human beings, about time constraints such as the "critical period" of language acquisition, about the interplay between syntax and semantics, and so on. Many of these questions have an empirical character, and will be resolved only through much further research in biology, neuroscience, linguistics, psychology, and elsewhere. The connectionist approach may, to be sure, be able to contribute to this research, but the scope of such contribution should not be overestimated. For instance, when a connectionist researcher makes a claim about the relation between learning and development, it should be clear what aspects of this relation they are trying to simulate: temporal aspects (sets of skills acquired at particular stages), biological aspects (physical changes in the nervous system), or mental aspects (changes in representations of the outside world), a combination of these, or some other aspect? Similarly, when connectionists talk about "semantic constraints," it should be clear whether what they mean is the relation between their language-like representations and the outside world, or the relation between those representations and the internal (computational) processes that they generate (respectively, relations β and α in Figure 6.5; cf. Smith 1998).

Unfortunately, most connectionist literature is silent about such distinctions, making it hard to discern the intentions and objectives of model builders. For instance, it is not clear how connectionist models of language capture the semantic aspects of language (in the sense of relation to the outside world), as claimed by Rhode and Plaut. The debate between Elman and Rhode and Plaut, I believe, illustrates this point quite well. This debate has created an unresolved dilemma for connectionism concerning the modeling of language learning by children. Is either the model of Elman or that of Rhode and Plaut truly reflective of the situation faced by children? Or is neither relevantly accurate?

This dilemma, I believe, cannot be resolved within the connectionist framework, mainly because of the disconnection of connectionist models from the outside world (Clark 1997; Ekbia, Goldberg, and Landy 2003). What

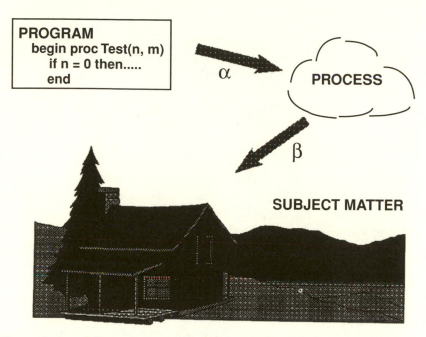

Figure 6.5. Two different meanings of "semantic relation" (from Smith 1997, with permission).

can be resolved, of course, is which of the two approaches can learn the limited idealized grammar used in the training of these networks. But, as I want to argue next, there is such a gulf between these models and how real language is learned that drawing firm conclusions about language learning in children is simply not possible.

Performance, Competence, and Communication

The works of Elman and of Rhode and Plaut both represent the view of language learning as a statistical process – namely, "that language learning depends critically on the *frequency* with which forms occur in the language and not simply on whether or not they occur at all" (Rhode and Plaut 1999: 98).[16] This view contrasts with the view due to Chomsky – that learning a language involves converging on the single, correct grammar of the language (which is associated with language "competence"), and that any deviation from this grammar in the actual behavior of language learners is due to "performance" factors. According to the Chomskian view, "given that all learners of language must acquire competence in equivalent grammars, it is critical to have formal guarantees that this will happen" (ibid.: 70). From the statistical perspective, on the other hand, "the grammars acquired by members of a language community need not be identical but only sufficiently similar to permit effective communication" (ibid.). According to connectionists, this view of language as a medium of effective communication erases the distinction between "competence" and "performance" proposed by Chomsky (1957). However, I want to argue that the erasure is very partial and incomplete, and that it introduces a dichotomy similar to the one between competence and performance.

In order to see how this happens, we should go back to the original intuitions behind Chomsky's competence/performance distinction. The idea of "competence" involved an *ideal* model of language and grammar that was totally divorced from "performance" – that is, from the real language used by people as a means of communication. This allowed the classical model of grammar to remain isolated from real issues of language learning. According to critics of the classical view, this happened because the classical model considered only positive data and paid no heed to negative data from real language – for example, false starts, hesitations, errors, blends, and so on – making it irrelevant to empirical studies of language.

A similar story, I believe, applies to connectionist models, because they too are isolated from real-language data. A close look at the experiments conducted by Elman and by Rhode and Plaut, for instance, reveals just how impoverished are the notions of meaning, context, and time that these experiments deal with. As I suggested previously, there is a very weak relation, if any, between these models and the outside world and, hence, no semantics in any serious sense of the word. In terms of time, the input is a discrete set of symbols that do not happen in real time (despite the fact that recurrent networks capture temporal context in a crude sense). In terms of context, the input data is a set of isolated sentences with no relation among them. The notion of "context" used in the description of recurrent networks is, in fact, a very narrow linguistic notion, which refers solely to the immediate language structures (words and phrases) that surround a word, and not to the circumstances of the world around the speaker.

Elman (1990), however, has made the following argument to show that context is indeed incorporated in his model (described earlier). Imagine that after the network has been trained, a novel word – "zog" – with a new bit pattern is presented to it. Assume also that ten thousand sentences are generated with (the bit map for) the word "zog" replacing (the bit map for) the word "man" in all previous occurrences. Training the network with the new sentences (without further training) and analyzing the activations would show that the new word had been assigned an internal representation that is consistent with what the network had already learned – that is, it bears the same relationships to other words as "man" did. Elman concludes from this thought experiment that, "in certain contexts, the network expects *man*, or something very much like it." He then relates this to the capability of human learners to make "use of the cues provided by word order to make intelligent guesses about the meaning of novel words" (ibid.). In other words, he suggests that the meaning of "zog" is determined by the network in a fully context-dependent manner.

This reasoning, as I said earlier, is based on a particular conception that takes context to consist of the immediate linguistic surrounding, and not the circumstances of the outside world. The intuition underlying Elman's reasoning is what I earlier called "decoupling" – namely, that purely symbolic patterns (in the present case, the patterns of grammatical regularities) are as rich in information for the system as would be the web of connections to the outside world (in the present case, spoken language). And this, as we saw, imposes serious limitations on the capabilities of neural networks, making them inflexible and passive processors of built-in primitives.

In short, these connectionist models are too idealized and abstracted from the features of real language, and this, I believe, makes them susceptible to similar criticisms as are directed at classical competence models. To show this even more clearly, I would like to discuss a theory that sheds further light on the statistical approach to language learning.

The Statistical Approach: A Naked View

The study of models of language learning thus far reveals a tension within connectionist research – namely, that between architectural and representational constraints. While the former constraints pull connectionist models "downward," toward neural-level explanations, the latter draw them "upward," toward high-level constructs such as grammatical categories, lexical classes, linguistic errors, and so on. This tension has, in fact, resulted in two major trends in the study of language in connectionist research: one is "symbolic approximation," advocated by, among others, Paul Smolensky, whereas the other is a purely statistical approach.

Roughly speaking, symbolic approximation is the idea that symbolic theories are roughly to connectionist models what classical mechanics is to quantum mechanics – the former are a high-level compression of the latter. Smolensky is an advocate of this view. "In the domain of language," he says, "the patterns of activation constituting mental representations admit abstract, higher-level descriptions that are closely approximated by the kinds of discrete, abstract structures posited by symbolic linguistic theory" (Smolensky 1999: 594). This view does not have many proponents among hardcore connectionists.

The more orthodox connectionist approach, which insists on the idea that connectionist networks are "statistical inference machines," finds support in certain data from language development in children. In recent years, experiments with very young children (eight months old) have suggested that statistical regularities might play a more prominent role in the learning of natural language than was traditionally thought (Saffran et al. 1996; Seidenberg and MacDonald 1999). This suggests, in turn, that knowledge of grammar may not play as major a role in language learning as classical theory would have it, and that what matters most is merely which words occur in which local contexts and with what frequencies. In short, the intuition goes, language might be a "bag of words" where some items are found more often in certain places than in others. This line of thought has been pursued in earnest by a number of researchers in linguistics, developmental psychology, and computer science (Seidenberg and McDonald 1999). Since written texts are discrete and therefore are far more amenable to statistical analysis than recorded samples of speech, which are continuous, these researchers have focused on mathematical models of text processing that depend solely on statistical data retrievable from pieces of text.

Language as a Bag of Words

One group of such models is called the theory of *latent semantic analysis* (LSA; Landauer, Folz, and Laham: 1998). The purpose of LSA, according to its creators, is to provide "a method for determining the similarity of meaning of words and passages by analysis of large text corpora" (259). LSA does this by representing words or sets of words (a sentence, paragraph, or essay) as points in a high-dimensional "semantic space" (e.g., between fifty and fifteen hundred dimensions) and reducing the dimensions to a much smaller number by mathematical techniques. This method of text representation is not new. What is new in LSA is that it creates associations not between successive words but between words and larger meaningful utterances in which they occur. The intuition is that the meaning of a word is "a kind of average of the meaning of all the passages in which it appears," and the meaning of a passage is "a kind of average of the meaning of all the words it contains" (ibid.).

For instance, given the article titles in Figure 6.6(a) as input text, LSA creates a matrix of nine columns, each corresponding to one input passage, and twelve rows, each corresponding to a content word (i.e., any word except

c1: *Human* machine interface for ABC *computer* application
c2: A *survey* of *user* opinion of *computer system response time*
c3: The *EPS user interface* management *system*
c4: *System* and *human system* engineering testing of *EPS*
c5: Relation of *user* perceived *response time* to error measurement

m1: The generation of random, binary, ordered *trees*
m2: The intersection *graph* of paths in *trees*
m3: *Graph minors* IV: Widths of *trees* and well-quasi-ordering
m4: *Graph minors*: A *survey*

(a)

	c1	c2	c3	c4	c5	m1	m2	m3	m4
human	1	0	0	1	0	0	0	0	0
interface	1	0	1	0	0	0	0	0	0
computer	0	1	1	0	1	0	0	0	0
user	0	1	1	0	1	0	0	0	0
system	0	1	1	2	0	0	0	0	0
response	0	1	0	0	1	0	0	0	0
time	0	1	0	0	1	0	0	0	0
EPS	0	0	1	1	0	0	0	0	0
survey	0	1	0	0	0	0	0	0	1
trees	0	0	0	0	0	1	1	1	0
graph	0	0	0	0	0	0	1	1	1
minors	0	0	0	0	0	0	0	1	1

r (human.user) = −.38, r (human.minors) = −.29

(b)

	c1	c2	c3	c4	c5	m1	m2	m3	m4
human	0.16	0.40	0.38	0.47	0.18	−0.05	−012	−0.16	−0.09
interface	0.14	0.37	0.33	0.40	0.16	−0.03	−0.07	−0.10	−0.04
computer	0.15	0.51	0.36	0.41	0.24	0.02	0.06	0.09	0.12
user	0.26	0.84	0.61	0.70	0.39	0.03	0.08	0.12	0.19
system	0.45	1.23	1.05	1.27	0.56	−0.07	−0.15	−0.21	−0.05
response	0.16	0.58	0.38	0.42	0.28	0.06	0.13	0.19	0.22
time	0.16	0.58	0.38	0.42	0.28	0.06	0.13	0.19	0.22
EPS	0.22	0.55	0.51	0.63	0.24	−0.07	−0.14	−0.20	−0.11
survey	0.10	0.53	0.23	0.21	0.27	0.14	0.31	0.44	0.42
trees	−0.06	0.23	−0.14	−0.27	0.14	0.24	0.55	0.77	0.66
graph	−0.06	0.34	−0.15	−0.30	0.20	0.31	0.69	0.98	0.85
minors	−0.04	0.25	−0.10	−.0.21	0.15	0.22	0.50	0.71	0.62

r (human.user) = −.38, r (human.minors) = −.29

(c)

Figure 6.6. The application of LSA to an sample of text data: (a) titles of some technical memos (b) a word-by-context matrix; (c) the reconstruction of the matrix in (a) (from Landauer et al. 1998, with permission).

pronouns, articles, prepositions, etc.) used in at least two of the input passages (see Figure 6.6[b]). Using the mathematical technique of *singular value decomposition*, LSA constructs a new matrix that contains some information about the correlations among words and passages (see Figure 6.6[c]). To understand the difference between the two matrices, notice, for example, that the word "trees" did not appear in title m4, hence it had a value of zero in the original matrix (prior to analysis). However, since m4 did contain "graph" and "minors," and since these have shown to be correlated to "tree" (in other text samples), after the analysis the entry has a value of 0.66. This figure can be viewed as an estimate of the percentage of occurrences of the word "tree" in a very large sample of text containing "graph" and "minors." By contrast, the word "survey," which had an original value of 1 for the entry under m4, now has an estimate of 0.42, reflecting the fact that it is unexpected in this context. In short, by reducing the dimensions and extracting information from the reduced representation, this method gives an estimate of the likelihood that a certain word occurs in certain contexts. The creators of LSA describe the method in the following (anthropomorphic) manner:

This text segment is best described as having so much of abstract concept one and so much of abstract concept two, and this word has so much of concept one and so much of concept two, and combining those two pieces of information (by vector arithmetic), my best guess is that word X actually appeared 0.6 times in context Y. (Landauer, Foltz, and Laham 1998: 272)

The important point to note about these guesses and estimates, according to Landauer et al., is that they "are not simple contiguity frequencies, co-occurrence counts, or correlations in usage, but depend on a powerful mathematical analysis that is capable of correctly inferring much deeper relations (thus the phrase 'Latent Semantic')" (p. 263). This has led the creators of LSA to claim that LSA not only is a useful practical tool for text analysis but also constitutes "a fundamental computational theory of the acquisition and representation of knowledge [in human beings]" (p. 265). They suggest that "from both engineering and scientific perspectives, there are reasons to try to design learning machines that can acquire human-like qualities of human-like knowledge from the same sources as humans" (Landauer, Laham, and Foltz 1998).

A Statistical Model Beats Human Beings

Some practical applications of LSA seem to support such a claim. For example, LSA has been applied to measure similarity of meaning among words – that is, their proximity in the semantic space; and it fared rather well in this task. After one scanning of an encyclopedia by LSA, for instance, "physician," "patient," and "bedside" were all tightly clustered in the semantic space crated by the LSA process. Or, as another example, after being trained on some introductory psychology textbooks, LSA was tested with multiple-choice comprehension tests provided by the textbook publishers, and "performed well above chance in all cases" (it scored 60 percent) (279). In all of these cases, LSA was first trained on a large text corpus intended to be representative of the text from which humans learn about the topic, and was then tested with four-alternative multiple choice tests used to test students for their understanding of the material.

Most interesting, perhaps, is the use of LSA to assign scores to written answers to essay questions on a vast array of topics (from heart anatomy through psychology to American history, current social issues, and marketing problems). In these tests, university students were asked to write short essays to cover an assigned topic or to answer a posed question. In each case, LSA was first trained either on a large sample of instructional text from the same domain or on combined text from the very large number of essays themselves. It then produced a high-dimensional semantic space. The experimenters then represented each student essay as the vector average of all the vectors for the words it contained, and used a mathematical formula whose input parameters were the length and angle of the average vector to assign a letter grade to the essay. The grades were then compared to those assigned by two to four human experts (university course instructors or professional exam readers from the Educational Testing Service). Landauer et al. (Landauer, Laham, and Foltz 1998) report that it "correlated significantly better with individual expert graders than one expert correlated with another." LSA has been further applied to many other tasks – for example, comprehension of metaphors (Kintsch, 2000) and categorization (Laham 1997).

LSA and similar theories, which adopt a "bag-of-words" approach to language, pose interesting questions about language learning and understanding. Probably the most interesting issue is how well a passage's meaning can be derived without paying any attention to word order (Landauer et al. 1997). Although processes that depend on word order and syntax undeniably play important roles in the comprehension of sentences, Landauer et al. (1997) argue, "it is difficult to know just how much people's extraction of information in ordinary discourse for ordinary purposes depends on such processes over and above what is derived from the combination of lexical items alone." Theories such as LSA may help us find answers to such cognitive questions.

Landauer et al. (1997) point out that LSA's learning mechanism is equivalent to a linear neural network. Laham (1997) even speculates whether "brain structure corresponds to LSA structure." He takes the case of a specific group of neuropsychological patients – namely, those who exhibit disnomias (inability to name) for certain categories of objects (ones that occur in nature), while retaining the ability to name other (artificial/synthetic) objects – as evidence that the brain may make use of a process similar to LSA. In short, if these authors are right, the success of LSA may supply a boost of support for the connectionist approach to modeling the mind.

Of Nuns, Sex, and Context

> It is hard to imagine that LSA could have simulated the impressive range of meaning-based human cognitive phenomena that it has unless it is doing something analogous to what humans do.
>
> – Landauer and Dumais (1997)

As this sentence suggests, the developers of LSA seem to believe in a certain degree of (biological and cognitive) realism for their model of knowledge representation. Of course, they also show a certain degree of ambivalence when they call LSA's representations of reality "somewhat sterile and bloodless," but, on the other hand, they go as far as to claim, "One might consider LSA's maximal knowledge of the world to be analogous to a well-read nun's knowledge of sex, a level of knowledge often deemed a sufficient basis for advising young" (ibid.).

So, how could a "bloodless" model have "knowledge of the world"? The answer to this question, I suggest, lies in a very narrow conception of "knowledge" that is, in turn, based on a particular view of semantics, as the relation between computer programs and processes, which is often confused with the relation between process and the world (see Figure 6.5). Sliding slipperily back and forth between these two notions of semantics is at the root of claims such as that mentioned earlier. The analogy between a nun and LSA, although appreciable to some extent, does not hold a lot of water if we note that the nun, despite a lack of direct sexual experience, is an embodied individual with experiences similar to sexual desire – a crucial dimension that is not available to LSA.

In addition to these semantic problems of the statistical approach, connectionist models face another difficulty that did not exist with such strain in the classical case – namely, the problem of evaluating models. This, as we shall see next, introduces a new tension.

A New Tension: How to Evaluate Models

The statistical approach to language learning may in fact be a step toward more realistic models of language learning, but it deprives connectionists of the universal measure provided by the notion of competence.[17] While this might not be a serious problem in discussing language learning in human beings, it becomes a problem in evaluating computer models, simply because, as they stand now, these models are too far from real language as a means of effective communication. The performance of computer models, in other words, cannot be measured in terms of communicative ability, but no other agreed-on measure seems to be available either. This is best illustrated by the contrastive results reported by Elman and by Rhode and Plaut.

The discrepancy between their results and those of Elman prompted Rhode and Plaut to try to replicate Elman's results directly in two separate simulations, one that used an identical grammar and that gradually increased the complexity of input sentences, and the other that incrementally increased memory size. Surprisingly, in both cases they arrived at opposite results to those of Elman – that is, they found out that "there was a significant advantage for starting with the full language" (Rhode & Plaut 1999, 94). Although the authors state, "we do not yet understand what led Elman to succeed in these simulations when we failed," they make a number of interesting observations.

First, they point out that they started their simulations with larger initial random connection weights, and that this contributed to the variation in the learning behaviors (ibid.). Next, they note that the networks trained (by Elman and others who purportedly replicated his experiments) exclusively on complex inputs were not allowed sufficient training time given the initial random weights, and hence failed to learn the complex patterns in that limited time (ibid.). Finally, they suggest that "the learning parameters chosen" (by Elman and others) might have resulted in poor performance of their networks, and claim that, "given appropriate training parameters," a recurrent network can effectively learn language without external preparation of input data of the kind performed by Elman. Furthermore, in assessing their networks, Rhode and Plaut use a different statistical measure of error from Elman's, and claim that their measure is a better indicator of performance (80).

Whether or not these claims are correct, they reveal a number of crucial points about connectionist research. First, connectionist models seem to be very sensitive to the initial parameters chosen by the designer. The fact that two research groups, using the same architecture, input data, and training regimen, arrive at opposite conclusions poses serious questions – for example, how one should decide which initial parameters to use, what combination of training data to use, how long to proceed with training, and so on.

Variability in performance under similar conditions may, of course, be a desirable adaptive trait and a hallmark of intelligence. Hence, it might be argued, the unpredictability of neural networks' behavior is an advantage over deterministic models. While there is merit to this argument, it brings up the question of the goal of research done within the connectionist framework. If the goal is to demonstrate that simple architectures such as a recurrent network can manifest variable behavior under varying circumstances, then we should agree that connectionist research has, indeed, achieved this goal. If, on the other hand, the purpose is to resolve such basic questions as starting large versus starting small in language learning, then it seems that connectionism has so far failed to answer such questions. This is alarming because the main point of AI research is presumably to discover and pinpoint distinct mechanisms that produce intelligent behavior. And *simple* recurrent networks seem to be too simple to provide such mechanisms. That is, while these networks reveal basic structures that may be part of the recurrent brain processes of the type suggested by neuroscientists (Edelman 1987), they lack sufficient structure to capture the complex processes involved in the learning of language.

In sum, as far as the debate between nativists and empiricists is concerned, connectionism seems to have taken a step in the right direction, especially by trying to erase the competence/performance distinction. But this step has not been sufficiently decisive to overcome some of the old problems. As Smolensky (1999) remarks, innate learning rules and innate architectural features, or what I earlier called "prewiring," is one of the core assumptions of the connectionist approach. One of the problematic consequences of this assumption is that it reduces the flexibility of the network in response to variations in input. The next section discusses a connectionist model of language comprehension that addresses the issue of flexibility.

NEURAL REDUCTIONISM: A THIRD PASS ON CONNECTIONISM

True human comprehension of language involves so many perceptual, psychological, and social capabilities that it would be absurd to claim for any of the existing models in AI, symbolic or connectionist, that it understands language. In a typical AI microdomain, dealing with language involves the capacity to use a small, well-defined lexicon with a strict and rigid grammar, whether written or spoken, and to answer questions about certain types of situations involving the given concepts. The linguistic capability of the model would then be relative to the size of the lexicon and the complexity of the potential situation. Jupiter, the model introduced at the outset of this chapter, for example, uses a vocabulary of two thousand words for the domain of weather forecasting.

No stand-alone connectionist model of language understanding is presently claimed to understand a human language or a subset of it. What connectionist models do instead is take input streams and parse them into words, phrases, and sentences, and even this turns out to be difficult in and of itself, as the models studied in previous sections demonstrated. The models studied in this section, developed by Stephen Grossberg and his colleagues at Boston University, face similar challenges. These models belong to a large class of connectionist networks – namely, the class of unsupervised models (and competitive learning) introduced in Appendix B.

Another Dilemma: Flexibility versus Stability

Appendix B discusses some of the advantages of competitive learning models – for example, the application of these models in the generation of topographical maps similar to those found in the brain. However, competitive networks also have certain drawbacks, the most important of which is their use of so-called *grandmother-cell* representations – namely, localized representations that encode whole concepts in a single unit (a neuron in the brain or a node in a connectionist model). This type of representation results in, among other things, the losing of a whole category if a single output unit fails[18]. Conversely, there is always a chance that certain units in the output layer will turn into "dead" units – that is, will never represent any category. Furthermore, these networks are not capable of representing hierarchical structures. "Two input patterns are either lumped together or not; there is no way to have categories within categories" (Hertz et al. 1991). These are all important issues, some of which (e.g., the problem of dead units) have fairly reliable solutions, and others of which (e.g., nonhierarchical representation) threatens the biological plausibility of these models, especially in light of recent findings about the hierarchical structure of cortical maps, as well as their plasticity (Edelman 1987). Grossberg (1987) has addressed this problem, which he calls the "stability–plasticity dilemma," by suggesting a variation of canonical models of competitive learning called "adaptive resonance theory" (ART). He formulates the stability–plasticity dilemma in the following way:

How can a learning system be designed to remain plastic in response to significant new events, yet also remain stable in response to irrelevant events? How does the system know how to switch between its stable and its plastic modes in order to prevent the relentless degradation of its learned codes by the "blooming buzzing confusion" of irrelevant experience? How can it do so without using a teacher? (1987: 30)

Rumelhart and Zipser (1985; see Appendix B) sidestepped this dilemma, Grossberg says, by using an overly simple input environment. Critical of such an approach, Grossberg (1987) sought to face the dilemma head-on, and suggested ART (originally proposed in Grossberg 1976) for this purpose.

The main idea behind ART is to use bottom-up and top-down processes that constantly "resonate" with each other – that is, they closely interact in a coupled manner so that the outcome of one process reinforces, and is reinforced by, the outcome of the other. Figure 6.7 shows an ART model of *speech integration* – namely, a system that takes as input a continuous stream of phonemes and returns as output ensembles of those phonemes (as words). There are two subsystems that functionally complement one another: the *attentional* subsystem processes familiar inputs, while the *orienting* subsystem deals with unfamiliar ones. The attentional subsystem is basically a competitive learning network that develops increasingly precise categories and representations of all previous phonemes. Furthermore, this subsystem has a top-down direction of processing that helps the system judge the familiarity of a new input – that is, the degree to which it fits into one of the previously formed phonological categories. If the input is judged to be familiar, it is used to adjust and tune even further the category to which it belongs (in the sense of settling on the constituent phonemes of the category); if not, its processing is delegated to the orienting subsystem, resetting the attentional

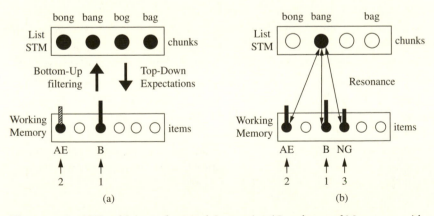

Figure 6.7. An ART architecture for speech integration (Grossberg and Myers 1999, with permission) (a) bottom-up and top-down processes; (b) the finalization of the process.

subsystem, preparing the conditions for creating a new category. In sum, the system gradually builds phonological prototypes that can accommodate new input, becoming further stabilized, or in the case of nonaccommodation, can create new prototypes.

In this way, Grossberg argues, the network manages to be, on the one hand, stable enough not to ceaselessly change its encoding of the inputs, and, on the other, to be flexible enough to respond to novel situations appropriately. What makes this possible is the presence of top-down processes that focus attention on the relevant features of the input. The crucial point is that the network achieves this without an outside teacher that corrects its errors – that is, it operates in an unsupervised mode.

ART has been used to model and analyze various linguistic (and nonlinguistic) tasks, typically at the level of phonological processing (Grossberg 1987). A recent example is a model of speech perception based on ART. Speech perception in a real situation requires numerous skills – a significant one being the ability to focus exclusive attention to a particular speaker in a noisy environment such as a party. "Auditory scene analysis," as this is called, is a very complex skill that involves a combination of cues such as proximity and direction of the source, continuity and pitch of the signal, and so on. None of these is sufficient in itself because the task involves both grouping and segregation of sounds – namely, the ability to tease apart the incoming sounds into different streams, and then to segregate each stream into words, phrases, and so on. Using the basic ART architecture, Grossberg and his colleagues have made models to simulate these behaviors. Based on results obtained with various ART models, Grossberg (1995) suggests that similar principles and mechanisms may play important roles in the human brain.

Has ART Solved the Stability–Plasticity Dilemma?

The original motivation behind connectionism was to bring inquiry about cognition down to a level much closer to the neural substrate than traditional AI ever had. The idea was that this is the right level for understanding and formalizing cognition, and that analysis at the symbolic level should be considered as merely an approximation to this basic level, just as Newtonian mechanics approximates quantum mechanics (Smolensky 1988). In short, the idea was that connectionism is a theory of cognition, not of implementation – that is, it is not simply a different way of building systems that could be built using the techniques of symbolic AI. Were it not for this claim, everyone would be a connectionist, because everyone agrees that mental processes are somehow implemented in the brain (Christiansen and Chater 1999).

But since many connectionists insist that the right level of computationally realizing cognition is subsymbolic, an internal tension is generated between cognitive-level constructs (e.g., grammars) and neural-level explanations. The tension becomes especially acute when connectionist models are used to explain high-level behaviors such as language in terms of neural interactions.

ART seemingly avoids this tension by simulating tasks that are, by and large, well below the symbolic level. The language employed in describing these models uses such words as "energy," "frequency," "pitch," "resonance," "location," and so on, and describes processes as sending waves back and forth between physical layers. There is hardly any claim about symbols, concepts, or other high-level constructs. This is manifest, for instance, in the discussion of *relevance*, where ART is described as discriminating between "irrelevant noise" and an "informative signal" (Grossberg 1987: 30). What makes such language possible is mainly the restriction of the targeted behaviors to phonological analysis, and a reluctance to extend them to language understanding. For more than twenty years, Grossberg and his group have built ART models that closely simulate various visual and auditory behaviors, but none of them has dealt with language comprehension *per se*. Although conservative, this is a sound research strategy, especially in contemporary AI, where a desire to leap to complex domains tends to be the dominant trend.[19]

ART models integrate top-down and bottom-up processes in a resonating fashion, a feature that is believed to be widely present in the mammalian brain – for example, in the visual pathways (Varela, Thompson, and Rosch 1991: 96). But these models still deal with language phenomena at a relatively low level – namely, at the level of phonemes. In this manner, they dodge the problem of bridging the gap between low-level processes and high-level symbolic phenomena, which is often a lack in connectionist networks. These are clear advantages of ART models that are gained thanks to what I called "neural reductionism." A close look at an ART model clarifies what this means.

ARTSTREAM, designed to carry out auditory scene analysis, has three processes running in parallel: a bottom-up process that activates spectral components (i.e., assigns numerical amplitudes to different frequencies in the auditory input), a top-down process to prime specific spectral components in the absence of bottom-up input, and a resonating process that goes back and forth between the two levels in order to amplify the matching components between them (Govindarajan et al. 1994). Likewise, ARTPHONE, designed to carry out the segmentation of speech (into phonemes) and the integration of the speech (into words), has two main subsystems – a working memory for processing phonetic items and a high-level category stage. It chunks items such as phonemes, letters, syllables, or words into larger groups, and selects the most predictive chunks – that is, those having the highest degree of match with the phonetic input in the next stage – to generate top-down contextual pressures to guide perceptual processing. As items enter, work space (what is called "working memory" in Figure 6.7), the nodes send priming signals to those in the short-term memory (STM), activating several potential categories.[20]

For example, a word that begins with "ba . . ." (/bæ/) sequentially activates chunks responsive to the /b/ and then to the /æ/. These, in turn, activate chunks starting with /b/ and /bæ/, with the caveat that bigger chunks take longer to be activated because they have higher threshold values. Furthermore, larger chunks, when activated, inhibit or mask smaller ones. Thus, the /bæ/, which can only be activated after /æ/, suppresses the /b/ chunk, and sends top-down feedback to associated items (e.g., /ng/), representing an expectation for the pattern "bang," which is stored in the short-term memory. Those chunks whose top-down signals are best matched to the sequence of incoming data reinforce the working memory items and receive larger bottom-up signals from them, and so on. As Grossberg et al. put it, "a resonance wave travels across the network that embodies the speech code and percept" (ibid.). In this way, the completion of the word "bang" extends the pattern in working memory, and terminates the resonant process. This process also could terminate if there is a mismatch between the top-down and bottom-up signals, in which case other small chunks are activated and the whole process starts over again.

As we see, an implicit assumption in this model is that the phonological aspect of processing is autonomous and independent from other levels – for example, semantic and syntactic levels. This is a major simplification, given what we know about the relationships among these various aspects of language (see the next section). What ART models have achieved thus far is, therefore, a solution to Grossberg's stability–plasticity dilemma by staying close to low-level *signals*, and avoiding high-level *symbols*. In short, ART does not quite provide a mechanism that successfully links the syntactic (signal) and semantic levels, and hence does not overcome what seems to be a major obstacle in AI research; it merely avoids the problem by staying close to one level. The next section introduces models of language production that aim to tie phonological and semantic aspects more tightly together.

ADEQUACY: A FOURTH PASS ON CONNECTIONISM

Naively speaking, production of language is the process of translating thought into speech. Understood in this way, it can be thought of as involving different stages and components. Levelt (1989), for instance, recognizes three main components of language production:

i.   a *formation* component in which a "message", a nonverbal represen-
     tation of the utterance, is formed;
ii. a *formulation* component that takes a message and turns it into lin-
     guistic form;
iii. an *articulation* component that involves the movements of the articu-
     latory organs for producing sounds.

According to this theory, lexical access is that part of formulation where words are retrieved for the expression of a thought. On the surface, this seems to be a simple mapping between the meaning and the sounds of words. If this were the case, a simple pattern associator (of the kind discussed in Appendix B) would be able to model lexical access. As Gary Dell and colleagues have observed, however, "characterizing lexical access as just a mapping from the semantic features of a concept to a lexical item ignores the fact that such features do not uniquely identify a word" (Dell et al. 1999, §2). Because of this, more complex models of lexical access are required. Many theories, for instance, assume that the mapping occurs in two steps (ibid.): (i) lemma selection, during which a concept is mapped onto a *lemma*, a non-phonological representation, often assumed to be associated with the grammatical properties of a word; and (ii) phonological encoding, during which the lemma is transformed into an organized sequence of speech sounds.

Language Errors: A Gateway to the Brain?

One of the common phenomena that support two-stage theories like this is the tip-of-the-tongue phenomenon, where a speaker seems to be aware of the existence of a word but cannot access its sound. One way to explain this phenomenon is to assume that lemma selection has taken place but phonological encoding has not. This interpretation is further supported by studies that have shown that speakers in the tip-of-the-tongue state know the grammatical properties of the word being sought – for example, its grammatical gender. This, of course, does not necessarily imply that the two stages are temporally separated, as is suggested by the error of saying "Hungarian restaurant" instead of "Hungarian Rhapsody" (ibid.). What triggers this error is, of course, that both "restaurant" and "Rhapsody" begin with "r," but notice that both of these words temporally happen after the word "Hungarian."

The *aphasia model*, originally reported by Dell et al. (1997), simulates the tip-of-the-tongue phenomenon. The architecture of the model includes

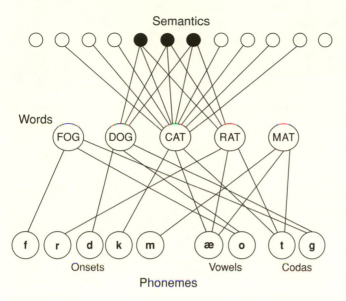

Figure 6.8. The aphasic model (from Dell et al. 1999, with permission).

three layers: semantic features, words, and phonemes (Figure 6.8). Each unit in the middle layer corresponds to one word. Assuming monosyllabic words of consonant-vowel-consonant form, the units in the phoneme layer are divided into three groups: one for the first consonant (the "onset"), one for the middle vowel, and one for the final consonant (the "coda"). Each word unit is connected via bidirectional excitatory links to up to ten semantic units and three phoneme units.

The model works by interactive spreading activation that proceeds in two steps, corresponding to lemma selection and phonological encoding. Processing begins by adding activations to the semantic features of the target word, say, CAT. The bidirectional connections spread the activation, for a fixed number of steps and according to a linear activation rule, to the units on the other two levels. Thus, words such as DOG get activated because of shared semantic features, and words such as MAT get activated through shared phonemes with the target word CAT. A "mixed" word such as RAT, on the other hand, gets activation from both sources, becoming thereby more activated than the previous two. Under perfect processing, the word with the highest activation, namely, CAT, would be selected as the answer. By introducing some noise into the activations, Dell et al. open the door for other candidate words to be selected on occasion. In any case, the selection of the word brings the lemma-selection stage to a conclusion. The second step, phonological encoding, begins with a large boost of activation to the chosen word unit, which spreads activation for another fixed period of time. The phonemes with the highest activation are then selected and fed to a buffer, concluding the encoding process. Again, errors may also occur in this stage if and when the wrong set of phonemes is activated by noise.

To use the model as a probe to understand aphasia in human beings, Dell et al. compared the error pattern of the model with those of aphasic human beings. In doing so, they first made careful adjustments to the parameters (noise, size of the activation boost to the selected word during lemma selection, connection weights, decay rate, etc.) in order to match the error pattern of the model with that of a normal human being. Furthermore, to create aphasic error patterns, they *lesioned* the network in two different ways: (i) limiting its ability to transmit activation (by reducing connection weights); and (ii) limiting its ability to maintain its activation patterns (by increasing a decay parameter). These so-called lesions gave rise to various error patterns.

"Stupid" Errors

Reducing connection weights makes the activation patterns on each level less consistent with each other (because now the two levels will not communicate with each other as effectively as they should, so changes in one may not trigger similar changes in the other), resulting in "stupid" errors – for example, the production of either a non-word such as LAT or an unrelated word such as FOG for CAT. According to the authors, these reflect inconsistencies between the word and phoneme layers in the former case, and between the semantic and word layers in the latter.

"Smart" Errors

When the decay rate is increased, errors occur because noise dominates the decayed activation levels, but spreading of activation among layers is still strong. This results in what Dell et al. call "smart" errors, in which there is consistency between at least two levels. A combination of both lesions results in an error pattern that is roughly the overlap of these two.

Dell et al. (1997) used this model to classify aphasic patients, according to the pattern of their errors, as suffering from pure decay lesion, pure weight lesion, or both. They claim that by using this model they have been able to predict both the kinds of errors that a specific patient is likely to make and the pattern of recovery that would follow a specific course of training. Despite this, according to Dell et al. (1999), the aphasia model has certain limitations – for example, the nonsequential character of its output, the pretailored architecture, and the assumption of prestored phonological frames that specify the syllabic structure of each word. They discuss another model, the phonological error model, originally reported in Dell, Juliano, and Govindjee (1993), that presumably overcomes the above limitations. This model, as its name implies, is mostly concerned with the kinds of errors that might arise in phonological encoding. Since it uses a variation of a simple recurrent network, I will not discuss it here.

Who Makes Errors – The Person or the Brain?

Dell et al.'s models provide useful insights as to the possible causes of certain language errors and maladies such as aphasia among human beings. They demonstrate, for instance, how certain errors might arise from an unusually high decay rate of activation or from unusually low connection weights. Does this mean that we should seek to explain all language errors by looking at levels close to neural processing? Or that we should be looking for brain lesions whenever we observe some language disorder in a human being? Probably not (and Dell et al., in my judgment, would likely agree with this answer).

That any cognitive (dys)function has a correlate in some neural (mis)happening cannot be disputed. However, it does not follow from this that there is a simple one-to-one relation between the mind and the brain, between behavior and architecture, or between function and substrate. This point is at the root of many objections against "simple connectionism" (to borrow a term used by Clancey 1997). The study of speech errors and disorders provides a good case for highlighting this question.

Humans commit many different kinds of speech errors (see Hofstadter and Moser 1989 for a very wide-ranging survey of such errors). Current connectionist models, however, do not have very many sources of variance that could explain this diversity of errors. Decay increase and weight reduction, suggested by Dell et al. (1999), are about the only ones. In other words, there is a serious mismatch between the diversity and richness of the phenomenon (errors) and the theoretical apparatus that seeks to explain it. So one of two things must be the case. Either the multiplicity of errors is only apparent – that is, all errors originate in fact in a very limited number of neurological events – or else the theory is too weak to fully explain the situation – that is, we need a theory that could make more distinctions and handle more complexity. Preliminary observation, I want to show, suggests that the latter is the case – that is, current connectionist models are inadequate for explaining the full range of speech errors.

For starters, neurological evidence portrays a very complicated picture of speech disorders. Based on research on aphasic patients, for instance,

Gazzaniga et al. (1998) suggest that it is lexical *integration* that is impaired in these patients rather than lexical *access*. The patients have difficulty integrating the meaning of words into the current context established by the preceding word in the sentence (312). In the sentence, "The man planted a tree on the bank," the context tells us that "bank" refers to the side of a river and not a monetary institution. It is this information that gets lost for the aphasic patient, and, to explain it, neuroscientists invoke higher-order structures well above the level of neurons. On the other hand, existing connectionist models have inherent limitations that make it impossible for them to develop high-order structures. These limitations cannot be overcome by architectural modification of the present schemes – a fact that is most clearly revealed by the difficulties faced by connectionists in tackling the *binding problem*. For instance, if there is a red-colored pen on a round blue table, the binding problem is the challenge of ensuring that the features "redness" and "longness" get linked ("bound") to the pen, and the features "roundness" and "blueness" to the table, and not any other combination (Anderson 1995: 290; see Appendix C).

The units of a simple connectionist model only have one numerical dimension – namely, an activation value that shows the degree to which a specific input (e.g., a morpheme) is present. What is needed, in addition, is at least one other dimension to represent *correlations* among units. Having a threshold is one way of doing this (because all the units that are activated below a given threshold can be thought of as being correlated, as do the units above the threshold), but it provides only a binary choice. Adding more layers would not help either, because it has been formally proven that a three-layer architecture can simulate any architecture with more than three layers. Some models of binding have added a phase angle to the units in order to add this dimension (Gasser and Colunga 2000). The idea is to have different groups of nodes fire at different times ("phases"), hence binding those that fire at the same time to the same object or event. This is biologically plausible because it simulates the relative timing of interneuronal firings, which have been postulated to play a major role in the brain. But even with such an extra "phase" dimension, connectionist researchers are still encountering great difficulty in modeling basic binding relations in their models – for example, the example about the spatial relation between a red pen and a blue table (ibid.; Gasser personal communication). This is symptomatic of the inherent limits of simple connectionism, and serves as a reminder that the relation between cognitive behavior and the brain is much more complicated than these models suggest.

In short, language errors, like many other cognitive behaviors, are often the outcome of high-level events above the neuronal level, and to find explanations for such errors, it is crucial to look at those higher levels rather than at the microstructure of the brain. We have seen, furthermore, that the simple nodes of current connectionist models are too limited in their capabilities to handle the full range of speech errors.

CONCLUSION: ELIZA, NETtalk, AND MYSTICISM

> AI programs are notorious for being impenetrably complex. Sometimes this feature is painted as a virtue, as if the mystery of intelligence ought to be preserved in computational models of it. But a model that we don't understand is not a model at all, especially if it works on only a handful of examples.
>
> – McDermott (1990)

"Science is about understanding" – this is the conventional wisdom, and it is what McDermott is defending in the above excerpt. Ironically, however, the appeal of the connectionist movement is at least in part due to its revolt against this dogma. "Neural network mysticism," as James Anderson (1995: 277) dubbed it, represents a rebellious rejection of the traditional scientific commitment to tractable analysis, and this, according to some authors, resonates well with the so-called postmodern sensibilities of our times (Turkle 1995: 134–36). W. Daniel Hillis, the inventor of the Connection Machine, refers to this mysterious quality as "the appealing inscrutability of emergent systems" (ibid.).

NETtalk is the epitome of such emergent behavior and of the performance-orientation of connectionism (see Appendix B). Anyone who listens to a session in which NETtalk progresses from initial babbling sounds to semirecognizable words, and then to a fair simulacrum of human speech, cannot help being heavily impressed (Clark 2001). NETtalk, in this sense, is – or was – the Eliza of connectionism. Like its notorious predecessor, however, it gradually faded in people's memories, and with it the initial fever of excitement has declined, like a node decaying in a neural network. Therefore, we are now in a better position to judge the promises of connectionism than we were a decade or two ago.

What We Have Learned *about* Connectionism: The Alchemist's Pledge

> This kind of investigation cannot prove how the brain works. It can, however, show that some models are unworkable and provide clues to how to revise the models to make them work.
>
> – Rochester et al. (1956)

These sentences were written almost half a century ago about neurally inspired Perceptron models, and they still hold true, I believe, about the descendents of those models – namely, the present-day connectionist models. Connectionism is now about two decades old, with literally thousands of researchers working under its banner. The fruit of their efforts has, by and large, been the discovery of many types of subtle mechanisms, each of which is suited to a handful of tasks. This is by no means a trivial accomplishment. Every established science began with the creation of simple methods and tools, many of which started out off target but proved to be useful in later development (The purification methods and apparatus developed by alchemists, for instance, are still in use in chemistry).[21]

On the other hand, intense focus on performance and output has moved most of these mechanisms away from biological realism. An interesting example of this is the effort invested in models such as NETtalk to produce language before comprehending it, in sharp contrast to language learning in human beings where comprehension precedes production. Seen in this light, connectionist models are more like demonstrations (or, in the lingo of computer professionals, "proof of concept") of the kinds of performance that tinkering with networks can achieve, rather than models of mental activity, brain architecture, or human cognition as such. For this reason, no "lifesize chunk of behavior" has been exhibited by connectionists (Harnad 1990). Our survey of connectionist models of language processing confirms this assessment.

As we have seen throughout this chapter, of the original intuitions behind connectionism – namely, what I called architecture over function, decoupling, learning, neural reductionism, prewiring, and adequacy (of connectionism as a theory of cognition) – none survives critical scrutiny. The first four need rethinking of some of their underlying premises, for we have seen that function is as important in connectionism as it is in classical models, that decoupling from the environment is in fact the Achilles' heel of connectionism and not a point of strength, that learning cannot be totally divorced from conceptual knowledge, and that no one level of analysis should be given priority over others. Prewiring, by contrast, is a debatable notion that, in some interpretations, brings connectionism close to classical views about innateness. Finally, the adequacy of connectionism as a complete theory of mind is a disputable suggestion, as was illustrated by the story of the connectionist treatment of linguistic errors.

What We Have Learned *from* Connectionism: The Experimenter's Regress

> The problem with experiments is that they tell you nothing unless they
> are competently done, but in controversial science no-one can agree on

a criterion of competence. Thus, in controversies, it is invariably the case that scientists disagree not only about results, but also about the quality of each other's work. This is what stops experiments from being decisive and gives rise to regress.

— Collins and Pinch (1998: 3)

This chapter was devoted to connectionist models of language learning, and although, as I mentioned earlier, this is not the domain where artificial neural networks fare best, it is certainly an area that has attracted much attention in connectionist research. It is fair, therefore, to ask what we have learned about language from such research. To be sure, connectionists have discovered mechanisms that can learn certain simplified grammars and languages. As Christiansen and Chater (1999), two researchers who work in this area, point out, the progress involves "drastic simplifications." While simplification is at the heart of all scientific work, the art of a scientist is to do this in such a way that crucial aspects of the studied phenomenon are not thrown out. This, as we have seen, is not true of most connectionist models of language learning, which are based on impoverished notions of context, semantics, time, and so on. Consequently, the relevance of these models to issues of real language is quite contentious. Furthermore, issues of scaling-up remain a major challenge, as do criticisms such as that of Reeke and Edelman (1988) concerning biological realism.

A broader issue for all of connectionism is *replicability* of results, which is a cornerstone of scientific methods. The discrepancy among the results obtained by Elman and by Rhodes and Plaut, for instance, illustrates the difficulty of replication in connectionist networks. Many groups (e.g., Joyce 1996) have reported replications of Elman's work, obtaining results that are compatible with it. Rhode and Plaut, on the other hand, also claim to have replicated Elman's work. Yet, as we have seen, they arrive at contradictory results and so they question the validity of previous replications by speculating that maybe the "networks . . . were not allowed sufficient training time," or maybe "the learning parameters chosen resulted in poor overall performance," and so on. The point again is not whether such assessments are correct, but that one cannot simply declare by fiat which aspects of an experiment should be mimicked in order for us to be able to claim that it has been replicated. Who should decide which aspects are crucial and which ones are not?

This is a thorny issue at the heart of science, which Collins and Pinch (1993: 98) have dubbed the "experimenter's regress." The problem for difficult science, according to these sociologists of science, is "What is the correct outcome?" However, the knowledge of the correct outcome cannot provide the answer, simply because we don't know what the correct outcome should consist of. Experimental work can be used as a *test* if we find a way of breaking into the circle of the experimenter's regress – something that happens in science when the appropriate range of outcomes is known at the outset, providing a universally agreed criterion of experimental quality (ibid.). In the absence of such criterion, some other means should be found that is independent of the outcome. In the current debate, for instance, is it starting small or starting large that constitutes the right outcome? Connectionism fails to answer this question because there is disagreement on the proper training set from the outset.

The experimenter's regress is an issue for all AI (and cognitive science), but connectionism is more vulnerable to it largely because of the implicit and complex character of its representational schemes. As some have suggested, the connectionist style of work may, in fact, exemplify a new way of doing science, but even novel methods need some criteria of evaluation. And this is something that we do not yet have.

7   Mathematical Models: Dynamical AI

Hume's Majestic Dream

Here is then the only expedient ... to leave the tedious lingering method, which we have hitherto followed, and instead of taking now and then a castle or village on the frontier, to march up directly to the capital or center of these sciences, to human nature itself; which once being masters of, we may every where else hope for an easy victory.

– David Hume (1739): *A Treatise of Human Nature*

C omplex systems and processes evade simple analysis. Cognition, for example, is a complex process that emerges from the joint activity of the brain, the body, and the environment. Each of these is, in turn, a complex system with millions and billions of components – neurons, cells, individuals – which, to make things even more complex, are also diverse in form and capability. Would it not be ideal if we could treat all of these complex systems, subsystems, and sub-subsystems using a single analytical tool? Advocates of the dynamical approach in AI and cognitive science take this question seriously. Their approach is strongly motivated by the search for a universal tool – or, as Scott Kelso, a leading light in the dynamical school, has put it, for "a common vocabulary and theoretical framework within which to couch mental, brain, and behavioral events" (Kelso 1995).

Cognition, furthermore, is a temporal event, so it should be studied as such – that is, as a process that unfolds in time. This is a key intuition behind the dynamical approach. The static representations and discrete methods of the classical approach, dynamicists[1] argue, fail to capture this crucial aspect of cognition, and need to be replaced with alternatives that can do so. The dynamical approach, they claim, provides the natural alternative.

This chapter opens with a brief introduction to the historical and intellectual background behind the dynamical approach, gives a sketch of Dynamical Systems Theory, and presents *HKB* and *DFT*, two of the best-known models built in this framework. It then examines the main bones of contention between advocates and opponents of the dynamical approach – most notably, the explanatory role of the dynamical approach in AI and cognitive science, the suitable level for such explanations, and the question of meaning. It reexamines these issues in the light of, respectively, the main thesis of this study, the views of Henri Poincaré (the originator of dynamical systems theory), and the work on complexity (especially by John Holland) and agent-based modeling.

BACKGROUND: A LOVE FOR MATHEMATICS

Thomas Savery, an eighteenth-century engineer from Wales, was the builder of the first steam engine put to practical use in industry (c. 1700), and also the first person to use the term "horsepower" in approximately its modern sense. Joseph Weizenbaum, who reports this historical piece of information, speculates that "perhaps the term [horsepower] arose only because there were so many horses when the steam engine replaced them, not only in its first incarnation as a stationary power source, but also in its reincarnation as a locomotive" (1976: 32). Weizenbaum uses this example to impart a possible suggestive role to the term "horsepower" in the invention, almost one hundred years later (1804), of the locomotive by the British engineer Trevithik, who thought of replacing flesh-and-blood horses with steel ones. I want to use the same example to venture another suggestion: perhaps the story of the invention of "horsepower" is not unique, but is a typical exercise of human intuitive powers in the realm of science.

"Horsepower," history tells us, was later standardized and defined as the equivalent of precisely 746 watts, shedding all its arbitrary reverberations in the process. Welsh horses continued to be as unruly and diverse as before, but "horsepower" was ruled in and standardized forever. Perhaps, like "horsepower," all scientific concepts are the outcomes of human intuition and inventiveness. Perhaps a similar process of standardization could take place in sciences such as psychology, if we could only find the right set of primitives and units. Perhaps we could standardize and quantify "decision," "attention," "awareness," "will," "love," "hatred," "moral," and so on – and perhaps we could even establish quantitative and mathematical relations among them. Given that such a process of formalization took place with "energy," "force," "power," "resistance," and so on in physics, why not in psychology?

This was a question that occupied David Hume's mind around three hundred years ago, and that will engage us throughout this chapter. Based on the premise that "all the sciences have a relation, greater or less, to human nature," Hume argued that the "science of man" (what we call psychology today) should be given top priority in our intellectual investigations, which "must be laid on experience and observation" (ibid.). The central goal of Hume's proposal was to put mathematical garb on psychology, as Newton had done for physics. In this chapter we shall examine whether the Humean Dream can be realized in any conceivable manner, and I shall try to say if so, how, and if not, why. The modern dynamical approach will be our focus.

"Dynamics," as a word, refers to the way a system evolves with time, where by "system" we loosely mean some collection of related parts that we perceive as a single entity. Familiar examples are the solar system, the central nervous system of mammals, the immune system of our bodies, the postal service of a big or small town, a nationwide power supply network, or even a socioeconomic arrangement such as the capitalist or socialist systems. The dynamics of each of these systems, then, has to do with the way they change in time: How, for example, does the solar system evolve in terms of the positions, speeds, and accelerations of individual planets? Or how has the capitalist system evolved in terms of production and distribution of goods, labor relations, economical cycles, and so on?

This meaning of "dynamics" as the evolution of a system in time is accepted by almost everybody in AI and cognitive science. One could, in fact, argue that the dominant view in cognitive science is quite compatible with this broad understanding of a dynamical approach, because it is obvious that cognitive systems change with time.[2] If we define cognition as the processes that take place when intelligent beings think – that is, when they sense, perceive, remember, imagine, plan, predict, decide, understand, interpret, act, and so on – then there is no question that it happens in time. It is probably this broad meaning that Hofstadter, for instance, has in mind when he repeatedly uses the word "dynamic" to describe the workings of the Copycat model of analogy-making – for example, "dynamic conceptual proximities," "dynamic spreading of activation," "dynamic emergence of pressures," and "dynamic mixture of bottom-up and top-down processing" (1995: 266–67; see Chapter 9).[3]

There are, however, more specific flavors of the dynamical approach that constitute points of contention, and these are the ones that will engage us for the bulk of this chapter. Most notable among them are models that seek, in keeping with the Humean Dream, to capture human thought and behavior in an elegant mathematical formalism.

The contemporary origins of the mathematical approach to the study of mind and behavior go back to the 1940s and 1950s, when, under the rubric of *cybernetics* (Wiener 1948), ideas such as "feedback" and "control loop" were shown to play an important role in science and engineering, and when serious attempts were launched to explain human behavior in similar terms. After the 1950s, this strand of ideas was overshadowed by computational notions and metaphors, but it nonetheless continued to lurk in the background in AI, cognitive science, and psychology. The resurgence of dynamics as a main scientific contender in the study of mind is, however, a rather recent event, born out of the attempts of a number of researchers in the above disciplines to apply dynamical methods to the study of behavior and cognition and to the design of intelligent artifacts. Today, as a result of such efforts, one sees dynamical models of sensorimotor behavior, language (phonology, morphology, audition), visual perception, decision-making, growth and development, and so on. Port and Van Gelder (1995) constitutes an example of such work in cognitive science, and Thelen and Smith (1994) constitutes a cogent attempt to understand infant development in dynamical terms.

The dominant framework in most of these works is known as *dynamical systems theory*, with which we now acquaint ourselves.

FROM FINGER WAGGING TO DECISION MAKING

In mathematical accounts of the dynamical approach, a dynamical system is defined as a set of time-dependent variables that collectively constitute the system's "state." The focus in such approaches is on the change of the state with time, which is generally expressed in the form of *differential equations*. A differential equation is one that formulates the change in time of system *variables* in terms of system *parameters*.[4] The formula $m\, d^2x/dt^2 = -kx$ for a spring-mass oscillator, for instance, is a differential equation that relates the oscillator's position (x) in time (t) to its mass (m) and the spring's stiffness (k). Simple variations of this formula are also used to model various muscle and limb movements in humans and animals (Latash 1993; see also Chapter 8). The challenge for mathematical accounts is to develop similar equations that would govern more complex bodily and mental behaviors.

A Geometrical Outlook

The basic idea of mathematical dynamics is that if we can determine the relevant variables of a system, and if we know its initial state, then, by applying the equations that govern its evolution, we can predict the state of the system at any later time. If the rules are expressed mathematically in the form of differential equations, we can do this by solving the equations. The solution of the differential equation for spring-mass system, for example, is a periodic function that gives the state (position and velocity) of the oscillating mass at any given moment. Similarly, a system of differential equations for the solar system determines the state of the system (position and velocity of each planet) at any given time. The appeal and elegance of this technique is such that eighteenth-century philosophers such as Laplace and Leibniz proposed to think of the entire universe as one giant system, governed by a set of differential equations.[5]

This dream turned out to be unrealizable for many reasons, the most obvious of which is the enormousness of such an undertaking. But there are also more technical reasons, such as the fact that most differential equations do not have closed-form solutions in terms of a standard set of primitives – for example, the simple-seeming case of the motion of just three point masses in space under the influence of their mutual gravitational force (Norton 1995).[6] In addition, complex systems often involve nonlinearities – that is, the disproportionate change of system behavior due to minor changes in initial conditions or in parameter values.

It was in response to such difficulties that the great French mathematician Henri Poincaré (1854–1912) devised a method known today as "dynamical systems theory" (DST). DST is a *qualitative* method for studying differential equations – that is, instead of seeking exact numerical solutions, it uses geometrical notions such as "(state) space," "motion," "trajectory," "proximity," "attractor," . . . and so on to describe and predict certain aspects of the behavior of dynamical systems. Using this approach, one can study the trajectories that a system may follow in a space of possibilities, and one can also deal with qualitative questions such as the long-term stability of a system or its behavior in the face of outside perturbations.

In the case of the solar system, for instance, typical questions for DST would be: "Is the solar system stable? That is, will two planets ever collide, or will one ever escape from or fall into the sun? If we could alter the mass of one of the planets or change its position slightly, would that lead to a drastic change in the trajectories?" (Norton 1995). As we see, unlike quantitative questions about the exact positions and velocities of the planets, the above questions bypass the need for precise numerical solutions of the equations of motion; it would seem that a description in terms of general trends, accessible and inaccessible regions, and other more visual or geometric notions would suffice.

The Self-Organization of Behavior

Mechanical systems and planetary systems constitute a small and simple group of phenomena, and historically the first phenomena, to be studied using the DST formalism. A more interesting group consists of the so-called self-organizing systems that arise in many diverse situations. The central feature of such systems is their capability of reorganizing themselves and adapting to new conditions without direct involvement of a central executive. It is well known, for instance, that our bodies lose millions of dead cells and replace them with new ones every day, without this affecting their functioning as living organisms in any obvious way, and without the brain or any other controlling organ having any obvious and direct role in the process. But our bodies are not the only systems with such capabilities; there are similar systems in fluid dynamics, astrophysics, neuroscience, ecology, sociology, and economics.

Consider, for instance, the supply and consumption of goods in a city like New York. In the absence of any central planning commission or large reserves for buffering the fluctuations, the smooth and continued supply of goods is "sort of a magic that everywhere is taken for granted" (Holland 1995). Every time we go to a supermarket shelf, confident of finding our favorite pickles, Holland suggests, we depend on this magic to reign – the magic of self-organized, adaptive behavior in the large-scale scope of a huge city and with the unsupervised coordination of millions of individuals and hundreds of organizations (suppliers, retailers, consumers, transporters, etc.).[7]

Similar patterns are observed in even simpler physical phenomena. Consider the formation of patterns in cooking oil when it is heated (Kelso 1995). Initially, there is no large-scale motion; all that happens is the random motion of oil molecules, called "heat conduction." If a large-enough temperature gradient is established, however, the liquid begins to move as a coordinated whole, giving rise to an orderly pattern of "convection rolls" – namely, the circular motion of oil molecules in a coherent and organized fashion. An even more telling version of this phenomenon occurs when the liquid is heated from below and cooled from above.

The explanation for the formation of these interesting patterns is rather simple: the cooler liquid at the top is denser and tends to fall, while the warmer liquid at the bottom is less dense and tends to rise. In the terminology of DST, this event is called an "instability," which is driven by the temperature gradient (called the "control parameter"), and which gives rise to macroscopic convection rolls (called a "cooperative effect" or "collective effect") that have a fixed amplitude (called the "order parameter"). Physicists explain the phenomenon by assuming that the initially random starting pattern is a superposition of a number of different vibratory modes, some of which are damped out for any given temperature gradient, and others of which gain amplitude and come to dominate the prevailing pattern. This "selection mechanism" turns out to be a basic principle of nature: from random initial conditions a specific form of motion is favored. The stable points or regions in the space of all possible states towards which a system travels are called *attractors*, because any trajectory that passes close to such a point or region will be sucked in. The opposite of an attractor is a *repellor*.

Chance also plays a major role in a system such as this. An accidental fluctuation or perturbation, for instance, might make the fluid follow one of the two possible (clockwise and counterclockwise) directions of motion. Such "symmetry breaking" is also widespread in nature. A good example is the process of embryogenesis in metazoans – organisms that develop from a single cell (a fertilized egg) into a multicellular organization having a great diversity of cell types. This happens via successive division of cells, which adhere to each other and create a ball that has an interior and an exterior. However, this cluster of cells soon loses its spherical symmetry, as it goes through a series of stages where physical symmetries are broken one after another (Holland 1995).

The dynamical characterization of a system is principally based on notions such as: instability, collective variables, control parameters, selection mechanism, symmetry breaking, attractors, and so on. The system is thought of as being driven by a collective control parameter through a state space in which there are distinct regions such as attractors, repellors, and so on.

The dynamical systems approach affords a viewpoint that, at least superficially, is in sharp contrast with the way traditional AI and cognitive science view things. For example, in contrast to the "filing-cabinet view" of the brain as a repository of text-style information (Clark 1997: 67), a dynamical view portrays it in the following way:

[T]he human brain is *fundamentally* a pattern-forming, self-organized system governed by nonlinear dynamical laws. Rather than compute, our brain "dwells" (at least for short times) in metastable states: it is poised on the brink of instability where it can switch flexibly and quickly. By living near criticality, the brain is able to anticipate the future, not simply react to present. (Kelso 1995: 26)

Some dynamicists suggest that this viewpoint constitutes a revolutionary step in the study of cognition. A close look at some dynamical models will help us assess this opinion.

Finger Movement: The HKB Model

Much has been said about the complexity of the human brain and its variegated structures. But the story of bodily movements and their underlying

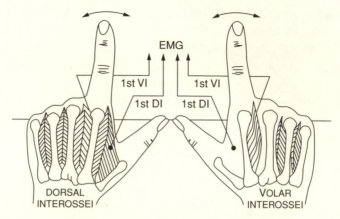

Figure 7.1. Finger-wagging experiment (from Kelso 1995, with permission).

complexities is no less interesting. The human body contains roughly 10^2 joints and 10^3 muscles (not to mention 10^3 cell types) – many orders of magnitude less than the number of neurons (10^{11}), but still very complex if one considers, on the one hand, the degrees of freedom of movement generated by these figures and, on the other, the multiple functions performed by each bodily organ – for example, the multiple roles of the mouth in speaking, chewing, breathing, and so forth. Still more surprising is the number of anatomical components involved in the simplest of bodily functions. A baby, for example, must coordinate approximately thirty-six muscles to be able to say "ba" (Kelso 1995). The orchestration among these many components is a fascinating story yet to be accounted for. An account of a simpler but similar phenomenon might be a first good step toward that direction. One such account is provided by the HKB model, named after its originators H. Haken, J. Kelso, and H. Bunz.

The HKB model was initiated by a simple observation of rhythmic behavior in human hands (Kelso 1995; see Figure 7.1). Most people can wag the index fingers of both hands in only two stable patterns: *out-of-phase*, where both simultaneously move right, then left (like the windshield wipers on most cars), and *in-phase*, where the fingers approach one another at the midline of the body (like the wipers of very rare car models). The relative phase of motion between the two fingers in these two cases is, respectively, 180 and zero degrees (see Figure 7.2).[8] A more interesting observation is that, starting out of phase and increasing the speed of finger movements gradually, people cannot sustain the pattern, and, above a certain threshold frequency, spontaneously switch to the in-phase movement. The reverse process, however, does not occur; that is, starting in phase and decreasing the speed, the

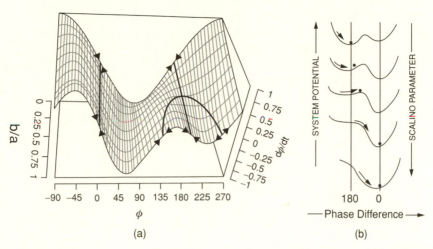

Figure 7.2. (a) The vector-phase diagram of the finger-wagging experiment; (b) The analogy with a ball in a potential well (from Kelso 1995, with permission).

movement does not switch back to out-of-phase. In the jargon of dynamical systems theorists, one could say that the system consisting of the two hands is bistable (has two attractors) in the low-frequency states, and monostable (has one attractor) in the high-frequency ones, and it makes a transition between them at a critical point (but only going from low to high, and not in the reverse direction).

The HKB model tries to explain this behavior parsimoniously in dynamical terms. The first step in the construction of the model is to find collective variables that relate the individual components. Having ruled out other possibilities such as frequency ratios – because they do not have the property of coupling the two fingers in a single variable – the model takes the relative phase Φ as the collective variable. This variable is symmetric in space (as is verified by imagining the experiment in a mirror) and periodic in time. As with all periodic behaviors, this allows writing a function V as a Fourier series expansion in terms of the relative phase. Taking only the first two terms of the expansion, one gets:

$$V = -a \cos \Phi - b \cos 2\Phi$$

Figure 7.2(a) shows the "vector field diagram" of the HKB model obtained by plotting the derivative $d\Phi/dt$ in terms of Φ with b/a as the control parameter. The diagram clearly exhibits the transition from antisymmetric ($\Phi = \pm 180$) into the symmetric mode ($\Phi = 0$). Figure 7.2(b) provides an intuitive understanding of the behavior by using an analogy with a ball in a well. The ratio b/a represents the depth ratio of the wells, and its decrease changes the bistable state into a monostable one (in this case, at the threshold value of 0.25).

Kelso has used this model to predict many of the behaviors (critical fluctuations, critical slowing-down,[9] etc.) manifested in a self-organizing dynamical system, and has verified these predictions in experiment. He has also applied the model to other limb motions. More recently, others have used HKB to model and to make predictions about other phenomena such as the rhythmic behavior in speech (Kaipainen and Port 2001).

In sum, the HKB model seems to fulfill some of the typical expectations of a scientific model – it predicts, formalizes, generalizes, and so on. Furthermore, as Chemero (2000) has argued, it suggests a general strategy for providing mathematical and dynamical explanations of behavior – namely:

- first, observe patterns of macroscopic behavior.
- then look for collective variables (like relative phase) and control parameters (like rate) that govern the behavio.
- finally, search for the simplest mathematical function that accounts for the behavior.

This strategy might be therefore claimed to constitute the core of a mathematical approach to the study of mind and behavior. This, as we shall see, is indeed the claim put forth by the strongest advocates of the dynamical approach (van Gelder 1998).

Such a proposal may elicit a number of doubts on the part of a skeptic – for instance:

- finger-wagging is a "low-level" behavior, and it is not clear (indeed, it is very unlikely) that the above strategy would apply to "high-level" behaviors such as reasoning, planning, remembering, and so on.
- models such as HKB are mere descriptions, not explanations: they do not tell us *how* a system works.
- the variables (such as V) in dynamical models of behavior are devoid of meaning; they do not refer to any specific object or quantity in the outside world.

Let us call these, respectively, the questions of "level," "adequacy," and "reference." To counter the "level" criticism, the advocates of the dynamical approach have introduced models of high-level behaviors – for example, a dynamical model of decision-making called "Decision Field Theory" (DFT). Although DFT is, by and large, a psychological model of decision making having little to do with AI, it is nonetheless of considerable importance in the dynamical approach, and so I would like to introduce it briefly here before considering the other objections.

A Mathematical Model of Decision Making

Decision Field Theory (DFT), developed by Townsend and Busemeyer (1995), is a dynamical model that deals with decision processes in human beings. Unlike traditional models of decision making, which are often under the influence of the classical *expected utility* model, DFT seeks to describe how preference states evolve over time by incorporating gross factors such as the anticipated values of different choices. According to the classical utility model, people make decisions by assigning utility values and expectations (probabilities) to each possible outcome of a decision, and by comparing the weighted sum of the values. For instance, if you need to travel between Boston and New York, and want to decide among car, train, or air travel on the basis of time, cost, comfort, and risk, what you supposedly do is to assign values to these factors, and weigh them by their respective probabilities (of flight delay or traffic jam, for instance; or of chances of collision, terrorist attack, etc.). This gives you an overall utility figure for each alternative, the comparison among which would lead to a decision.

The main features of utility-based models are their being: (i) *static*, in that they assume that the preferences do not vary with time; and (ii) *deterministic*, in that they assume a simple binary relation between actions and utilities ("either this, or that"). From a psychological point of view, what is missing in these models, Townsend and Busemeyer suggest, is the deliberation *process* often involved in a real situation: Planning for a trip from Boston to New York, for instance, one might initially think that traveling by car is the right thing to do; the next day, a friend reminds one of the heavy traffic jams around New York; later, one hears bad news about gasoline prices; and so on.

Townsend and Busemeyer (1995) proposed the DFT model as a remedy to these problems. Unlike the classical utility models, DFT assumes that deliberation is both *dynamic* and *stochastic*. That is, it views motivations, preferences, and consequences of actions as functions of time, and it assumes that behaviors and actions emerge as a result of the stochastic processing of pressures coming from different directions. Like the HKB model, DFT uses differential equations to show how the combined effect of motivations and preferences lead a decision maker toward a stable state that triggers a specific action.

The analogies to physical quantities such as position, movement, and approach/avoidance, which are at the heart of this model, make it difficult to differentiate between its metaphorical and literal aspects. Most commentaries on DFT also limit themselves to the kinds of explanations afforded by this model, and stop short of discussing the significance of the metaphorical language employed in its elaboration (see Clark 1997: 124–5, van Gelder 1998: 616, and Chemero 2000). Clark, for instance, mentions the generalizations, explanations, and predictions that fall out of "the specific equations they use to model the evolution of the chosen parameters and variables over time" (1997: 124). He further observes that DFT "provides a vocabulary and a level of analysis well suited to capturing patterns in the temporally evolving behavior of intact well-functioning agents," but he does not comment on how this vocabulary relates to the decision processes that are observed in human beings.

Dynamicists, on the other hand, point to DFT to counter the "level" critique – namely, the claim that dynamical models are suitable only for explaining low-level behaviors. But the creators of DFT do not seem to make such claims. They explicitly point out that DFT is not a full model of decision making, and the physical analogies of their model demonstrate that their goal, far from the replacement of all high-level models of decision making, is intended merely to capture the temporal processes that give rise to decisions. Given that these authors also do not discuss the meaning of the physical analogies, that leaves unresolved the question of the adequacy of the dynamical systems approach for high-levels types of behavior.

Having seen HKB and DFT as two popular models that use the dynamical systems theory to study (low- and high-) level human behavior, we can now examine the issues that surround DST more closely.

DYNAMICAL SYSTEMS THEORY: ITS DEFENDERS AND THEIR CRITICS

Dynamical systems theory (DST), as was explained earlier, provides a qualitative method for the study of systems. In AI and cognitive science, two contrasting views seem to have emerged about the potentials and capabilities of this method – namely, radical advocacy and moderate corroboration. In some interpretations, the radical view takes the form of an ideology that might be called "dynamicism" (see note 1).

Radicals: The Dynamical Systems Theory as an Ideology

Radical dynamicists, in my definition, are those who are not content with portraying the dynamical approach as being suited to one limited facet of cognition, or as one among a number of theories contributing to a full understanding of cognition. Rather, they advocate the wholesale replacement of all talk of computation and representation by the language of geometry and dynamical systems (van Gelder 1998; cf. Clark 1997: 101). Van Gelder (1998), for instance, introduces what he calls the "Dynamical Hypothesis in Cognitive Science" as a contender for "the status of the 'law of quantitative structure' concerning the nature of cognition" (615).[10] He compares and contrasts his Dynamical Hypothesis with what he calls the "Computational Hypothesis," which he characterizes as having four major components: (i) digital variables and states; (ii) discrete and ordered time; (iii) algorithmic behavior; and (iv) semantic interpretation.[11] While the emphasis in computational approaches, van Gelder claims, is on structures that transform according to rules, the dynamical perspective emphasizes change, geometry, timing, etc., as well as the quantitative nature of these features. In his conception, a system is dynamical to the extent that it is quantitative in terms of state, time, or the rate of change of state with time (619).[12]

Skeptics: The Dynamical Approach as Fundamentally Inadequate

Earlier, I outlined three possible criticisms of the dynamical approach – namely, what I called the "level," "adequacy," and "reference" critiques. The "level" criticism, as we saw, is not quite handled by the introduction of a model such as Decision Field Theory. Let us now examine the second criticism – namely, the one that challenges the adequacy of the dynamical approach as a scientific tool for the study of cognition. This is usually stated as the argument that dynamical models are "descriptive" and not "explanatory." This distinction calls for a technical discussion in the philosophy of science that I cannot enter into here, so let me approximate it by offering an example. Suppose that you have not seen lasers and want to learn about them, so you ask a friend, and, depending on how you phrase your question and how they interpret it, you might get any one of the following answers (for the sake of exposition, I am assuming a gas laser):

1. A laser is a device that produces coherent electromagnetic radiation.
2. A laser works by the stimulation of radiation in the following way: You excite the molecules in a medium from their ground state to a higher energy level by injecting energy into the medium, and the molecules, in decaying back to their original level all in phase, return the energy in the form of radiation.
3. A laser is an oblong cavity filled with a gas, enclosed by two mirrors on both ends, and equipped with an energy source.

These are very terse descriptions, but hopefully they convey my point – namely, that they constitute different types of answers to different types of questions. The first one simply says ("describes") *what* a laser is, the second one tells us ("explains") *how* a laser works, and the third says ("explains") *how* to build a laser. Therefore, the first one could be called a "description", and the other two "explanations." In this case, answer (2) is (the beginning of) a "mechanistic" explanation that takes for granted both atomistic theories of matter (a gas is made of molecules) and the laws of quantum mechanics (energy levels are discrete), and answer (3) is (the beginning of) what I, following Clark (1997), am going to call a "componential" explanation, in a sense that is very familiar in AI and cognitive science. Properly understood, this kind of explanation provides a decomposition of a system in terms of functional components and how they interact and cooperate in giving rise to an overall behavior.

Given this distinction between "descriptions" and different types of "explanation," what the critics charge is that the dynamical approach fails to provide componential explanations of the kind that is of interest to AI and cognitive science. In other words, they argue that one cannot build an AI system by simply adopting a dynamical perspective; more is needed. This debate, I argue, is a manifestation of the tension between scientific and engineering aspects of AI. Before examining it from this perspective, however, let me expand the debate a bit further.

Moderates: Dynamical Systems Theory as a Supplement

A majority of scientists who have adopted dynamical systems theory as their framework consider it superior to other approaches, but they do not see it in opposition to those approaches. Townsend and Busemeyer, who created decision field theory as a dynamical model of decision making, for instance, reject the claim that "static theories are irrelevant to the understanding of human decision-making" (1995).

The relation between dynamical and computational approaches, according to conciliatory views such as these, is often a division of labor between two modes of analysis that inform each other, each one explaining certain aspects of a phenomena and leaving the rest to the rival theory. A parallel in physics is provided by the complementary theories of light: the wave theory and the corpuscular theory. Someone with a similar view in physics, then, would argue that the two theories actually supplement each other, and are therefore both needed for our full understanding of the nature of light.

Such is the spirit of the position that Dietrich and Markman (1998) advocate. Instead of physics, however, they use an analogy with biology in which Darwinians and Mendelians, "rather than cooperating, battled it out for whose theory would win in the contest to explain the emergence of new species" (637). After nearly thirty years of pointless wrangling, the authors report, biologists realized that "Mendelian genetics and Darwinian natural selection actually needed each other, and that both were true, being explanations at different levels" (ibid.). In order to avoid a similar fate in cognitive science, Dietrich and Markman propose a kind of compromise, according to which "the dynamical approach is best for *some* of the sensory and motor functions, especially those with tight feedback loops, whereas the computational approach is best for higher cognitive processes as well as some perceptual – motor processes" (ibid.).

Mitchell (1998: 645), building on a similar analogy with the selectionist/structuralist debate in evolutionary biology, recommends "rapprochements between theories of change and theories of structure" in cognitive science, and provides as an example of such an attempt the work done on "complexity" at the Santa Fe Institute (discussed later in this chapter). Similar views are presented in Clark (1997) and Bechtel (1998). These authors compare dynamical descriptions with other forms of explanation, which, they believe, complement dynamicism in affording us a fuller understanding of the many aspects of cognition.

In short, as these examples indicate, there is a trend in AI and cognitive science to accord the dynamical perspective a significant role in the study of the mind. However, as we will see in the next section, there are also critiques that seem far less reconcilable with dynamical systems theory.

SCIENCE OR ENGINEERING: THE SAME OLD TENSION

The point of the "adequacy" critique, as we saw, is that the dynamical approach fails to provide recipes for *how* to build cognitive systems. Cognitive scientists are accustomed to a particular kind of explanation, which is variously called "mechanistic" (Bechtel and Richardson 1992), "componential" (Clark 1997) or, probably more widely, "functional" (Putnam 1975) – that is, one that breaks the system up into component parts and assigns functions to them. Such an explanation makes it possible to build a system from the ground up. This is what renders this type of explanation appealing to people in AI, who tend to think of their job as that of building working models and systems, but also to cognitive scientists who generally subscribe to this kind of explanation.

For someone with such a viewpoint, descriptions are just that – descriptions: they do not tell you how to build systems, and that is why cognitive scientists tend to be dismissive of descriptive accounts as being non-scientific or essentially inadequate. Clark (1997) articulates this deficiency of "pure" dynamical systems in the following way:

[T]hese pure models do not speak to the interests of the engineer. The engineer wants to know how to build systems that exhibit mind-like properties, and, in particular, how the overall dynamics so nicely displayed by the pure accounts actually arise as a result of the microdynamics of various components and sub-systems. (1997: 120)

The HKB model, for instance, provides a differential equation for the change of some quantity V in terms of the phase angle Φ and the ratio a/b. It does not tell the engineer how to build a system that exhibits the finger-wagging behavior. This, I suggest, is another manifestation of the main tension of AI proposed in this study, a tension that seems to evade resolution despite the best intentions and efforts of people like Clark to effect a compromise between different approaches. To see why it is difficult to make a genuine compromise, let us take a look at a robotic model inspired by the dynamical approach.

A Robot Avoids Obstacles: Engineering Prevails

Think of an automatic door in a supermarket. The door has a pad in front to detect a person approaching it, and a pad to the rear to hold it open until the person is all the way through, and also to make sure that the door does not strike someone standing behind it (assuming that the door is a swinging, not sliding, type). The part that controls the operation of the door, the controller, has two states: OPEN and CLOSED, representing the corresponding condition of the door (see the state diagram in Figure 7.3). As is shown in the figure, there are also four possible outside conditions: FRONT (a person on the front pad), REAR (a person on the rear pad), BOTH (people on both sides), and NEITHER (no one on either side). At any given moment, the state of the controller depends on its previous state and the input from the environment. For example, starting in the CLOSED state, if the input is FRONT, the state changes to OPEN, but if the input is BOTH it stays in CLOSED. This type of controller is a *finite-state automaton* – a computer with, in this case, a single bit of memory (one bit is enough for representing two states). Controllers for other devices, such as an elevator or a washing machine, need larger memories, but they are still finite-state automata working on similar principles.

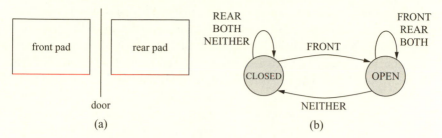

Figure 7.3. (a) an automatic door; and (b) a state diagram for its controller.

Now, assume that you want to build a robot that moves toward a specific object, say a desk. This may, in fact, need a simple controller, not very different from that of the automatic door. Assume that you somehow manage to represent the desk with a small number of bits in the robot's memory (in the ideal case of a world with only desks, even one bit would be enough), equip the robot with a camera and a motor, plug it in, and let it loose. A finite-state automaton with three states can easily perform this task (see Figure 7.4). If there is a desk present, the robot detects it, the memory bit representing the desk is turned on, the robot moves to the desk, the state changes to SUCCESS, and the robot has finished. If not, it keeps looking for a desk until it finds one; if it does not find one, it transits to the FAILURE state.

Bajscy and Large (1999) have built robots on these principles. One of their robots is equipped with a stereo camera pair used for obstacle detection,

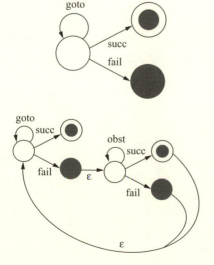

Figure 7.4. The schematic of a finite-state automaton for a simple navigation robot (from Bajscy and Large 1999, with permission).

a third camera mounted on a turntable for tracking objects, and several computers used for processing sensory signals, generating control signals, and making decisions. The job of the controller is to transform visual input into control signals, and this is done by using differential equations that describe the rate of change of behavioral variables, such as heading direction and velocity.

According to Bajscy and Large, the behavior of the robot is controlled by the configuration of attractors and repellors – desired actions (such as moving toward a target) are attractors, and undesired actions (such as moving toward an obstacle) are repellors. The dynamical mode of operation, according to the authors, makes for a smooth coupling between the robot and the environment. For example, if a target moves, the location of the corresponding attractor will move as well; or if a new obstacle comes into view, a repellor forms where there was none before. In this way, the robot's perceptions and actions are closely coupled with environmental features (such as obstacles and targets), and all are incorporated into a single set of differential equations. The integrated treatment of the system and the environment is a positive feature of the dynamical approach that is manifested in this example.

In the case of this simple behavior, the objection that dynamical descriptions cannot contribute to design seems to be defeated. The robot does, in fact, operate successfully on the basis of dynamical principles. But how about more complex behaviors, which need many perception–action loops and which involve more complex environments? As we shall see, much more needs to be done in order for a system to function under such circumstances.

A Robot Makes a Decision: Science Prevails

Despite the level of flexibility observed so far, the dynamical system of the robot can model only one simple perception–action behavior at a time, whereas complex tasks typically involve sequences of behaviors. This happens if, for example, the robot needs to pick up an object x and then move toward a target, in which case another perception–action loop would be required. Dropping x at the target and returning to the original starting point would require yet another loop, picking a second object y on the way back yet another loop, and so on. In short, as things start to get more complex, more and more loops come into the picture, and the utility and applicability of the dynamical formulation becomes increasingly dubious and problematic. To see why, let us follow Bajscy and Large in their effort to add one more loop to the previous one. Interestingly, they have done this in two ways – the old symbolic way, and the dynamical way – and this provides us with a chance to directly compare symbolic and dynamical approaches.

The symbolic system basically involves a finite-state automaton of the type we described for the automatic door, where individual states at the upper, so-called *symbol* level (i.e., the level at which the robot "decides" what to do next), correspond to elementary behaviors at the lower signal level (i.e., the level at which electrical current flows in the control circuitry of the robot) – therefore, the authors call it a *discrete-event system*. The idea here is to have "atoms" of behavior, such as GoTo (a target) or ESCAPE (from an obstacle), which can be compounded into more complex behaviors such as navigation.

In the *competitive dynamic system*, on the other hand, both signal-level control and symbol-level decisions are modeled using differential equations. The major difference with the discrete-event system is that, according to the authors, "Rather than defining multiple elementary perception–action behaviors, a single master equation is defined containing all possible task constraints" (ibid.). The outcome is a close mutual coupling between the two levels of the system – each variable at the symbol level controls the weight of a task constraint at the signal level, in such a way that the upper-level system can activate and deactivate the contributions of attractors and repellors to the behavior, "synthesizing control laws on the fly" (63).

The authors provide a "bifurcation diagram" to explain the above behavior. Such a bifurcation diagram could, in fact, be helpful as a visualization tool in understanding the behavior of the robot.[13] As such, it might also be a valuable design tool for the engineer, as it seems to have been to Bajscy and Large. As valuable as this might be, however, this visual and technical utility is limited to low-dimensional (typically three-dimensional) cases. An increase in the number of dimensions would make the diagram unusable for a human, because our intuitive geometric understanding breaks down after a certain point. This problem of scaling and tractability, which is one of the major challenges that the dynamical systems approach faces, is one of the roots of the skepticism about the contribution of the dynamical approach to the building of systems – whence, the "adequacy" critique (cf. Clark 1997: 101).

In sum, although it seems that the description-not-explanation criticism breaks down in very simple cases such as Bajscy and Large's robot, it retains its force when we move on to more realistic situations. The simple robotic model, however, faces another major problem, which is reflected in the "reference" critique of the dynamical approach.

The Question of Reference

After testing a number of increasingly complex systems, Bajscy and Large reported that the dynamic ones "perform tasks faster and more reliably," whereas the discrete ones "obey task constraints more faithfully, reluctant to relax constraints regardless of environmental complexity" (64). They attribute these differences to the "the model of decision making" (which seems, in essence, to be similar to the Decision Field Theory model introduced earlier), and to the fact that the dynamic system changes state less frequently, especially in the face of noisy sensor readings. Despite these advantages, the authors discard radical interpretations of the potentials of the dynamical approach, and basically arrive at a conclusion that is now familiar to us from our studies in the previous chapters:

Intelligent agents must be capable of bringing to bear a rich variety of perception–action strategies but, at the same time, reasoning and solving problems to perform familiar and unfamiliar tasks in novel environments. (Bajscy and Large 1999: 64)

Put as a criticism, this statement would take the familiar form of the argument that what makes something (e.g., the human mind) cognitive is its ability to interact *meaningfully* with the world – that is, its ability to have a semantic interpretation of its environment. The dynamical perspective, it is often argued, fails to capture this characteristic feature of cognitive systems. Thus, even if the dynamical approach could deal more effectively than traditional AI with some aspects of cognition – such as interactive physical relations with the environment – it fails, the argument goes, to capture this crucial aspect of cognition. Dennett (1998: 637) eloquently articulates this point:

[B]oth good, working cognitive systems (brains) and defective, hallucinating cognitive systems are dynamical systems. . . . Similarly, both a trained acrobat at his best and a drunk lurching down the road bumping into things are dynamical systems. You cannot begin to explain why some dynamical systems have evolved and others, just as dynamical, have not, until you introduce informational (or semantic) considerations of some sort that let you distinguish between when an animal is getting it (roughly) right and when it is getting it wrong.

Dennett here raises a very serious objection. The question, as always, is how to introduce *semantic* considerations into AI systems, whether they are described in dynamical terms or in some other language. As Bajscy and Large point out, the question is "how to integrate models of perception–action behavior with models of problem-solving behavior" (ibid.). To this question nobody has offered an answer. What we have instead are question-begging replies such as the following:

The quantities invoked in dynamical accounts often differ fundamentally from ordinary physical quantities. "Valence" and "preference" [of Decision Field Theory], for example, do not appear in textbooks of mechanics. (van Gelder 1998: 620)

Such answers obviously do not tell us what the variables and quantities in dynamical models of human behavior mean; they just tell us what they are *not* – namely, that they are not the same as physical quantities. One way of avoiding such answers, I submit, given the little that, despite so many decades of psychology, we still know about the human mind (and given the state of the art in mathematics), is basically to give up on the Humean Dream of "mathematizing" psychology, and to aim for a more realistic option. Such an attitude, I believe, is perfectly compatible with the origins of dynamical systems theory as formulated by Poincaré.

RECONSIDERING THE DYNAMICAL APPROACH

The aim of science is not things themselves, as the dogmatists in their simplicity imagine, but the relations between things; outside those relations there is no reality knowable. (Poincaré 1905/1952: xxiv)

As mentioned earlier, Henri Poincaré was the originator of dynamical systems theory, and he also made other significant contributions to science and the philosophy of science – for example, to the theory of special relativity in physics and to group theory in geometry. Many of his ideas were, as a matter of fact, absorbed by logical positivists and incorporated into their systems (Friedman 1999). In particular, he had a remarkable view of science that has come to be known as "conventionalism." Dynamical Systems Theory could arguably be viewed, and is probably best understood, as just one element in the bigger cluster of ideas due to Poincaré. It would be reasonable, therefore, to revisit the dynamical approach in this light, and to see what Poincaré has to say about the relation of sciences to each other, especially given that many advocates of the dynamical approach seem to be supportive of his views (van Gelder (1998: 621), for instance, nominates Poincaré as "the Newton of the mind").

In Poincaré's view, scientific thinking (and, one may add, all thinking) is a process in which the mind projects structure onto the world in order to extract empirical laws (patterns) from it. The sciences, according to this picture, are tied together like the links in a chain, where each link presupposes all the ones preceding it. However, unlike the more common hierarchical and reductionist accounts of science (e.g., Hempel and Oppenheim 1949), this structure does not rest on the foundation of physics. Rather, it is a *conceptual* structure that relates different domains of human knowledge, where no single domain (e.g., physics) attains ontological priority over others – a relationship among "equals," so to speak. This non-reductionist character makes

Poincaré's view appealing to dynamical theorists, who are inclined toward multilevel explanations.[14] More important, however, are the differences that Poincaré observes between different sciences in terms of the role of intuition and experiment. Let us examine this further.

Poincaré's account of science stops at experimental physics, and does not move on to, for instance, psychology, despite the fact that he was deeply interested in cognition, and despite the fact that many of his contemporaries (most notably Ernst Mach) insisted on including psychology in their accounts of science. We do not know why Poincaré excluded psychology from his account of science, and venturing a guess would be precarious. However, one point is definite in his thinking: a science of the mind should be built on a model that best suits its subject matter, which consists, I think, in intelligent behavior in its many different manifestations. Notwithstanding some overly ambitious claims about having a "unified theory of cognition" (Newell 1990), it turns out, nobody is in possession of such a theory. This does not imply, of course, that we have to give up on the goal of understanding cognition and intelligent behavior. Nor does it imply that there are no lessons to be learned from other disciplines. What should be given up is the idea of having a "quick-and-dirty" unified theory built on the model of physics, biology, and so on.[15]

There are alternative approaches, both within and outside psychology, that are reminiscent in spirit of the dynamical approach, but that are not in any sense committed to a specific mathematical formalism such as differential equations. These approaches take *complexity* as the distinctive feature that makes cognitive systems similar to other heterogeneous, multilevel adaptive systems. As the following discussion shows, the study of cognition from the perspective of complexity reveals some of the key aspects of cognitive systems, and may help give rise to a more genuine science of mind.

Cognition as Complexity

Much is said and heard about complexity these days: its ubiquity, its importance, and its elusive nature. In fact, the harnessing of complexity has been a recurring theme and challenge in all of the approaches that we have examined so far – from the staggering computations of Deep Blue through the millions of assertions of Cyc to the vast number of nodes, connections, and training cycles of connectionist networks. In the present chapter, we also faced complexity when discussing self-organizing systems such as the regeneration of cells in living organisms, the distribution of goods in big cities, and the formation of patterns in boiling oil.

Traditionally, in order to study complex phenomena, scientists have broken them up into more elementary phenomena, and there are, roughly speaking, three different ways of doing so: in time, in space, or into constitutive components. This method of decomposition is based on a number of simplifying assumptions, such as, for instance, that the system is homogeneous – that is, it is made up of roughly identical particles. Take the propagation of heat in a gas, for example, where it is assumed that each molecule interacts with its neighbors through collisions whose details are hidden from us. But this does not matter; all that matters is that the effects average out, and that all differences are leveled thanks to the homogeneous composition of the gas. As Poincaré said, the reason "why in physical science generalization so readily takes the mathematical form is because the observable phenomenon is due to the superposition of a large number of elementary phenomena which are *all similar to each other*" (1952: 158; original emphasis).

The other simplifying assumption in the traditional treatments of complexity is that phenomena are considered "ahistorical." Thus, instead of studying the entire temporal trajectory of a phenomenon as a whole, scientists connect each moment solely with the moment immediately preceding it. They assume that the present state of the world depends solely on the *immediate* past, without being directly influenced by the recollection of a more distant past, or by its history, so to speak. This assumption allows physicists to write down a system of differential equations, instead of studying the whole phenomenon over all of time. This is, for instance, what made it possible to replace the global laws of Kepler by the local laws of Newton. Having painstakingly tabulated the position of the planets for long stretches of time, Kepler discovered that they follow an elliptical path around the sun. Newton, on the other hand, formulated the motions of the planets in differential equations that captured the local change of position and he was, therefore, able to predict future states. It is this kind of purely local formulation that makes it possible for us to model a three-body gravitational problem to any desired degree of accuracy, despite the fact that no closed-form solution exists for this problem.

The question that we are presently faced with is whether a similar decomposition strategy will work for cognitive systems without distorting their essential character. In other words, are cognitive systems (e.g., brains) also homogeneous and ahistorical? These, I believe, are crucial questions for cognitive scientists to answer, and fortunately, a good fraction of the research at centers such as the Santa Fe Institute and the Argonne National Laboratory can be understood as dealing with these questions. John Holland's account of complex adaptive systems, to which I have alluded before, is an example of such work.

Heterogeneity of Components

Drawing on examples of systems in genetics, ecology, neuroscience, economics, and so on, Holland has shown how these systems, despite differences in other respects, exhibit great similarity in their patterns of behavior and in the mechanisms that they employ for adaptation. He lists seven basic commonalities among complex adaptive systems, among which are the emergence of complex large-scale behaviors from the aggregate interactions of less complex agents, the prevalence of nonlinearity, and the possession of special mechanisms for anticipation. The objective of work on complex adaptive systems, Holland believes, is "to uncover general principles that will enable us to synthesize complex adaptive systems' behaviors from simple laws" (1995: 38).

One such principle, in Holland's view, is "diversity" of the components, as opposed to the homogeneity of, for instance, the atoms in a gas or the nodes in today's connectionist networks. One implication of this principle is that systems with heterogeneous components may not be easily amenable to mathematical formalisms such as differential equations. Holland, in fact, considers the use of partial differential equations unnecessary, and believes that "a move toward computer-based models that are directly described, rather than PDE-derived, will give handsome results in the study of complex adaptive systems." Such models, he further notes, "offer the possibility of controlled experiments that can suggest both guidelines for examining real organizational processes and guidelines for mathematical abstractions of organizational dynamics" (124–25). Other researchers, of more formal persuasion, have arrived at similar conclusions about the limitations of present mathematical formalisms such as differential equations (Petitot et al. 1999, Introduction; Axelrod and Tesfatsion 2007).

The Historicity of Social Life

As with homogeneity, it is not obvious that the assumption of ahistoricity holds in cognitive phenomena in any serious sense of the word. In fact, there are reasons to believe the contrary. The notion that the state of a cognitive system like the human mind – however we define a "state" – should depend only on its immediate preceding state is rooted in purely *physical* conceptions of such phenomena as "memory," "remembering," and so on. Indeed, a brain, being a physical system, *can* be understood as evolving from one split second to the next. However, cognition, *psychologically* understood, takes place in individual minds, and an individual mind is the culmination of a unique personal history of interactions within a social and cultural background. Therefore, if we jump from the *physics* view of a brain (a collection of particles) to the *psychological* view of a mind (a collection of concepts, thoughts, images, memories, etc.), then the split-second-by-split-second view might not be very helpful. In order to understand a mind, one might need to go beyond recent happenings.

This idea of "historicity" involves a more radical claim than the idea of "path-dependence" often underscored by dynamical theorists. Clark (1997) has articulated the latter notion as follows:

Human learning . . . appears to be hostage to at least some degree of path dependence. Certain ideas can be understood only once others are in place . . . you can't get everywhere from anywhere, and where you are now strongly constrains your potential future intellectual trajectories. (1997: 205)

Clark notes, however, that this basic form of path-dependence finds much more complex and intricate forms in human beings because of language and the social dimension that it adds to human cognition. Language and social life make it possible for individual human beings to share the experience of others, going beyond the paths formed in their own experience. This capability renders human behavior unpredictable, making it perilous to predict its future development.

In sum, the differences between cognition and the phenomena traditionally studied in physics and other more basic sciences are of such depth and import that we should be highly suspicious of attempts at building psychology on the model of physical sciences. The most important of such differences, from the perspective of complexity, as I have suggested here, are the diversity of the constitutive components of cognitive systems and the historical character of cognition (as manifested in culture and language). These differences suggest that we might need to take a fresh look at the Humean Dream.

Revisiting Hume: Generative Explanations

The properties of heterogeneity and historicity are not unique to cognitive systems; they are also common in social systems. The social sciences seek to understand how the interaction of many individuals leads to large-scale outcomes (Axelrod and Tesfatsion 2007). To explain macroscopic regularities such as social norms, institutions, and political systems they try to figure out how the autonomous local interactions of heterogeneous agents generate the given regularity (Epstein 2005: 1). Traditionally, social scientists approached this question by gathering qualitative data from interviews, observations, and surveys or by conducting studies that use quantitative data. While these methods can illustrate effectively the emergence of regularities, they are rather limited by the static nature of their data and by the inevitably impressionistic character of their analyses (Gilbert 2004).

Computer simulations provide a useful way to overcome these limitations and to develop models of high clarity and precision. By making it necessary to think through one's basic assumptions, simulations force the analyst to specify every parameter and every relationship in an exact manner, also allowing others to inspect the model in great detail (ibid.). One approach to implementing computer simulations is called "Agent-Based Modeling." This approach conceives complex systems as a set of agents that interact and adapt to changing environments. Starting with a description or theory of individual agents, it seeks to formulate rules of behavior that can be captured in computer programs. Based on these rules, the simulation can then be used to study the behavior of a system as a whole – that is, of how the system could evolve in time.[16]

In this fashion, agent-based models play a similar role in the social sciences to that of mathematics in the physical sciences (Gilbert and Troitzsch 2005: 5). Rather than providing mathematical models, however, what they do is to provide "generative explanations" of phenomena. To explain a pattern, a model shows "how a population of cognitively plausible agents, interacting under plausible rules, could actually arrive at the pattern on time scales of interest" (Epstein 2005: 1). The motto, in other words, is: *If you didn't grow it, you didn't explain it* (ibid.). The impact of AI-style of thinking is evident in this motto. It seems that we have come back full circle to a situation where AI practitioners can learn from techniques to which AI itself has made key contributions.

CONCLUSION: WHO IS DOING GOOD SCIENCE?

The philosopher Hilary Putnam once denounced the functionalist hypothesis in cognitive science (to which he had previously subscribed) as an illusory dream of a "Psychological Physics" – "the dream of laws and concepts as rigorous as those of physics" (1990: 41). Putnam's criticism may not be quite on target, because explanations in cognitive science can perfectly well be *not* modeled on foundations of physics (cf. Bechtel and Richardson 1992, Haugeland 1997). But Putnam's criticism nonetheless hits upon scientists' deep-rooted belief in special kinds of explanations that could be broadly called "formal" or "mathematical." This belief is, in turn, based on a number of age-old convictions about "good science" and "bad science." Good science, according to these convictions, is general, universal, law-based, and formal. Bad science, by contrast, lacks one or more of these attributes – that is, it is particular, local, lawless, or non-formal, or a combination of these. Many of the debates that one sees in less mature sciences (such as AI and cognitive science) boil down to the question of who is actually doing good science in the above sense.

What We Have Learned *About* the Dynamical Approach: Formality Versus Generality

> Mathematics, rightly viewed, possesses not only truth, but supreme beauty – a beauty cold and austere, like that of sculpture, without appeal to any part of our weaker nature, without the gorgeous trappings of painting or music, yet sublimely pure, and capable of a stern perfection such as only the greatest art can show.
>
> – Bertrand Russell (1957)

The problem with the above debates is not only their black-and-white character (general versus particular, universal versus local, etc.), which is often too simplistic to reflect the subtleties of the natural order, it is also that they are built on deep conceptual conflations. One such conflation is between generality and formality – that is, in the presupposition that to be general is to be formal. Formalists (who believe in the indispensability of mathematics for good science) will insist that science is impossible without generalization. From this premise, however, they leap to the conclusion that, because mathematics is our best generalizing tool, it is imperative to apply mathematics as extensively as possible to all types of phenomena. The power of mathematics, as Russell seems to suggest in the earlier excerpt, is its ability to harness our unruly and fallible intuitions and to turn them into rigorous models and theories. It does this, formalists argue, by forcing us to make our assumptions explicit, to prune spurious elements, and to focus our attention solely on relevant components.[17] Poincaré, who was, of course, a great mathematician, agreed with this: "Every generalization is a hypothesis.... By the precision which is characteristic [of mathematical physics], we are compelled to formulate all the hypotheses that we would unhesitatingly make without its aid" (1952: 150–51).

While mathematics is certainly a generalizing tool, the converse does not in any way follow. That is, it does not follow that mathematics is the *only* way to generalize. The work of John Holland demonstrates this point clearly. Holland, as we saw, is in search of general principles and properties for complex adaptive systems, but he does not draw solely on mathematics, partly because he finds the existing mathematical formalisms inadequate for his purposes, and partly because he finds the methods of computer simulation more effective and useful. These methods are recently adopted and expanded by such approaches as agent-based modeling, which provide "electronic laboratories" for multilevel explanations. Of course, there are also limits to what these methods can offer. As Epstein (2005: 5) has argued, a simulation is not a sufficient condition for explanation – merely to generate is not necessarily to explain. The usefulness of these method "resides in the far-reaching generative power of [their] simple micro-rules, seemingly remote from the elaborate macro patterns they produce" (ibid.: 18).

What We Have Learned *from* the Dynamical Approach: Theory Versus Subject Matter

This last point about computational methods points to another conflation that is made by some advocates of the dynamical approach: that between the theory of computing and the phenomenon of computing. This is best illustrated by the sharp contrast sometimes drawn between computers and dynamical systems (van Gelder 1998). The claim, as we have seen, is that computers are *not* dynamical systems because they have discrete states, time, and so on. As a matter of fact, however, it is the *theories* of computers that describe them as discrete by making abstractions from certain features (such as continuous voltages and currents, for instance). The failure to notice this difference between computing and its theories, it seems, is at the root of many unnecessary contentions between dynamicists and their opponents. The point is not whether computers, as physical systems, are or are not dynamical systems; it is whether the discrete approximations made in theories of computers are adequate for describing those dynamical systems. The history of science has shown that discrete systems can approximate continuous ones so well that the *in-principle* distinction between discrete and continuous becomes irrelevant for most practical purposes. Whether or not the same is true of cognitive systems is a question that needs to be answered by looking through the appropriate lens – e.g., through the study of the nature of "digitality" and digital phenomena (Lewis 1971; Goodman 1976; Haugeland 1981; Smith 2000).

Conflations such as this – between formality and generality, and between theory and subject matter – drive many a dynamicist, I believe, to seek to do what seems to be impossible: to materialize the Humean Dream of putting mathematical garb on thought and cognition. In the dynamical approach, this has led to an exaggerated focus on low-level behaviors or the ignoring of crucial attributes of cognitive systems – for example, the heterogeneity of components, historical path-dependence, and, most importantly, their meaningful (semantics-laden) relation to the world. Staunch defenders of the dynamical approach usually respond by saying that their way of doing things is new in AI and cognitive science, and that, given sufficient time, it will prevail. Notwithstanding the empirical character of this claim, however, the odds seem to be against them. The gulf between the Humean dream and the complex reality is too wide to be bridged by projections such as this.

8   Cog: Neorobotic AI

La Mettrie's Mechanical Dream

Let us conclude bravely that man is a machine; and that there is in the universe only one kind of substance subject to various modifications.

– Julien Offray de la Mettrie: *L'Homme-Machine*

C og is a robot with an upper-torso humanoid body that learns to interact with people through various "senses" (Figure 8.1). It is different[1] in many respects from any other artifact that we have seen so far. In the vocabulary used by its designers, Cog is:

- *embodied* – it has a body (or some fraction thereof) similar to the human body;
- *embedded* – it is "socialized" (in a very minor way);
- *developing* – there is a "baby" version of it, Kismet, that is meant to go through development;
- *integrated* – it is equipped with, and is meant to integrate the data from, the equivalents of various sensory organs.

Furthermore, Cog is different from a typical robot in being "general-purpose" – it is meant to become the dream household robot that could act as a pet, a baby, a servant, and, ultimately, as a companion. "The distinction between us and robots is going to disappear" (Brooks 2002a: 236).

Even this briefest of introductions to Cog seemingly points to a radical departure from everything that has heretofore happened in AI. Classical AI, we should recall, views cognition as *abstract* (physical embodiment is irrelevant), *individual* (the solitary mind is the essential locus of intelligence), *rational* (reasoning is paradigmatic of intelligence), and *detached* (thinking is separated from perception and action) (Smith 1999). Connectionism, having remained committed to most of the above principles, did not mark

Figure 8.1. The robot Cog.

nearly as radical a departure, especially because it did not reject the notion of representation, so central to classical theories of mind. However, neorobotics, which is what the approach behind Cog is called, may be driving AI in a whole new direction – or so its advocates suggest.

The purpose of this chapter is to assess the sweep of this promise. Following a brief history of robots before and after AI, we mull over the four major themes of the Cog project in the list at the beginning of this chapter, and discuss some of the challenges facing the neorobotics approach. Throughout, we will witness how the products of engineering ingenuity combined with AI techniques have introduced into AI both new dimensions and new tensions, without genuinely solving the old tension between the scientific and engineering aspirations of the field.

BACKGROUND: A LOVE FOR MECHANISM

Human beings seem to have been forever fascinated by the idea of building automata – artifacts designed to mimic or replicate the bodily behaviors of animals, especially of human beings. Excavations at the temple of Susa in Persia have uncovered a five-thousand-year-old limestone pig and lion that, pulled by a string, gave the impression of moving autonomously. Ancient Egyptians used statues secretly operated by priests to choose their new pharaoh. Closer to our times, in 1738, Jacques de Vaucanson introduced a flute-playing automaton to the Académie des Sciences that could produce musical sound "in the same way a human would produce it" – that is, by the manipulation of air flow through "mouth," "lips," and "fingers"; and Pierre Jaquet-Droz, a Swiss, "in 1774 . . . created a life-sized and lifelike figure of a boy seated at a desk, capable of writing up to forty letters of the alphabet" (Mazlish 1993).

These inventions caused sensations not only among laypeople but also among natural philosophers of the time, who wondered whether, for example, the automaton was just "mimicking" human beings or was "replicating" them: whether it just appeared human or indeed incorporated the same mechanisms of sound production. Among the hot debates around topics such as these, Julien Offray de la Mettrie, a French physician and materialist philosopher of the eighteenth century, wrote a bold book entitled *L'Homme-machine* ("Man the Machine") to advance his thesis that humans are machines (entities that are mechanical, i.e., fully explicable via the laws governing physical matter). He even argued that if apes could be taught language they would not differ from primitive humans.

Over the past three centuries, these projects, which were aimed at testing the essence of life and intelligence, have transformed our perceptions of both humans and machines (Riskin 2007). Today, we are still grappling with similar questions and issues, not only in the realm of artifacts, but also in our attempt to explain animal behavior.

The Early Robots: Navigating with Maps

> It is difficult to imagine how any system that did not store and retrieve the values of variables and apply to them all of the operations in the system of arithmetic could do sun compass holding, dead reckoning, and the determination of distance from parallax.
>
> – Gallistel (1998)

Social insects possess a rather complex faculty of communication among themselves. Honeybees, for instance, have marvelous methods of communication when they discover a new source of food. A successful forager bee, carrying nectar in its crop and pollen on its leg and body hairs, flies back to the hive and performs a waggle dance in the form of a figure eight. According to some accounts, the waggling part of the dance constitutes the segment common to the two loops of the "8," and its angle with respect to the gravitational vertical equals the angle formed by the hive, the sun's azimuth, and the food source. The number of waggles danced is also believed to be proportional to the distance from the food source. According to these accounts, other foragers that use this "information" to get to the food source repeat the same behavior, informing yet others, and so on and so forth.

The psychologist Charles Gallistel takes this behavior as evidence that the bee can store in its nervous system the value of an "allocentric angle" – that is, an angle that does not have the bee at its apex (1998). Since this angle cannot be directly determined at the point where it is recorded in memory (the food source), Gallistel argues, the bee must *compute* this angle during its foraging flight by its dead-reckoning mechanism.[2] He seeks to explain this, and other similar behaviors in insects such as the digger wasp, ants, locusts, and so on, in terms of "cognitive maps" – that is, learned representations in the nervous system of the animal that mirror the geometry of the terrain.

This same viewpoint underlay early AI projects in robotics, such as Shakey, which we saw in Chapter 5, and SHRDLU, which was briefly mentioned in Chapter 6. SHRDLU was a simulated robot, built at MIT, that operated in a simulated blocks microworld. It was equipped with a graphic interface and a video screen that displayed its operations in a visual manner. Furthermore, it had an impressive (written) language interface through which it not only followed commands given in ordinary English but also answered questions about its "motivations" for doing things in a certain sequence. When asked why it picked up the little pyramid among its blocks, for instance, it replied, "To clear off the red cube." Moreover, it was also able to remember and report its previous actions, such as touching a particular pyramid before putting a particular block on a particular small cube (Crevier 1993).

Shakey and SHRDLU differed in terms of design and capability, but they shared a very fundamental principle: both operated on the basis of an accurate model or representation of their blocks world. Both needed a description of the current situation and of the desired goal (e.g., to collect cans or to arrange blocks in a particular way), a precise plan for how to get from one situation to the other, and a set of rules to carry out that plan. In more realistic situations, this strict dependence on internal representations, preset plans, and precise rules could generate insurmountable problems. Indeed, the analysis of this gave rise to the notorious "frame problem" (see Chapter 4).

To illustrate the frame problem, Dennett (1990) introduces three fictitious robots R_1, R_1D_1, and R_2D_1, each of which is meant to be an improved version of the previous one, but all of which fail because of the same underlying difficulty – namely, the frame problem. These robots are designed to fend for themselves by rescuing their spare battery supply that is on a wagon locked in a room with a time bomb set to go off soon. For each of these robots, Dennett sketches a possible scenario – rather amusing, but sobering – where it would fail. The first robot fails because it "didn't realize that pulling the wagon would bring the bomb out along with the battery," although, ironically, it "*knew* that the bomb was on the wagon in the room" (ibid.: 147). The second robot, which was made "to recognize not just the intended implications of its acts, but also the implications about their side-effects [e.g., carrying the bomb along]", also failed because it spent too much time making all sorts of *irrelevant* deductions about the possible side-effects – for example, "that pulling the wagon out of the room would not change the color of the room's walls" (ibid.). Finally, the third robot, which was even taught "the difference between relevant and irrelevant implications," also failed because it was busy setting aside some thousands of irrelevant implications while the clock was ticking away!

Although Dennett's examples may not represent typical circumstances for either robots or insects, they do demonstrate a core difficulty faced by all early robots: it is impossible for such systems to assume anything that was not explicitly stated and to avoid making irrelevant deductions. And, as we discussed at length in Chapter 4, there are simply too many things going on in the outside world for any intelligent system to state and keep track of explicitly. This key stumbling block, among others, led many researchers in AI to look for radically different approaches.

The New Robots: Navigating Without Maps

> The ability of bees to use the sky as a directional reference, to measure flight distance, and to integrate directions and distance flown means that the radial coordinates of each foraging site within the colony's considerable flight range can be successfully communicated to recruits that have never flown there before. A map-based system, by contrast, would be limited by the extent to which the dancer and the recruit overlap in their experience of the landscape.
>
> – Dyer and Seeley (1989)

The view expressed in this passage is radically different from Gallistel's view about bee foraging. Clancey (1997), who opens the chapter of his book on neorobotics with the same passage, raises the following questions: How are physical coordination and behavior sequencing possible without stored procedures? How is attention possible without words to describe goals and features? Could a robot develop its own criteria for what is interesting and what is an error, so that it is not bound by its designer's ontology? If Dyer and Seeley are correct in their hypothesis, and if there are feasible answers to Clancey's questions, then Gallistel's map-based explanation of bee behavior might be mistaken. In other words, researchers such as Gallistel may be confusing a particular *theory* of how things work with how things *actually* work in the bee world. That is, perhaps such theorists project their own understanding onto the "minds" of the insects. Early AI research, similarly, tried to build the scientists' understanding of possible mechanisms into the programs that controlled the robots – for example, they built robots that could work only by using explicit reasoning mechanisms, and, as with Dennett's fictitious robots, the products were often feeble.

To show that alternative ways of doing things are possible, therefore, many researchers have tried to build robots that do not store maps of the world inside their "brains," but that perform tasks similar to the old robots. Examples abound, and the following is a small sample of such work:

- Toto is a robotic cat that navigates the corridors of an office building without an *a priori* map. It uses a compass and keeps track of its ordered interactions with various landmarks (a wall on the right, a corridor, etc.). The landmarks are used to construct a map that is not explicit; it is part of the robot's mechanism – that is, it builds a set of little local directional cues, but nothing global (Mataric 1992).
- Luc Steels designed a simulated society of robots that cooperate in collecting ore samples. They do this by dropping "electronic breadcrumbs," which self-organize into a path and attract other robots. The core idea is that descriptions of paths are not built into the robot mechanism (Steels 1990).
- Pengi is a simulated robot that plays an arcade video game without a bird's-eye view of its world. It uses indexical descriptions such as "the ice cube that the ice cube I just kicked will collide with" in order to keep track of changes in its world (Agre and Chapman 1987; see also Chapter 5).
- Genghis is a robotic insect that walks toward any moving source of infrared radiation, steers to keep its target in sight, and scrambles over obstacles in its way, all without any internal notion of "toward," "ahead," or "over" (Brooks 2002a; see also Figure 8.2).

These are but a few examples of robots that operate on principles totally different from those of Shakey and SHRDLU. These principles constitute

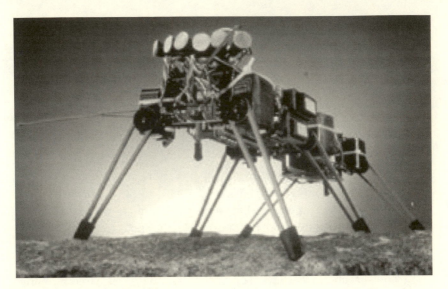

Figure 8.2. The robot Genghis.

what has come to be known as "neorobotics" or "nouvelle AI" (connoting the allegedly novel and minimal character of the new approach, as in "nouvelle cuisine," famous for its spartan portions of food).

NOUVELLE AI

The AI lab at MIT, which until recently was directed by Rodney Brooks, is one of the pioneering sites for neorobotics. In the mid-1980s, vexed by the dilemma that AI tries to build expert physicians and engineers while at the same time failing to build a machine that can tie, so to speak, its own shoes, Brooks (1986, 1991) suggested that AI should aim for the more modest goal of insect-level intelligence. Following what he called an "engineering methodology," Brooks proposed the building of "creatures" that are let loose in the world, that learn to cope with the environment, and that pursue multiple goals. Taking natural evolution as a guide, Brooks argued that high-level behaviors such as language and reasoning "are all pretty simple once the essence of acting and reacting are available" (ibid.). Building on this evolutionary trope, Brooks made an argument that appeals to contemporary sensibilities: It took natural evolution much longer (billions of years) to perfect behaviors having to do with perception and mobility than to develop the capacities of abstract thought and reasoning (millions of years). He even postulated that 97 percent of human activity (whatever such a figure might mean) is concept-free – that is, does not involve concepts of the kind assumed in traditional AI (cf. Kirsh 1991).

Therefore, the first step, according to Brooks, was to turn the tables on the central tenet of both classical and connectionist AI – namely, the idea of representation. Adopting the motto "the world is its own best model," Brooks argued that an intelligent being would be better off taking direct advantage of the information available in the environment than trying to compute and reason using a mental model of the world. The focus of research at MIT thus shifted to a set of new ideas and principles, the most important of which are the following (Brooks 1997: 417; 1999: 165–70):

1. *Situatedness*: A situated creature or robot is one that is embedded in the world, and that does not deal with abstract descriptions (such as logical sentences, plans of action, etc.), but through its sensors with the here and now of the world, which directly influences the behavior of the creature.
2. *Embodiment*: An embodied creature or robot is one that has a physical body and experiences the world, at least in part, directly through the influence of the world on that body.[3]
3. *Intelligence*: Although vague, this is intended to highlight the point that, "Intelligence is determined by the dynamics of interaction with the world" (ibid.). In imitation of natural evolution, AI should focus its efforts on "low-level" intelligence.
4. *Emergence*: Complex behavior should emerge as a result of interactions among simple and primitive tasks and modules: "Intelligence is in the eye of the observer" (ibid.).

Brooks made the case for these ideas at the 1991 International Joint Conference on Artificial Intelligence, where he also won the prestigious Computers and Thought award. Many of these ideas, of course, had parallels and precedents in other places. The emphasis on body and interaction, for instance, goes back to the views of earlier cyberneticists such as Gregory Bateson and Heinz von Foerster and of Continental philosophers such as Heidegger and Merleau-Ponty, and their supporters such as Hubert Dreyfus, and Varela, Thompson, and Rosch (Clancey 1997). Similar ideas were arguably also present in early writings on AI, such as Turing's seminal 1948 paper "Intelligent Machinery" (Brooks 1999: 141). But, for reasons that were sketched in the Prologue, in the early years of AI these ideas did not find as much acceptance as the alternative views of the Boolean-dream ilk. In the hands of the MIT group and other technically minded people, however, not only were these ideas articulated in a new idiom, they were transformed into engineering techniques and artifacts.

The MIT Approach: The Subsumption Architecture

One new technique was based on an idea known as "subsumption architecture." This type of architecture consists of different layers, the states of which indicate what the robot is currently doing – for example, "sensing something in front," "moving to the right," "backing up," or just "walking." Each layer is composed of a network of finite-state machines (see Chapter 7), which communicate by sending numerical messages to each other. A first, *collision-avoidance* layer, for instance, has a finite-state machine called *collide* that simply "watches" (using an ultrasonic signal, for instance) for anything directly ahead, and when something is detected it sends a *halt* message to another finite-state machine in charge of running the robot forward (Brooks 1997: 410). Another layer makes the robot *wander* about, a third layer makes it *explore*, and so on. In this way, each layer forms a complete perception–action loop, built on top of (and "subsuming") previous layers that perform more primitive behavior – whence the name of the architecture.

What makes the subsumption architecture different from traditional designs is that perception and action are tightly coupled in each layer, obviating the need for a central processor to link and control them. In particular, what makes it qualitatively different is that it is based on the decomposition of intelligence into individual modules that can generate complete behaviors, and whose cooperation can give rise to more complex behaviors, as opposed to the decomposition of traditional AI systems into functional modules that could not generate a behavior on their own (Brooks 1999: 112).

This novel architecture, of course, has its own issues and problems. Whereas traditional systems typically demonstrated sophisticated reasoning in rather small and sharp-edged domains (e.g., chess, theorem-proving, the blocks world), and the challenge for them was to generalize to robust behavior in more complex domains, the new robots tend to demonstrate less sophisticated behaviors, but in relatively complex environments (e.g., avoiding obstacles, following walls, wandering around), and the challenge for them is to generalize to more sophisticated behaviors (ibid.: 129).

In brief, the promise – or the hope – of the new robots, especially those built at MIT using the subsumption architecture, was that they would gradually manifest increasingly complex behaviors that would emerge as the result of interactions among simpler behaviors and modules.

A "MUTATIONAL" LEAP: TODAY THE EARWIG, TOMORROW THE HUMAN

The original plan of Brooks's group was to build primitive robots with "insect-level intelligence," and the hope was to ratchet up the performance *incrementally* in the manner of natural evolution – an idea that led philosopher David Kirsh (1991) to ask rhetorically if it would be possible to make a transition from earwigs to humans within the robotic framework.

According to the original plan, there was "no particular interest in demonstrating how human beings work" (Brooks 1997: 401). However, very soon, and without the coming-about of the intervening stages, the insect-like creatures yielded their place to humanoid-seeming robots such as Cog. Behind the scenes there lay a personal reason for this switch in research program, best stated by Brooks himself:

I had been thinking that after completing the current round of insect robots, perhaps we should move on to reptilelike robots. Then perhaps a small mammal, then a larger mammal, and finally a primate. At that rate, given that time was flowing on for me, just as for everyone else, it was starting to look like, if I was really lucky, I might be remembered as the guy who built the best artificial cat. Somehow that legacy just did not quite fit my self-image. (2002a: 65)

In this manner, the MIT group leapfrogged to the far end of the evolutionary order (Castañeda and Suchman 2005). At the same time, the engineering ambition was supplemented with "a scientific goal of understanding human cognition" (Brooks and Stein 1994; Brooks et al. 1998; Scassellati 2000). These, as we see, are very ambitious goals: a mutation in research program from insects to humanoid robots, and, at the same time, a serious new commitment to conduct psychologically relevant research. In fact, not only are these ambitious goals, but they are somewhat contradictory.

On the one hand, the MIT group upped the ante by jumping from insect- to human-level intelligence (a brief look at Figures 8.1 and 8.2 illustrates this drastic leap). On the other hand, as have many others in AI, they have added a scientific goal to their original engineering project. In other words, in taking up this challenge, the MIT group has made two moves in opposing directions. The tension between these two divergent moves, as we shall see, has had specific consequences: it has regenerated the old tensions of AI in new forms; it has introduced new tensions into the field of AI; and it has resulted in the undoing of some of the original intuitions that motivated the neorobotics approach – most notably, the principle of the emergence of complex behaviors from simpler ones.

The revision of principles is clearly manifest in the major themes that constitute the topics of the more recent writings about Cog. In particular, whereas "embodiment" and "situatedness" are still considered central issues, as they were before, "intelligence" and "emergence" have been replaced by "development" and "integration." In Brooks et al. (1998), which is one of the most comprehensive reports on Cog, for instance, the word "emergence" does not appear even once. The evaporation of the term "emergence," as we shall see, is not simply a result of an innocent or casual choice of vocabulary; the reasons behind the switch have deep roots in the new design principles. To show this, in the next four sections I turn to an examination of the four central themes behind the Cog project, and the way in which they are incorporated in the design of the robot.

THE FIRST THEME: EMBODIMENT

The motivation behind creating Cog is the hypothesis that:

> Humanoid intelligence requires humanoid interactions with the world.
> – Cog's homepage

The main idea motivating the building of physical (as opposed to virtual or software) robots is that the detailed physical nature of the world matters in how creatures deal with it. A creature should not only accommodate and respond to this structure, it should exploit it for its own purposes. The fact that there is gravity of a certain strength on Earth, or that air, earth, and water present varying types and degrees of resistance to motion, for instance, crucially affects the way terrestrial creatures move around. On the one hand, a moving object must spend energy to overcome friction and viscosity. On the other hand, it can exploit the very same forces to move around in certain ways (e.g., flying, walking, swimming, sliding, skating, or leaping). One consequence of this is that, rather than calculating its motions in every detail, a creature can simply move around by relying on such physical properties.

Similar effects could be obtained for free – that is, without any computation – in a robot that is physically coupled to its environment.[4] Furthermore, and this is a corollary to the above idea, the *form* of the body is also critical in how a creature utilizes the physical structure of the world. Hawks, dolphins, people, ants, and lizards use gravity and friction in extremely different ways. This, in turn, may provide different perceptions of the world, and may consequently account for different cognitive processes among different species (Lakoff 1987; Varela, Tompson, and Rosch 1991).

An obvious implication of these observations is that if we want to build systems that have human-level intelligence, we had better build robots that have not merely a physical body but in fact a humanoid form (Brooks et al. 1998). In so doing, we too, as designers can exploit the physics of the world for various purposes, dispensing with the need to explicitly model or simulate many of its features; the physical structure of the world is there to help us. Cog was designed according to this principle.

COG: THE EMBODIED CREATURE

Cog is an upper-torso humanoid robot with a number of motor, perceptual, and computational systems (see Figure 8.1). The physical structure of Cog is designed so that it can manifest human-like motion, with its sensory systems providing information about its immediate environment, allowing it to interact with humans (albeit in a very primitive way so far).

Cog has a total of twenty-one mechanical degrees of freedom: two six-degrees-of-freedom arms, a torso with a two-degrees-of-freedom waist (side-to-side and front-to-back), a one degree-of-freedom torso (spine) twist, a three-degrees-of-freedom neck (side-to-side, front-to-back, and twist) and three degrees of freedom in the eyes. The arms are built on a mass-spring model that arguably has some biological plausibility to it (MacKay et al. 1986). As Brooks et al. (1998) emphasize, the spring-like property gives the arm a sensible "natural" behavior that not only allows it to move smoothly at a slow command rate, but also makes it simply deflect out of the way if it is bent or hits an obstacle.

The ultimate goal of the Cog project in terms of motor behavior is a robot that can move with "the speed, dexterity, and grace of a human." The approach adopted for doing this is to exploit the "natural dynamics" of components such as arms – a feature that humans and animals seemingly exploit as well. Adult and young humans, for instance, swing their arms at comfortable frequencies close to their natural resonant frequencies (if they were pendulums), and use the same dynamics to learn new motions (Thelen and Smith 1994). Similarly, infants perform the same leg motions when they are laid down, held in water, or trying to walk (ibid.). Using design methods based on similar dynamical principles, Cog currently performs a number of delicate movements – for example, turning a crank or manipulating objects such as a slinky.[5]

In sum, the physical structure and the motor capabilities of Cog reflect the high-level engineering skills involved in its creation. But it would be naïve to assume that engineering is all that is involved. For instance, as we shall see later, art and artistic expression contribute heavily to Cog's appearance and bodily structure – a fact that should not be overlooked in understanding the reactions of human beings toward the robot. Furthermore, the notion of embodiment implies many other ideas, which need to be fleshed out. Most notable among these is the idea of cognition being at the core of life, as captured in the equation "life = cognition" (Stewart 1992).[6]

Life = Cognition?

The notion of humans as machines is an old one, going back at least to the Enlightenment and materialist philosophers such as La Mettrie. The same idea is also at the foundation of AI, where humans are usually taken to be the paradigmatic case of intelligent machines. More recent trends in AI, such as Artificial Life (ALife) and neorobotics, have expanded the scope of the field to include not only cognition but life in general.[7] According to Lars Risan (1997: 70), an anthropologist who closely studied the ALife research group COGS at the University of Sussex, the intuition common to all these approaches is that being alive is equivalent to having cognitive and intelligent capabilities. This is an obvious departure from earlier notions of life based on the possession of such properties as equilibrium and homeostasis, which originated in physics and biology. The simplest form of such capabilities, according to those who seek to define life in terms of cognition, is self-replication: the ability to make copies of oneself. Although it is not clear why self-replication involves cognition – it is basically a process involving DNA and enzymes, not cognition – the purpose of "Life = Cognition" formula is to challenge the boundary not only between humans and life in general, but between life and machines (ibid.). The ALife researchers, for instance, seek to contribute to the science of biology by simulating life in computer models. Chris Langton, an ALife researcher at the University of Sussex, gives voice to the above intuition as follows:

By extending the empirical foundation upon which biology is based *beyond* the carbon-chain life that has evolved on Earth, Artificial Life can contribute to theoretical biology by locating *life-as-we-know-it* within the larger picture of *life-as-it-could-be*. (Langton 1989: 1)

This project, as Risan (1997: 46) points out, introduces the tension between science and engineering to ALife research. The robotic approach, being suspicious of mere (software) simulations (Brooks 1999: 109–10), pushes this project in another direction, and tries to find intelligence in special

assemblages of electric motors, cogs, bolts, nuts, and, of course, computers. In particular, humanoid-robot projects such as the one at MIT seek to
achieve human-level intelligence in the body of a robot like Cog. What matters, according to this view, is "embodiment" in the sense of having a physical
reality, not "body" in the sense of a blend of flesh, blood, hormones, genes,
and so on; what matters is *physical* interaction with the world, not *bodily*
experience in the sense of hunger, thirst, sleep, sex, caressing, aging, and
dying (and all the complex feelings that accompany these).

This difference between having a body (in a biological sense) and being
embodied (in the physical sense) can be a source of tension in one's views,
especially if one steps out of the world of pure engineering and into the world
of a science such as biology. While Brooks the engineer did not have such
concerns, Brooks the engineer/scientist expresses this tension in the following
way (2002a: 68):

The robots we build are not people. There is a real danger that they bear only a
superficial relationship to real people. . . . Perhaps we have left out just too many
details of the form of the robot for it to have similar experiences to people. Or
perhaps it will turn out to be truly important that robots are made of flesh and
bone, not silicon and metal.

To resolve the tension, Brooks argues as follows: Generally, our tendency
to ascribe a special status in the universe to the human species derives from a
kind of primitive tribalism. This tendency, he reminds us, has been defeated
twice in modern times: first by Galileo and Copernicus when they drove Earth
out of the center of the universe, and then by Darwin when he discovered our
common origins with other animal species. The third and last step in this
direction, according to Brooks, has been under way for the past fifty years –
ever since machines (computers) started to challenge us in unprecedented
ways. To show how, he provides two major arguments,[8] which, for the sake
of brevity, I will call the "scientific" and the "engineering" arguments.

The Scientific Argument
Brook's first argument, which has a scientific and philosophical tone, begins
with simple axioms – for example, that "we are nothing more than a
highly ordered collection of biomolecules" and that "the body, this mass
of biomolecules, is a machine that acts according to a set of specifiable rules"
(2002a: 172–173). The problem, Brooks maintains, is that there is some "new
stuff" that we are missing in biology. Unlike philosophers such as Searle,
Penrose, and Chalmers, with whom he contrasts his views, Brooks claims

that "the new stuff is something that is already staring us in the nose, and we just have not seen it yet" (2002a: 187). Furthermore, he muses:

My version of the 'new stuff' is not at all disruptive. It is just some new mathematics, which I have provocatively been referring to as 'the juice' for the last few years. But it is not an elixir of life that I hypothesize, and it does not require any new physics to be present in living systems. My hypothesis is that we may simply not be seeing some fundamental mathematical description of what is going on in living systems. Consequently we are leaving out the necessary generative components to produce the processes that give rise to those descriptions as we build our artificial intelligence and artificial life models. (ibid.)

This argument, therefore, boils down to our ability "to come up with some clever analysis of living systems and then to use that analysis in designing better machines" (2002: 191). However, Brooks asserts, our success in this endeavor is threatened by "the limits of human understanding" in confronting the human mind itself. But notice that discovering this limit is somehow the main challenge of AI, because human understanding is correlated, if not coextensive, with human intelligence. Brooks' resort to the "new stuff" reveals, among other things, the inadequacies of physicalism as a model for bodies or worlds. Brooks' initial assertions notwithstanding, the world does not ground regress (Suchman 2007: 231).

Let us look at his second argument.

The Engineering Argument
Unlike Brooks's first argument, the second one has a clear engineering spin to it. It is a long discussion spread over two chapters of his book, so I shall give only the gist of it here. The main axiom is that computer technology has revolutionized our lives during the last fifty years, and there is no going back. Not only has this brought about prosperity for most of us, but moreover, we now can, for the first time in history, incorporate technology inside our bodies. This began with cochlear implants and pacemakers, is moving toward retinal implants and vision enhancement devices, and will continue with electronic chips in our skulls. "[H]umankind has embarked on an irreversible journey of technological manipulation of our bodies" (2002a: ix). Robotic technology will merge with biotechnology to a point where "The distinction between us and robots is going to disappear," and "there won't be any us (people) for them (pure robots) to take over" (2002: 236; ix). This should, according to Brooks, bring comfort to those (such as Bill Joy and Jaron Lanier; see Chapter 3) who "worry about mere robots taking over from us" (2002a: 236).

Notice how different this argument is from the previous one, and how it leads to very distinct conclusions. The first argument is skeptical of our capability to fully understand and simulate our biology, whereas the second one, following a deterministic technological logic, is most definite in its prediction of the final outcome – namely, the emergence of "cyborgs" that are hybrids of humans and robots (see Chapter 3). In practical terms, the two arguments would lead to very different research programs and predictions. The first would prescribe building humanoid robots to help us understand our biology, while the second would predict flesh-and-metal cyborgs, without much concern for their scientific significance.

In short, the scientist and the engineer in Brooks arrive at contrasting conclusions and prescriptions. Note the practical uncertainty hidden in these views: Should AI research focus on the building of humanoid robots, or should it concentrate on auxiliary devices such as implants to enhance *human* intelligence? If both, how would these research programs be related to each other? In other words, should the goal of AI be defined as the understanding of human intelligence, the creation of alternative intelligence, or the enhancement of human capabilities?

Notice, furthermore, that expanding the scope of AI to include biological questions about life has introduced a new dimension into AI, and, at the same time, new tensions – for example, between the ideas of "life" and "cognition," or between the organic and the engineered. Haraway (2003) has suggested that, despite attempts to erase the boundaries of organism and artifact, the ultimate target of these robotic projects is to approximate human-level capabilities. This reveals a new form of hyper-humanism, which replaces "an *a priori* commitment to human uniqueness with an equally essentialist investment in fundamental mechanism" (Castañeda and Suchman 2005). This stands in obvious tension with the thesis that as humans we are machines. A thoroughly embodied view of cognition would frame its projects not as the importation of mind into matter, "but as the rematerialization of bodies and subjectivities" in ways that challenge familiar assumption about the relationship between the mind and the body (Castañeda and Suchman 2005).

THE SECOND THEME: SITUATEDNESS

The second major idea in the Cog approach is that meaning can arise only through a cognitive entity's direct interaction with the world, where "interaction" is broadly understood as perception and action. This description, of course, is very broad, and allows a wide range of interpretations. No one, and certainly not AI practitioners, denies that perception and action matter for cognition. But earlier approaches in AI, as we have seen, either marginalized these as secondary issues that could be accounted for in due time, or else provided a very limited view of perception and action, typically embodied in an eye–arm system in earlier robots. More importantly, perception and action were considered as separate processes, mediated by a "brain" or central processor.

The situated approach, to the contrary, takes perception and action as the centerpiece, and pushes central processing and internal representations of the world to the margin. There is, of course, great variation among the views within the situated approach about the role of representations. Smith (2000, 2002), for instance, suggests a "rehabilitation of representations" in ways that would make them compatible with the situated view. Brooks (1991), on the other hand, proposed the subsumption architecture to argue for "intelligence without representation" (1991).[9] This view underlies the design of Cog, but to a much lesser degree than it *used* to be. According to Brooks et al. (1998), for instance:

There are representations, or accumulations of state, but these only refer to the internal workings of the system; they are meaningless without interaction with the outside world.

This notion of representation is best manifested in Cog's perceptual system, which consists of five subsystems. Equipped with these subsystems, Cog performs tasks that require coordination among different perceptual and motor systems. For instance, it mimics all the movements of the human eye – namely, three voluntary movements (saccades, smooth pursuit, and vergence) and two involuntary movements (the ocular reflex and the opto-kinetic response).[10] It also demonstrates strikingly life-like behaviors: it orients its head and neck in the direction of its gaze; it points with its arm to a visual target; it locates faces and eyes; it even nods and shakes its head in imitation of a human being. In addition, Cog has a central processor or "brain," consisting of a heterogeneous network of PC's that can be expanded at will by adding new computers. There are also dedicated local motor controllers that operate the joints, as well as a separate network that processes audio and video signals.

This distribution of control mechanisms diminishes the role of the central processor. This is more or less compatible, with some adjustment, with the original "principle of minimum representations," outlined in Brooks (1991). But I want to show that, mainly because of the sudden leap in research plans to humanoid robots, the notion of emergence, which was the other central principle of the original view, has been largely undermined by the design of Cog.

Do We Need Concepts to Make Sense of Perceptions?

One of the features of traditional AI systems was that "they will need an objective model of the world with individuated entities, tracked and identified over time" (Brooks 1999: 166). The early robots such as Shakey, for instance, could only recognize objects for which they had built-in descriptions in their memory. What they did was to simply *match* that description, according to specified features, with the visual input in order to detect the presence of objects – for example, a straight body with circular extremities was a cylinder for them. LABMATE, the dynamic robot introduced in Chapter 7, had a similar limitation: the world had to be given to it precategorized and prelabeled. Bajscy and Large acknowledge this caveat in their work, but do not provide a solution:

> In our view, the main unsolved problem is how to segment the continuous signal into states, strategies, labels, and so forth, and how to arbitrate among states for effective interaction with the environment. (Bajscy and Large 1999: 59)

This problem of segmenting the continuous flow of input and of making sense, in William James's words, of the "booming and buzzing confusion" of the outside world has been a vexing scientific question in psychology, and a major challenge for AI. Neorobotics essentially sought to bypass this problem by adopting a different approach "where a mobile robot used the world as its own model – continuously referring to its sensors rather than to an internal world model" (Brooks 1999: 166). Frogs, after all, do not need a "fly-concept" in order to flip their tongue out for a passing fly (Clancey 1997: 195). Why should robots?

Early neorobotics models actually followed this strategy rather faithfully, and were able to handle simple tasks quite successfully. Robots that could navigate corridors without a concept of "wall" (Toto), or that could follow moving objects without a notion of "toward" or "object" (Genghis), provided examples of such success stories. However, the extension of these "quick wins," as Clancey dubs them, to "a cockroach to a bird or a cat is incredibly difficult" (ibid.). Clancey's skepticism turns out to be justified, and some of the techniques used in the design of Cog show this clearly, as I will presently argue.

Today the Face, Tomorrow the World?

In order to find faces (of people, dolls, etc.), Cog uses built-in representations (templates) to distinguish between face-like objects and other items in the

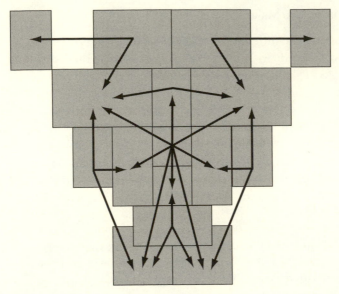

Figure 8.3. A template for the detection of faces (from Scassellati 1998, with permission).

environment. First, it employs a ratio-template-matching algorithm to find potential face locations (targets) in the scene (Scassellati 1998; see Figure 8.3).[11] Then the eyes saccade to the target with the highest score, using an unsupervised learning algorithm (see Chapter 5). Finally, a mapping takes place from the peripheral image (outside) into the foveal image coordinates (inside) in order to establish the location of the face.[12] In this way, the robot detects and locates faces in the environment.

Such an approach to face detection raises a number of issues. First, it is in obvious contrast with the idea of "emergence" that was among Brooks' initial principles – namely, the idea that complex behaviors and systems should emerge from the interaction of simpler ones. The face-detection mechanism in Cog, as we see, basically consists of special functional modules that detect face-like objects (and nothing else) by comparing them with built-in representations. Neither the mechanism nor the representations emerge from simpler ones; they are simply hardwired.

A second issue is that this approach cannot be generalized to other objects. Faces constitute only one class of objects that a human (or a humanoid robot) has to classify in a real-world environment, and so the approach adopted for Cog would require the addition of other modules dedicated to the recognition of other classes of objects. This would amount to hundreds or thousands of modules just for the classification of objects – an idea that seems rather infeasible. Moreover, *detection* is a much simpler task than *recognition*: whereas the former only involves the generic classification of objects as, for instance, "faces," "books," and "chairs," the latter involves the recognition of *individual* objects such as John's face, Mary's book, and my chair.[13]

The final issue that comes up about Cog's face-detection mechanism is that a good part of the task has effectively already been solved for the robot by ingenious engineering techniques. While this might be acceptable for a purely engineering project, it certainly undermines the original philosophy that was inspired by the model of biological evolution. Cog, according to that project, would have been the last link in a chain of simpler robots that were to be developed through a long and painstaking research program – a vision totally counter to the shortcut method that was subsequently adopted. It bears pointing out that faces are not merely one of many types of entity that Cog can recognize at this point. The fact is that Cog recognizes *only* faces – not blocks, boxes, cans, or a myriad of other simpler objects. Cog is a carefully engineered artifact with narrow functionality, and its perceptual capabilities are the outcome of a kind of engineering that amounts to little more than spoon-feeding. As such, Cog cannot evolve, bootstrap, or ratchet up its current capabilities to acquire more sophisticated ones, and one is hard pressed to attribute much significance to its very limited repertoire of visual categories. Despite nouvelle AI, which understands *situated behavior* as adaptation to particular stimuli and environments, behavior is not simply reactive and contingent on the external world. Rather, it reflexively constitutes the world's significance, which in turn gives behavior its sense (Suchman 2007: 15).

THE THIRD THEME: DEVELOPMENT

The shift to humanoid robots has brought about a shift in perspective in the Cog group from *natural selection* to *child development*. In other words, the painstaking process of *evolving* creatures from simple to complex has yielded to the *development* of "adult robots" from "baby robots." "Developmental approaches to robot construction," the Cog group argues, "produce systems that can scale naturally to more complex tasks and problem domains" (Brooks et al. 1998; Scassellati 2000). So the issue of scaling-up that was originally seen as an evolutionary process has metamorphosed into a developmental one, and this is what motivates the intense focus on face detection in their work.

To explore the theme of development, the MIT group has built, in addition to the main humanoid robot, three development platforms for testing and debugging purposes. One of these platforms, named "Kismet," according to

Figure 8.4. One of Kismet's facial expressions.

the Cog group, is a "vision and emotive response platform" for exploring the nature and possibilities of social interaction between robots and humans. Kismet is said to have capabilities for emotive facial expressions indicative of anger, fatigue, fear, disgust, excitement, happiness, interest, sadness, and surprise (see Figure 8.4). For this purpose, Kismet's face is embellished with what might have otherwise seemed like rather frivolous or superfluous features: eyebrows (each one with two degrees of freedom: lift and arc), ears (each with two degrees of freedom: lift and rotate), eyelids and a mouth (each with one degree of freedom: open/close). Two microcontrollers, one for driving the robot's facial motors and one for implementing the "motivational system" (emotions and drives) as well as the behavior system, are also present in this junior robot. Some might protest, at this point, that such additions would be likely to contribute to an Eliza effect on the part of perceiving humans. I shall discuss this presently.

Kismet the Infant Robot

Kismet in its current incarnation exhibits novel interactive behaviors. For instance, using the face- and eye-finding routines discussed earlier, it can establish "eye contact" with a human being. The capability to create eye contact is believed by some psychologists to be essential for *joint attention*, which is, in turn, believed to be the precursor to any social interaction. Joint attention is the capability of two living beings (mostly mammals) to simultaneously pay attention to the same object by pointing to it or by simply directing their gazes toward the object. This, in turn, requires the capability of the two creatures to establish eye contact with each other. In fact, some psychologists seek to explain developmental disorders such as autism in terms of the failure to establish eye contact with people (Baron-Cohen 1995).

In addition to eye contact, Kismet can also imitate the head-nodding of a human being who stands in front of it. (Curiously, the Cog group calls a researcher who interacts with Kismet a "caretaker," not an "observer" or "experimenter," and not even a "trainer," as is usually said of people who interact with animals in a similar fashion.) That is, if the experimenter nods yes, the robot responds by nodding yes, and similarly for shaking one's head in denial. This is achieved by adding a tracking mechanism to the output of the face detector. By keeping track of the location of a salient feature on the face (such as the mouth or the eyebrows), this mechanism provides information about the direction of movement (roughly, horizontal and vertical), which is further classified as a *yes*, a *no*, or as *no-motion*. Since the nodding and shaking mechanisms get their input from the face-detection module, the robot reacts to the movement only of a face-like object (human or doll), not other objects. This kind of reaction to the presence of human beings, which motivated the focus on face detection, also provides what the Cog group considers to be the beginnings of social interaction. Let us pursue this latter idea further, in order to discover the motivations behind it.

Psychology and Robotics: A Path to Be Trodden

Development is typically thought of as a progressive process where previously learned behaviors and skills enable the learning of new ones. Jean Piaget, probably the most respected child psychologist of the twentieth century, formulated this incremental process in terms of successive stages that follow a quite strict progression (1952). Other psychologists, with varying degrees of support for this idea, have tried to discover mechanisms that could give rise to such a progressive process. In Chapter 6, we saw one such example in Elman's idea of "starting small," which focused on the gradual increase in "external complexity" – for example, in the structure of the language input. A parallel idea is to assume a gradual increase in "internal complexity" – that is, in perceptual and motor skills. A stepwise increase in the acuity of both sensory and motor systems, for instance, has been shown to facilitate learning motor skills significantly (Thelen and Smith 1994). In either case, social interaction is thought to provide the circumstances for development, through imitation, direct tutelage, or "scaffolding," where a caretaker guides the infant through the learning process.

The MIT group seeks to implement this idea of progressive development in Kismet, focusing mostly on the processes of imitation and joint attention. In order to implement these processes, they have decomposed them into four stages – namely, maintaining eye contact, gaze-following, imperative pointing (trying to obtain an object that is out of reach by pointing at it), and declarative pointing (drawing attention to a distant object by pointing at it) (see Figure 8.5). Kismet's face- and eye-detection mechanisms are basically

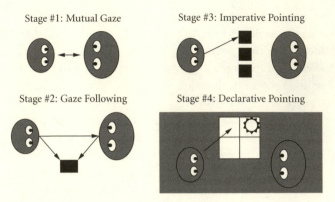

Figure 8.5. The importance of imitation in learning in children (from Scassellati 1999, with permission).

those of Cog, which we have already seen. The rest of these skills are also implemented in Kismet using similar engineering techniques and algorithms, the details of which are beyond our interest here.

The proclaimed goal of this research is to construct systems that both inform, and are informed by, psychological theories of development (Brooks et al. 1998; Scassellati 1999, 2000). The problem is that there is a wide spectrum of views in developmental psychology on the issue of the driving mechanisms behind change in children. Development has to do with change, and the main question for a theory of development is what the origin of change or of new form is (Lewontin 1998; Oyama 2000; Thelen and Smith 1994). It is mainly in how they answer this question that theories of development differ. While it might be safe, therefore, to say that most developmental psychologists nowadays consider the process of change to be progressive, there is enormous variation among their views as to *how* this process takes place.

Child Development: A Synopsis

Theories of child development are numerous and vary greatly. One example is the "theory-of-mind theory," or *theory theory*, which is very close to common folk psychology, according to which people's actions result from such internal mental states as their hopes, wishes, beliefs, doubts, and desires (Wellman and Gelman 1992).[14] Children in the age range of three to five years are starting to acquire an understanding of other people's beliefs, and of the role those beliefs play in causing their behaviors – something that is not manifest at earlier ages. The proponents of theory theory take this as evidence that development has mainly to do with the formation of theories about why people behave the way they do. In other words, the idea is that children, in the course of development, acquire a "theory" of other persons' behaviors, and are able to predict and explain those behaviors in terms of mental states that "cause" them, pretty much in the spirit of what scientists do when they create theories to account for natural phenomena – whence the name "theory theory." In this view, impairments such as autism would result from the lack of a theory of mind in the afflicted. In short, theory theory "can be seen as attempting to base social cognition in a mentalistic belief–desire psychology" (ibid.).

On the opposite extreme, there are views based on a dynamical theory of development, similar to those we discussed in Chapter 7 (Thelen and Smith 1994). According to this theory, we recall, development is a continuous process of change that takes place because of the physical interactions of the child with its environment. The dynamical view, as we saw, avoids the usage of mental constructs such as "beliefs" and "desires" to explain learning and development in children.

From Psychology to Robotics

The above views in developmental psychology are in clear opposition to each other: one is purely mentalistic (it explains behaviors in terms of internal mental states), whereas the other is largely behaviorist (it explains behaviors without recourse to mental representations). Interestingly, however, the MIT group draws upon both of these views as sources of insight. Scassellati (2000), for example, gives the example of hand–eye coordination in Cog. Without human supervision, it is said, Cog learns to point to an object by using its own errors in mapping among different coordinate systems – for example, retinal image, head-centered gaze, arm-centered motors, etc. In short, and this is the crucial point, the learning process occurs in real time, without using an explicit representation of the coordinates for the outside world (Scassellati 1999, 2000). This technique, as we see, is inspired by the dynamical view that sees motor skills as building on each other successively, using the dynamics of interaction between the system and the environment.

On the other hand, in the same paper Scassellati (2000) discusses the example of the development of joint attention in Kismet. In this case, the inspiration comes from Baron-Cohen's model, which is a model based on the theory-of-mind theory. Elsewhere, acknowledging the theory of mind as "the most relevant studies" to their purposes (Scassellati 1999), the Cog group outlines the work on joint attention as "part of a larger project to build a theory of mind for the robot, which would allow it to attribute beliefs, desires, and intentions to the model [the human being whose behaviors the robot is to imitate] . . . " (Breazeal and Scassellati 2000).

In short, the Cog group borrows liberally from clashing psychological theories of development to inform their views, and this can be justified in one of two ways: either one believes that there is in truth no incompatibility between the rival psychological theories, or one does not concern oneself with such theoretical issues, and, adopting a purely engineering attitude, draws upon whatever theory serves one's design best.[15] Given that the proponents of the theory-of-mind and the dynamical views see their camps as seriously incompatible, the latter seems to be the case with the Cog group's use of psychological theories. That is, as before, the Cog group seems to have adopted a purely engineering attitude in this respect as well. The question is, why do they need to discuss theories of development at all? What is the relevance of these theories to their project? Do these theories serve as sources of inspiration for design principles?

It seems that there are no definite answers to these questions. While one might argue that the dynamical approach provides insights about design for the robotic approach, there is nothing in theory theory that would help the Cog group with design issues. It seems that these discussions about psychological theories serve more as a justification and a means to enroll allies within the psychology community for the work done at MIT. While this might be understandable as part of the way things work in science, it leaves the MIT group in an odd situation, not only because it damages their theoretical consistency, but also because it contradicts some of their original intuitions (about the undesirability of mental models).

From Robotics to Psychology

How about the reverse direction, from Kismet to psychology? It is not clear, I argue, how the robotic research at MIT could inform developmental psychology in any serious way. It has been suggested that "humanoid robotics research can also investigate scientific questions about the nature of human intelligence" (Scassellati 1999, 2000). Specifically, it is claimed, robots provide a testbed for evaluating the predictive power and validity of psychological theories through controlled, repeatable experiments. A close look at the possible outcomes of such experiments, however, reveals that the informative role given to robotics research is far from obvious.

Take the example of the joint-attention mechanism discussed earlier. One possible outcome of experiments on this mechanism is that the robot will manifest the behavior predicted by the model of joint attention – for example, it will learn to follow the gaze direction of a human being toward an object, or to point to an object to "attract attention" to it. This, as Scassellati notes, "provides a *possible* explanation for the normal (and abnormal) develop-ment of joint attention ... it says nothing about the underlying biological processes" (ibid.). What if the robot does not show the predicted behavior? Scassellati considers two possible scenarios: (i) the failure is a result of a "logical flaw in the [psychological] model," in which case, he suggests, "we can identify shortcomings of the proposed model and potentially suggest alternate solutions"; or (ii) the failure is a result of significant differences in environmental conditions of the robot and a human infant, in which case, he suggests, one could draw conclusions about the robotic implementation, "not the model or the underlying biological factors" (ibid.).

The question is, how could we distinguish between these two scenarios? That is, how could we know whether the failure is a result of the shortcomings in the model or to environmental differences? Suppose that Kismet learns to follow the gaze direction but fails to show "interest" in the object. Is this a failure on the part of the psychological model, or is it because there are pos-sibly other salient objects around, or simply because the control mechanisms of the robot have become unstable? There seem to be no definite answers to such questions.

In summary, the relation between research on humanoid robots and devel-opmental theories seems to rest on very "shakey" grounds, so to speak. At the present stage, there is little substantial finding in this research that could possibly inform psychological theories of development. Conversely, the way in which research on Cog (and Kismet) is informed by theories of psychology also seems to be burdened with inconsistencies and irrelevancies. This leads to an "apparently circular trajectory," where neorobotics materializes current theories in developmental psychology and then represents itself as a testbad in which to assess their adequacy (Keller 2007; cf. Suchman 2007: 239). We see a clear example of *inscription error* at work here (see the Epilogue). The attempt by the Cog group to establish such links, therefore, could be largely understood in terms of a desire to endow their engineering projects with scientific relevance to boost up the legitimacy of these projects and to enlist allies within different scientific communities. In early-twenty-first-century technoscience, nature has become "a source of certainty and legitimacy for the designed and the engineered" (Haraway 1997: 103).

Does this mean that there are no lessons to be learned about us, human beings, from the work done on Cog? I think there are, but in ways that have little to do with the arguments made by the Cog group. Actually, I want to argue, projects such as these say much more about us than they say about robots, and I would like to discuss this in the context of the fourth, and final, major theme in Cog research: social interaction.

THE FOURTH THEME: SOCIAL INTERACTION

Kismet, as I said, engages in interactions with human "caretakers." The purpose of these interactions is to provide learning episodes for the robot to be able "to manipulate the caretaker into satisfying the robot's internal drives (fatigue, social stimulation)" (Brooks et al. 1998). The robot reportedly does this by showing one of three "consummatory" behaviors ("sleep," "social-ize," "play"), and displaying through facial expression one of its five emotions ("anger," "disgust," "fear," "happiness," "sadness") or two expressive states ("tiredness," "interest").

In a typical episode, a human interacts with the robot in a face-to-face manner, either by waving a hand at the robot, or by using a toy (a small black-and-white cow or an orange slinky) to engage in "play" with it. The facial expressions of the robot provide visual cues that tell the human participant whether to switch the type of stimulus and whether the intensity of interaction should be increased, diminished, or maintained at its current level. To give a concrete picture of how this works, it pays to quote at length from Brooks et al. (1998; the boldface words are from the original):

For instance, if the robot is under-stimulated for an extended period of time, it shows an expression of **sadness**. This may occur either because its **social drive** has migrated into the "lonely" regime due to a lack of social stimulation (perceiving faces near by), or because its **stimulation** drive has migrated into the "bored" regime due to a lack of non-face stimulation (which could be provided by slinky motion, for instance). The expression of **sadness** upon the robot's face tells the caretaker that the robot needs to be played with. In contrast, if the robot receives an overly-intense face stimulus for an extended period of time, the **social** drive moves into the "asocial" regime and the robot displays an expression of **disgust**. This expression tells the caretaker that she is interacting inappropriately with the robot – moving her face too rapidly and thereby overwhelming the robot. Similarly, if the robot receives an overly-intense non-face stimulus (e.g., perceiving large slinky motions) for an extended period of time, the robot displays a look of **fear**. This expression also tells the caretaker that she is interacting inappropriately with the robot, probably moving the slinky too much and overstimulating the robot.

Brooks et al. go on to describe this as an ongoing "dance" between the robot and the human aimed at maintaining the robot's drives within homeostatic bounds:

If the robot and human are good partners, the robot remains **interested** and/or **happy** most of the time. These expressions indicate that the interaction is of appropriate intensity for learning. (ibid.)

The question that immediately comes to mind from reading a passage such as this is what justifies the use of emotion-laden words such as "sadness," "fear," "disgust," and so on in talking about Kismet. The key words in this passage that might lead to an answer to this question are, in my opinion, "expressions," "partner," and "learning"; and I would like to briefly pause on these one at a time.

Emotions: Expressions and Impressions

Kismet, as we have seen, manifests facial features that, when observed by human beings, can be interpreted as expressions of happiness, sadness, fear, and so on. Although, in talking about this capability, the creators of Cog "do not claim that this system parallels infants exactly," they do assert that "its design is heavily inspired by the role motivations and facial expressions play in maintaining an appropriate level of stimulation during social interaction with adults" (ibid.).

It is, of course, quite reasonable for a humanoid-robot designer and engineer to be "inspired" by certain ideas about human psychology. Ancient doll makers, as I mentioned earlier, also took inspiration from the way (they thought) animals work. So do artists and painters (at least those with a realist bent) who take inspiration from natural or social phenomena. The question is what lessons can be drawn from these artifacts about the original source of inspiration – that is, about animals, humans, or objects. It is one thing to be inspired by a certain phenomenon (and even, I am going to venture, to seek to understand *what* it is), but it is quite another thing to try to understand *how* it works. This, in a way, is what differentiates science from other modes of knowing: scientists seek to understand *how* the world works (Giere 1999).

The question, therefore, is not whether the design of Kismet is inspired by *what* children do; it is what the design tells us about *how* they do it – in this case, of how emotions, motivations, and facial expressions are related. It is the answer to this question, I believe, that determines the scientific significance of the Cog project. And the answer to this question, it turns out, is not straightforward. As a matter of fact, a number of answers to such a question are conceivable.

One possible answer is to say that Kismet's facial patterns in reaction to human behavior are genuine expressions of genuine feelings. Such an answer

seems to be in agreement with the views of behaviorist psychologists such as
B. F. Skinner, who believed that we do not need to "experience feelings and
then express them" (1985: 38). Feelings, according to Skinner, are not causes
of behaviors, but the "collateral products of the causes of the behavior." For
example, to pull one's hand away from a hot object, Skinner argued, one does
not need to have "a desire not to be burned, a belief that the hot object exists,
and a belief that pulling the hand away will terminate the stimulus" (ibid.).
Such behaviors, according to Skinner, are simply "flexion reflexes" caused
by what he called "the contingencies of reinforcement." To claim that there
are feelings behind Kismet's facial patterns is, in principle, compatible with
Skinner's view, although, to be entitled to be called expressions of feelings,
they should be the products of reinforcement by the environment or the
human experimenter.

Another possible answer to the question of how Kismet's facial patterns
are related to feelings, and so on, is to argue, as critics such as Searle do, that
since our feelings are closely linked to the organic chemistry of life, robots
that lack such chemistry are necessarily devoid of feelings, and any apparent
expression of such feelings, facial or otherwise, is in fact devoid of meaning
and significance. This viewpoint is at odds with our earlier decision to take
AI's fundamental assumption for granted – namely, that intelligence is not
necessarily carbon-based.

Yet another line of thought regarding this question is to agree with critics
that feelings are important, but to disagree with their claims that feelings can
originate only from organic chemistry, and also to disagree with mainstream
AI that feelings can emerge from a sufficiently complex cognitive architecture. This line of thought, which is sympathetic to projects such as Cog, is
advocated by some sociologists who argue as follows:

What we "feel" is given to us by language and through our conversations. At the
end of the day, feelings may not at all be straightforward matters of our bio-
electro-chemical composition but rather of our profoundly social lives. (Restivo
2001: 2112)

From this sociological perspective, then, "Electro-mechanical entities will
turn out to be just as susceptible to an internal life as humans once they have
developed language, conversation, and awareness – that is, once they have
developed a social life" (ibid.). Whether or not we agree with this position,
the fact of the matter is that Kismet is *not* a social robot in the sense intended
in this view, because it does not have language, does not socially interact or
converse in a significant way, and does not yet have awareness in any serious
sense of the word.

A last line of thought about the question of the significance of Kismet's "expressions," I propose, is to examine the relation between them and (observers') "impressions" of them. To motivate this, let me quote the social psychologist Sherry Turkle, who reports on her first visit to Cog in the following manner:

Cog's mobile torso, neck, and head stand on a pedestal. Trained to track the largest moving object in its field (because that will usually be a human being) Cog "noticed" me soon after I entered its room. Its head turned to follow me and I was embarrassed to note that this made me happy. I found myself competing with another visitor for its attention. At one point, I felt sure that Cog's eyes had "caught" my own. My visit left me shaken – not by anything that Cog was able to accomplish but by my own reaction to "him." (Turkle 1995: 266)

Turkle's reaction to Cog, I believe, reminds us of the fundamental tendency on the part of human beings (even the most sophisticated among us) to anthropomorphize or, to put it in terms that I find more explanatory, to *attribute* intelligence and other human qualities to other objects, artifacts, animals, and so on. In a way, Turkle's reaction to Cog is not different from typical reactions to Eliza or to NetTalk (see Chapter 6), in that they all reveal the act of attribution of human qualities by human observers to various kinds of expressions (written, verbal, facial, etc.) manifested by machines. Precisely, this phenomenon, I believe, lies behind the ongoing "dance" between humans and Kismet reported by the Cog group. The dance, as such, says much more about us than about the robot, and, if anything, we should be shaken, as was Turkle, by our own reactions, and not by the robot's accomplishments.

Social Life: Communication and Communion

What about the communicative (and so-called social) aspects of Kismet's behavior? What is their significance for our understanding of human social life? To answer these questions, I would like to suggest a distinction between two major aspects of social life, which I shall call the "communication" and "communion" aspects. Both aspects, I will argue, are crucial for genuine social interaction, and lacking either, as Kismet does (partly in the former aspect and wholly in the latter), will make the behaviors devoid of social significance not only in the human sense, but also in the more limited animal sense.

To be sure, one aspect of the interactions among social species can be roughly characterized as *communication* – namely, the exchange of messages (or signs or information) among individuals. This aspect of social interaction is very important, and has been extensively studied by communication theorists, linguists, social psychologists, and semioticians. The social psychologist George Herbert Mead, for instance, constructed a theory of mind on the basis of communication. Mead's views have many facets, especially concerning the relations between individual and social aspects of intelligence. I would like here to highlight a distinction that he makes between different types of communication.

Insects such as bees and ants, Mead reminds us, have a kind of communication that is based on physiological distinctions – for example, on some members of an ant colony beings queens, and others beings fighters, workers, and so on, according to the specific physiological properties of each group. This is analogous to the differentiation of organs in a body. This kind of communication gives rise to the kind of cooperative behavior that we saw among bees at the beginning of the chapter or that is widely known and discussed about ant colonies (see, for instance, Wilson 1971; Hölldobler and Wilson 1990; Hofstadter 1979). Mead calls this "unconscious communication," and contrasts it with "self-conscious (or significant) communication," which, he argues, is predominant among human beings. The outstanding feature of this latter kind of communication is that it requires what Mead calls "participation in the other" – that is, "the appearance of the other in the self, the identification of the other with the self, and the reaching of self-consciousness through the other" (1934: 253). For this kind of communication to happen, furthermore, "one has to have something to communicate before communicating" (259). Finally, Mead argues, "the process of communication cannot be set up as something that exists by itself, or as a presupposition of the social process" (260). On the contrary, he believes that the social process is a precursor of communication.

It is self-conscious (or *conscious* or *deliberate* or *premeditated* or *intended*) communication that gives rise to what I call the *communion* – namely, the sharing of goals, interests, values, responsibilities, and commitments. While the communicative aspect of human relations provides the "syntax" of social interaction, the communion aspect provides its "meaning" – so much so that speaking of "social interaction" would be vacuous in the absence of this content. Common goals, norms, trust, and responsibilities constitute, to a large extent, the glue that keeps communities and societies together.

Now, the question is, which kind of communication (if any) does Kismet engage in when it interacts with human beings? Kismet's interactions arguably involve elements of the communication aspect, albeit in a very primitive form. Although there is no verbal language, the fact that it reacts to the presence of human beings by manifesting certain behaviors or expressions can be roughly taken as a form of communication. But notice that, unlike in bees and ants, these behaviors do not have any grounding in Kismet's specific physiology. So they cannot be of the unconscious kind. On the other hand, since Kismet's interactions are not built on prior social relations, they cannot be of the conscious kind either. Kismet's behaviors being devoid of content, it seems, one would be hard pressed to attribute communion (i.e., conscious, intended communication) to Kismet at all, in the same way that one hardly attributes any significance to a parking garage's well-wishing to the driver, "Thank you! Have a safe trip!" (Hofstadter 1997: 508).

One might, of course, speculate that infants' behaviors are also devoid of content in a very similar way. That is, it might be argued, children, too, initially lack a sense of goal, interest, value, and responsibility – these are instilled in them only in the process of social development. So why shouldn't we expect, it might be asked, a similar process to take place in Kismet? The answer, if Mead is correct, lies partly in the fact that children, unlike robots, have genuine biological needs that drive them toward interaction with their environment, and, more importantly, in the fact that they aredeeply embedded in a network of social relations (Gell 1998). .

Learning and Memory

What if we were to build the equivalents of those biological drives into robots (as the Cog group seems to be trying to do), and then were to let them loose in real social environments to interact with people and possibly other robots (again as the Cog group and others have begun to do)? This would obviously require, among other things, the capability of learning by the robot – and learning crucially depends on having what cognitive psychologists (as well as lay people) call a "memory." While there are serious differences of opinion about the mechanisms of memory and remembering (some of which we have already noted in previous chapters), nobody would deny that memory is an indispensable component of learning and of intelligent behavior.

Given that Kismet does not have memory to learn from its experience and interactions, it is not clear what its creators mean when they talk about it "learning from interacting" with human beings.[16] Social learning, like any other type of learning, depends on memory because, for instance, an important aspect of engaging in social interaction is to "know" individual people. (We can now see why it is a stretch to describe people who interact with Kismet as its "caretakers.")

There seem, therefore, to be major problems with any claim about the social significance of Kismet's interactions with its environment, and with the idea that Kismet can be used as a testbed for studying social behavior in human beings. To show that these are not simple features that could be easily added on later, the next section considers examples of some of the kinds of things that any robot built on similar principles ought to, but will not be able to, accomplish.

Overcoming the Semantic Barrier

The lack of memory in Kismet and its concomitant inability to recognize individual people is only part of a much bigger problem that could be called "overcoming the semantic barrier" – namely, the challenge of "reaching out" to those parts of the environment that are spatially or temporally distant. Think of things that a normal human being can easily do, but that Kismet, Cog, or any enhanced version of them built on the above four principles (embodiment, embeddedness, development, social interaction) would fail to perform, even if it could freely walk around and presumably converse in natural language (Smith 2000):

- Deal with hypotheticals: "Are you going to be sad if I leave you right away?" Or, "If you take that route, do you think you'll get through before they shut the last section at 5:00?"
- Report on what one did: "Before I came in, were you talking to someone else?" Or, "When you came by the door, did you see a backpack on the floor next to the door?"
- Plan sensibly: for example, pick up something that one should know one is going to need in the near future;
- Make deliberate adjustments to one's behavior: for example, realize that even though some route is geometrically shorter, there are usually so many obstacles along it that it would take less time to take by a longer but less crowded route.

One might surmise that the creators of Cog would respond that these are unfair expectations to have of their robots given the stage of development that they are in (Brooks 1999), but in fact, they seem to see their major problem in a totally different light:

Our ultimate goal is to understand human cognitive abilities well enough to build a humanoid robot that develops and acts similar to a person. To date, the major missing piece of our endeavor is demonstrating coherent global behavior from the existing subsystems and sub-behaviors... (Brooks et al. 1998)

What these authors call a "missing piece," however, is much more than a mere "piece": it is, according to many cognitive scientists, a central attribute of cognition and intelligence that "nouvelle AI" sought to overthrow – namely, discrete representations (symbols). As Smith (2000) has put it, the MIT robots, as they stand now, might be *in* the world (embedded) and *of* the world (embodied), but they are certainly not *about* the world (cognitive). And this, it seems, is a major shortcoming of Cog and company.

CONCLUSION: WHO WANTS HUMAN ROBOTS?

Nouvelle AI, as its name implies, is one of the latest trends in AI research, and Cog is one of the most visible projects conducted within this framework. Let us see what lessons we have learned about Cog, and from it.

What We Have Learned *about* Cog

AI's perennial fascination with embodied automata has both theoretical and practical justifications. Theoretically, robots provide effective testbeds for ideas, and they presumably should have a justificatory and evidential power that would be hard to match in any other type of modeling. From early on, therefore, building robots was on the agenda of many AI researchers. The "cybernetic turtles" realized by the brain physiologist Grey Walter are among the early examples of how the combination of few nonlinear elements can give rise to complex behavior (Crevier 1993: 31; Brooks 2002a: 17–21).

Another example of theoretically motivated research on robots comes from the book *Vehicles* by Valentino Braitenberg (1984). This short, light-hearted book is a very interesting exercise by a neurologist to demonstrate how intelligent behavior, at least in the eyes of the beholder, can emerge from very simple machines that operate on very simple principles. Braitenberg starts with basic machines (e.g., ones with just one or two light sensors) that have wheels, and, in a carefully worked-out series of thought experiments, he upgrades them in a stepwise fashion by introducing an element of chance and nonlinearity and using two mechanisms – one for association and chunking, the other for succession and chaining. In each small step, he describes the new behavior that would be manifested by such "vehicles" with a simple addition or modification. Eventually, Braitenberg's imaginary vehicles reach a surprising degree of behavioral sophistication.

Both of these examples come from outside AI – namely, from neurology. However, eye–hand robots that can manipulate simple geometrical objects, such as blocks, should probably be considered the first products of attempts in AI in building robots. The problem with these early robots, as we have seen, was the very impoverished character of the environments in which they could successfully operate. Furthermore, early AI researchers "cheated," to use Brooks' word (1997: 417), by basically solving many of the serious problems for their systems beforehand, and the principal mechanism for this, according to Brooks, was "abstraction" (by which he essentially means "perception" or even "filtering of raw input data into preexistent categories") whose usage, according to Brooks, "is usually considered part of good science, and not (as it is used in AI) as a mechanism for self-delusion" (Brooks 1997: 398). In AI, however, he complains, abstraction is usually used to factor out all need for either perception or motor skills (ibid.). So the malady, according to Brooks, is "abstraction," and the remedy is to squarely face the need for perception and action, and to let the artifact itself perform the abstraction (ibid.).

The neorobotic approach sought to fix the situation by using "subsumption" architectures that allow the gradual buildup of complex behaviors from simpler ones. And, as a brief look at the list of physical or simulated robots that have been built would verify, genuine contributions have been made in this direction. Many research labs around the world still diligently pursue this line of research on robots, and there have been worthwhile findings. Maris and te Boekhorst (1996), for instance, report experiments in a microworld populated by very simple Braitenberg vehicles, which act collectively to build heaps of simple objects. What seems to the observer to be a complicated collective behavior is, in fact, the result of a very simple mechanism for avoiding obstacles (using a light sensor). The Artificial Intelligence Laboratory at the University of Zurich is also engaged in similar experiments on the collective behavior of robots (Pfeifer and Scheier 1999).[17]

There are also other streams of research conducted under the rubrics of Affective AI and Human-Robot Interaction (HRI) (e.g., Sloman 2001; Minsky 2005; Scheutz et al. 2007). Although some of this work is subject to similar pitfalls highlighted in the current writing (cf. Scheutz 2002), it still can make significant contributions to an integrated understanding of emotions, language, perception, and action. In one such study, Brick and Scheutz (2007) report on a robot that interacts with humans face-to-face using natural language. Building on "the human tendency to anthropomorphize artifacts," this approach is based on the premise that "people will base their expectations about a robot's capabilities (perceptual, linguistic, etc.) on their observations of its appearance and behavior."[18] For instance, a robot with two "eyes" on a movable "head," will be expected to see objects and to direct its gaze to them. Such expectation will be violated, the argument goes, if the robot does not use perceivable context in its language behavior. A robot that is designed on these premises can bring the material context to bear in language processing, integrating language and perception in an interesting way.

This is not to say that such experiments show the feasibility of a purely "nouvelle" approach for achieving full human-level AI. As Scheutz et al. (2007) point out, even natural human-like interactions between robots and humans is not achievable in the foreseeable future; "in fact, we are not even close." As was pointed out earlier in the chapter, the major challenge for the robotic approach is to be able to generalize to more sophisticated behaviors. Over time, it has become ever clearer that there is only so much that can be done with the purely bottom-up designs of robots such as Genghis. At some point, in order to get more interesting results, one has to consider bringing in top-down elements, as in traditional AI. This is basically what the Cog group has done halfheartedly, and without explicitly admitting it – for example, the introduction of template-matching algorithms for face-detection, the use of the theory-of-mind theory to explain their project, and so on.

But my concern is not one of intellectual honesty; my concern is that the MIT group made a leap from the "modest" goal of insect-level intelligence to the very sophisticated goal of human intelligence, and never justified it theoretically. Not only that, they have tried, as we have seen, to link the Cog project to human biology, psychology, and sociology in inconsistent and unwarranted ways. In doing so, the Cog group has reintroduced some of the old tensions in AI, and has introduced new tensions as well. Examples of the former are the tensions between inside and outside or between representation and perception/action; examples of the latter are those between (physical) embodiment and having a (biological) body, between life and cognition, between expressions and impressions, between communication and communion, and so on and so forth.

These observations illustrate how notions such as "embodiment," "situatedness," and "development" have been incorporated into business as usual within AI research, reviving some of the main tenets of initial AI (Suchman 2007: 230–31): the primacy of the mind over the body; the positing of a "world" that preexists independent of the body; and the understanding of the body as a kind of receiver for stimuli given by the world. Based on these tenets, the figure that has emerged from neorobotic AI is "a bodied individual in a physical environment, rather than a socially situated individual" (Adam 1998: 136).

What We Have Learned *from* Cog

But have you ever heard of an AI failure?

    – Brooks (1991/1997: 397)

There's this stupid myth out there that AI has failed.

    – Brooks (2002b: 82)

In the late 1980s and early 1990s, when Rodney Brooks started to criticize mainstream AI, he blamed the AI community for what many others before him (e.g., Hubert Dreyfus) had charged: failure to admit failure and, to use his own term, "(self-) deception":

They partition the problems they work on into two components. The AI component, which they solve, and the non-AI component, which they don't solve. Typically, AI "succeeds" by defining the parts of the problem that are not solved not-AI. (Brooks 1997: 398)

Some time later, when Brooks's own approach and the neorobotics research at MIT (and elsewhere) had moved into the limelight, he seems to have changed his opinion altogether, arguing that "AI is everywhere" (Brooks 2002b: 82). Brooks's examples of an omnipresent and successful AI are things such as regulating the fuel injectors in cars, finding the gates that we need to board airplanes at the airport, and competing against humans in video games (ibid.). On the basis of such examples, Brooks now charges critics for advancing the "stupid myth ... that AI has failed," notwithstanding the fact that the major point of these debates, as Brooks himself was once eager to point out, had to do with "replicating the full power of human intelligence," not with fuel injectors, airport gates, and video games. I would like here to speculate about the possible reasons for this drastic shift of perspective.

One of the charges that the young Brooks used to advance against the AI community was that, because of the funding crisis:

AI researchers found themselves forced to become relevant. They moved into more complex domains, such as trip planning, going to a restaurant, medical diagnosis, and such like. (1986/1997: 397)

The internal desire and external pressure to become relevant, I want to suggest, is also behind both the shift of perspective at MIT and the concomitant change in research projects. DARPA, as the main source of funding for AI, has always been interested in robots – first as "mechanical spies" (devices that could collect information behind enemy lines) in the Cold War era, and later as "electronic combatants" (mechanical soldiers that can fight in high-risk frontlines) in electronic warfare, or as antiterrorist agents that can operate under hazardous conditions. Therefore, it seems likely that the surge of interest in humanoid robots has much to do with the rising interest on the part of funding agencies for robotic soldiers.[19]

What reinforces this conjecture is that, while the neorobotics approach has found global support, the push toward humanoid robots is prevalent largely in the United States and in Japan. In the Japanese case, this is motivated mainly by a drastic increase in recent years in life expectancy, on the one hand, and by the forecasted shortage of nursing staff for the elderly, on the other. A similar motivation does not seem to exist in the United States, where it is instead the military that is the major driving force behind this kind of research. Most research centers in Europe, by contrast, have stayed faithful to the original agenda of the situated approach. As a look at the work of places such as the AI labs at the University of Birmingham, the University of Zurich, and Darmstadt University of Technology would demonstrate, the purpose in most of these labs is to evolve artificial creatures from very simple capacities to increasingly complex and autonomous ones. As another example of this difference, the European Commission's Cognitive Systems initiative has explicitly made it clear that the primary aim of the project is to advance *scientific* understanding (Sloman 2005: 15).

Some of the research groups in Europe are, in fact, critical of the Cog project because they fear that, in its rush toward complex robots, it may damage the reputation of the whole robotics effort. One such critique comes from the group at Sussex, which, ironically, calls itself, COGS. Risan (1997: 125) reports from his close observation of the COGS group:

Rodney Brooks at MIT, the most famous "insect builder" in the AI community, has recently challenged the "insect approach" by starting to make a humanoid, a human robot, called Cog. This project, when it became known in COGS, received a lot of attention and was fiercely criticized, by ALifers and non-ALifers alike. AI has throughout the years been much criticized for making "wild" claims about what their machines will soon be able to do. . . . Brooks' Cog project, especially the very optimistic time schedule – consciousness was to be achieved by the end of 1997 (Brooks and Stein 1993: 15) – seemed to be another example of the extravagant claims of AI, possibly making the whole discipline, people at COGS feared, look ridiculous.

In summary, careful study of the Cog project once again confirms the central thesis of this writing that the opposing demands of scientific and engineering practices are the main source of tension in AI, and that to understand these tensions one needs to look at the broader social and historical context of phenomena.

9   Copycat: Analogical AI

Hofstadter's Romantic Dream

I am a romantic who tends to see the power and depth of human creativity as virtually limitless. . . . I hope thereby to convey the attitude that in AI . . . , one should not expect full success overnight – nor should anyone want it.

– Douglas Hofstadter: *Le Ton beau de Marot*

Copycat is a computer model of analogy-making in the domain of letter-string puzzles. Given an analogy problem such as "**abc** ⇒ **abd**; **iijjkk** ⇒?"[1], for example, it comes up with a set of various answers such as **iijjll**, **iijjdd**, **iijjkl**, **iijjkd**, **iijjkk**, **iikjkk**, **iidjkk**, or even **abd** or **aabbdd**.

Puzzles such as these are common in aptitude tests because apparently they provide useful measures of people's intelligence and creativity. Copycat, by the same token, is believed to have some degree of creativity, albeit a minute one. This model, its successor Metacat, and its siblings Letter Spirit, Tabletop, Phaeaco, and others owe their original conception to Douglas Hofstadter and his Fluid Analogies Research Group. Hofstadter believes that analogies are at the core of human cognition and creativity, and that computer models of analogy-making can provide useful insights into the mechanisms underlying the marvels of human intelligence, from art to science and from language to music. In this chapter, we study a few models of creativity and analogy-making, in particular Copycat, which is based on Hofstadter's views.

BACKGROUND: THE QUESTION OF LEVEL

In the early years of seventeenth century, in a classic experiment on falling bodies, Galileo tested the fall of a smooth-surfaced object on a lubricated inclined plane to find the correlation between speed and time of travel. The reason for this experimental setup was to achieve a "frictionless" world – that is, to minimize the effects of friction in order to be able to control for key parameters such as height and slope. Galileo could have, for instance, rolled a rock from a peak in the Alps to find the above correlation, but he did not (Although he famously did a similar experiment at the Tower of Pisa, but that is a different story). Instead, he chose to do this in a "carefully-designed and highly-restricted" domain. This kind of controlled experimentation, according to historians of science, marks the beginning of modern science as we know it today. Almost four hundred years after Galileo and kinematics, we might ask, What is the equivalent of what he did in the realm of AI?

This question is at the heart of a debate in AI, including the research done on analogies. Briefly, the debate has to do with the proper domains of research in AI in terms of the *real* or the *ideal* character of the problems investigated. Some researchers advocate idealized domains because they believe that such domains provide useful insights about universal *mechanisms* of analogy-making that we can then use to understand real-world problems (Hofstadter 1985). Others advocate real-world domains, and argue that the significance of analogy is as a mechanism for conceptual change, "where it allows people to import a set of ideas worked out in one domain into another" (Forbes et al. 1998: 247). They charge that domain-specific models such as Copycat cannot capture this significant aspect of analogy-making. The first group counterargue that current computer models of analogy-making which are claimed to work in real-world domains lack flexibility and genuine analogical mechanisms because too much of the solution is already built into these model by the modeler.[2] This debate brings up many thorny issues about research in AI, which we will try to address in this chapter.

CREATIVITY: THE ELUSIVE MIND

Creativity, in art and music but also in daily activities, is considered a mark of intelligence. Studying creativity might indeed provide an "acid test" for cognitive science: "cognitive science cannot succeed if it cannot model creativity, and it is here that it is most likely to fail" (Dartnall 2002: 14). Psychologically speaking, traditional accounts of creativity – from the inspirational view that considers creativity as essentially mysterious to the romantic view that attributes creativity to exceptional gifts such as insight or intuition – are inadequate because they beg the question by simply replacing one name (creativity) with another (divine gift, insight, etc.). Arthur Koestler (1964) recognized this shortcoming and tried to give a more principled account of *how* creativity works but, as Boden (1990: 5) points out, his own view was no more than suggestive. Henri Poincaré (1982) adopted a more systematic approach, and formulated a four-phase process of creative thinking – roughly, conscious preparation, subconscious incubation, abrupt insight, and evaluation. Like Koestler, his account highlights the significance of "long, unconscious prior work" preceding the creative act.

The four phases of creativity suggested by Poincaré only give a departure point for the new sciences of the mind – functionalism starts where phenomenology stops. If creativity is, at least partly, the outcome of "long, unconscious prior work," the question is, What does this "work" consist of? And how could it be best studied? In their attempt to answer these questions, studies in AI and cognitive science focus on mental *processes* that give rise to creativity. As Dartnall has argued, most of these belong to the so-called *combinationist* accounts according to which *nothing can come of nothing*, "so that what we have must be a *combination or recombination of what we already had*" (2002: 15). The problem with these accounts is that they do not tell us *which* combinations are novel and *how* novel combinations can come about (Boden 1994; cf. Dartnall: ibid.). Dartnall further argues that there is a close link between combinationism and mentalism, in that they both rely on an atomistic view of cognition where simple entities are syntactically manipulated to produce more complex wholes. The only difference is that mentalism is committed to the manipulation of *interpreted* entities, whereas combinationism is not (ibid.: 18–19). Dartnall seeks to provide an account of creativity that draws upon knowledge and judgment, rather than mental combination of syntactic elements.[3]

To this end, Dartnall distinguishes three distinct types of creativity. First is the type of creativity that trades in *uninterpreted* components (e.g., in music and architecture). Second is the type of creativity that involves *interpreted* components, whether the components are representational in themselves (as in certain styles of painting) or by convention (as when we say, "let this pepper pot represent Napoleon"). Finally, the third type of creativity, according to Dartnall, does not have components at all (e.g., pottery). The idea is that combinationist accounts can at best explain the first two types of creativity but not the third type, which does not rely on the combination of previous components. The challenge, then, would be to show "how creative products can emerge, not out of a combination of basic elements, but out of our knowledge and skill – out of what we know about them and their domains" (ibid.: 21).

In what follows, we will see examples of computer models of creativity roughly for each of these types: Emmy composes music is a purely combinationist style, Aaron has evolved to produce figurative paintings that seem meaningful to the human eye, and Copycat solves analogy problems using organizing concepts and themes, maybe pointing to a direction for AI and cognitive science to meet the challenge mentioned in the previous paragraph.

Emmy: The Combinationist Composer

Experiments with computer composition in music abound (Loy 1989; see Cope 1991: Chapter 1 for a brief history). One of the most interesting and celebrated of these is David Cope's Experiments in Musical Intelligence, EMI or Emmy. Imagine feeding in Beethoven's nine symphonies to a machine, and it coming out with Beethoven's Tenth. That is almost what Emmy is all about. Initially conceived in 1981, Emmy has moved on to produce music in the style of such revered musicians as Bach, Brahms, Chopin, and Mozart, and with a quality that the most sophisticated musicians find impressive and "deceitful." Hofstadter (2002) reports a set of auditions in which students and faculty at reputable schools such as Indiana, Julliard, and Eastman Rochester listened to the music composed by either these great composers or by Emmy in *their* style, and were not able to guess the provenance with better than a chance probability. Hofstadter himself describes his first encounter with an Emmy mazurka in the style of Chopin in this manner:

I was impressed, for the piece seemed to *express* something. . . . It was nostalgic, had a bit of Polish feeling to it, and it did not seem in any way plagiarized. It was *new*, it was unmistakably *Chopin-like* in spirit, and it was *not emotionally empty*. (ibid.: 72; original emphasis)

As we note, some of the concepts that emerged in discussing the robot Kismet in the previous chapter – impression, expression, feeling, emotions – are brought up here in high relief. Given the close association between music and human spirit, this has caught music aficionados by surprise: "I was truly shaken," continues Hofstadter. "How could emotional music be coming out of a program that had never heard a note, never lived a moment of life, never had any emotions whatsoever?" This reaction is similar in kind but stronger in depth to some of the responses that we saw to Deep Blue's victory over Kasparov (see Chapter 2). Writing about this similarity between Emmy and Deep Blue, Hofstadter expresses his concern about "the profundity of the human mind's sublimity being taken away, being robbed, by the facile victories of programs that *seemed totally out of touch with the essence of the domains* in which they were operating so well" (2002: 73–74; emphasis added). Our interest here is in the relationship between Emmy and its domain, which Hofstadter characterizes as seemingly "out of touch." Before discussing this, however, we need to know a little bit about Emmy's inner working.[4]

Very briefly, the basic idea behind Emmy is what Cope calls "recombinant music" – finding recurrent structures of various kinds in a composer's music, and reusing those structures in new arrangements, so as to construct a new piece *in the same style* (Hofstadter 2002: 74). Being given a set of input pieces (usually by a single composer and belonging to the same general form, such as mazurka), Emmy chops up and reassembles them in a principled and coherent way. The guiding principles in this process are very similar to those followed by someone solving a jigsaw puzzle – namely, to simultaneously observe the local fit of each piece with other pieces and the global pattern of the whole picture. Hofstadter calls these syntactic and semantic meshing, as they deal, respectively, with form and content. In addition, in each composition Emmy incorporates *signatures* – a characteristic intervallic pattern that recurs throughout a composer's *œuvre* – as well as another sophisticated mechanism that captures and manipulates repeated motifs at different levels of the input pieces.

The computer implementation of the above techniques and mechanisms has taken the programming of roughly twenty thousand lines of code in Lisp by David Cope, who writes "There is no magic in my work, only long hard hours of programming, a lot of musical experience, and some lucky guess-work at certain junctures" (1991: x). Of course, the composer does not claim to be an AI researcher by any measure, and one should not hold him account-able for the "cannons" of AI. Neither does Hofstadter criticize Cope for taking on an immature project by stepping outside the realm of microdomains. He only expresses his bafflement with the total disconnect between the (mecha-nistic) method and the (impressive) results. "It gave me a fright, and I talked honestly about that" (personal communication).

Aaron: The Figurative Painter[5]

In art, too, people have tried to test computers in terms of creativity. One of the first experiments in computer-generated art is Harold Cohen's *Aaron*, a computer-artist whose products have enjoyed the approval of the art world, being exhibited in respected museums around the world. A well-established painter himself, Cohen was originally interested in abstract, nonrepresen-tational art. Cohen's early view, which is sometimes referred to as "abstract symbolism," was influenced by both the Modernists' denial of meaning in art and by Abstract Expressionists' fascination with universal themes; although he adhered to neither, arguing that art should be a "meaning generator not a meaning communicator" (Cohen 1995). In other words, rather than receiv-ing a specific meaning codified in the artwork, the viewer of art should create meaning *de novo* – a feat that human beings seem to excel at in various degrees. This propensity of humans to assign meaning became a central theme for Cohen, who wanted to answer the question "How is it that the marks you make take on certain kinds of meaning?" (McCorduck 1991: 16). In the

Figure 9.1. Aaron's early drawings.

context of our discussion, Cohen's work can be considered an experiment in what I have called the Generalized Eliza Effect in this book.

Cohen experimented with these ideas first by creating map-like paintings produced by splattering a canvas with paint and then drawing lines between the dots of paint according to certain rules, and later by generating child-like paintings from ink and crumpled Dacron cloth. The desire to exclude himself from execution led Cohen to computers on the presumption that this "would permit a rigorous test of ideas about art-making and would demonstrate their validity if their execution produced art objects" (ibid.). For this purpose, Cohen encoded a set of hierarchical rules that he called "cognitive primitives" – for example, figure-ground rules, closure, similarity, division, repetition, and spatial distribution. The drawings produced according to these rules were crude mixtures of closed and open figures scattered about the allotted space (Figure 9.1).

To improve Aaron's artistic abilities, Cohen added more cognitive primitives inspired by observations about human children. He noticed that two events often coincide when children are learning to draw: the moment that a line migrates out from the center scribble to enclose the rest, and the first

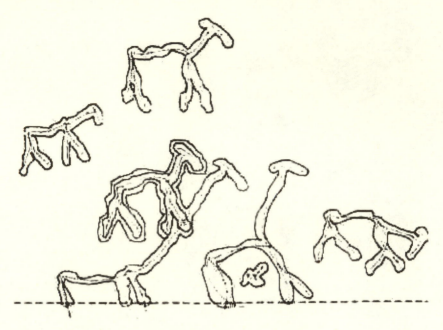

Figure 9.2. The first "meaningful" objects in Aaron's paintings.

instance when the child attributes symbolic meaning to the picture – for example, when the child thinks, "This is a picture of Mommy." Changing Aaron's drawing strategy to one where it first constructed a "core figure" and then enclosed it with an outline increased the thing-likeness of the drawings (see Figure 9.2). Cohen was reluctant for Aaron's paintings to become more figurative. He feared that the power of Aaron's drawings derived from their abstract nature, allowing the viewer greater freedom in assigning meaning. He was also unsure how much information Aaron would need in order to produce representations of objects in the real world. These reservations were both resolved by practical circumstances – Cohen was asked to modify Aaron so that it could produce drawings of the Statue of Liberty as part of an exhibition at the New York State Museum. Given sufficient descriptions of the Statue, Aaron could produce endless variants of core figures, reconfirming the basic claim of this writing that:

Evocation rests upon the viewer's propensity to assign significance to events. Far from diminishing the exercise of that propensity, the new drawings evidently shifted it to a higher site, where significance is assigned to the dramatic relationships generated by what the elements – the explicit figures – seem to stand for, rather than the simpler act of simply identifying the elements themselves. (McCorduck 1991: 100)

Aaron's drawings continued to improve in terms of balance, perspective, and accuracy, acquiring a rough resemblance in subject and treatment (though not style) to primitivist paintings of Gauguin and Rousseu (see Figure 9.3). Although Cohen views Aaron as merely a means of producing his art on a par with other machines that artists use to make art, he makes an argument for the significance of Aaron to cognitive science. He claims that the reason Aaron's paintings function as art is deeply buried in how humans see the world – "we skew what we see in the direction of what we know" (ibid.: 104). Aaron's productions might have to say more about what humans bring to the experience of art than about computers acquiring human abilities.

Whether we are talking about Aaron or Emmy, therefore, we need to resolve this gap between their algorithmic and purely mechanical method and the impressive (to a certain extent, at least) results. Indeed, Hofstadter (2002) addresses this very point in discussing Emmy. Having considered and refuted a few "standard" arguments – for example, that Emmy lacks personal style, idiom, or originality; it is the *performance* of Emmy's music by a human with a heart and a soul that gives meaning to the piece; the credit should mainly go to the original composers whose styles Emmy mimics; music happens in the brain of the hearer, as John Cage taught us decades ago; and so on – he ultimately addresses the question which is at the heart of the issue: *Is there such a thing as musical meaning?* To this he replies:

I personally think that I hear meaning all over the place in music, but it is very hard for me to explain this meaningfulness in words. That's what makes music so important in my life. Were it just formal gestures, I would tire of it very quickly. But I cannot explain what it is, exactly, that I hear in a given piece, no matter how much I love that piece. I believe, as much as I believe anything, that musical semantics exists, but I don't think it is much like linguistic semantics. (Hofstadter 2002: 100–101)

I share the sense of awe and bewilderment expressed in the above sentences, and do not pretend to have an answer to the question of meaning in music. However, as suggested earlier, I take Aaron and Emmy as glaring demonstrations of what I earlier called the Generalized Eliza Effect. I would like to suggest that maybe in music, as in art and elsewhere, the attribution of meaning by the listener and observer plays a much greater role than we tend to believe. If this phenomenon manifests itself in art and music, one could imagine that it might be at work in many other places as well. I want to further suggest, along with social scientists, that the attribution might be more an outcome of sociocultural practices (partly embodied in individual minds) than cognitive science is currently inclined to grant.

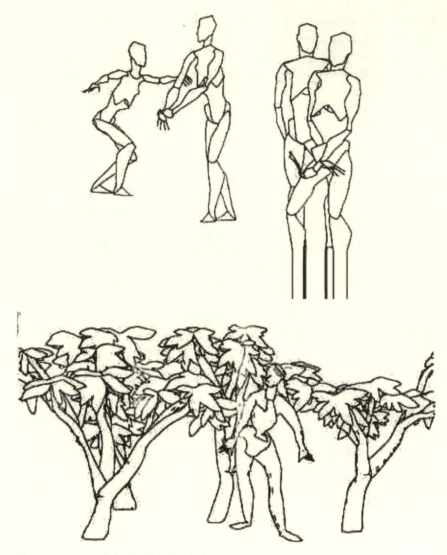

Figure 9.3. Aaron's "primitivist" paintings.

Mundane Creativity

Art and music constitute idealized domains in the same sense that chess does
(see Chapter 2), except maybe that they involve a semantic component that is,
by and large, absent from chess. As Hofstadter (1985: 181) put it, in addition to
syntactic "head pattern," art and music also have a semantic "heart pattern."
This latter component is probably what makes art and music inspiring to

people, but neither music (harmony) theory nor the science of psychology have adequately explained the origin of this inspirational power. How about more "mundane" creativity of the kind that human beings manifest throughout their daily lives (Prinz and Barsalou 2002)? Are we in a better position to understand this kind of creativity? The answer is yes, if we look at the work that is done on this topic in AI and cognitive science.[6]

As mentioned earlier, a major strand of ideas in cognitive science invokes analogy-making as the key process behind creativity. One way to be creative is to look at new situations as similar to previous, more familiar situations – that is, to make analogies between situations. Analogies have reportedly played a key role in the creation of new scientific theories (Koestler 1964; Boden 1990). But in the context of everyday thinking, scientific discoveries might just be the tip of an iceberg. That is, analogies might indeed be at work at a much more mundane level than examples of scientific creativity suggest. This is the view held by many cognitive scientists (e.g., Gentner 1983; Holyoak and Thagard 1995; Hummel and Holyoak 1997; Forbus et al. 1998; Hofstadter 2001). Hofstadter is among this group.

Hofstadter is interested in high-level perception or, rather, he believes that this is the level where most interesting cognitive processes take place. By high-level perception, I mean the level of perceptual processing at which semantically-defined concepts play a critical role (Chalmers et al. 1992). It is the level where you see something and call it a "fire," you meet someone and think "looks sort of like Louis Armstrong," sniff something and remark "Mexican restaurant," hear a piece of music on the radio and recognize "Big band jazz," and so on. In short, this is the level where prior mental categories are invoked by some kind of input (sensory or abstract), giving rise to meaning. According to Hofstadter, what happens in all of the above situations is an act of analogy-making, "because whenever a set of incoming stimuli activates one or more mental categories, some amount of slippage must occur (no instance of a category ever being precisely identical to a prior instance)" (2001: 501).

A Concept Is a Package of Analogies

The notion of *conceptual slippage*, alluded to in the above sentence, is central to Hofstadter's view. Concepts and categories, according to this view, are quintessentially fluid entities with ill-defined and blurry boundaries that adapt to the context and align themselves with it. The concept of Vietnam which simply refers to a particular country in Southeast Asia, for example, is tightly associated in the average American mind with the huge political debacle in which the United States got mired in the late 1960s and early 1970s. Along with the accompanying social and cultural strife, this complex historical situation is referred to as "Vietnam," being associated with other concepts such as war, communism, social unrest, 1968, rice, the Pentagon, President Nixon, dominos, rice, and so on. It is on the basis of these associations that phrases such as "Iraq: Bush's Vietnam" or "Windows-95: Microsoft's Vietnam" start to make sense. The idea is that, "It is the complex, fluid nature of concepts in the mind that allows such analogies to be effortlessly perceived and understood" (Marshall 1999).

Similarly, the concept "shadow" illustrates a great deal of fluidity, as shown by the following examples:

- "rain shadow" – the arid zone to the one side of a mountain range;
- "snow shadow" – a circular patch of green seen underneath a tree after snowfall;
- "in the shadow of his father" – George W. Bush coming to office in 2001;
- "in the shadow of 9/11" – the New York city after 2001;
- "out of the shadow of her cancer" – a breast-cancer survivor;
- "in the shadow of the war" – Iraq after the U.S. occupation.

In other words, the domain of the word "shadow," and basically any other concept, is a blurry region in semantic space. As these examples show, the blurriness derives from a process where new situations are mapped onto prior categories and situations, and this is analogy-making *par excellence*. A concept, in other words, "is a package of analogies" (Hofstadter 2001: 503), and conceptual slippage is what allows apparently unrelated situations to be perceived as being fundamentally "the same" at a deeper, more abstract level (Marshall 1999: 4). But if analogy-making takes place at an abstract level, the question still remains as to *how* this works – that is, how is the abstract level implemented on lower-level mental mechanisms?

Subcognition Is Computational

The question of level, as we have seen before, is central in cognitive science. Roughly speaking, this is the question of, "What is the *best* level of studying cognition?" Or, given the ambiguity of the qualifier "best," a more useful way of putting the question is to ask, "At what level do most interesting cognitive events take place?" Leaving aside the obvious and pluralist reply that my undergraduate students typically give to this question – namely, that *all* levels of cognition are interesting and we should hence study them all – there are more useful ways of thinking about it. One is to think about *frequency*, and ask what it is that people (and other intelligent beings) do most of the time. The other is to consider *rigor*, and ask how we could best create formal and mathematical theories of cognition on a par with other "hard" sciences. The third alternative is to focus on the *distinctiveness* of particular cognitive behaviors, and look for distinguishing properties that separate them from other behaviors. Yet another way of thinking about the question of level is to start with the basic premise of AI and cognitive science – that cognition is computation – and ask at what level the premise is most meaningful. This last approach is roughly what Hofstadter adopts. In his seminal paper *Waking Up from the Boolean Dream*, Hofstadter (1985) motivates his approach by suggesting a sharp contrast between two points of view. One is attributed to Herbert Simon, who allegedly had said the following:

Everything of interest in cognition happens above the 100-millisecond level – the time it takes you to recognize your mother.

The other is Hofstadter's own view, which he provocatively phrases as follows:

Everything of interest in cognition happens below the 100-millisecond level – the time it takes you to recognize your mother.

The intended pun notwithstanding, these opposite statements point to a very basic difference of viewpoints in regards to the question of level. "Am I really computing when I think?" asks Hofstadter, to which he implicitly gives a negative answer, especially if we take "computing" to mean what computers do:

Admittedly, my neurons may be performing sums in an analog way, but does this pseudo-arithmetical hardware mean that the epiphenomena themselves are also doing arithmetic, or should be – or even *can* be – described in conventional computer-science terminology? Does the fact that taxis stop at red lights mean that traffic jams stop at red lights? One should not confuse the properties of objects with the properties of statistical ensembles of those objects. (Hofstadter 1985: 643)

The notion of "epiphenomenon," which others call *innocently emergent* (Dennett 1977) or simply an *emergent* (Clark 1997) phenomenon, is a key concept that has gained tremendous traction in cognitive science and elsewhere in recent years. The point of the taxis-traffic and neurons-thoughts analogy is to emphasize that "what you see at the top level need not have anything to do with the underlying swarm of activities brining it into existence" (Hofstadter 1985: 643). Hofstadter's point, in short, is that, "*something can be computational at one level, but not at another level*" (ibid.; original emphasis).

The goal of AI models, then, would be to show how these levels interact or collaborate in giving rise to meaningful interpretations of perceptions and events. This is the idea behind models such as Copycat.

COPYCAT: THE MICROWORLD OF LETTER STRINGS

Built on the above principles, Copycat is designed to be a model of fluid concepts, high-level perception, and analogy-making that simulates the complex, subconscious interplay between perception and concepts underlying human creativity (Mitchell 1993; Marshall 1999). Copycat, as mentioned at the outset, seeks to do this in the abstract and idealized domain of letter strings. The architecture of Copycat consists of the *Workspace* (roughly a short-term memory, where all perceptual activity takes place), the *Slipnet* (roughly the long-term memory, where the program's concepts reside), and the *Coderack*, where agents called *codelets* collectively work in parallel, at different speeds, on different aspects of an analogy problem, without a high-level executive process directing the course of events. The main structures created in the Workspace are *bridges* created through a mapping, *groups* created by a chunking process, and *rules* that capture the way in which the initial string changes.

Given the analogy problem "**abc** ⇒ **abd; iijjkk** ⇒?," for instance, codelets work together to build up a strong, coherent mapping between the initial string **abc** and the target string **iijjkk**, and also between the initial string and the modified string **abd**. Codelets also build hierarchical groups within strings, which serve to organize the raw perceptual data (the letters) into a coherent chunked whole. For example, in the string **iijjkk**, codelets might build three "sameness-groups" **ii**, **jj**, and **kk**, and then a higher-level "successorship-group" comprised of those three groups. A mapping consists of a set of bridges between corresponding letters or groups that play respectively similar roles in different strings. Each bridge is supported by a set of *concept-mappings* that together provide justification for perceiving the correspondences between objects. For example, a bridge might be built between **a** in **abc** and the group **ii** in **iijjkk**, supported by the concept-mappings leftmost ⇒ leftmost and letter ⇒ group, representing the idea that both objects are leftmost in their strings, and one is a letter and the other is a group. Nonidentity concept-mappings such as letter ⇒ group are called *slippages*, a concept that is at the core of this view of cognition, as we saw earlier.

Finally, once a mapping has been built between the initial and the modified strings (i.e., between **abc** and **abd**), a rule such as the following is created: "Change letter-category of rightmost letter to successor" or "Change letter-category of rightmost letter to d." It is to be noted that different ways of

Workspace

(Codelets run: 882)

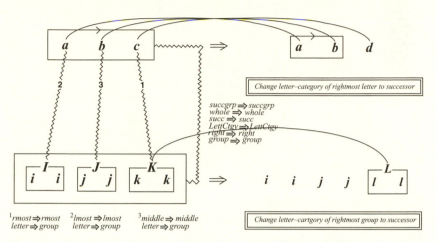

Figure 9.4. Copycat's Workspace, while working on the"**abc ⇒ abd; iijjkk ⇒**?" analogy (from Marsall 1999, with permission).

looking at the initial/modified change, combined with different ways of building the initial/target mapping, give rise to different answers. A bridge from the letter **c** in **abc** to the group **kk** in **iijjkk**, based on a letter ⇒ group slippage, may yield the answer **iijjll** or **iijjdd**, depending on the rule used to describe **abc ⇒ abd**. However, a bridge from **c** to the rightmost letter **k** in **iijjkk** may instead yield **iijjkl** or **iijjkd**, again depending on the rule. In short, to produce an answer, the slippages underlying the mapping between **abc** and **iijjkk** are used by codelets to "translate" the rule describing **abc ⇒ abd** into a new rule that applies to **iijjkk**, such as "Change letter-category of rightmost group to successor" (see Figure 9.4).

METACAT: FROM SELF-EVALUATION TO SELF-WATCHING

An interesting feature of the domain of Copycat analogies is that there is no single "right" answer for any given problem; rather, a range of answers is always possible. In the example discussed earlier, as we saw at the outset, there are about eight possible answers. People often make consistent judgments about the quality of some of these answers, but the ones judged "best" are not at all the most obvious answers. Copycat has a feature that allows it to evaluate its answers to particular problems. Called *temperature*, this is a simple numerical measure of overall Workspace "coherence," which reflects,

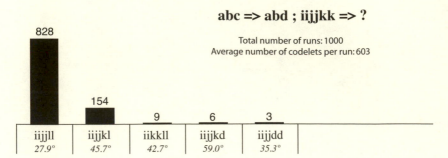

Figure 9.5. Copycat evaluates its satisfaction by using "temperature" (from Marshall 1999, with permission).

at any given moment, the amount and quality of structures built so far – the lower the temperature the higher the organization of the Workspace and the higher the quality of the relevant answer (Figure 9.5). Temperature is computed on the basis of the *strength* values of all of the structures existing in the Workspace, measured by their overall fit with the current set of mappings and weighted by each structure's relative importance. For example, if the *group* concept in the Slipnet is highly activated, a bridge between **a** in **abc** and the leftmost letter **i** in **iijjkk** will have a lower strength than a bridge between **c** and **kk**.

However, the concept of *temperature*, despite its usefulness, is crude because Copycat is still unable to explain *why* it considers particular answers to be good or bad; it cannot explain its choices. In other words, the program does not have the capability to *watch* and evaluate its own processing. This shortcoming is the main motivation behind *Metacat*, the successor of Copycat that has a "self-watching" capability as well as a memory to retain answers to a given problem for the purpose of comparing and contrasting them. For example, given the problem "**abc** $\Rightarrow$ **abd; xyz** $\Rightarrow$?," two possible answers are **xyd** and **wyz**. The second answer derives from the observation that **abc** and **xyz** start at the opposite ends of the alphabet, with **abc** going to the right based on successorship and **xyz** going to the left based on predecessorship.[7] In other words, this answer is associated with the notion of symmetry between the "opposite" letters **a** and **z**, which makes it qualitatively superior, in most people's minds, to the literal-minded answer **xyd**. People who make such a judgment are often also capable to explain it in terms of the notion of symmetry, as does Metacat. In addition, people also see the contrast between the above problem and "**rst** $\Rightarrow$ **rsu; xyz** $\Rightarrow$?," in which the notion of symmetry is absent, making the literal-minded **xyu** superior to the alternative **wyz** in this case. In other words, **xyd** and **xyu** play essentially identical roles in their respective problems, and are thus of comparative quality, whereas the two **wyz** answers are quite different, even though on the surface they appear to be identical. Metacat is also capable of making similar judgments, demonstrating its ability to "see" similarities and differences between problems as well as answers.

FROM SUBCOGNITION TO COGNITION

The capability of making comparisons such as the above in Metacat is related to another feature – namely, that it can build *explicit* representations of the ideas underlying the answers it finds. This is what the program designers mean by *self-watching*, and what many cognitive scientists and philosophers consider a property of conscious behavior (e.g., Karmiloff-Smith 1992). The explicit representations called *themes* are memory structures getting built in Metacat's *Themespace* as the program works on an analogy problem. Themes are comprised of the concepts that are in the Slipnet, and can take various activation levels, depending on the extent to which the ideas they represent are being used in the Workspace. For instance, in the problem **"abc ⇒ abd; xyz ⇒?"**, an **a-z** bridge built between strings **abc** and **xyz**, supported by the concept-mappings first ⇒ last, leftmost ⇒ rightmost, and letter ⇒ letter, gives rise to three *bridge themes* – Alpha-Pos: opposite, representing the idea of alphabetic-position symmetry; Direction: opposite, representing the idea of left-right symmetry; and ObjectType: same, representing the idea of mapping objects of the same type (i.e., letters) onto each other. As yet another type of explicit representation, Metacat also maintains *traces* of the most active themes throughout the solution of an analogy problem, keeping stock of themes important to the problem (Figure 9.6).

It should be noted that themes as discussed earlier are intended to represent the awareness of particular aspects of an analogy problem at the *cognitive* level, not the subcognitive level. Given the original premise in Hofstadter's view about the significance of the subcognitive level, this move to a higher level can only be justified by noticing the narrow domain under investigation here, as the developers of the model acknowledge themselves:

Copycat's concepts, to be sure, are but a crude approximation to the true power and flexibility of human concepts. Still, there is a sense in which its concepts really are active, semantic entities within its tiny, idealized world – not just empty static symbols shunted around by the program. (Marshall and Hofstadter 1997)

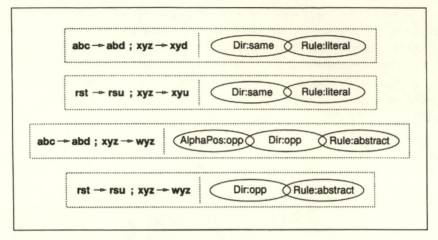

Figure 9.6. Metacat's Themespace (from Marshall 1999, with permission).

LETTER SPIRIT: THE FLIGHT OF IMAGINATION

The philosophy on which Copycat and Metacat are built, as well as the resulting architecture, do not only work in the domain of letter strings; they are also
applied to other domains such as the design of letter forms, the simplified
arrangement of a table top, the geometrical domain of Bongard problems, and
so on (Hofstadter and The Fluid Analogies Research Group 1995; Foundalis
2006). Letter Spirit, for example, focuses on the creative act of artistic letter design. Such design should take into account two orthogonal aspects of
letterforms: *categorical sameness* of instances of the same letter in different
styles (e.g., the letter "a" in Times and Baskerville) and the *stylistic sameness*
of instances of different letters in the same style (e.g., the letters "a" and "f" in
Times). Figure 9.7 shows the relationship of these two aspects. Given one or
more seed letters, the goal of Letter Spirit is to design the rest of the alphabet
in their style, or *spirit*. Rehling (2002) provides details of how the program
does this, and I am not going to repeat them here.

Clearly, Copycat and Letter Spirit operate in different domains but deep
down they have something in common. The question is, what is that common "thing"? If one were to apply the underlying method to the programs
themselves, one should ask, "What is it to be a program like Copycat, Letter
Spirit, Phaeaco, etc.? What is it to be a program in Hofstadter's lab? What is
the spirit of Letter Spirit?" Broadly speaking, the answer to these questions is:
the principles upon which they are built. We have already discussed two such
principles. The first one has to do with the question of level, and the second

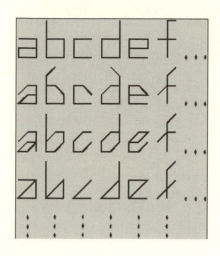

Figure 9.7. Items in any column have letters in common; items in any row have styles in common (from Rehling 2002, with permission).

principle, as articulated by Hofstadter (see the Prologue), is that all of these programs work in "carefully-designed and highly-restricted microdomains." While the creators of these programs consider this second principle the source of the strength of their models, their critics, as we have seen, are skeptical of the claim. This debate leads to other interesting issues about the nature of work in AI that I will discuss later in the chapter.

In addition to this, McGraw and Hofstadter (2002: 253) discuss a number of other principles, especially as they relate to programs that model creativity – namely, that the program must make its own design decisions, that its knowledge of the domain must be rich, that its concepts must be flexible and context-dependent, and that it must be able to continuously judge and modify its own output in an converging process of iteration. All of these principles might be important in building models of creativity but, following Dartnall (2002), I would like to highlight a related epistemological shift in our understanding of the notion of representation.

The combinationist accounts of creativity, as we saw earlier, assume that (what seem to be) novel creations are nothing but assemblages of prior elements stored as mental representations in the creator's mind. This view is intuitively appealing because it accords with our basic intuition that nothing can be created from nothing. According to this intuition, a letterform designer, for instance, can produce a new font by drawing upon bits and pieces of previous letters and styles, or variations thereof. This intuition is sensible to the extent that it reasserts that basic metaphysical principle that nothing can be generated *ex nihilo*, but it brings with it a whole epistemological baggage that might not be as thorough – especially in its reliance on the view of representations as static, mirror-like copies of sensory experience. The combinationist view of creativity shares with the mentalist view of cognition this basic understanding of mental representations as subconsciously stored copies of prior experience.

We saw the various limitations of the mentalist notion of representation in previous chapters. As far as creativity is concerned, the main problem of mentalism is that it cannot adequately explain those instances of creative act that trade in a large dose of "imagination." These are cases where the distance between the created product and previous experience is so complex and convoluted that a simple reassembly of prior elements cannot possibly explain what happens. In fact, far from being novel, these flights of imagination are manifested all the time by all human beings – that is, whenever we make analogies, or whenever we manage to visualize our favorite politician on a donkey with yellow grin on their green face (try and do that right now). As Dartnall has demonstrated, explaining these imaginative acts requires a new epistemology in which representations, "rather than copied or transduced from experience, are generated 'in the imagination' by our knowledge about a domain. They are the created products of such knowledge, rather than stored repositories or representations of what we know" (2002: 51). Dartnall has explained at length how this view is partially, but successfully, implemented in Letter Spirit, especially in its "central feedback loop of creativity" where the program constantly evaluates and modifies its products. According to this alternative view, "we first learn to make judgments about the world and then deploy this ability offline to construct representations in our minds" (ibid.: 2). In short, creativity is at the bottom a continuous process of making sense of the world, generating representations in the imagination, and using them to make even more sense of the world (which now includes our own products and artifacts).

CONCLUSION: TAKING CONCEPTS SERIOUSLY

This chapter introduced us to AI models of creativity, especially those that employ analogy-making as their main mechanism, and in particular models such as Copycat and Metacat, which are based on Hofstadter's views. In order to better understand and appreciate these models of creativity, we first looked at Emmy and Aaron as examples of recognizable types of creativity. We learned that these two models, while inspiring and impressive, might have to say more about human impressions than about computer expressions. However, there might be more significant lessons to be learnt form the models of analogy-making.

What Have We Learned *about* Copycat? To Rehabilitate Representations

Analogy-making forms a broad area of research in AI and cognitive science with numerous models and approaches – for example, the ARCS and ACME models (Holyoak and Thagard 1989), the SME model (Falkenheiner et al. 1990), and the case-based models of CBR (Leake 1996). Among these, the distinctive feature of the approach taken in Copycat and other models like it is probably that they take concepts seriously. The core assumption underlying this approach is that only by understanding the nature of concepts will other important aspects of cognition (such as perception, memory organization, reminding, creativity, and self-awareness) become understandable. Understanding concepts, according to proponents of this approach, "is the central problem of cognitive science and artificial intelligence" (Marshall 1999). Whether or not we agree with this, the fact of the matter is that there is not much research done on "concepts" in either AI or cognitive science. Concepts are simply not taken seriously, and to the extent that they are the questions that people ask about them often remain philosophical. We still do not know much about cognitive mechanisms involved in the formation, grouping, and processing of concepts. We do not have, in other words, much to say about "thinking" and thought processes.

There are, to be sure, many reasons for this deficiency. Theoretically, I believe, one of the things that we need in order to alleviate this is a new account of representation. The classical accounts that take cognitive representations as static, passive, and faithful mirror-like copies of the outside world have certainly failed but, as we have seen in the previous chapters, recent antirepresentationalist accounts also have proven inadequate. What we need is an account that strikes a middle ground between these, and does justice to the dynamic, active, and fluid character of representations. Rather than discarding representations, as radical critics of the classical view suggest, we need to rehabilitate them (Smith forthcoming). The architecture and mechanisms of Copycat-style models, as I discussed earlier, provide the beginnings of such a rehabilitated account.[8]

To give an example of such an account, consider the work of Thompson, Oden, and Boysen (1997) on a type of chimpanzee called *Pan troglodytes*. These chimps were trained to associate a simple plastic token (such as a red triangle) with any pair of identical objects (a pair of shoes, for instance) and another plastic token with any pair of different objects (say, a cup and shoe). The chimps could then solve the more abstract problem of categorizing pairs-of-pairs of objects in terms of higher-order relations of sameness or difference – for example, "shoe/shoe and cup/shoe" should be judged as "different," whereas "shoe/shoe, cup/cup" should be considered the "same." As Clark (2003: 70–71) points out, this is a task beyond untrained chimps and even some human beings. Clark explains this on the basis of "the association of the lower-order concepts (sameness and difference) with stable, perceptible items" (namely, plastic tokens), and argues that language and linguistic labels play a similar role in human cognition. These "cognitive shortcuts," as Clark calls them, provide an interesting parallel with the kind of representational structures used in Copycat. This, in my view, is the key contribution of Copycat and its sibling models.

WHAT HAVE WE LEARNED *FROM* COPYCAT? EMERGENCE

> Artificial Intelligence research is fundamentally concerned with the intelligent behavior of machines. In attempting to create machines with some degree of intelligent behavior, AI researchers model, theorize about, predict, and emulate the activities of people. Because people are quite apparently social actors, and also because knowledgeable machines will increasingly be embedded in organizations comprising people and other machines, AI research should be concerned with the social dimensions of action and knowledge as a fundamental category of analysis. But current AI research is largely a-social, and because of this, it has been inadequate in dealing with much human behavior and many aspects of intelligence.... AI research must set its foundations [to] treat the existence and interaction of multiple actors as a fundamental category.
>
> – Gasser (1991)

Another major theme that comes to light from our study of Copycat-style models is *emergence*. The notion of emergence surfaces frequently in different places in computing, AI, and cognitive science (e.g., Hofstadter 1985; Forrest 1991; Clark 1997; McDonough 2002); it points to a new way of understanding and a new approach to modeling. This approach comes in different names and flavors, the common insight behind all of which is that "what you see at the top level need not have anything to do with the underlying swarm of activities brining it into existence" (Hofstadter 1985: 643). Copycat and Letter Spirit implement this approach by having various "agent-based analogy engines" (Dartnall 2002: 48) interact in a decentralized environment, with the overall behavior having little similarity to what each agent does. To make these models genuinely creative, the Hofstadter group limits them to idealized microdomains. On close scrutiny, however, stripping down the domain is not the only way to achieve emergent behavior. In fact, as Les Gasser suggests in the above excerpt, another alternative is to move *further out* and to create simulated environments, which provide idealized situations far less complex than the real world.

Like Hofstadter, Gasser advocates an approach to AI that would focus on "the existence and interaction of multiple actors," but instead of mental entities it seeks to understand these actors as social entities. This approach has given rise to agent-based modeling and simulation, which we looked at in Chapter 7. A similar view is advocated by what has come to be known as "swarm intelligence" (Kennedy and Eberhart 2001). This approach derives insights from the study of species such as ants, where the collective behavior of simple agents interacting locally with their environment gives rise to coherent global patterns. These approaches have found applications in many theoretical and practical projects, although not in the study of creativity. However, even in this area, AI and cognitive science will be well-served if they take "the social dimensions of action and knowledge" more seriously. The challenge is to show how collective action and knowledge may contribute to individual creativity. Recent models of creativity such as ACE (Leclerc and Gosselin 2004, 2005), which are based on the situated on-site practices of human artists, might be early examples of such attempts, although it remains to be seen how successful they will be in applying, as they do, traditional tools such as production rules to the findings of their studies.

Moreover, social science has indicated that the creative acts of the human mind cannot be separated from the cultural and material conditions of their production (Becker 1982). Our study of Emmy and Aaron clearly demonstrates this: the success of these models crucially derives from a cultural environment that is receptive to certain types of artistic and musical production, from technologies that provide the material tools of such productions, and from institutional norms and practices that promote them. We cannot fully explain the success of these programs without taking note of these parameters. This observation applies equally well to more academic projects such as Copycat – for instance, in their dealing with funding issues. Pragmatically, Hofstadter's emphasis on microdomains might be impractical when it comes to the raising of funds for AI projects. As in most other technoscientific disciplines, large projects require considerable amounts of resources that can be secured only through the support of federal or private funding agencies. And in order to secure such funds, researchers often find themselves in the position of "translating" their objectives so as to match the goals of funding agencies (see the Epilogue).[9] Hofstadter is a romanticist, and he does not hide it. He seeks to understand human creativity in ways that are faithful to both conceptual and emotional aspects of human cognition. The passage cited earlier from him on meaning in music continues as follows:

I think that when we understand musical semantics ... we will know a great deal more about how human emotionality is constituted. But I think that will be a long time in the coming. (Hofstadter 2002: 101)

One can hardly disagree with Hofstadter on this last point. It will be a while before AI and cognitive science would be able to figure out how to approach the questions that programs such as Aaron and Emmy bring up about creativity and about the way that we collectively discover or construct meaning in and through our artifacts.

EPILOGUE

Democritus' Atomic Dream

THE FUTURE OF AI

Nothing exists except atoms and empty space; everything else is opinion.
— Democritus (ca. 460–370 BCE)

Criticism is not as common in science and engineering as it is in art and literature. Scientists review each other's writings, write commentaries on them, or try to replicate a reported experiment, but they rarely criticize each other's work in the sense intended here – that is, in the sense of *a reflexive evaluation of background assumptions, biases, and principles, and an examination of the way they guide the creation of theories, models, and technical systems*. Traditionally, scientists leave such criticism to "outsiders" – philosophers, sociologists, or even to religious or political ideologues. This is not to say that science totally lacks critical practices. Scientists also have dedicated venues – societies, workshops, conferences, committees, panels, journals, as well as very rigorously established procedures of peer review – whose function is to keep things in constant check, presumably mitigating the need for self-criticism. Nevertheless, it is not common to find reflexive accounts of science from within the scientific community. Science changes, but the driving engine of change is seldom an explicitly critical encounter on the part of scientists themselves.

Contrary to this received tradition in science, the present work conducts a critical assessment of a scientific and technical field, Artificial Intelligence (AI), from a constructive standpoint that aims to contribute, rather than refute. My purpose throughout this study was to show that such a critique of AI is both necessary and useful, whether the concern is scientific (that is, it is concerned with a better understanding of the phenomenon of intelligence), or related to engineering (that is, it is intent on the creation of better devices).

309

In particular, as someone deeply interested in human cognition, I intend to draw lessons that cognitive scientists will find useful in their study.

The account provided in the preceding chapters hints at the broad context, but it is mainly focused on the intellectual aspects of the development – that is, on how guiding principles and theories have evolved over decades and have reached their present shape, and how they have been at least partially captured and realized in particular AI systems. To provide a more comprehensive picture, I would like here to pull together the different strands of ideas that are scattered throughout the chapters. As we did in Chapter 1, I am going to present these as a set of "threads" that together create the colorful fabric of AI that we have examined throughout this study.

THE THREAD OF IDEAS: THE ATTRIBUTION FALLACY

The first chapter detailed some ideas predating AI that have had a long-lasting influence on its development – for example, the idea of a mind separated from the body, the idea of thinking as consisting mainly of the logical manipulation of symbols, the idea that meaning is independent of form (as captured in the dictum "You take care of the syntax, and the semantics will take care of itself"), and so on. We have observed clear impacts of these ideas on various approaches to AI, and thus do not need to repeat them here. What I would like to do instead is to highlight a prevalent idea that is usually expressed as "Intelligence is in the eye of the beholder," but could be understood more accurately as a predisposition to attribute intelligence to various artifacts around us.

Human beings have the capability to identify with other human beings, and to experience themselves from the standpoint of other individuals – to read others' minds, to put themselves in others' shoes, so to speak (Mead 1934: 138; Enfield and Levinson 2006). This special capability is closely linked with the deeply social nature of human life, and is of utmost significance in the development of the self (ibid.: 140). There is a flip side to this central capability, however, which is manifested in our strong predilection to believe this is just as valid to do in the case of animals and other natural and artificial things: we attribute, overgeneralize, and anthropomorphize, in other words. The AI community has, often inadvertently, taken advantage of this human tendency, turning what could be called *innocent* anthropomorphism to a *professional*, and often unjustified, technoscientific one (Risan 1997: 57).

The earliest well-known manifestation of this phenomenon is the case of Eliza, the computer program designed by Joseph Weizenbaum in the mid-1960s to act like a Rogerian psychotherapist, responding to typed lamentations of patients by asking canned questions that echoed strategically chosen words back at them (see the Prologue). This simple trick convinced many people who interacted with Eliza that the program not only understood them but even empathized with them. In reflecting on this human weakness almost a decade later, Weizenbaum made some general observations about its origins in the predilection mentioned in the previous paragraph. It is worth quoting several sentences from his musings:

On a much higher level, each participant brings to the conversation an image of who the other is. Since it is impossible for any human to know another completely, that image consists in part of attributions to the other's identity, attributions which must necessarily be based on evidence derived from independent life experiences of the participant. Our recognition of another person is thus an act of induction on evidence presented to us partly by him and partly by our reconstruction of the rest of the world; it is a kind of generalization. We are, in other words, all of us prejudiced – in the sense of pre-judging – about each other. And, as we have noted we all find it hard, or even nearly impossible, to perceive – let alone to accept and to permit to become operative – evidence that tends to disconfirm our judgments. (1976: 190)

As was mentioned in the Prologue, this type of prejudice or illusion, when directed toward artifacts, has come to be known in AI as the *Eliza effect*. Due to the medium of interaction between people and the program (typed language), the Eliza effect is often understood as "the susceptibility of people to read far more understanding than is warranted into strings of symbols – especially words – strung together by computers" (Hofstadter 1995: 157). I want to suggest, however, that there is what could be called the "Generalized Eliza Effect" (GEE) that applies to all forms of interaction (verbal, gestural, social, etc.) and to all media of communication (written, spoken, pictorial, etc.) between potentially intelligent beings (humans, other animals, artifacts, etc.). GEE is manifested when we inadvertently talk to our pets, when children take the canned utterances of Furby dolls as genuinely meaningful, when people deludedly attribute empathy to Eliza, when they conflate a diagram used in describing an AI system with a representation in the program itself (as we saw in the case of Coach; see Chapter 5), when they come to believe that there are genuine emotions involved in the behaviors of Kismet, and so on. GEE is, in short, a clear manifestation of what I call the "attribution fallacy," for the sake of a specific term that applies to the unwarranted use of our tendency toward identification.[1]

It is surprising how much AI researchers, wittingly or unwittingly, both fall for and take advantage of this common fallacy. Above, I expressed the Generalized Eliza Effect in a somewhat positive manner – namely, "intelligence lies in the eye of the beholder," but in fact, GEE is often exploited in a manner so as to intimate that AI systems are far more intelligent than they really are. We have seen examples of this in almost all the preceding chapters, ranging from Deep Blue through Cyc, Cog, and Coach, and including some connectionist and dynamical models.

THE THREAD OF THEORY: TRIALS OF STRENGTH

The moment of truth is a running program.

— Herbert Simon (1995)

But why, the reader might wonder, should this kind of attribution fallacy be so prevalent in AI, as compared to other places in science and engineering? The answer, I believe, lies in the fact that AI, despite its multidisciplinary origins, is only loosely connected to other sciences, which are usually linked together in ways that tend to make them more accurate, more verifiable, and more accountable to each other (Latour 1999: 18, 97). This relative isolation of AI from the rest of science is manifested in at least two ways – namely, in terms of method and in terms of evaluation criteria.

In terms of method, AI seeks to explain the workings of the human mind or the phenomenon of intelligence in general. The study of cognition has traditionally been the realm of psychology, epistemology, and philosophy, and, except for psychology, the modes of inquiry of these disciplines rarely overlap with those of science. There are, therefore, not many historical precedents in the scientific tradition in dealing with this subject matter. As for psychology, while it might have been the original dream of AI to contribute to it, we have seen that a clear majority of current AI research is not concerned with that goal. This has severed AI's relation with psychology in serious ways.

Similarly, despite efforts of AI researchers to make their work relevant to other sciences – neurological, biological, social, and so on – the best that has happened is that AI models have been *inspired by* the findings of these sciences, but the opposite direction of influence is largely blocked. That is, the findings of AI rarely have implications for those sciences, and this makes their evaluation rather difficult. We have seen why this is the case with connectionist networks (Chapter 6), but it is more generally true of most AI. The intuition shared by some AI researchers, especially those who still care about the psychological realism of their models, might be phrased as follows:

My system is inspired by phenomenon X (the brain, a behavior, a protocol, a process); my system also works; hence the mechanism that in human beings gives rise to phenomenon X must be similar to my system.

This is a flawed reasoning with deep-going consequences, and we have seen many instances of it in the preceding chapters – for example, Coach, LSA, and Kismet in, respectively, Chapters 5, 6, and 8.

This brings us to the second way in which AI's link to the rest of science is weak – namely, its evaluation criteria. Many years ago, Cohen and Howe (1988) conjectured that evaluation is not a standard practice of AI, "because our methodology is vague." They wrote:

Where other sciences have standard experimental methods and analytic techniques, we have faith – often groundless and misleading – that building programs is somehow informative. Where other sciences expect specific aspects of research to be presented (for example, hypotheses, related research, experimental methods, and analyses and results), empirical AI has no comparable standards. (p. 35)

In other words, in AI the *working* of a system is the main measure of evaluation, and "truth," according to the quote from Herbert Simon, is equated with a running program. However, the notion of "working," as we have seen, is obscure and murky in many situations. Many connectionist models, for instance, "work" in the sense that they capture some narrow aspect of human behavior. Does this mean that the human brain also uses the same mechanisms as a connectionist network in order to generate the same behavior? We found in Chapter 6 that the answer is negative. Kismet, by contrast, "works" by responding in superficially meaningful ways to human presence. Does this mean that human social development follows a similar pattern? Again, we found that this is not necessarily the case. Moreover, in cases such as Cyc, the criterion of "working" hardly applies at all, because its developers insist that its performance will only be able to be evaluated when the total encoding of common sense has come to an end (or at least surpassed a certain critical mass) – and this stance has apparently provided room for the Cyc group to postpone the evaluation of their system to a shimmeringly vague future (with a caveat to be discussed shortly).

Philosophers of science traditionally think of the verification of scientific work either as the evaluation of *models* by checking their predictions against observed or experimental data (Lloyd 1994), or as the deduction of *laws of nature* from data and the checking of new data against the predictions of those laws (Giere 1999). Therefore, what Cohen and Howe (1988) say about other sciences is in accord with this traditional view in philosophy of science. Because of the differences between AI and other disciplines, however, these authors suggest that AI must develop its own evaluation methods appropriate to its practice, and they actually present their own methodology for this purpose (ibid.).

The idea that AI is different from other disciplines and is, therefore, in need of its own evaluation method is compatible with one of the basic premises of this writing – namely, that AI, unlike most other disciplines, is involved in multiple practices that are in tension (see the Prologue). However, AI is also similar to other scientific disciplines in a more basic sense – that is, in the sense that it is a *collective activity*, something people do together. Why is this important?

The sociologist Howard Becker addresses this question in a comparative discussion of the sociologies of deviance, art, and science (Becker forthcoming).[2] What is common among all these cases, according to Becker, is that in all of them, "a field of empirical research (a science) has replaced a field of philosophical discourse." Many classical topics in psychology, for instance, have been superceded by empirical investigation, and although philosophers and epistemologists continue to debate many such topics, "much of their territory has been colonized by social scientists, covering the same ground from a different standpoint" (ibid.). A similar thing has happened in AI, I suggest, where researchers have colonized part of the territory that traditionally belongs to philosophy. So there might be insights in sociology that AI practitioners might find useful.

One such insight has to do with the nature of scientific "truth." Becker elaborates on this in an eloquent manner:

Something is "real" – and therefore has to be taken seriously as the touchstone which tells us whether what we think is true should be accepted as such or not – when what I say about it will withstand all the criticisms and questions people can bring up to discredit it . . . You anticipate what serious critics – people who really don't want your conclusion about whatever-it-is to be true, people who have a stake in showing you are wrong in any way they can do it – would say. Then you do whatever is necessary to counter those criticisms, so that the critics can no longer make their criticism. (ibid.)

Science studies thinkers have made similar observations about how scientists validate their findings to their colleagues. Bruno Latour, for instance, suggests that one of the things that scientists do is subject their finding to tests of various kinds, "trials of strength," which it must withstand (Latour 1987; cf. Becker ibid.). In contrast to the philosophical view attributed to Karl Popper, where scientists are supposed to always try to falsify their theories, this sociological view leads to the notion of truth as a practical matter that scientists have to deal with in order to convince friends and foes to accept what they say as true, or true enough. And in contrast to classical epistemology that tells us what we should count as "real knowledge" and what as spurious, this sociological view doesn't tell us what "real" knowledge is, "but rather what kinds of organized activities produce the results scientists prize as scientific" (Becker forthcoming: 5). Broadly understood, this view applies to science as it does to art, ethics, and even the management of information (Ekbia and Kling 2003).

Latour (1999) provides a useful example of this view at work in his investigation of how soil scientists made the leap from an observation A (an unmarked patch of forest) to an abstract idea B (the shift between two ecological systems). How does this happen? This epistemological problem is difficult to solve if you frame it as getting from A, way over here, to B, unimaginably far away over there. Working scientists, as Latour shows, do this by taking very small incremental steps – from a marked-off piece of land, to a soil sample dug out of the ground, to a box full of such samples, to classification tags, to a chart based on the tags, to a journal article. "Each step makes sense to the community the results are presented to, and the epistemological mystery is solved" (Becker ibid.).

It is this type of incremental work and its presentation to the community that, by and large, is missing from AI, as Cohen and Howe pointed out many years ago. In order for a running program to really represent "the moment of truth," as Simon had suggested, the practitioner needs to make explicit and share more and more details of the intervening steps between their theory and their "working" system. The absence of these details from much of the work in AI, together with the loose connection between AI and the rest of science, account for a good fraction of the problems that we have discussed in earlier chapters. The point to notice is the earnest attempts by some AI researchers to disguise these problems by engaging in a form of discourse that allows a very liberal use of language. And this, as we shall see next, is a subtle matter.

THE THREAD OF WORDS: MAKING UP INTELLIGENCE

> Although it is quite possible, and perhaps even appropriate, to talk about a "proud IBM 360–50 system," the "valiant 1800," or the "sly PDP 8," I have never observed anyone using this style of language. Instead, we romanticize what appears to be the intellectual functions of the machines. We talk about their "memories," we say that these machines store and retrieve "information," they "solve problems," "prove theorems," etc.
>
> – Heinz von Foerster (1970: 28)

Were there any perverts before the latter part of the nineteenth century? The answer is NO, according to the philosopher Arnold Davidson who believes that, "Perversion was not a disease that lurked about in nature, waiting for a psychiatrist with especially acute powers of observation to discover it hiding everywhere. It was a disease created by a new (functional) understanding of disease" (Davidson 1990). The philosopher Ian Hacking uses this example and a few others – for example, the cases of "split personality," "homosexual," and "suicidal" persons – to show how through the practice of naming and *labeling* we literally "make up people," and "how social reality is conditioned, stabilized, or even created by the labels we apply to people, actions, and communities" (1999: 163). For instance, although there has been plenty of same-sex activity in all ages, *there were no same-sex and different-sex people* until the society started to apply these labels to people. It was such that a kind of person called a "homosexual" (and, for that matter, another kind of person called "heterosexual") came into being at the same time as the kind itself was being invented. In short, our labels change the space of possibilities for personhood. "Who we are is not only what we did, do, and will do but also what we might have done and may do" (ibid.: 165). How about artifacts such as computers and AI models? How much does their space of possibilities change by our labels?

Hacking does not talk about computers, but he makes a careful distinction between people and things. He argues that, unlike intentional human actions that must be *actions under description*, "what camels, mountains, and microbes are doing does not depend on our words" (ibid.: 166). A century ago we would have said that tuberculosis is caused by bad air, and today we may say that it is caused by microbes. However, according to Hacking, what is happening to the microbes and the patients is entirely independent of our correct or incorrect description (although it is not independent of the prescribed medication). Hence, the "microbes' possibilities are delimited by nature, not by words (ibid.: 166). Curiously, in the current technophile culture, on the spectrum suggested by Hacking where people and things are two defining points, computers are closer to people than they are to microbes and camels. In other words, I argue, our culture has drastically changed the space of possibilities for computers by its use of labels, metaphors, and even "quotes." Part of this space, of course, is "conquered," so to speak, by computers due to their novel capabilities, but the overall space is much larger than what they are entitled to. How so?

Metaphors are ubiquitous not only in ordinary language but also in scientific discourse. Physicists talk about "chain reactions," "rotation" (in an abstract space), "excited states," "white noise," "monochromatic neutron beams," and so on, and do not apologize for these liberal usages of concrete familiar terms. Mathematicians likewise talk about "imaginary," "rational," and "irrational" numbers, and biologists talk about "selfish genes," "jumping genes," "gene expression," and so on. What, then, is wrong with the use of metaphoric language in talking about the capabilities of computers that worried von Foerster three decades ago?

The answer, I suggest, lies in the difference between computers and the entities studied by other disciplines. The character of the entities they study prevents physicists and biologists, for instance, from taking the meanings of the terms literally. Physicists do not conceive of an atom in an excited state as being in the grip of emotional forces. This, however, is not true in AI, where the borderline between the literal and the metaphorical is often blurred in unwarranted ways. Winograd's SHRDLU, for instance, used a language called PLANNER, which was developed for the purpose of facilitating programming. Carl Hewitt, the developer of the language, explained his motivation in creating this language as follows:

There was this big disparity between the way people programmed in LISP using things like lambda and other specialized functions, whereas in fact they were talking in terms of goals, subgoals, and plans. So I decided, "We'll have a programming language that has plans, goals, and assertions." (Crevier 1993: 100)

In this way, Hewitt and others facilitated the task of AI programmers in developing their artifacts, and diminished the disparity that Hewitt talks about. In so doing, however, they also facilitated, albeit involuntarily, the usage of anthropomorphic language in the description of such artifacts beyond reasonable limit, adding to the disparity between the literal and metaphorical meaning of words.

This argument is very delicate and I have taken extreme care not to present it in a misleading way. The point is *not* to question the legitimacy of using the language of "plan" and "goals" in talking about computers in certain limited cases – a computer that is used for planning does plan after all, and using a distinct term (such as "c-plan"; see Chapter 2) for computers is not only impractical, it is senseless. The point is to be careful about the limits of legitimate use, and this, as I have tried to clarify throughout, is very tricky business. A thermostat, for instance, controls temperature, but we would not usually say of it that it *tries* to make the temperature 70 degrees. Similarly, we should be very careful when we say of Deep Blue that it *knows* about forking its opponent, of Coach that it *understands* football strategies, of Kismet that it expresses *emotions*, and so on and so forth (McDermott 1976).

The imprecise and unheeded usage of terms, as I suggested in the Prologue, is at the root of the recurring tensions in AI, where the gap between the reality of artifacts and their putative capabilities has been wittingly or unwittingly reduced by metaphorical language. A brief look at the way the usage of quotation marks in AI literature has developed illustrates this point.

If one looks back at the history of AI, an interesting pattern emerges in the way quotation marks are used in the AI literature (and in conversations among AI people) from the time that Turing put together the words "machine" and "think," through the 1950s–1960s when, thanks to the von Neumann architecture, computer were endowed with "memory" and thought of as "information-processors," the 1970s when computers began to "plan," "know," and "learn," and the 1980s when they could "associate," "recognize," and "talk," to the 1990s when they were given "life," "body," and "senses," and were portrayed as "sad," "happy," "angry," and so on. The pattern, in other words, is that, with the passage of time, more and more human-like features of increasing subtlety and complexity are attributed to computers, first with quotation marks, and later without them. What happens as a result of this tempting slippery slope is that people get used to this way of using language, and this in turn seduces many people into uncritical acceptance of claims that would have been hard to even think about otherwise.

In this manner, society collectively undergoes a conditioning process wherein its members unconsciously slip into metaphorical usage of anthropomorphic terms to describe the behavior of computers. Thanks to a gradual slide along this slippery slope, some computer experts can today write, in a relatively unchallenged manner, about such things as "spiritual machines," "emotional robots," "virtual sex," and so on, whereas just thirty years ago von Foerster balked at the idea of applying even the words "memory" and "information" to computers. Indeed, in a surprising twist, over the course of just a few decades, certain terms have become so strongly associated with computers that words such as "information," "knowledge," and "problem solving" are just as likely to conjure up an image of machines these days as of human beings.

The significance of these sociolinguistic phenomena is that some AI people, rather than becoming aware of and fascinated by this slippery slope (and its implications for how cognition works), have instead simply accepted it and now are largely exploiting it as a promotional tool – that is, as a means to promote their claims about the capabilities of their programs and products. The most prominent examples of this tendency are people like Ray Kurzweil (Chapter 3), but they are also found in many other places in AI. In no sense has there been any *systematic* effort on the part of the AI community to counter this type of slippery linguistic slope. That someone like Kurzweil has become established as a spokesperson of AI is, indeed, a telling fact in this regard. In reacting to Kurzweil's public pronouncements, most AI researchers are quick to remind us that he is *not* one of them. Nonetheless, the AI community has been more accommodating to the likes of Kurzweil than to those like Dreyfus who have approached AI claims with caution or skepticism.

One might, of course, ask if the AI community would have been capable, in any case, of stopping the slide down the slippery slope, given the overall trend of the dominant culture. This is a difficult question to answer, but the following discussion might provide the beginnings of an answer.

THE THREAD OF CULTURE: THE PRICE OF POPULARITY

For better or worse, AI has come to occupy a special place within the popular culture, in ways that other computer-related areas have not. The extent of the popularity has turned not only certain AI practitioners into public figures, but also robots such as Cog and Kismet into celebrity robots. As Suchman (2007: 237) observes, these robots are represented through a wide corpus of media renderings: stories, photographs, videos, websites, and so on. Suchman considers these artifacts as recent manifestations of "the very old dream of a perfect, invisible infrastructure" – a dream that she locates within the historical frame of the current "service economy" (ibid.: 217). Along with this historical understanding, I suggest, there are other reasons why the public is fascinated with AI. One of the reasons is, of course, that people sense that the issues raised by AI are directly related to their self-image as human beings (see the Prologue). The flip side of this is that those issues are commonly considered fair game for lay philosophizing (Crevier 1993: 7). It is thus that AI finds a host of casual commentators among reporters, advertisers, moviemakers, and the general public – something that is not possible in physics, for example (although to some extent it happens nonetheless).

Each group of such commentators engages in discourses about computers that are specific to their particular goals, strategies, and roles. Politicians, for instance, usually talk about computers as vehicles of progress and social well-being (the extensive discussion by high officials of the U.S. administration in the early 1990s of the so-called *information superhighway* was a prominent example). Businesspeople, Wall Street consultants, and the vendors of computer technology, on the other hand, typically highlight the impact of computer-related technologies (e.g., expert systems and "smart" products of all sorts) on efficiency and productivity. To advance their agenda, all of these groups usually depend on the claims of the AI community about the outcomes of their research (of the kind we have studied in the preceding chapters). Although the relation between the research community and the outside commentators might often be indirect and mediated, its significance can hardly be overestimated. Two examples of such relations might illustrate this more clearly: the film industry and the public press.

The first example comes from the film industry. As I mentioned in the Prologue, film and fiction have played a major role as the interface between AI and the popular culture. For reasons that are beyond our scope here, somewhere during the 1960s and 1970s the film industry (as dominated by Hollywood in the United States) made a turnaround in its portrayal of technology (especially computer technology), and of its vision of the role of computers in the future of human society. Even a superficial comparison between two famous movies will demonstrate this point. One is Charlie Chaplin's *Modern Times* – a dark comedy made in 1946 that is a vivid portrayal of the implications of automation and assembly lines for the social, economic, and cultural aspects of life in mid-twentieth century. The other one is Stanley Kubrick's *2001: A Space Odyssey* – a science-fiction movie that introduced to the popular culture, through HAL, the notion of coexistence of humans and intelligent machines.[3] Although HAL is finally driven out of existence by being unplugged by the human protagonist, the very idea of the "death" of a computer (dramatized by the emotional outbursts of HAL) was in sharp contrast with Chaplin's cold and lifeless portrayal of modern technology. In terms of style, contrary to Chaplin's realistic account of modern times, Kubrick's *2001* mixes science and science fiction in a more delicate way. Both of these elements – Kubrick's futuristic and sensationalistic style – have been picked up and amplified in later movies that involve computers or AI as central themes – e.g., the film *Artificial Intelligence* by Steven Spielberg, in whose production the AI pioneer and MIT researcher Marvin Minsky was closely involved as an advisor). Except for a couple of movies that largely appeal to the intellectually sophisticated audience (e.g., *The Net* or *Brazil*), we have yet to see a popular film similar to *Modern Times* that will provide a realistic view, albeit in comic fashion, of the impacts of computer technology on the lives and attitudes of people.

The second example concerns the relation between AI and the public media. The media also has played an especially prominent role in the promotion of utopian discourses about AI. Journalists, typically looking for eye-catching and news-making stories, have found in AI a plentiful source of titillating stories, and AI researchers, especially those with the opportunity to make it to the front pages, have seldom refrained from providing them. We have seen examples from interviews with Douglas Lenat about Cyc or with Rodney Brooks about Cog. Publicizing one's views and projects is not, of course, reproachable in and of itself. It becomes so, however, if it feeds into and increases confusion on issues of public interest. Brooks, for instance, on a PBS documentary on the subject of HAL and *2001* (November 27, 2001), used the phrase "in principle" at least three times while discussing the possibility for robots to become as intelligent as human beings. This kind of cautious approach was laudable, setting Brooks apart from the more utopian futurists. However, there is a problem even here: For someone with sufficient knowledge of the issues, the term "in principle" suggests a vast gap between current robots and human consciousness, but the casual observer typically does not realize how much of a hedge lies buried in the words "in principle," and thus takes this argument as evidence for an around-the-corner realization. The hedge becomes evident, however, when we notice that Brooks's examples of successful AI are fuel injectors, airport gates, and the like (see Chapter 8). It also becomes evident in the types of media presentations of the artifacts themselves – for instance, when Cog is portrayed only from the "waist" up, hiding the extensive array of machinery, cables, computers, and software that "support" it. That this kind of presentation also erases the enormous human labor that is invested in the design, implementation, and minute-to-minute operation of the robot is the another important side of the story that rarely gets media attention (Suchman 2007: 238).

The confusion generated by these kinds assertions and presentations was quite manifest during Ray Kurzweil's interview on National Public Radio's Talk of the Nation Science program (December 23, 2005) about his more recent book *Singularity Is Near: When Humans Transcend Biology* (Viking Press, 2005), which, building on the same assumptions as we saw in Chapter 3, now discusses the possibility of eternal life, eradication of illness and poverty, the solution of energy problems, and so on. During this program, both the host and calling listeners raised important questions about the social, philosophical, economical, and technical feasibility of Kurzweil's claims, only to receive the repetition of the same ideas in response: the law of increasing returns, exponential growth, nanotechnology, and so on. Interestingly, Kurzweil was very adamant that his views are "not utopian," pointing out as evidence that he himself has not aged in the last fifteen years. In the light of the absurdity of such claims, one could imagine the kind of confusion that is generated when Viking Press prints the following on the jacket of Ray Kurzweil's previous book:

This is not science fiction. This is the twenty-first century according to Ray Kurzweil, the "restless genius" (*Wall Street Journal*) and inventor of the most innovative and compelling technology of our era. . . . *The Age of Spiritual Machines* is no mere list of predictions but a prophetic blueprint for the future.

As these examples illustrate, various groups, with various degrees of technical savvy, engage in their own styles of discourse about AI, but they often draw upon the claims of AI researchers to support their own assertions. Such claims often provide the raw material for these other groups to mold them in their own fashion and to develop their own interpretations – for politicians to talk about progress, for filmmakers to present their futuristic visions, for journalists to create eye-catching headlines, and so on. These interpretations, in turn, serve (most of) the AI community to publicize their projects, to become relevant, and to garner support from the government and funding agencies (more on this shortly).

In this fashion, the AI community feeds into, and is fed by, a popular culture with a strong penchant for technology and a deep-rooted predisposition to believe in technology as a panacea for all ills. A historical analysis of the roots of these cultural attributes is beyond our scope here, but we have already seen a brief synopsis of its main ingredients in the words of David Noble (see Chapter 1). It is thanks to this kind of worldview that "prophetic blueprints for the future" are widely embraced by a largely ignorant, unreflective, and uncritical audience.

THE THREAD OF PEOPLE: THE MORAL ECONOMY OF AI

> AI has had problems from the beginning. It is a new field in which people came from many different directions. That has meant they didn't always know where things came from, because many people imported them. And we still haven't established a set of norms of responsibility, of referencing, that keeps us from reinventing wheels all the time.
>
> – Herbert Simon, in *Crevier* (1991)

The historian of science Robert Kohler, in his study of the *Drosophila* community that I referred to in Chapter 2, makes a case against the "standard story" of the working of science, which is based on a "myth of tribal heroes" (1999: 245). Against this widespread myth, Kohler argues that neither heroes nor tools and material alone make a productive research community: "The production of knowledge also requires an effective *social* technology"[4] (ibid.: 249). This social structure involves, among other things, a workplace culture that encourages original and thorough work, a means to spread the word of new practices and of their worth, a way to recruit new talent, and so on. Most important among these, however, is a "moral economy" (a term introduced by the historian Edward P. Thompson) that refers to the moral (as distinct from economic and organizational) principles underlying productive activities. In the case of science, Kohler highlights three such principles as especially central: "access to the tools of the trade; equity in the assigning of credit for achievements; and authority in setting research agendas and deciding what is intellectually worth doing" (ibid.). "*Access, equity,* and *authority* – much of the success or failure of research groups," Kohler argues, "depends on their ability to manage these crucial elements of communal work" (ibid.). He compares and contrasts the moral economy of exchange that prevailed in genetic biology in the early years of the twentieth century (best exemplified by Thomas Morgan group's work; see Chapter 2) with the secrecy, competitive races, and bitch-the-other-guy-if-you-can morality of current research on new vitamins and hormones, genes, and infectious agents (like the AIDS virus). He attributes the recent decline of open exchange among molecular biologists to "their being involved in the highly lucrative biotechnology industry," and postulates a causal link between material culture and moral order (ibid.: 255–56).

It seems to me that in terms of moral economy AI is more similar to current biotechnology than to early fly genetics, especially in terms of the issues of authority. The easy explanation for this state of affairs would be to attribute it to the field's youth. AI is a relatively young field, and the AI community has been more accommodating to the influence of individuals than more established scientific disciplines tend to be. Thus "icons," "wizards," "gurus," and "geniuses," as they are typically labeled by the media, are the visible and trusted spokesmen of the field (and I mean this literally: almost all major figures in AI are men), who, in Simon's words, are usually "hankering for respectability" for the field (and, often, for themselves) (ibid.). AI is also a multidisciplinary field, with people coming from computer science, engineering, linguistics, mathematics, neurology, philosophy, physics, psychology, and so on. This, as Simon pointed out, contributes to conceptual dissonance, to lack of disciplinary rigor, and to the divergence of views within the field.

Although youth and multidisciplinary origins might have been principal reasons for widespread confusion and individual impacts during the early years of AI, they certainly are not any more (after all, AI has been around for half a century already). A more serious reason why certain individuals enjoy this much influence, as I suggested in Chapter 1, has to do with the entrepreneurial spirit that is so common among AI people who make it to the higher echelons (and they are the ones who are typically sought out by the media). While some are very explicit about their entrepreneurial ambitions – "We are merchants and engineers, not scientists," say Lenat and Feigenbaum (1991) – and while some (such as Kurzweil) are professional entrepreneurs who market their products as AI artifacts, the entrepreneurial aspirations of another group are subtler. Rodney Brooks, for instance, devotes a full chapter of his book *Flesh and Machines* to the story of the business ventures of the building of a commercially viable robotic doll, and a good part of another chapter to the promotion of his (company's) version of a household robot: "A robot offers a single point of investment that automates your whole house" (2002a: 139).[5]

This kind of entrepreneurialism, in its "healthy" form, might indeed benefit AI, as it would drive exploration and innovation. However, if it turns into the principle that governs the moral economy of the field and the way researchers deal with issues of access, equity, and authority, then it might become an obstacle against transparency, openness, and collaboration.

THE THREAD OF MONEY: THE TRANSLATION OF DREAMS

> Our mission is to build smart machines, but ultimately, our scientific mission is to *understand intelligence*.
> – Chuck Thorpe, Director of the Robotics Institute at
> Carnegie-Mellon University

This is an excerpt from an interview reported in *The Tartan*, Carnegie Mellon University's student newspaper, under the title: "Robotic Love: Those Who Build Robots for a Living and Those Who Live to Build Robots" (Brenda Reyes, December 9, 2002). In the interview, Thorpe elaborates on the Institute's involvement with the Department of Defense: "We are involved in basic research and in educating students. If you are looking to build robots for a military purpose, this is the wrong place to do it."

The report also includes an interview with Hans Moravec, a former director of the Robotics Institute who characterizes the research goals of the Institute as follows:

What we want is to give robots a sense of their surroundings, so they can *know where they are and move through the world*. (emphasis added)

These statements, by a well-known AI researcher and the director of a key research center, suggest the scientific motivations of the work conducted at their lab. An examination of the kind of work done by Moravec, however, reveals a significant gap between the putative goals and the actual work. In July 2002 (the same year as these interviews were given), for instance, DARPA (the Defense Advanced Research Projects Agency) awarded CMU's National Robotics Engineering Consortium (the commercial arm of CMU's Robotic

Figure E.1. The unmanned ground combat vehicle developed by a consortium of CMU's National Robotics Engineering Center and Boeing Corp.

Institute) and its industrial teammate Boeing $5.5 million to build and test a prototype robotic "unmanned ground combat vehicle" (UGCV). The vehicle will be the first attempt at an autonomous ground combat vehicle that *can operate on all types of terrain* (see Figure E.1).[6]

This is just one example of a pervasive pattern in scientific research – namely, a tight alignment between research labs, especially in "technoscience" (Latour 1987), and the outside world, especially funding agencies. What typically happens is that, in pursuing pure scientific objectives, scientists find themselves involved in the "impure" activities of seeking external help, support, and recognition. Bruno Latour has provocatively characterized the situation as follows:[7]

This sounds paradoxical: when scientists appear to be fully independent, surrounded only by colleagues, obsessively thinking about their science, it means that they are fully dependent, aligned with the interest of many more people; conversely, when they are really independent, they do not get the resources with which to equip a laboratory, to earn a living, or to recruit another colleague who could understand what they are doing. (1987: 158).

Table E.1. The funding received by Hans Moravec for military-related projects

Project	Period	Amount	Funding agency
Robust Navigation by Probabilistic Volumetric Sensing	June 1999–Dec. 2002	$970,000	DARPA
Probabilistic Sensor Interpretation	Sept. 1990–June 1995	$700,000	ONR
Autonomous Mobile Robots	Jan. 1985–Sept. 1990	$1,000,000	ONR
Road-Following Vision System	Jan. 1985–Jan. 1987	$2,000,000	DARPA
Autonomous Underwater Robots	April 1981–Dec. 1984	$2,000,000	ONR

The alignment between a laboratory that seeks "to understand intelligence" and DARPA, which probably has little interest in this question, is made possible by *translating* the scientific dream of building robots that "know where they are and move through the world" into the military dream of building vehicles that "can operate on all types of terrain." It is this type of dream-translation that makes it possible for costly AI projects and research institutes to be funded on a continuous basis. Table E.1 shows a list of more than $6.6 million in funding received from the military agencies DARPA and ONR (Office of Naval Research) by Hans Moravec between 1981 and 2002.

How the original scientific goals of a research lab are affected by such alignments is a question with no single answer. To reduce "boundary-work" – the term that the sociologist Thomas Gieryn uses to characterize the strategic practical action of scientists "to appeal to the goals and interests of audiences and stakeholders" (1999: 23) – to interests is "too crude by half":

Boundary-work is surely instrumentalist. But is it merely so? Is it fair to accuse scientists seeking to protect autonomy or secure research funding of duplicitous behavior, as they concoct a representation of themselves tailored to maximize whatever returns are on the line? Can boundary-work – and the specific contours of science then and there – be *reduced* to interests? Too crude by half.

The question, Gieryn suggests, "is not whether science is pure or impure or both, but rather how its borders and territories are flexibly and discursively mapped out in pursuit of some observed or inferred ambition – and with what consequences, and for whom?" (ibid.). The question, I concur, applies to all science, as it does to AI. The point of my discussion, therefore, is *not* to single out Moravec (whose work is interesting in many respects) or even AI (to the improvement of which I am trying to contribute through this work). The point is that "the appeal to the goals and interests of audiences and stakeholders" does have an effect, and this could be hardly disputed.

Sometimes, as I suggested in Chapter 8, a whole research program is revamped so as to accommodate to the goals of the funding agencies. Other times, the impact is subtler. To give one example, the Cyc project was originally introduced as having the ultimate goal of achieving and surpassing human levels of commonsense knowledge. The dominant vision of the Cyc group at that time was for it to be a long-term project with no immediate payoffs, and the standard rejoinder to critics involved the "pond metaphor" – namely, that because of the exponential character of the growth of the knowledge base, Cyc's ultimate capability will not be obvious until the very end (just as the covering of a pond by exponentially-reproducing algae will be barely noticeable until the last moments). Today, however, this type of argument could no longer be invoked by the Cyc group because, as they need money to keep the project going, they have to make Cyc relevant to the current goals of funding agencies – whence the new descriptions of Cyc as a "database integration tool" (see Chapter 4).

THE LONG ROAD AHEAD: UNDOING THE DEMOCRITEAN DREAM

> The conviction persists, though history shows it to be a hallucination, that all the questions that the human mind has asked are questions that can be answered in terms of the alternatives that the questions themselves present. But in fact, intellectual progress usually occurs through sheer abandonment of questions together with both of the alternatives they assume, an abandonment that results from their decreasing vitalism and a change of urgent interest. We do not solve them, we get over them.
>
> – John Dewey

Artificial Intelligence, as I said at the outset, is heir to a modernist mandate of a purified world with sharp boundaries between mind and body, subject and object, nature and culture, science and politics, and so on – a dream that is ripe with tensions, asymmetries, and misalignments (Latour 1993). The triple (scientific, engineering, and discursive) practices of AI not only embody these tensions, they regenerate them, the various examples of which we have seen in the preceding pages. Taking these examples as witness, our survey so far has been focused on the bumpy road traveled over the last few decades. It is now time to draw upon our findings to look at the roads ahead, in the hope that perhaps we can develop an outlook that is less tortured in its practices, more perceptive in its aspirations, and perhaps realistic in its ambitions.

AI has come a long way from the days when its founders thought of cognition as consisting mainly of abstract mental activities, manipulation of logical symbols and representational states, or the passive retrieval of built-in frames and scripts. Today, we understand that intelligence arises from the coordination of the mind, the body, and the world (Clark 1997). Though it may appear modest, this shift in point of view is a major accomplishment of AI, even if it did not come about in the most efficient, beautiful, and reasonable way, even if it is just as much a result of a long series of failures as a result of a string of incremental successes, and even if AI has raised more questions than it could answer. In this last part of the book, I would like to briefly assess both the accomplishments and limitations. I would also like to explore a radical alternative that would arise if, following Dewey's lead, we abandon the original question of AI – whether and how machines can be as intelligent as humans – in favor of an alternative question: How are humans and machines mutually constituted through discursive practices?

What We Have Learned *about* AI

I suggested at the outset that AI finds itself in a problematic situation today. The gap that I have documented between dreams, claims, and promises, on the one hand, and realities, achievements, and successes, on the other, demonstrates that this is, indeed, the case. In a way, having a gap between dream and reality is desirable, because it might provide an impetus for further research and hard work. The problem is in the approach that is adopted in narrowing the gap. This chapter's portrait of AI in the making was provided principally to show prevalent and potential pitfalls in AI's approach, but it may also point to alternative approaches. One such alternative is what Agre (1997b) calls the "constructive path," which, in his outline of a similar vision for AI, he describes as follows:

The constructive path is much harder to follow, but more rewarding. Its essence is to evaluate a research project not by its correspondence to one's substantive beliefs but by the rigor and insight with which it struggles against the patterns of difficulty that are inherent in its design. Faced with a technical proposal whose substantive claims about human nature seem mistaken, the first step is to figure out what deleterious consequences those mistakes should have in practice. If the predicted impasses have actually been detected in the technical work, then the next step is not to conclude that AI, considered as a static essence, has been debunked in a once-and-for-all fashion. Instead, research can now proceed on the basis of a radical interpretation of their significance ... (Agre 1997b)

Agre goes on to describe the "painstaking middle way" needed in order for this type of constructive research agenda to succeed. This is the stance taken throughout the present work. My purpose here was not so much to generate antigens (or "antifactors") against the prevailing threads and influences discussed in the preceding pages, but to understand, assimilate, and mobilize those threads in the right direction. I further believe that this kind of approach, if widely and persistently pursued, is what is needed to improve the current situation in AI, and the following is the minimum that needs to be done:

- to pay attention to the hidden assumptions, presuppositions, and prejudices that we have about artifacts, especially computers;
- to make explicit as much as possible the steps that lead from a theory to a system (artifact or program), and to present those steps to the community of AI scientists in great detail;
- to clean up the anthropomorphic language that we use to talk about artifacts, to pay close attention to the metaphorical character of this language, and to recognize the limits of the efficacy of the metaphors;
- to check the results of AI models and theories against the findings of other (physical, biological, and social) sciences in a systematic bidirectional manner.[9]

This mix of technical engagement and reflexive criticism might ameliorate unrealistic science-fiction-style fantasies that envision new technologies as giving rise to ever-greater scientific understanding, technological supremacy, artistic expression, organizational efficiency, cultural development, social well-being, and so on. Such utopian fantasies, in turn, trigger dystopian fears about the risks involved with the growth of technologies such as those pursued in AI research. The anti-utopians' characterizations of the tragic possibilities of AI and other technoscientific work "provide an essential counterbalance to the giddy-headed optimism of the utopian accounts" (Kling 1997: 51). These extreme visions, as we have seen, are greatly exaggerated, and are thus in need of serious revisions. A social realist approach of the kind Kling advocated would be in sharp contrast to utopian and dystopian views, both of which paint their portraits with monochromatic brushes: white and black. The middle road in which taking account of sociomaterial context allows shades of gray to enter the picture has been a central principle of the present work.

What We Have Learned *from* AI

Where does this leave AI in the big picture? What is the overall contribution of AI to science, engineering, and philosophy, to our inquiry into human mind, behavior, and agency, and to the continuing quest for nonbiological intelligence? I suggested at the outset that we can learn from AI in *novel* ways, both from its successes and failures. If an AI system "works," it can provide insights into the mechanisms of cognition, interaction, communication, and so on. If it doesn't, a reflexive analysis such as what we saw in the preceding chapters would illustrate particular manifestations of attribution fallacy or preemptive registration, as the case might be, highlighting concrete aspects of human cognition (see the Prologue). The notion of Generalized Eliza Effect (GEE) points to these dual possibilities that can be meaningfully exploited in AI work.

I emphasize "novel" here because many of these lessons could only be attained through AI models, approaches, and techniques. As Smith (1996) points out, "Midway between matter and mind, computation stands in excellent stead as supply of concrete cases of middling complexity ... against which to test specific metaphysical hypotheses" (1996: 20). AI models occupy a unique place in this middle realm, as they face the mind-matter question head-on. The models and approaches discussed in the preceding chapters illustrate this point clearly. From the issues of knowledge, language, and representation to those of experience, emergence, and embodiment, AI confronts longstanding questions of ontology, epistemology, and metaphysics, which have eluded scholars and philosophers for centuries. AI does this with a kind of rigor and doggedness that is only affordable with the material and generative character of its artifacts. In so doing, AI and computing in general provide novel ways for rethinking the entrenched conceptions of the human (Hayles 1999; Suchman 2007), raise interesting questions about the relationship between humans and nonhumans, introduce new concepts and vocabularies for thinking about these questions, and enrich the current intellectual landscape is unprecedented ways. In this thinking, the question of whether AI regenerates conservative humanism (Suchman 2007: 242) or presents a challenge to received conceptions of the human (Hayles 2005: 143) becomes moot. For by bringing the tensions of modernism into high relief, by capturing and illustrating those tensions in its systems, AI creates the possibility of the demise of modernist views in a dialectic manner. *AI dismantles the modernist mandate by mimicking it.*

A radical interpretation of current AI research would, of course, not stop here. Rather it would question some of the fundamental assumptions and presuppositions that AI has inherited from Cartesian and Hobbesian traditions – namely, what we earlier dubbed *mentalism* and *logicism* (see Chapter 1). A shared feature of these traditions is their adherence to a particular understanding of individual representations as static mirror-like replica of pre-existing entities. Situated approaches such as neorobotics sought to overturn these traditions, but, as we have seen, they stop short of accomplishing their stated goal for various conceptual and practical reasons. What is the alternative?

Scholars from various fields of inquiry – science studies, cultural studies, feminist studies, queer studies, critical theory, and others – have dealt with this question, trying to shift the focus from the issue of *representation* to that of *action* – that is, from the question of whether and how representations correspond to reality to how reality is enacted through sociomaterial practices. My own thinking on these issues has been largely influenced by Brian Smith's *philosophy of presence* (Smith 1996; see the Prologue), by Michel Foucault's ideas on knowledge and power (Foucault 1977; cf. Ekbia and Kling 2003), and by writings of philosophers and science studies scholars on representation, intervention, and mediation (e.g., Hacking 1983; Latour 1993, 1999, 2005; Rouse 1999 – see this Epilogue, the Prologue, and Chapter 3, respectively). Recent writings by the anthropologist Lucy Suchman (e.g., 2007) and the feminist philosopher Karen Barad (2003) provide provocative articulations of a similar line of thought.

The common thread that I would like to extract from these lines of inquiry is this: in order to understand X in humans or artifacts – where X would be "intentionality," "cognition," or "agency," depending on whether you are a philosopher, psychologist, or social scientist, respectively – we need to *rethink* some of the most deeply entrenched assumptions and ideas that have come down to us from Western analytic tradition in both science and philosophy. In its most radical form, the rethinking would take us all the way back to Greek philosophy and the *atomistic* view of Democritus. What we see as a stone, Democritus told us, is just an appearance; the *real* stone is made of atoms that move in a void and that give the stone its properties. In this fashion, he postulated a world consisting of individually determinate entities with inherent properties. This Democritean dream, as Hacking (1983) dubbed it, put our thinking on a path that has led to the present situation. Descartes and Hobbes, as we saw earlier (Chapter 1), pushed this idea further by, respectively, erecting a wall between the atomist world and our representations of it and turning the representations into individually manipulatable formal tokens. In this fashion, a gap was created between representation and reality that we have tried to bridge ever since. Given that all attempts in building this bridge have failed, it might be time to go back to the beginnings and reconsider the original question.

Today, scientific theories and liberal social theories alike are based on the individualistic tradition that Democritus founded and Descartes fortified

(Barad 2003). And AI is no exception to this. The problem facing AI, as Suchman argues, "is less that we attribute agency to computational artifacts than that our language for talking about agency, whether for persons or artifacts, presupposes a field of discrete, self-standing entities" (2007: 263). An alternative that suggests itself strongly would be to think of agency (or intelligence or intentionality) in *relational* terms – that is, in terms of an ongoing "intra-activity" that involves both humans and machines. In other words, rather than taking these as attributes of individual humans or machines, rather than assuming a boundary between humans and machines that needs to be crossed (through the practices of AI, for instance), we should start with the assumption that the human-nonhuman boundary shifts dynamically, reconfiguring both in the process (Barad 2003). The solution, as Smith (1996: 347) argued, is to be committed to "One world, a world with no other, a world in which both subjects and objects – we and the things we interact with and think about and eat and build and till and are made of and give away as presents – are accorded their appropriate place." This, I concur, is the way out of the current situation.

Looking back at the preceding chapters, it would seem ironic that a journey that started with Turing's dream and continued with Descartes, Hobbes, Hume, and others, should take us all the way back to Democritus. However, as Hacking points out, "Democritus transmitted a dream, but no knowledge" (1983: 142). To turn this dream to knowledge – of humans, of the world, and of their relationship – we have no alternative but to undo it. Such a project would reformulate the AI project on different levels. Theoretically, the question of AI changes from whether and how machines are intelligent to how intelligent behavior emerges in the interactions between humans and machines. Technically, the project would be redefined from one of constructing "smart" machines to one where effective arrangements are sought in which humans and machines engage in an entangled web of meaningful activities. Ethically, this perspective is more honest and rewarding because, rather than denying the differences between humans and machines, it understands them as historically and materially constructed. By refusing to fix the category of human and excluding a range of possibilities in advance, it opens up new horizons to a *posthumanist* future – that is, "one that incorporates important material and discursive, social and scientific, human and nonhuman, and natural and cultural factors" (Barad 2003: 808).

This posthumanist future might well be upon us already. However, it would take time for our worldview, our thinking, and our theories to come to grip with it. That seems to be a distant point in the future.

Afterthought: A Posthumanist's Pragmatic Dream

The human heart has hidden treasures,
In secret kept, in silence sealed –
The thoughts, the hopes, the dreams, the pleasures,
Whose charms were broken if revealed.

– Charlotte Brontë

In wrapping up my thoughts, I notice that we might not have been able to meaningfully resolve many of the tensions and dilemmas that are built into modern thinking, and that AI captures and regenerates so forcefully in its practices. By revealing longstanding dreams of human beings, this writing, despite Brontë, is not meant to break any charms, but it has, I hope, shed some light on the tensions embedded in those dreams. We all experience the impact of these tensions in our daily lives, especially in dealing with unresolved social issues such as access, equity, justice, and freedom. Having lived in opposite corners of our planet – partly in Iran and partly in the United States – I myself experience this tension most lucidly in my reaction to modern science and technology, as the attentive reader might have noticed throughout this writing.

The optimist technophile in me suggests that human beings will someday achieve sufficient collective intelligence and wisdom to create the circumstances for the development of sciences and technologies whose sole purpose would be to better the human condition. Artificial Intelligence might well be an important part of that endeavor. AI is going to stay with us, my utopian half suggests, in the foreseeable future, not only because it is heir to our perennial dreams but also because it bears with it the seeds of a liberating future. In that future, Cyc and Deep Blue might be remembered as extinct dinosaurs lost to the impact of fresh ideas and new technologies, while Cog, Coach, Copycat, NetTalk, and others might serve as amoeba-like entities that have contributed, through their successes or failures, and in varying degrees, to the development of our cyborg existence.

The social dystopian in me, on the other hand, is wary and, at times, fearful and nervous. Even if the human race survives the calamities of political adventurism and environmental capriciousness, I think, the increasing number and complexity of issues that partly derive from technoscientific artifacts and their uneven distribution according to class, race, gender, and geography renders the probability of their fair, rational, and meaningful solution to infinitesimally low. The future of our cyborg species, my dystopian half suggests, is one of more inequality in access to both material and nonmaterial goods, in which technology plays a significant role – perhaps most importantly, in the production, dissemniation, and access to information. In that perilous future, those who are willing to take bigger risks, those who find themselves in positions of power, and those who talk louder will run the show, giving course to later developments, and increasing even further the inequalities and injustices, which, in turn, prepare the ground for more adventurism... *ad infinitum.*

The pragmatist posthumanist in me, heedful of both, however, invests trust in the capability, ingenuity, and resilience of the human species, in its quest to understand and shape the world in an image that is more caring, accomodating, and responsible.

Minimax and Alpha-Beta Pruning

THE MINIMAX ALGORITHM

In order for the evaluation process discussed in Chapter 2 to bottom out, the designer of a chess-playing machine chooses a certain look-ahead depth at which to stop the recursion. This depth depends on such factors as the speed and processing power of the hardware. In the case of Deep Blue, as was mentioned, the depth was fourteen. What this means is that, at each step, Deep Blue looks ahead fourteen plies (seven moves) into the game until it reaches a level in the tree where it should apply the scoring function to evaluate the nodes (leaves), and assign a number to each one. These numbers are then backed up to the top in order to choose the best move. Figure A.1(a) demonstrates how this is done in a two-ply game tree. (Notice that at every point in the middlegame, each player has more than thirty moves to choose from. Thus, each branching point in the tree actually splits into about thirty-five nodes, only a small number of which are shown in the figure, for the sake of simplicity.)

Assume that levels I and III in the tree represent the possible moves for the machine, and level II those for the opponent. Suppose also that the numbers on level III have been obtained by directly applying the scoring function to the board positions. (In other words, we are assuming a look-ahead depth of two here.) Using these numbers, the machine should back them up to level II, which represents possible moves for the opponent. It should, however, evaluate the nodes at level II from the opponent's point of view – that is, it should find the worst that could happen from its own viewpoint. This means that, out of all possibilities, node A would inherit the smallest score from all its children at level III – namely, the score of one, belonging to D. A similar thing happens to node B, which gets five from E (see Figure A.1[b]). (If we call the nodes at each level the "children" of the node directly above them, we could

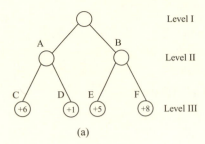

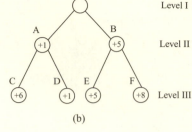

(a)

A two-ply game tree with the scores
assigned at the lowest level

(b)

The scores backed up by the minimax
algorithm to level II

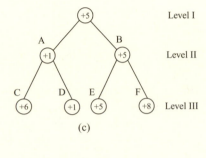

(c)

The score backed up to level I tells the
machine to follow the branch leading to B

(d)

The horizon effect: A possible scenario
where minimax fails

Figure A.1. Minimax algorithm.

think of the backup algorithm as a strict rewarding mechanism for child-rearing that rates parents according to the worst among their children.) Next, the numbers should be backed up to level I. This time, however, the machine should choose the move that maximizes its score. Thus, it would make the move that leads to B, whose backed-up score is five (see Figure A.1[c]).

The minimax algorithm may, of course, fail terribly under special circumstances, which might arise, for instance, as a result of the so-called *horizon problem*. In order to understand how this happens, look at Figure A.1(d), where the evaluation at level IV shows a drastic change compared to the one at the previous level. Since, according to our original assumption, the look-ahead had stopped at level III, the algorithm fails to detect the danger hidden beyond the "horizon," leading thus to the trap indicated in node H. Looking one level further ahead, in other words, the score of five promised by the static evaluation of node B turns out to have been a mere mirage. Such a situation — one that could arise, for instance, if an opponent's pawn is turned into a queen by being advanced to the last row – could be avoided by looking ahead one more ply, but that only pushes the horizon off by one ply, rather than eliminating it; there is no guarantee that the same kind of problem won't occur with the deeper horizon somewhere else in the tree. Shannon's idea of a *quiescent* or *stable* situation is actually meant to address this problem: to explore the possibilities until one arrives at a situation where the evaluation function does not fluctuate drastically.

ALPHA-BETA PRUNING

As we noted, the number of possible moves (or the branching factor) of the game tree begins to explode in the middlegame, because a player has thirty to forty moves to choose from in a typical middlegame position. After one move (two plies), there are roughly a thousand positions to be evaluated, after two moves about a million, after three moves about a billion, ... and so on. In other words, the number of evaluations increases by a factor of about thirty for each ply. For a computer that can evaluate one terminal position every microsecond, this implies sixteen minutes to make a move with a look-ahead of six plies. As it turns out, looking six plies ahead is totally inadequate, and, moreover, sixteen minutes is far too long to take for a move. Therefore, for any serious chess match. Thus, the big challenge for a chess-playing program is to narrow down the number of positions examined to a bare minimum so that the choice of the best move is made manageable.

Since backup is always carried out in conjunction with a depth-first search of the game tree, improving the performance requires a "pruning" method that eliminates a large number of nodes from consideration. Shannon proposed a "forward pruning" heuristic method that was meant to eliminate the "obviously bad" moves – for example, to eliminate from the thirty possible legal moves the worst ten from the point of view of the static evaluator. Surprisingly, this notion turned out to be too elusive to be captured in rules. Other methods that could be formalized and executed easily on the computer thus were needed.

As we noticed earlier, the main challenge for a chess-player is to try to figure out the *worst* that could happen to them in any given situation. This is the origin of the idea of the minimax algorithm. The so-called alpha-beta pruning technique is based on essentially the same idea. Suppose that you have three possible moves, one of which is moving a knight. If this move leads to the capturing of the knight by the opponent's queen (or pawn or any other piece), you certainly do not consider it as a reasonable option, even if the knight move could lead to a checkmate of the opponent's king in a later step. Put differently, if there is the possibility of a devastating reply to a move, then

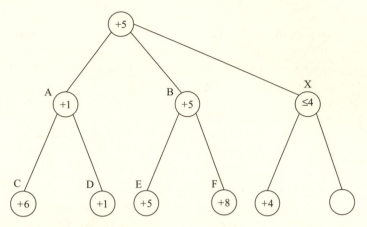

Figure A.2. Alpha-beta pruning.

you simply don't make it. The alpha-beta algorithm works exactly on this principle, and is, thus, trivially plausible. The way it works is demonstrated in Figure A.2, which shows a tree similar to the one in Figure A.1(a) except for the additional subtree X. Assume that after backing up the values to nodes A and B, you move on to X. If, on examining a child of X, you hit a node with a score of five or less, you are entitled to drop consideration of the rest of X's children immediately because you know that the backed-up value to node X is going to be five at best. Since you already have this much available in node B, there is no point in pursuing the search in X any further. In this way, all of the nodes in subtree X get pruned at once before even being examined. If we recall that each node has more than thirty children on the average, the saving in time due to this simple insight becomes manifest. Ordering the nodes in terms of their threat (by using static evaluation) would result in even further efficiency because the lowest numbers are backed up earlier in the process.

An Introduction to Connectionism

Chapter 6 briefly introduces connectionist models and their functioning. The purpose of this appendix is to go into more detail about how these systems work, and to give the unfamiliar reader a feel for their various capabilities. As discussed in Chapter 6, the connectionist approach is motivated by the low-level architecture of the brain – whence the term "artificial neural networks" applied to connectionist models. The first essential idea about artificial neural networks is that, like the brain, which is a network of a huge number (10^{10}) of tightly connected neurons, artificial networks are composed of a large number (typically ranging from tens to hundreds) of interconnected "nodes." Far from being an architectural analogue of a biological neuron, however, the node of connectionist networks is "an abstract neuron" – that is, it lacks many of the structural and functional details of a real neuron such as the large number of synapses (10^4 on the average), differentiated input and output channels, distinct electrical and chemical processes, three-dimensional space distribution of neurons and distal connections among them, the time lag involved in interneuronal communication, and so on (Rumelhart 1989: 207). It is a simple processing element that communicates by "sending numbers along the lines that connect it [to other] processing elements" (the equivalent of firing rate in brain neurons) (ibid.). This, according to Rumelhart, is what accounts for the similarity of artificial neural networks to their natural counterparts.

The other essential idea about neural nets, which follows from simple considerations of processing times in human behavior,[1] is "massive parallelism." This is motivated by the fact that the brain has very many components that operate simultaneously (although each one by itself is very slow).

This setup is based on two major assumptions:

i. Almost all "knowledge" in a connectionist system is taken to be *implicit* in the connections among units, rather than being explicitly encoded in the units themselves (as was the case in classical models such as Cyc).

ii. Mental activity mainly consists of changing the strengths of the connections among basic units in appropriate ways. An organism is born with a brain (a set of neurons that are wired and interconnected in a specific way), and it changes the strength of these connections in the process of learning and interacting with its environment. This is the crux of cognition and thinking in the connectionist view.

Smolensky (1999) has summarized the above points in what he calls the "commitments of connectionism" (of PDP style):[2]

a. Mental representations are distributed patters of numerical activity;

b. Mental processes are massively parallel transformations of activity patterns by patterns of numerical connections;

c. Knowledge acquisition results from the interaction of:
   i. innate learning rules
   ii. innate architectural features
   iii. modification of connection strengths with experience.

HOW TO BUILD A SIMPLE CONNECTIONIST NETWORK

Suppose that we were to construct a simple network to recognize between capital "G" and capital "Q," or, put more succinctly, to associate "G" ("Q") with a circular shape with (without) an opening that has a slanted (horizontal) short bar on the southeast corner. The construction of such network would proceed in three stages – design, training, and testing.

In the design stage, a number of basic decisions have to be made. First, we need to specify the number of units. This, in turn, depends on the number of relevant "features" in the domain and the number of distinctions we want to make. A reasonable number for feature ("input") units in this case would be three – one for the overall circular shape, one for the opening gap, and one for (the angle of) the stem; and a reasonable number for the letter ("output") units would be two – one to represent "it is a G," and one to represent "it is a Q" (usually, one should not distinguish between "input" and "output" nodes in this model, because it is an associator that can run in both directions). We also create a link between every feature unit and every letter unit, getting a total of six connections. Finally, we assign random connections weights – numbers between "–1" and "1" to these links.[3]

These were all structural decisions. We also need to make some other decisions or assumptions about the operation of the network – for example, the output function, the activation rule, the discrete or continuous (integer- or real-valued) character of inputs and activations, and so on. In this case, we assume that the inputs are real-valued numbers that represent the conspicuousness of the relevant feature on a continuous scale. Thus, a value of .9 on the node for the opening size means that there is a big opening in the input shape. We assume further that the activation rule of a unit is the weighted sum of all of its inputs, and that the output function is a "threshold function" – that is, the unit will only be activated if the sum of its inputs is above a certain value, say, .8.

In the training stage, we present the network with a series of matching inputs to the two groups of units. That is, we vary the features on the input side, and tell the network whether this combination represents a G or a Q on the output. The network's task would be to *learn to associate* novel feature combinations with either G or Q. It would do this by adjusting the connection weights in such a way that it could *generalize* to unfamiliar feature combinations. The training should continue until the network settles on an almost fixed set of connections weights, in which case we could advance to the test phase, and demand performance from the network. And, in fact, this is precisely what happens if we test the network on either previously familiar inputs or unfamiliar ones.

We have just constructed, in so many simple steps, an effective *pattern association* network that distinguishes among possible combinations of features by classifying them as either a G or a Q. This is a remarkable feat, if we notice that it can be extended to more complex domains. The task of constructing this network was made easy by the artificially simplified character of the domain – that is, a domain with just two output patterns and a small number of features. For a more complicated domain, we would have had to find network parameters in a tedious process of trial and error, typical of connectionist practice. However, and this is the major source of connectionist appeal, the same basic technique can, in principle, be generalized to increasingly complex tasks and domains – for example, the recognition of written text, spoken words, faces, and so on.

This partly explains the allure of the connectionist approach to many researchers in AI and cognitive science: Not only do the models "program themselves" by adjusting the connection weights; they also are easily generalizable across tasks and domains. There are, to be sure, other reasons for the attraction that our simple model cannot fully explicate. A more complicated

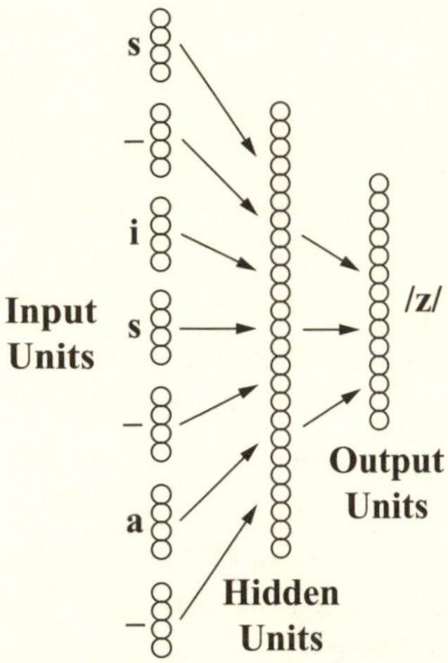

Figure B.1. The NETtalk model of text reading (from Sejnowski and Rosenberg 1987, with permission).

example – namely, the famous NETtalk model – can bring some of the capabilities of connectionist models to light.

NETtalk: LEARNING TO PRONOUNCE WORDS

Languages are full of inconsistencies in terms of pronunciation rules. In the English sentence "This is a book," for example, the letter "s" occurs in two places, with identical immediate contexts – that is, it is sandwiched between "i" and a space. However, the "s" in "this" is unvoiced (it is pronounced /s/), and the "s" in "is" is voiced (it is pronounced /z/). To overcome such difficulties, a system built to learn English pronunciation must either keep each case in rote memory and follow fixed rules for applying the case in each specific situation, or it should develop a kind of representation that makes the decision on the fly by looking, for instance, farther than the immediate context of a letter in order to get its pronunciation right. Both of these alternatives have been experimented. DECtalk, developed by Digital Equipment Corporation, is a commercially available example of the first, rule-based, approach. Connectionist models, such as NETtalk (Sejnowski and Rosenberg 1987; see Figure B.1), use the other, emergent, approach.

NETtalk takes English text as input and produces a coding for speech at the output. The encoded output could be then fed to a standard speech synthesizer that transforms it into real speech sounds. The model uses a three-layer, feed-forward architecture with a back-propagation learning algorithm (see Chapter 6 for the definition of these terms). The input layer involves seven groups of units, each consisting of twenty-nine nodes assigned to one character. It thus can look at a seven-character window of text, enough for pronouncing most English words. At each time step, the fourth letter in the input string is the target letter whose phonemic contribution should be determined and given as output. The rest of the input letters basically provide the context for fixing the precise pronunciation of the target letter. The representation of characters at the input layer is localized, with one active unit for each character, space, or punctuation mark. There are about two hundred input, eighty hidden, and twenty-six output units, giving rise to a total of about twenty thousand connections.

In terms of performance, NETtalk has been one of the most impressive connectionist models ever. If trained on samples of transcribed speech in child language literature, it can produce phonemes from the training set 95 percent, and from an unfamiliar text sample 80 percent, of the time. In both cases, during a typical demo, the speech output could be heard to progress from initial babbling sounds to semirecognizable words, to a fair simulacrum of human speech (Clark 1997).

UNSUPERVISED LEARNING AND COMPETITIVE NETWORKS

NETtalk falls into the general class of *supervised learning* models, so named because they get direct feedback about the correctness of their output from an outside "teacher" – that is, from the modeler. Another major class – namely, *unsupervised learning*— involves architectures that do not get such feedback. Tasks are assigned to these networks so that they can learn by making direct associations between a previous set of (training) inputs and a new group of (test) stimuli, without anyone telling them directly how well they have done. Given a large enough number of patterns (e.g., letters of alphabet), for instance, the network learns how to categorize an unfamiliar shape as belonging to one or the other category (a particular letter). Speech processing and reading, which deal with repeated patterns of phonemes, syllables, and so on, might thus be good candidates for such networks. This idea has given rise to connectionist models of "competitive learning," a subcategory of unsupervised learning.

Another feature of models such as NETtalk is the mutual inclusiveness of categories represented by the output units – that is, two or more output units may stand for the same letter of alphabet. We can change this situation by adding *inhibitory* links between the output units, making it impossible for them to be activated at the same time (see Figure B.2). Should we do this, we have built a network in which the output units compete for firing – hence, the name "competitive" for the network, and the name "winner-take-all"

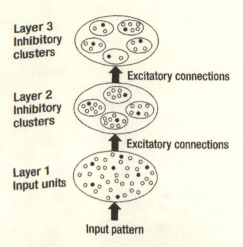

Figure B.2. A competitive network for detecting position-specific letters (Rumelhart and Zipser 1985, with permission).

or "grandmother cells" for the units (Hertz et al. 1991: 217). The aim of the network would, then, be to generate categories rather than making associations.

Such a competitive network was built by Rumelhart and Zipser (1985). Instead of the local encoding of features, however, they used a 7 × 14 grid "retina" to represent letter patterns, presented to the network one pair at a time. The network consists of ninety-eight input units, each corresponding to a point on the grid, and two output units, each of which has ninety-eight connections to the whole set of input nodes. The task of the network is to determine which of the letter pairs AA, AB, BA, and BB is present at the input. The reason letter pairs, rather than single letters, are selected for input is the interest in position-specific letter detectors. For instance, one of the units responds whenever AA or AB is presented, and the other responds whenever BA or BB is represented. That is, one unit becomes an A detector for position 1, the other becomes a B detector for position 1, and so on. The model completed this task successfully.

In general, such networks divide up the input data into clusters that share specific features. In the simplest of competitive networks, this is done in the following way (ibid.):

1. the units in any layer are broken into a set of non-overlapping clusters, where each unit inhibits every other unit within the cluster;
2. the clusters are winner-take-all, such that only the unit with the largest input is maximally activated, and all the rest are off;
3. every unit in a cluster receives inputs from the same links;

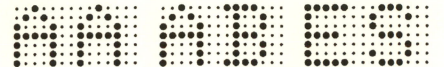

Figure B.3. The 7 × 14 retina used to present letter pairs to the network of Figure B.2 (from Rumelhart and Zipser 1985, with permission).

4. a unit learns if and only if it wins the competition within the cluster;
5. a stimulus pattern is represented as the collection of discrete elements that are either active or inactive;
6. the sum of the weights of each unit is fixed, and the unit learns by redistributing the weights among its input link, shifting weight from its inactive to its active input lines.

In comparison to supervised learning with backpropagation of error, competitive learning has a number of advantages, the most important of which, as suggested by some researchers, is biological plausibility (McLeod et al. 1998: 133). For instance, competitive learning uses a *local* learning rule – that is, the information required to change the weight of a connection is available at either side of the connection (there is no error signal coming from elsewhere). Moreover, there is no need for an explicit "teacher." Taking note of such properties, some connectionists have concluded that "competitive networks are a feature of many brain circuits" (ibid.). In fact, a variation of these networks, called "Kohonen nets," is used to model *topographic maps* known to be important structural components of the brain. These maps are parts of the cortex that preserve the topological relations (e.g., neighborhood or distance) among sensors on the surface of the body (such as the eyes, the ears, and the skin). Some neuroscientists have proposed that these maps are at the foundation of many brain functions such as memory, recognition, learning, and even consciousness (Edleman 1992).

APPENDIX C

The Language Acquisition Debate

The acquisition of language by children is an intriguing phenomenon and a fascinating topic in developmental psychology. It is a multifaceted process that involves the employment, coordination, construction, and mapping of many human faculties (perceiving, thinking, hearing, speaking, acting, etc.) as well as environmental resources (objects, relations, times, places, events, etc.). Language acquisition also constitutes an enormous task in terms of magnitude. To get an idea, adult speakers of English use between twenty thousand and fifty thousand word forms when speaking, and a considerably larger vocabulary when comprehending. In the case of young children, according to some estimates, they should master around ten new words a day on average in order to arrive at a vocabulary of fourteen thousand words by the age of six. The growth of vocabulary from then on to about age of seventeen averages at least three thousand new words a year (Clark 1994). Starting at age ten, children encounter about ten thousand new words a year, and at least one hundred thousand distinct word-meanings in their textbooks alone (ibid.).

The complexity and enormity of this phenomenon poses serious questions for linguists, psychologists, and AI practitioners who have worked hard to understand and explain it but who are, by far, remote from a comprehensive and concurred-upon theory of language acquisition. As a companion to our study of connectionist models of language learning, this appendix provides a brief introduction to some of the key issues of language learning. For simplification, and following normal practice, I will divide the discussion into two main parts – namely, the acquisition of the lexicon (words) and the learning of grammar. Each of these will be further divided into smaller subtasks and problems – for example, memory, processing, and so on.[1]

ACQUISITION OF THE LEXICON

Language consists of words, and language learning begins with the learning of words. Words are important because they arguably constitute the smallest semantic units of a language. Learning the lexicon is an important requirement for mastering the language because it is the stock of established words (dog, desk, destiny) or phrases (fit as a fiddle; flat as a board; free as a bird) that speakers can draw upon when they communicate by language. Lexical entries are stored both in dictionaries and in people's memories. While there is a clear "storage" scheme for dictionaries, no such scheme is known in human memory. We do not know, for instance, whether words are piled randomly as in a bag or listed in an orderly fashion as in a lookup table, are stay put as in a shelf or floating around as in a fluid, are clearly bordered and localized as in billiard balls or fuzzily fusing and drifting into each other as in clouds and electrons. These, and a host of other possible pictures, provide useful metaphors for us to think about lexical organization in human memory, but they are far from established theories. Indeed, a growing number of researchers find the storage metaphor totally misleading (Edelman 1992; Clancey 1997).

ISSUES OF MEMORY

Various theories of cognition provide and support different pictures of lexical memory. AI researchers Marvin Minsky (1974) and Roger Schank (1984) see it as a system of template-like "frames" or "scripts," the neuroscientist Pulvermüller (1999) as fairly localized assemblies of neurons, and cognitive scientist Gilles Fauconnier (1994) as "mental spaces" that drift, merge into each other, whereas Douglas Hofstadter (1999) provides a picture of lexical memory resembling that of fish swimming in a slime, and Edelman (another neuroscientist) thinks of it as a map of maps among disparate neuronal structures when "the brain constructs maps of its own activities" (1992: 109).

Connectionism also provides its own ways of portraying lexical memory. A number of connectionist models of memory structure have been put forth (Hopfield 1982; Kanerva 1988; Plate 1995), the most outstanding feature of which is the distributed character of representations. These are based on the notion of *content-addressable memory*, which, in contrast to classic accounts, does not use explicit addressing of memory items (Ballard 1997). Do not think, connectionists suggest, of phone books which use surnames as keys, of dictionaries that are arranged in alphabetical order, or of von Neumann computers that use serial addressing. Nothing similar to these, they argue, happens in human memory, which can use parts of the *content* to access a word. A partial description such as "a place for burning fire in the house for the purpose of heat generation," for instance, would trigger the word "chimney" in the minds of most human beings, whereas the most complete description of the same object does not make it possible to retrieve the relevant entry for it from a dictionary. This content-based aspect of memory is a characteristic feature of connectionist models of memory.

ISSUES OF PROCESSING

Lexical development in a human being manifests itself in two ways: (i) speech *comprehension* and (ii) speech *production*. These are related processes but, as research on different stages of development has shown, usually there are differences between them – adults' production vocabulary is always smaller than their comprehension vocabulary, and young children can understand words well before they can produce them. Infants under one year old, for instance, understand words for up to four months before they try to produce the same words (Clark 1993: 245). Eve Clark has even argued that this asymmetry is critical to the process of acquisition (ibid.: Chapters 2 and 3).

Connectionist research has been active in both aspects (comprehension and production) of lexical development. The main issues faced by connectionist models, as with other models of language learning, are usually framed as a set of problems, as follows:

- The *segmentation* problem: the problem of locating the boundaries between units of spoken language such as words, phrases, sentences, and so on within a continuous stream of speech.
- The *mapping* problem: the problem of isolating the word-forms of language, creating potential meanings, and mapping the meanings to the forms (Clark 1993).
- The *binding* problem: the problem of connecting high-level, general concepts and constructs to low-level features (Anderson 1995: 290).
- The *grounding* problem: the problem of grounding symbols, words and utterances in the events of the outside world (Harnad 1990).

Connectionist solutions to these problems are discussed in Chapter 6.

ACQUISITION OF GRAMMAR

Learning of grammatical regularities is one of the main challenges that a learner of a language faces. One such regularity exists in morphology – for example, the formation of the past tense of verbs in English. Received wisdom tends to explain this by the acquisition of *rules* – adding "–ed" to the verb stem – in the case of regular verbs, and by a kind of memorization in the case of irregular ones. This view is at the root of some theories of language acquisition – most notably, the so-called nativist theories that invoke innate capabilities of some sort in order to explain language learning (Chomsky 1957). Connectionists, by contrast, try to build models that learn both groups of verbs without using explicit rules.

Grammars vary across languages, but there are aspects of grammar that are more or less common to all languages – for example, all languages are comprised of units at different levels for encoding meaning (e.g., words, phrases, and clauses), which get arranged in various ways in order to express states of affairs (Hirsh-Pasek and Golinkoff 1996: Chapter 2). More specifically, all languages have the "same small set of grammatical categories and relations, phrase structure rules, inflectional paradigms, lexical entries, lexical rules, [and] grammatical features" (Pinker 1984: 25). It is possible, on this basis, to come up with a set of tasks that any learner of language has to fulfill before they could be called competent users of the language. As far as the acquisition of grammar is concerned, some of these tasks, in rough outline, are as follows:

- Learning of grammatical categories such as nouns, verbs, adverbs, and so on.[2]
- Learning of grammatical relations such as noun-verb, noun-predicate, and so on.
- Learning the "legal" phrase and sentence structures such as the subject–verb–patient structure of English.
- Learning the inflectional patterns such as tense formation, singular-plural, and so on.

The list is not exhaustive, but it gives a flavor of what is involved in the learning of grammar. In their endeavor to understand how young infants and children fulfill these tasks, psychologists and linguists face specific questions that need to be answered. Hirsh-Pasek and Golinkoff (1996) have summarized the questions as follows:

- What is present when grammatical learning begins?
- What mechanisms are used in the course of acquisition?
- What types of input drive the language-learning system forward?

The first question is concerned with what the child brings to the task of language learning. Given the enormousness of the task, this question is motivated by the idea that children should already have certain resources, innate or otherwise, at their disposal when they start learning language. The second question is concerned with the processes and mechanisms that are used in learning language. One of the interesting issues that arises, for instance, is whether these are the same *domain-general* mechanisms that are used in other cognitive functions (such as perception), or whether they are specific to language. Finally, the third question is concerned with the kinds of external resources that children employ in order to move forward in their learning – for example, their increasing knowledge of social conventions, or their increasingly sophisticated analyses of the linguistic input.

THE NATIVIST-EMPIRICIST DEBATE

Theories of language acquisition fall into different classes, depending on the answers that they give to these questions. One common classification is between empiricists – who argue that language structure exists outside the child in the social and linguistic environments, and the children need to pick these up with experience – and nativists – who believe that language acquisition occupies its own separate niche or module in the brain and has its own unique mechanisms (Hirsh-Pasek and Golinkoff 1996). Language learning, according to nativists, is a process of discovery instead of construction. Chomsky, the main figure behind this view, has written that, like puberty, learning a language is something that *happens* to the child, not something that the child does; and environmental input is just a "trigger" that sets off built-in functions (1988).

Many objections have been raised against extreme versions of both groups of theories. The main objection against empiricist views comes from the so-called poverty-of-the-stimulus argument: "As in the case of language, the environment is far too impoverished and indeterminate to provide this [language] system to the child, in its full richness and applicability" (Chomsky 1988: 153). A few examples might illustrate the point. First, consider the so-called empty categories such as the missing "you" in the sentence: "Go to bed!" Although "you" is implied in this sentence, it is not present in the surface form. Since children produce sentences such as "Go to bed yourself," but not ones like "Go to bed herself," they must be aware of the existence of "you," so the nativist argument goes, at some deep level. Furthermore, since no amount of pattern detection can explain the capability to retrieve the nonexistent "you," some other mechanism must account for it.

Second, according to nativists, the knowledge of structural dependencies of the type revealed in the following sentence could hardly be explained by bottom-up, empirical methods: "The man who will come is John." This sentence is composed of a main clause, "The man is John," and a subordinate noun phrase, "who will come," and only the "is" in the main clause may be fronted to form a question – that is, the only grammatical form is the question: "Is the man who will come John?" not the question "Will the man who come is John?" Speakers of language learn this distinction somewhere along the way and, according to nativists, no amount of encounter with surface structure will suffice to explain the acquisition of such structural knowledge.

Finally, another example in favor of the poverty-of-the-stimulus argument is that reliance on the surface cues provided in the input often leads to the wrong generalizations. For example, surface structure cannot teach us that the first sentence among the following three is wrong (Hirsh-Pasek and Golinkoff 1996):

- The chicken cooked the dinner.
- The chicken was cooked.
- The chicken cooked.

Examples such as these are used by nativists to support the poverty-of-the-stimulus argument. In the opposite direction, there are arguments against nativist views, especially radical versions of them that tend to attribute almost all aspects of language acquisition to an innate endowment. The most important of these arguments is the so-called bootstrapping problem. That is, assuming that there is indeed a skeletal syntactic system innately available to us, how do children start their purely syntactic learning? How do they start assigning grammatical roles (e.g., subject, object, etc.) to words? Answering these questions become more difficult in the face of huge variability among different languages in terms of grammatical relations. It is argued that nativist theories fail to comply with the empirical character of science, which should pay attention to variations among individual cases (here, among languages) and to experimental findings (in this case, of language acquisition among children). In other words, these theories are accused of providing too quick-and-easy answers to all questions by focusing on insipid universals.

Arguments such as these against both empiricist and nativist theories suggest that no radical version of either one might be able to fully explain the phenomenon of language acquisition (Hirsh-Pasek and Golinkoff 1996). Connectionism has turned into an important contender in the language-acquisition debate. As far as the nativist-empiricist debate is concerned, nothing in connectionist tenets commits it to either side of the debate, because the same connectionist architecture can be thought of as being the result of innate wiring (evolutionary process) or as the outcome of a developmental process. Therefore, while some connectionists land on the empiricist side (e.g., Quartz and Sejnowski 1998; Seidenberg and MacDonald 1999), others have adopted a position between the two poles. Smolensky (1999), for instance, has proposed a "grammar-based connectionist approach" to show that symbolic and connectionist approaches are mutually compatible.

Chapter 6 sketches some of the connectionist models that are built with the intent of contributing to this ongoing debate.

Notes

Prologue

1. The notion of "dream" in this work is similar to the word "imaginary" in recent cultural studies, which calls to mind both vision and fantasy but also emphasizes the historical character of our worldviews. The way we see and imagine the world is greatly shaped by the specific cultural and historical resources that are available to us (Suchman 2007).

2. Kuhn (1996) is indeed the most famous (and controversial) articulation of this historical truism.

3. Some authors use the terms "discourse" very broadly to "include techniques, technologies, metaphors, and experiences as well as language" (e.g., Edwards 1996: xiii). My usage of the term is, however, narrower, and includes mainly the metaphorical and linguistic aspects.

4. In daily life, too, we use anthropomorphic language to talk about artifacts, as well as technical language to talk about our experience. In English, "the radio plays music," "the camera captured the scene," and (even) "loudspeaker" are examples of the former, and "bubbly personality," "volcanic temper," and "magnetic charm" are examples of the latter. AI anthropomorphizes in a systematic way, thus making it an inherent part of AI practices.

5. Metaphorical language is prevalent in other scientific disciplines as well (for instance, physicists talk about particle "attraction" and "charm"), but the physical character of their subject matter protects these disciplines against literal interpretations of such metaphors. AI, because of its subject matter, does not have that kind of protection and, as we will see in the coming chapters, this leaves AI practitioners susceptible to a kind of literalism.

6. Simon (in Crevier 1993: 6) considers the interdisciplinary character of the field as the main reason for the problems in AI. I do not agree with this position, and I believe that, as is elaborated in the text, a multifaceted explanation is required.

7. I myself was attracted to AI through *Gödel, Escher, Bach* (GEB) in a life-changing way, the elaboration of which is beyond our scope here. It is ironic that the present critique should come out of a research lab that has undoubtedly been one of the Meccas of AI, by a "convert" who changed his life to study AI, and under the guidance of someone who has been a prophet of sorts for the field (in the Preface

to GEB, Hofstadter calls the views expressed in the book his "religion"). Whether the source of the irony should be sought in the character of AI, in the practitioners, or in the general circumstances of our times is a question that the present study might help us answer. In a deeply personal way, I consider the current work a fugal counterpoint to GEB.

8.   See, for example, Hofstadter (2002).

9.   Daniel Dennett characterizes Hofstadter's view in the following way:

> What Douglas Hofstadter is, quite simply, is a phenomenologist, a *practicing* phenomenologist, and he does it better than anybody else. Ever. For years he has been studying the processes of his own consciousness. . . . He is not a Phenomenologist with a capital "P." Dennett (1998: 235)

Dennett is not a friend of phenomenologists, and the fact that he labels Hofstadter as one is a curious fact that can only be understood in light of the distinction that he makes between phenomenology with capital "P" and with small "p," and in terms of the "sharp contrast" that he draws between the Husserlian school, which, in his opinion, "excuses the investigation from all inquiry . . . into the underlying mechanisms," and Hofstadter's work, which "stresses the need to ask – and answer – the question about how it works" (ibid.).

10.   This reflexive analysis is basically what I am doing in the current Prologue in terms of my own assumptions and ideas.

11.   Smith calls this "preemptive registration" (personal communication).

12.   I first came across Agre's work when I had written the bulk of this work, at which point I discovered a great deal of affinity in intuitions, goals, and even intellectual resources on which we have drawn. Despite the late exposure, I have still been able to draw extensively upon his ideas in refining my intuitions.

13.   Wherever possible, I have drawn on ethnographic studies by others such as Forsythe (2001) and Risan (1997).

Chapter 1

1.   I do not find the labeling of ideas as "ism's" a useful intellectual practice, and my usage of them is as mere conveniences that need to be explained and clarified in due course. The remainder of the section in the text is meant to do this for "mentalism" and "logicism."

2.   Why the views of Descartes and Hobbes, among all others, have been more strongly invoked in theories of computation is a fascinating question that, to the best of my knowledge, has not been fully explored. However, I will not address this question here, and will instead try to show how these two philosophers' views have influenced AI.

3.   Contemporary language and folk mythology still abound with expressions that testify to this alignment: "a soaring spirit," "I'm down," "down to earth," "in high spirits," "my spirits are sinking," and so on.

4.   Different authors use terms such as *formal* and *syntactic* in slightly different ways. Fodor (1980), for instance, takes *formal* to roughly mean "not semantic" and on that basis considers "syntactic operations a species of formal operations." Because it is not clear, as Fodor concedes, what "semantic properties" are, I prefer the

positive characterization given of the terms, which I owe to David McCarthy of Indiana University in his lectures on logic, to their negative characterization by Fodor.

5. Despite the many extant theories of computing, there is no single account that would cover all computational phenomena. Smith (forthcoming) enumerates seven such theories or "construals": "formal symbol manipulation," "effective computability," digital state machines," "information processing," and so on. The prevalent view in computer science takes all these theories as formally equivalent in an abstract mathematical sense – that is, in the sense that they could be proved to implement the same group of functions. As Smith takes pains to elaborate, however, this notion of equivalence is too abstract to be able to do justice to the realities of computation as manifested in the activities of practitioners worldwide. Smith's argument is, I believe, of great consequence for AI, and I will draw upon it later in the writing. For the purposes of this Prologue, however, I will follow the dominant view, assuming the equivalence of all theories of computation. In particular, I take as the basis of my argument the formal symbol manipulation view, which is closest in terms of both origin and issues to AI. Pylyshyn (1984) gives a lucid account of this view, and Fodor (1980) offers one of the best-known elaborations of its consequences for AI and psychology.

6. Almost all of what I claim here about the engineering culture pertains only to the United States. Although I know of no other comprehensive studies of engineering in other cultures, my personal experience elsewhere suggests that there are serious differences in the self-images and roles of engineers in other parts of the world.

7. Franklin Roosevelt is reported to have said that "the best American book to give every Soviet citizen" was the Sears Roebuck catalogue.

8. I have intentionally maintained the sexist language of the original text here, as AI has always been a male-dominated field.

9. As I indicated earlier, I am not a big fan of "isms", and I have tried in this writing to avoid them to the extent possible. The "-ist" words used in this section are only meant to be shorthand for what I have discussed in the previous sections.

10. A transducer is a mechanism through which an organism interacts with its environment – for example, sensory organs such as eyes and ears.

Chapter 2

1. Kasparov had previously lost a match to another program – Pentium Chess Genius developed by Richard Lang – in the context of the Intel Rapid Chess Tournament in August 1994 by the score of 1.5 to 0.5. This contest, however, did not gain as much publicity probably because, among other things, it was not conducted under the conditions of a world championship match and because the program was defeated by another grandmaster, Vishawanathan Anand, in the same tournament.

2. At Kasparov's request, the pieces were to be wooden, heavily weighted, not too glossy, without seams, and the king had to be 3.75 inches high. The colors of both the pieces and the board were to be dark brown and cream. The board was also to be not too glossy, with each square 2.25 inches on a side.

3. *New York Times*, May 12, 1997. Most of the information about the rematch is from IBM's Deep Blue Web site: http://www.research.ibm.com/deepblue

4. The ambivalent attitude in IBM had to do, on the one hand, with the company's vested interest in enhancing computer technology and, on the other, with its concern about the public's fear of "thinking machines" – to the extent that, according to a company spokesperson, "Artificial Intelligence" is not a term generally used at IBM. It is due to the latter concern that, according to Crevier, "the AI projects conducted at IBM fell victim to their own successes" (1993: 58, 221).

5. My apologies for the sexist language.

6. As a matter of convention and convenience, trees in computer literature are drawn upside down – hence the phrase "all the way down" in the text (see Appendix).

7. Deep Blue is much more complicated: its scoring function is reported to have 8,000 parameters.

8. Games like chess are called zero-sum because an advantage for one player means an equal disadvantage for the opponent. That is why the "best" move for the former can be defined as the "worst" move for the latter.

9. This, in turn, brings up the question of originality, a fundamental issue in AI – and, presumably, an effective tool in the hands of its opponents. We will come to this question later on.

10. An interesting aspect of Minimax that makes it different from human beings is that it does *not* distinguish among losing situations. In Minimax, a loss is a loss – it does not come in degrees. For a human being, it often matters how one loses.

11. Addressing a similar issue, Hofstadter (1998) alludes to Hearst's (1977) article as one source of his views, which were very similar to those of Hearst on the question of the prospects of computer chess.

12. The daughter of the poet Lord Byron, Lady Lovelace was a visionary and an "enchantress of numbers" (Toole 1992), who is believed to have played a major role in the creation of Charles Babbage's Analytic Engine.

13. I owe this analogy to Douglas Hofstadter.

14. With the increasing diffusion of the Internet, chess might go through another major transformation in the near future. During the world championship contest between Topalov and Kramnik in October of 2006, almost half a million observers and commentators around the globe followed and "watched" the game in real time. Like many other human activities, we are yet to grasp the deep transformative effect of this shift on the character of chess as a social activity.

15. Except in passing remarks such as this: "...one who knows the rules can play chess, but...a beginner 'can't play chess to save his life'" (Collins and Kusch 1998: 94). Also, in a debate with Hubert Dreyfus, Collins does not discuss chess directly, on the grounds that he finds it too confounded: "our criterion of good chess performance is *winning the game*, not mimicking human ability, and this creates confusion" (1992: 728). But from his arguments on other topics, one could venture a response close to that given in the text. Collins (1992), for instance, argues that, as a result of demands from machine-translation enthusiasts, our language might indeed become simplified and routinized so as to make it more susceptible to computerization. (This latter observation, I believe, is very significant, and I will come back to it in the Epilogue.)

16. In fact, this notion is closely related to our notions of Generalized Eliza Effect and Attribution Fallacy

17. The recent milestone achieved in the Human Genome Project provides a similar case. A simple-minded view might posit that once we have produced the so-called gene blueprint, we know everything that we need to know about hereditary mechanisms in human species. As many genetic experts have pointed out, however, that is an illusion. Ironically, it turned out that the number of genes was somewhat smaller (by 30 percent) than original estimates had it. That doesn't mean, however, that we are now in a more favorable position in our attempt to understand them, mainly because of the interactions that exist among genes. Much the same could be said about the brain and its building blocks. Interestingly, Kurzweil (1997) makes a similar point but proposes that we will soon be able to scan the human brain at the synaptic level and predicts, further, that we will be able to map the neural circuitry of the brain in the first half of this century, in a manner similar to what was done in the Human Genome Project.

18. The main communication mechanism in the nervous system is the transmission of action potentials, not electronic conduction. As Gazzaniga et al. (1998) remark, the latter is good only for short-distance communication. Long-distance communication requires active or regenerative electrical signals, which is what action potentials are.

19. Memory capacity is increasing proportionally. A hundred-gigabyte hard drive is also an over-the-counter product these days. Technically speaking, however, the most solid measure of computer performance in the field is *execution time* of programs. In the marketplace, other popular measures are adopted – for example, MIPS (million instructions per second), MFLOPS (million floating-point operations per second). My calculation here does not match any of these, and is done solely to provide a rough comparative estimate.

Chapter 3

1. I use the terms "possible" and "impossible," tongue in the cheek, with some caution here. Granting that the border between these is relative to capabilities and circumstances, I believe that there are physical, logical, and cultural constraints built into our environment that make certain things simply impossible, and these constraints must be taken into account in any grounded theory of intelligence. *Not anything goes*, in other words.

2. All of my examples come from Clark (2003). Numerous accounts of these technologies are available for the interested reader to follow (e.g., Gershenfeld 1999, Greenberg 2000).

3. The typical dimensions of a MOSFET today are tens of microns (e.g., the Intel 1 GHz Coppermine chip, which was demonstrated in February 2000, featured 0.18 μm interconnects with a silicon dioxide layer of about 200 Å). The wafer, for instance, cannot be made too thin for two reasons: (1) quantum tunneling (electrons may move in "leaps" rather than diffuse through the layer); (2) the thinner the layer, the slower the device (due to capacitance effects). Similarly, if the size of the gate is reduced to as low as 50 Å, quantum tunneling may occur across the gate (i.e., between the source and the drain of the transistor). At this point, we have left the classical regime and entered the quantum realm.

4. This brief sketch is by no means intended to be an introduction to quantum computing but, rather, to convey a feel for the potential of this new technology. The interested reader is invited to look at one of the following introductions to quantum computing:

   Meglicki, Z. (2000). *Introduction to Quantum Computing*; http://www.ovpit.indiana.edu/ B679;
   Nielsen, M. A. and I. L. Chuang (2000). *Quantum Computation and Quantum Information* (Cambridge University Press)
   Preskill, J. (1998). *Lecture Notes for Physics 229: Quantum Information and Computation*; http://www.theory.caltech.edu/people/preskill/ph229.

5. Of course, N bits can also assume 2^N different values, but one can easily represent these as binary strings of length N. The same cannot be done with a quantum system of N qubits.

6. In particular, we face the phenomenon called *teleportation* – the idea that the states of a system can be faithfully copied in another location without the need for material transfer, thus overriding the relativistic limit of the speed of light. The only theoretical explanation for this belongs to Bohm, who has tried to explain the nonlocal correlations in terms of a "quantum information field" that does not diminish with distance and that binds the whole universe together. As Meglicki mentions, however, this field is not physically measurable and only manifests itself through nonlocal correlations. Thus, he concludes, "at least at this stage, it is a matter of religion whether you want to believe in it or not" (Meglicki 2000).

7. In the terminology of complexity theory (which deals with the time and memory-space requirements of algorithms), an "intractable" problem is one where the amount of time or memory increases exponentially with the size of the input.

8. Bill Joy of Sun Microsystems wrote a call to arms in *Wired* magazine (8.04, April 2000).

9. In an issue of *Science* dedicated to the state of the art in nanotechnology, various experts stated: "Nanotechnology doesn't exist" (Don Eigler of IBM's Almaden Research Center); "My advice is, don't worry about self-replicating nanobots. It's not real now and will never be in the future" (Richard Smalley, a Nobel Prize–winning chemist at Rice University); "The technology is almost wholly on the drawing board" (John Seely Brown, head of Xerox PARC). *Science*, Vol. 290, No. 5496, November 2000.

10. Although Kurzweil uses *paradigm* very loosely to refer to different technologies as well as laws (e.g., Moore's Law), it seems that he has computational technology in mind most often when using the word.

11. As a working definition, Kurzweil characterizes intelligence as the "ability to use limited resources optimally" (1999, 18). This characterization, however, has more to do with the notion of evolutionary competition that is outlined in the second assumption in the text.

12. We have already talked about recursion and genetic algorithms, and will discuss neural nets in Chapter 6.

13. *Eschatological* literally means "having to do with the life after death and, especially, with the Day of Judgment." By using the term here, Lanier is presumably alluding to the predictions of the type we have seen in Kurzweil.

14. Clark mentions in passing that Moravec's view is "more subtle and interesting than his critics allow," but he does not discuss these subtleties and how they make this view different from the alternative "popular caricature." I am not as enthusiastically clear as Clark about the difference, but do not need to get into this discussion, as it is irrelevant to our purposes here.

15. The words "reality" and "resistance" have their common root in *res*, the Latin for "thing."

16. This is probably why Hollywood has shown more interest in this brand of AI than in any other. In a sense, various Hollywood productions –*2001: A Space Odyssey, The Bicentennial Man, Artificial Intelligence, I Robot, The Terminator* series, and so on – each seem to have been inspired or informed by one of the views examined in this chapter.

17. Asimov's three laws are as follows:

   1. A robot may not injure a human being or, through inaction, allow a human being to come to harm.
   2. A robot must obey orders given it by human beings except where such orders would conflict with the First Law.
   3. A robot must protect its own existence as long as such protection does not conflict with the First or Second Law.

Chapter 4

1. As we will see later in this chapter, the developers of Cyc take great pain to separate themselves from the logicist tradition. However, following Smith (1991), I will argue that despite their claim Cyc shares many of the tenets of the logicist approach. This also explains the allusion to the Boolean Dream in the title of this chapter.

2. Interestingly, Lenat and Feigenbaum (1991) name Carnegie Melon University's Soar project, MIT's robotics research, Stanford's work in logic, and all the connectionist school as examples of the formalist tradition in AI. Lumping all these together is certainly peculiar, and it reveals a very specific view of formalism. They seem to equate formalism with the attempt to *scale up* to human-level intelligence by starting from a simple mechanism (Soar and Robotics), a few examples (Logic), or high parallelism (connectionism). While this characterization of formalism is unique, it ironically brings Cyc itself under the same umbrella. For what is Cyc if not the hope of engendering intelligence by scaled-up knowledge? My notion of *formal* as used here, however, is close to the more standard use of the term – that is, "committed to formal logic." It is in this sense that I consider Cyc's approach formal.

3. In explaining why it is the expert's head that contains knowledge, Hayes says: "one knows it does because he is able to do the task one is interested in" (1990: 201).

4. Mass spectroscopy is a method in which the chemical composition and structure of a substance are determined through the spectral (frequency) analysis of the light produced by the burning of the substance.

5. The term *brittleness* was probably first used in the context of AI's weaknesses by John Holland, in his well-known article "Escaping Brittleness" (1986).

6. Although Gallistel's strictly computational view of insect navigation might not be agreeable to all cognitive scientists, his account is certainly compatible with the view behind Cyc and could not be discarded as irrelevant to Cyc's general framework.

7. Notice that the argument that is usually used in analogy to flight – namely, that we can learn about the general principles of intelligence by looking at domains such as chess – does not work here, because the goal in Cyc is to model human commonsense knowledge, which is species-specific. Incidentally, as a matter of historical fact (Lenat and Guha 1990), Cyc was originally introduced as a model of human intelligence. It was only later that this constraint was relaxed by Cyc's developers, probably as a tactical measure to avoid debates about the psychological realism of their project

8. The work of McCarthy and Hayes (e.g., 1990) may be the major exception. This author also made a very preliminary attempt in this direction in Ekbia (2002).

9. Pratt's report is available at: http://boole.stanford.edu/cycprobs.html (last visited in July 2003).

10. All references in this subsection are to Cycorp's Web site at the following addresses (accessed Dec. 16, 2002): http://www.cyc.com/tech.html and http://www.cyc.com/applications.html. I will refer to the Web site as "document" throughout this section.

11. "Microtheories," as we shall see later, are building blocks or modules of Cyc's knowledge base where consistency is maintained (see the main text). The notion of a "frame" was introduced by Marvin Minsky, who defined it as follows: "A *frame* is a data structure for representing a stereotyped situation, like being in a certain kind of living room, or going to a child's birthday party" (Minsky 1974/97). Inside each frame are several kinds of information, and *slots* are the substructures that keep this information. For instance, a frame for a student might have slots for name, year, grade-point average, etc. The frame that has "Joe Fox" as the value for its name slot, "2nd" for the year slot, and "3.4" for the grade-point-average slot represents a second-year student named Joe Fox with grade-point average of 3.4, and so on. Frames can also be nested within each other, so that a slot-filler in one frame may be another frame, which may have yet other frames as slot-fillers, and so on.

12. Because of the highly proprietary nature of the project, we do not know how much of Cyc's work involves finding synonyms. We simply know that it has a lexicon and that it consults it from time to time. This, however, is not a weakness in itself. People, after all, also use dictionaries when they don't know a word. Finding synonyms, by itself, is not a problem. It is the frequency of doing it and the ability to do it effectively and meaningfully that are important.

13. In fact, the description provided in the web page of how Cyc performs a similar task is not all that different from the above. The main difference is in the details of representation–instead of Fear(Person), they have:

```
(#$and
(#$isa ?x #$Person)
   (#$feelsEmotion ?x #$Fear #$High))
```

14. Microelectronics and Computer Consortium, founded in 1984 under the direction of Admiral Ray Inman, a retired staff member of DARPA (Defense Advanced Research Program Agency).

15. The list of questions prepared by Pratt also can be found on the aforementioned Web site.

16. These workshops (offered as a series Cyc101, 102, etc.), which are designed to introduce Cyc to present or potential customers, provide the opportunity of hands-on experience with the whole knowledge base for the first time in Cyc's two-decade history. After many years of waiting, I was very pleased and thankful to be able to take part in one of these workshops, as I was also impressed with the degree of enthusiasm and resourcefulness of some of the philosophers and knowledge engineers working on the project.

17. One such application was in the implementation of the Total Information Awareness system, a highly visible project sponsored by the Defense Department in the aftermath of September 11, 2001, under the supervision of Admiral John Poindexter: http://www.darpa.mil/iao/index.htm.

18. Some of these, such as incest taboo, are culturally relative, of course. But given that everything that is given to Cyc is part of a bigger microtheory called "inTheWorldWeLiveIn," it is rather puzzling that it does not provide immediate answers to such mundane questions.

19. This, in turn, might imply some significance for the number twenty. Given the binary (yes/no) structure of the question-answer tree, one might be inclined to infer that the number of concepts a person has in memory should be on the order of two to the 20th power – roughly, one million. The fact that guessers manage to win in a good portion of the games lends some plausibility to such an estimate for this limited version of the consensus reality, but it is not clear whether it also gives support to the same estimate suggested by Lenat and Guha (1990). Based on three different sources of calculation, these authors claim that the number of commonsense facts every individual knows is on the order of one million. For instance, a back-of-the-envelope calculation attributed to Minsky is based on there being one fact for every minute of short-term memory processing during an individual's lifetime.

20. That partly explains why the estimates of the size of Cyc's knowledge base have varied so drastically throughout the years. (Cyc's literature is, in fact, a bit fuzzy on what the real estimate is.) The estimate started out with one million assertions (Lenat and Guha 1990), and, later on, increased it to "about 1 million 'frame-fulls' or about 100 million assertions" (Lenat and Feigenbaum 1991), with the caveat that this is the estimate of the crossing point where "knowledge acquisition could be more profitably done by natural language understanding (reading online texts and 'discussing' the difficult parts) rather than continuing to build the KB manually, one assertion at a time" (233). It is also said that this is "the breadth of human knowledge, but of course not the depth" (ibid.). To the best of my knowledge, they have not yet approached this hoped-for crossing point. It remains to be seen whether any of the above estimates prevails in the future.

21. Note that *compiled* does not in any way mean "tacit." It is a technical term in computer science, meaning roughly that the data, rather than being directly accessible in the programming language, are stored as a lower-level representation.

22. On the face of it, the significant role of tacit knowledge in human cognition seems to point to a disadvantage for the human race. As one reviewer aptly wondered, why should our inability to explicate our reasons for what we do make us *more* powerful than a purely declarative system? Although this question is completely meaningful, it does not undermine the argument made in the text against Cyc. The point of the argument is to show why it is difficult, even impossible, to capture all of human commonsense knowledge and encode it explicitly, which is the self-proclaimed goal of the Cyc group. Whether or not this is a limitation of human cognition is not relevant to the argument.

23. The analysis given in this paragraph of the relation between "truth" and "relevance" is my reconstruction of an argument given by Lenat (1998), and its inclusion here does not mean that I necessarily agree with its premises. As a matter of fact, the whole point about making assertions in the present tense about a fact that belongs to the past or the future is very dubious, for the word "is" cannot be used in 1900 or 2100 to refer to a situation in 1997. It is also very contentious to say that "Bill Clinton will be president in 1997" was true in 1900. Who was Bill Clinton in 1900? In 1800? Was this sentence true in 3000 BC? Sixty million years ago?

24. Temporal logic is not unknown in AI. McDermott (1982) provides one such formulation.

25. As Dennett explains, there is less-than-perfect agreement within the AI community as to the scope of the frame problem. For instance, McCarthy and Hayes (1969), who introduced the term, apply it in a narrow sense to representation and planning. Dennett uses it in a broader sense, close to what people usually mean by the "relevance problem." I consider the frame problem to be an instance of the relevance problem, which specifically deals with temporal change in particular.

26. Proof by *construction* also constitutes a major method in the modern theory of computing, where theorems are proved by demonstrating how abstract mathematical structures called "machines" can be built in an algorithmic fashion (see, for instance, Cohen 1997, Zipser 2002)

Chapter 5

1. The terms "syntax" and "semantics" are very loaded words, used variably in different disciplines (logic, linguistic, computer science) – hence the quotes around them in the text. I try to avoid using the terms unless obliged to by the context, in which case they simply mean "form" and "meaning," respectively.

2. CBR people, as we shall see later, also consider their approach to be a scruffy version of AI, but for rather different reasons.

3. This may sound very similar to the "knowledge hypothesis" that underlies Cyc (see Chapter 4). But there is a fundamental difference that will become clear shortly in the text.

4. Lists are a fundamental type of data structure, and, as the name implies, a list consists of a set of items (possibly including other lists) in a specific order.

5. The expression 'PART-OF' indicates that the sense organ (eye) used for ATTEND belongs to the cornerback. The question mark indicates that the slot is not relevant or that there is no information available for filling it

6. Unfortunately, there is a minor confusion in Schank and Leake (2001), because the spelling of the word meaning "coat" is "mackintosh" with a lowercase "m" and a "k," but their point is understood in any case.

7. These examples are drawn from Collins 1989, which discusses Micro Coach, one of the models to be discussed in this chapter.

8. DEFMOP is a Lisp function that defines a MOP.

9. Micro Coach, as "a miniature version of the Coach program," is what is publicly available (Collins 1989: 291). The sample codes in this chapter are, therefore, from Micro Coach, but the discussions, being mostly conceptual, should apply to the full version of Coach.

10. It is a bit of a stretch to talk about "failure" in the course of a simulated game, especially given that there is really no game played between two teams. My use of the word "failure" in the text, therefore, should not be construed as a tacit confirmation that it comes anywhere close to the rich social and psychological meaning of the word.

11. Consider the following rather simplified scenario, for instance: If:

   - The U.S. government is in dispute with Iraq over the issue of weapons.
   - It has to decide between a full-fledged attack or the monitoring of Iraq's activities by the U.N.
   - Iraq picks the option of allowing the inspectors in.
   - Iraq can only pursue one counterplan – namely, either to allow the inspectors in or to prepare for war.
   - There is a deadline set by the U.N. resolutions on when the inspections happen.

   Then the United States should create a new plan that involves the following steps at the same time:

   - To run an anti-Iraq propaganda campaign (shared by both alternatives).
   - To mobilize troops and warfare to the region in the name of a cautionary measure (a modified form of the attack plan).
   - To carefully monitor Iraq's activities to see what choice it has made.
   - To decide whether to fully comply with the U.N. plan.
   - To be ready to attack, if deemed necessary.
   - To launch an attack with the help of U.S. allies before the completion of the inspections.

   Given the above strategy, it would be pointless for the United States, if it were to follow the Fork strategy, to wait until the U.N. deadline if it intends to invade Iraq because, with the world watching, an attack after the inspections were over (assuming they revealed no violations by Iraq) would be unjustifiable.

12. STRIPS stands for "STanford Research Institute Problem Solver."

13. The name "Shakey" was given to the robot as a revelation of its clumsy movements. Despite this, Shakey received publicity in *Life* magazine in 1970, when a sensation-seeking reporter dubbed it "the first electronic person" (Crevier 1993: 96). This is a good illustration of the kind of overstatement that AI tends to elicit in the media.

14. See, for example, the collection of essays in Glasgow, Narayana, and Karan (1995).

15. Barwise and Etchemendy (1994) developed an interactive computer program called *Hyperproof* that uses pictures such as those in Figure 4.2/3 to teach the principles of analytic reasoning.

16. The phenomenon of "free ride," according to Shimojima, "is due to a particular way in which a structural constraint governing representations matches with a constraint governing the targets of representation" (1996: 17). We need not go into the details of this, but the idea seems to be similar to what was briefly mentioned about constraints earlier in the text.

17. As an example of this internal incoherence, consider the following points from the same book (Schank et al. 1994). Although it is asserted that "knowledge structures function best if they are dynamic" (7), XPs and scripts are characterized as "fossilized" (59) and "frozen" (77) later on. It is, indeed, very difficult to reconcile these assertions.

18. A spin-off of this view, represented among others by Hammond and his colleagues, has actually moved in a direction that brings it very close to the views of Agre and Chapman (discussed earlier in this chapter), that put emphasis on the improvisatory nature of many of our routine activities.

19. These are from interviews reported in Brockman (1995). Dennett relishes Schank's role "as a gadfly and as a naysayer," describing him "a guerrilla in the realm of cognitive science."

Chapter 6

1. The term "connectionism," as first introduced by Ballard and Feldman (1982) and used in this chapter, is just shorthand. Connectionists constitute a large group of researchers who agree, at a general level, on a neural-modeling approach to the study and modeling of cognition, but who strongly disagree on many other things. Some, for example, believe only in biologically plausible training algorithms (such as Hebbian learning); others prefer settling and dynamical networks; some like fully distributed networks; others prefer local representations; and so on. The models studied in this chapter – for example, PDP and ART models – provide a sense of this diversity, but only in a limited way. The application of the term "connectionist" to all of them, therefore, should be understood in this loose fashion.

2. The discussion in the text assumes some familiarity on the part of the reader with connectionist terminology, as well as with the basic issues in language understanding. Appendixes B and C provide an introductory note on both topics for the uninitiated reader.

3. I asked these questions while at the MIT Museum in November 2001.

4. This is not to say that connectionist models do not play a role in extant commercial systems. (Both Jupiter and Claire probably involve key connectionist modules.) The point is that the general approach of connectionists has been to attack language processing in an incremental and divided fashion.

5. Small wonder that replication of results turns out to be a serious problem in connectionist research. A small change in any of the above steps – for example, in the order of presentation of the verbs – may lead to the failure to obtain identical results (by the same experimenter or, even more likely, by someone who intends to replicate the simulation) – more on this later.

6. The list in the text is cumulative but not inclusive. It involves the views of different connectionist authors and, as such, is not meant to suggest unanimity among them.

7. This is a broad definition of training. There are networks for which input and output nodes are not defined as such, but the basic idea of giving something to the network and getting output from it is still applicable to such networks.

8. Discussing the capabilities of networks with nonlinear output function, Churchland concludes: "there are no transformations that lie beyond the computational power of a large enough and suitably weighted network" (1997: 271).

9. In connectionist modeling, "local" means *one node* represents a concept, and "nonlocal" means that *many* nodes represents a concept.

10. There are also methods in classical AI of partially satisfying goals or of judging the level of progress toward a goal, but this kind of soft satisfaction is easier to implement in connectionist models because of the large number of degrees of freedom due the typically large number of processing units.

11. Of course, part of the vulnerability of classical models is due to lack of redundancy. One could, in principle build a classic model with enough redundancies in its language-like sentences so that it would not crucially depend on any single token of a sentence.

12. I myself have done this in Appendix B when describing the design of the simple association network. In the simple world of Gs and Qs, with rather well-defined features and boundaries, this might well be justifiable. But, in the real world of millions of objects and events with thousands of features and properties, it certainly is not.

13. We should notice that the impoverished form of the input (bits rather than phonemes) puts the model at a disadvantage compared to a human learner, because there are important temporal and phonological cues (such as stress patterns) that might make the task easier for a human language learner, but which are not available to the model. Observations like this show that, despite the focus in recurrent networks on issues of time, the notion of time is still too abstract in a model like this, making the task rather unrealistic.

14. The size of a memory "window" is roughly the number of stimulus inputs that are processed ("seen") at any given moment.

15. This example is from Elman (1993), but it sounds so unwieldy that the average speaker of English might have trouble parsing it. My purpose, as well as Elman's (I presume), in bringing it up is simply to communicate the point – not to demonstrate a real-life example.

16. The words "statistical" and "stochastic" are often used interchangeably, but I believe that they should be distinguished, the former referring to the type of *data* that is given to a model and latter to the kind of *processes* that take place in the model. Rhode and Plaut, for instance, call the connectionist models of language "stochastic" because these models are sensitive to frequency, but the right term, according to my suggestion, is "statistical."

17. Remember that the notion of "competence" in the Chomskian view is intended to provide an ideal model of language capability against which the real "performance" of individual speakers can be measured.

18. The term "grandmother cell" comes from criticisms of theories of brain architecture in which the representations in the brain are so localized that one could

pinpoint a single nerve cell as the site that represents complex object such as one's grandmother. This is generally believed to be far from true in brain architecture.

19. The pressure of the dominant trend is of such magnitude, however, that even Grossberg's group succumbs occasionally, as, for instance, when they make associations between their work and the phenomenon of consciousness (Grossberg and Myers 1999).

20. In cognitive psychology, the terms "working memory" and "short-term memory" usually refer to the same thing, but in ART models they are used differently.

21. I would like to thank David Landy for suggesting this analogy.

Chapter 7

1. The word "dynamicist" is not a common word in English. It recently has been put to use mostly in cognitive science literature, and I use it only as shorthand, for lack of a better term. As I shall explain later in the text, I use this term to refer to a special flavor of the dynamical approach that leans toward mathematical models of cognition.

2. The dominant view in cognitive science and AI is sometimes called "functionalism." The main idea of functionalism is that "the mental states of a human being are computational states," in much the same way that light is electromagnetic radiation of certain wavelengths (Putnam 1990). Functionalism holds that just as the view of light as electromagnetic radiation allowed us to understand and explain optical phenomena (reflection, refraction, etc.) in ways that were not possible before, the study of mental phenomena as computational states will allow us to explain them in novel ways.

3. The affinity of the dynamical and connectionist approaches is also quite obvious, because any connectionist model with continuous-valued weights and activations can, in principle, be thought of as a dynamical system that evolves in time. As we saw in Chapter 4, a whole generation of connectionist models has, in fact, been constructed with a built-in dimension of time in mind, making such models susceptible to dynamical analysis.

4. By definition, a "parameter" is a component of a system that affects, but is not affected by, the evolution of the system – for example, mass in Newtonian mechanics.

5. A caricature version of this dream, applied to the study of human beings, might look like this:

The Complete Set of Dynamical Equations
for Animus-sapiens

$$\partial(\text{SOUL})/\partial t = \alpha\, \partial\,(\text{WILL})/\partial t + \beta\, \partial\,(\text{LOVE})/\partial t + \gamma\, \partial(\text{THOUGHT})/\partial t$$
$$\partial(\text{WILL})/\partial t = \rho\, \partial(\text{DECISION})/\partial t + \sigma\, \partial\,(\text{POWER})/\partial t$$
$$\partial(\text{POWER})/\partial t = \tau\,(\text{BODY-STRENGTH}) + \omega\, \partial\,(\text{PSYCHIC-STRENGTH})/\partial t$$
$$(\text{BODY-STRENGTH}) = \xi\partial\,(\text{FOOD})/\partial t + \zeta\,(\text{VITAMIN})^2$$

6. One can see why even the solar system, with its nine planets, some of which have their own moons, would pose a serious challenge for mathematical analysis.

7. Sadly, in some parts of the world the magic is reversed: You will be surprised to *find* an item on the shelf ! Which one of these is a better example of adaptation, however, is a different question.

8. This convention for defining in-phase and out-of-phase motion is the opposite of the convention that physicists would tend to use. However, to maintain consistency, I have followed the conventions of the originators of the models.

9. Critical slowing-down means that it takes longer for the system to correct its behavior if it is perturbed near the critical value than away from it. For instance, Kelso and his colleagues applied a little torque pulse to perturb briefly (and unexpectedly) one of the oscillating fingers. They then measured the time it took to stabilize the phase relation again, and the results of such measurements fit the predictions of the model.

10. As van Gelder points out, this way of portraying the dynamical hypothesis is, in fact, a response to Newell and Simon's "Physical Symbol Systems Hypothesis", which was introduced as a "law of qualitative structure," allegedly on a par with the cell doctrine in biology and plate tectonics in geology (see Chapter 1).

11. Whether or not this is a fair and objective characterization of the computational approach to modeling the mind is a matter of serious debate. In fact, a number of computer scientists (Batali, Smith, Wegner) have argued that this conception is based on an inaccurate understanding of current theories of computing, which are themselves inaccurate accounts of the real practice of computing that permeates modern societies – "computation in-the-wild,", as Brian C. Smith calls it.

12. This emphasis on the quantitative form of theories of cognition is probably the most distinctive feature of radical dynamicism, and it has elicited many hard criticisms from opponents. Later in the chapter, I will address the question of quantification in the context of a closer examination of Poincaré's views.

13. I have not included these diagrams here in order to avoid a discussion of technical details. The interested reader is referred to the original paper (Bajscy and Large 1999).

14. As Quartz (1998) points out, the appeal of dynamical models is in providing what he calls "mixed-level explanations," and their success depends on "the denial of the autonomy of levels of explanation" (1998: 650).

15. It should be noted that physics seems to be also failing in its attempt to develop a unified theory.

16. See Gilbert and Troitzsch (2005) for an introduction and review.

17. This view was, for instance, expressed by the late Jon Barwise in response to skeptical questions about the role of mathematics and logic in cognitive science (personal communication).

Chapter 8

1. Dead reckoning is the computation of net displacement (i.e., position relative to starting point) by integrating (or summing up in increments) velocity with respect to time. It is an indispensable tool in navigation because, in unfamiliar terrain, it enables one to come back home.

2. Under this characterization, Pengi and Steels's crumb-collecting robots are situated but not embodied, and the same holds for an airline's computer reservation

system. However, a robot that mindlessly goes through the same spray-painting pattern over and over again on an assembly line is embodied but not situated (Brooks 2002a: 52). Toto and Genghis, by contrast, are both situated and embodied.

3.   This usage of the word "free," which is common in computer literature, is curious in two ways. First, contrary to the traditional usage, which meant "with no consumption of energy," this usage implies "no computation." Second, those who make such statements often fail to notice that a great deal of thinking (or computation, if you will) on the part of designers is invested in generating these so-called computationally "free" behaviors.

4.   Video clips of Cog doing these movements are available at: http://www.ai.mit.edu/projects/cog/.

5.   Note that the idea behind the shorthand "life = cognition" is totally different from the more traditional view that could be phrased as "cognition = life." Although the latter means that life is at the core of cognition (that is, in order to be cognitive, one has to be alive), the former means that cognition is at the core of life. This novel view that holds cognition as the key to life is at the foundation of Artificial Life (ALife; see the next note).

6.   ALife consists of techniques and methods of creating computer programs (software) that, when equipped and observed with the right visual interface such as a computer screen, exhibit life-like behavior (such as chasing, hunting, eating, reproducing, etc.) among software agents.

7.   What I call "arguments" are, in fact, various discussions and speculations scattered among the chapters of Brooks's book, summarized and restructured here for the purpose of clarification.

8.   "Intelligence without representation" was the title of a paper originally written in 1986 and published later in the journal *Artificial Intelligence* (1991). The title of the paper, as well as parts of its content, led many people to believe that Brooks and the MIT group were "anti-representationalists" – that is, against any use of internal representations in AI models. Brooks (1999: 79) grants that the title of this paper was "a little inflammatory," and claims that what he had in mind was, in fact, "intelligence without conventional representations." Although conceding that "this has led to much confusion about my position," Brooks asserts that he still likes the title!

9.   The quintuple eye movements have different functions, as follows. Saccades are high-speed ballistic motions that bring a salient object into focus on the fovea. In Cog, this is done by having the vision system learn a function that maps a change in the location of an object to a corresponding change in the position of the eye motor (Marjanoviç et al. 1996). Smooth-pursuit tracking keeps the image of a moving object in focus at low speed ($100°$ per second compared to $700°$ in saccades). Cog performs this by detecting a visual target and maintaining focus on the target. To reduce the computational load, only the central patch of an image is used for tracking purposes. Vergence movements adjust the eyes for viewing objects at varying depth. This is necessary for coordinating hands and eyes, discriminating figure and ground, and detecting collisions. Finally, the two involuntary eye movements are compensatory mechanisms to stabilize the eyes when the head moves slowly or rapidly. Cog uses its vestibular components (described in Appendix F) to carry out such movements.

10. A ratio template is divided into a number of regions and a number of relations. The relations are comparisons between region values, such as "the nose is brighter than the cheek." These relations are used to compare a stimulus and the template; the more matches, the higher the probability of a face (Scassellati 1998).

11. Remember that there are two cameras per eye – one that captures a wide-angle view of the periphery (approximately 110°), and another that captures a narrow-angle view of the central area (approximately 20°) with the same resolution.

12. A clarification is needed about the possible need for numerous modules, as I have suggested in the text. It might be argued, for instance, that one way to use the face-detection mechanism more generally is to change the template – for example, from face templates to car templates. Then, with most of the mechanism untouched, it can be used for a different purpose. Also, it might be possible to make the mechanism accept templates as input parameters, thus giving it more generality. Finally, because the eye-movement mechanism depends on unsupervised learning and is likely to be useful for other tasks, it can be thought of as a general mechanism. Although these might be plausible scenarios, they do not address my main point – namely, that the detection of faces does not *emerge* from the cooperation of simpler modules, as these scenarios would require.

13. This characterization of folk psychology might sound trivially obvious, but in fact it is not, for two reasons. One is that it is based on a representational view of mind, which is being disputed by, among others, the advocates of the neo-robotics approach. The other reason is that, even if one adopts the representational view, the elements of folk psychology vary from place to place and from time to time. Whereas the folk psychology of contemporary American society is often explained in terms of "goals, beliefs, and desires," for instance, the folk psychology of some other culture might better be explained in terms of "goals, beliefs, and commitments (or responsibilities)"; and these give rise to quite different systems of behavior.

14. A third possibility is also conceivable, and that is to say that rivalry between the psychology camps need not be taken very seriously by people outside psychology – that is, the outsider would simply select the correct pieces from either theory and would not pay attention to their differences. But this would make sense only if the Cog group was in fact indifferent toward what psychologists have to say – something that is not true, given that they even go so far as to suggest the relevance of their work to autism *as explained by the theory theory.*

15. Needless to say, Kismet has a memory in the sense that any computer has one, but that is totally different from the type of memory that is required for learning.

16. Visit http://www.ifi.unizh.ch/ for demonstrations of some of these systems.

17. To see the parallelism between DARPA's current objectives and the humanoid robot research at MIT, notice the following project announcement by DARPA (BAA #02–15) under the title: "Mobile Autonomous Robot Software (MARS) Robotic Vision 2020" (Due 04/03/03).

The Defense Advanced Research Projects Agency (DARPA) is soliciting proposals for the design, development, integration, and demonstration of perception-based autonomous robots that effectively operate in real-world environments and interact with humans and with other robots. The key enabling strategy for this effort is the structured incorporation into the system of operator intervention, machine learning, and other techniques so that the system's autonomous capabilities can be iteratively and methodically improved, resulting in the evolutionary development of the revolutionary capabilities needed to support the Joint DARPA/Army's Future Combat Systems (FCS) and other military transformational thrusts. The software being developed under the Mobile Autonomous Robot Software (MARS) program will create significant, asymmetric, military advantage by enabling the pervasive employment of an entirely new class of unmanned, autonomous military systems.

Chapter 9

1. To be read as: "If *abc* goes to *abd*, what does *iijjkk* go to?"
2. The spirit of the argument is similar to Hofstadter's observations about the Coach program and case-based reasoning (see Chapter 4).
3. I am sympathetic to most of what Dartnall has to say about the weaknesses of combinationist accounts and to his emphasis on knowledge, judgment, and sense-making as important elements of the creative process. However, as he points out himself, his account is just the beginning of a story to be told later (What is "knowledge-about" for example?). My use of his classification of types of creativity in the text only has heuristic value, and does not indicate my theoretical commitment. (Also, in terms of terminology, Dartnall uses the term "representationism" to refer to what I call "mentalism" in this writing (see Chapter 2).
4. Cope (1996) and Hofstadter (2002) provide detailed information about this, and we do not need to go into the technical details here.
5. I would like to thank Maia Bailey for useful information in this section.
6. I am not going to review this work here; the interested reader is invited to look at anthologies such as Dartnall (2002).
7. In Copycat's letter-string domain, the alphabet does not wrap around, therefore **a** has no predecessor and **z** has no successor, making it answers such as **xya** implausible for the problem.
8. Hofstadter, as an AI researcher, has been able to continue research in microdomains largely because of the generous support of Indiana University for his research, which relieves his group from the expectations of outside sources – a luxury that might be rarely available to other AI researchers (personal communication). What matters, though, is the motivation behind microdomains – namely, staying within the limits of the real capabilities of current AI systems. Simply put, microdomains are Hofstadter's method of (to borrow Brooks' phrase from the last chapter) staying "honest," and this is what matters. Any other method that accomplishes the same goal would be equally good, and finding such methods is, in fact, a challenge that the AI community needs to meet.

Epilogue

1. Attribution fallacy is, I believe, a special case of what Brian Smith calls "preemptive registration," in that his term refers to a general tendency (warranted or unwarranted) to inscribe meaning in artifacts.
2. This is not to say that "impression" does not play a role in other parts of science. To the contrary, as Giere (1999) has argued, visual models (diagrams, maps, graphs,

etc.) play a crucial demonstrative role in all of science, and, as Latour (1999: 105–06) has shown, public representation is a major component in the development of all scientific disciplines. The point is that in AI these turn into key justificatory elements, as we have seen in the case of pictures drawn for human consumption (see Chapter 5). A similar observation can be made about graphical interfaces that are widely used in AI.

3. Going beyond *2001: A Space Odyssey*, and the spate of more recent movies such as *Star Wars* (think of C370 and R2D2), *Matrix*, *The Sixth Sense*, and *Artificial Intelligence*, AI has come to occupy a special place in public discourse, in mass media (see, for instance, *Wall Street Journal*, Sept. 22, 2000, the *New York Times Book Review* of January 10, 2000, and numerous programs on National Public Radio and Public Broadcasting Services), and even, of all things, the pop-music world. In the United States, for instance, both the pop group Our Lady Peace and the rap group De la Soul have recorded CDs titled "Artificial Intelligence."

4. Kohler has borrowed this phrase from Steven Shapin.

5. The whole debate between Brooks and Kurzweil about the right future path for AI (roughly, software agents versus robots) can be seen, at least in part, as an entrepreneurial war between two business owners who manufacture goods that belong to these two categories.

6. http://www.machinebrain.com/articles/ugcv/ugcv01.html

7. Reprinted by permission of the publisher from *Science in Action: How to Follow Scientists and Engineers through Society* by Bruno Latour, p. 158, Cambridge, Mass: Harvard University Press, Copyright © 1987 by Bruno Latour.

Appendix B

1. Real neurons operate very slowly (in the time scale of milliseconds, about a million times slower than a computer component). Given that a typical human behavior of interest to psychologists – speech, perception, memory retrieval, and so on – takes on the order of one second, Feldman (1985) proposed that we should seek explanations of these phenomena that would not involve more than one hundred elementary sequential operations – hence his notion of "100-step-program." Because the processes that give rise to the same phenomena are typically very complex, this implies massive parallelism among processors.

2. There are two major brands of connectionist models: "localist" and "PDP (Parallel Distributed Processing)." The former, which was originally championed by a group of researchers at Rochester University (Feldman et al. 1985), favors "local" representations of knowledge – that is, the encoding of coarse-grained features in single nodes. As Smolensky (1988) has pointed out, this usually results in simple semantics and more complex operations in their models, as opposed to the simple processes and (normally) complex semantics of PDP networks. Despite some of the interesting features of localist networks, our emphasis in Chapter 4 is on PDP models. Thus, our use of "connectionism" is going to apply only to one brand of it. Ironically, the term "connectionism" was originally used and adopted by the Rochester group (Feldman and Ballard 1982).

3. Notice that we do not have any hidden units in this network. The reason is that, ambiguous cases notwithstanding, the space of all "Gs" and all "Qs" can be

effectively divided into two regions by a straight line – it is "linearly separable." This property alleviates the need for hidden units

Appendix C

1. Needless to say, this does not imply that real language learners also learn the language by dissecting it into different tasks; rather, they learn all aspects of language in unison. In fact, as some authors have argued (e.g., Clancey 1997), such partitioning (e.g., between memory and process) might be the source of a great many confusions in cognitive science.
2. This is not to say that children have an explicit knowledge of syntactic categories at an early age; in fact, they might not learn these as late as seventhgrade. The point is that, at least by the time they use multiword sentences, they demonstrate a tacit knowledge of these categories by using them correctly – for example, in question formation, in subject-verb agreement, and so on.

Bibliography

Agre, P. E. (1995). "The Soul Gained and Lost: Artificial Intelligence as A Philosophical Project." *Stanford Humanity Review* 4(2).

Agre, P. E. (1997a). *Computation and Human Experience*. Cambridge, UK, Cambridge University Press.

Agre, P. E. (1997b). Toward a Critical Technical Practice: Lessons Learned in Trying to Reform AI. *Bridging the Great Divide: Social Science, Technical Systems, and Cooperative Work*. G. Bowker, L. S. Star, B. Turner and L. Gasser. New York, NY, Erlbaum.

Agre, P. E. (2002). The Practical Logic of Computer Work. *Computationalism: New Directions*. M. Scheutz. Cambridge, UK, Cambridge University Press.

Agre, P. E. and D. Chapman (1987). *Pengi: An implementation of a theory of activity*. Sixth National Conference on Artificial Intelligence, San Mateo, CA., Morgan Kaufmann.

Agre, P. E. and I. D. Horswill (1992). *Cultural Support for Improvisation*. Tenth National Conference on Artificial Intelligence, Los Altos, CA., Morgan Kaufmann.

Agre, P. E. and D. Schuler (1997). *Reinventing Technology, Rediscovering Community: Critical Explorations of Computing as a Social Practice*. New York, NY, Ablex.

Anderson, J. A. (1995). *An Introduction to Neural Networks*. Cambridge, MA., A Bradford Book/ MIT Press.

Anderson, J. R. (1993). *Rules of the Mind*. Hillsdale: NJ, Erlbaum.

Athanasiou, T. (1985). Artificial Intelligence: cleverly disguised politics. *Compulsive Technology*. T. Solomonides and L. Levidow. London, UK, Free Association Books: 13–35.

Axelrod, R. and L. Tesfatsion (2007). A Guide for Newcomers to Agent-Based Modeling in the Social Sciences. *Handbook of Computational Economics, Vol. 2: Agent-Based Computational Economics*. K. L. Judd and L. Tesfatsion. Amsterdam, North-Holland, Available at http://www.econ.iastate.edu/tesfatsi/abmread.htm.

Bajscy, R. and E. W. Large (1999). "When and Where Will AI Meet Robotics." *AI Magazine* 20(3): 57–65.

Ballard, D. H. (1997). *An Introduction to Natural Computation*. Cambridge, MA., MIT Press.

Barad, K. (2003). "Posthumanist Performativity: Toward an Understanding of How Matter Comes to Matter." *Journal of Women in Culture and Society* 28(3): 801–831.

Baron-Cohen, S. (1995). *Mindblindness*. Cambridge, MA., MIT Press.

Bartlett, F. C. (1932). *Remembering: A Study in Experimental and Social Psychology*. New York, Macmillan.

Barwise, J. and J. Etchemendy (1994). *Hyperproof*. New York, Cambridge University Press.

Bechtel, W. (1998). "Representations and Cognitive Explanations: Assessing the Dynamicist's Challenge in Cognitive Science." *Cognitive Science* **22**(3): 295–318.

Bechtel, W. and R. C. Richardson (1992). *Discovering Complexity: Decomposition and localization as strategies in scientific research*. Princeton, NJ., Princeton University Press.

Becker, H. (1982). *The Art Worlds*. Berkeley: CA, University of California Press.

Becker, H. S. (forthcoming). What About Mozart? What About Murder? Accessed January 21, 2007 from: *http://home.earthlink.net/~hsbecker/mozart.htm*.

Biagioli, M., Ed. (1999). *Science Studies Reader*. New York and London, Routledge.

Bijker, W. E., T. E. Hughes, et al., Eds. (1997). *The Social Construction of Technological Systems: new Directions in the Sociology and History of Technology*. Cambridge, MA, The MIT Press.

Bloomfield, B. P. (1987). The Culture of Artificial Intelligence. *The Question of Artificial Intelligence*. B. Bloomfield. London, UK, Croom Helm: 59–105.

Bobrow, D. G. (1964). Natural Language Input for a Computer Problem-Solving System. Report TR-1, Project MAC, MIT, Cambridge, MA.

Boden, M. A. (1970). "Intentionality and Physical Systems." *Philosophy of Science* **37**: 200–214.

Boden, M. A., Ed. (1990). *The Creative Mind: Myths and Mechanisms*. New York, Basic Books.

Boden, M. A. (1994). Creativity and Computers. *Artificial Intelligence and Creativity: An Interdisciplinary Approach*. T. H. Dartnall. Dordrecht, Kluwer Academic Publishers.

Bolter, D. (1984). *Turing's Man: Western Culture in the Computer Age*. Chapel Hill, NC, University of North Carolina Press.

Born, R., Ed. (1987). *Artificial Intelligence: The Case Against*. London, Croom Helm.

Braitenberg, V. (1984). *Vehicles: Experiments in Synthetic Psychology*. Cambridge, MA., MIT Press.

Breazeal, C. and B. Scassellati (2000). Challenges in Building Robots that Imitate People. *Imitation in Animals and Artifacts*. K. Dautenhahn and C. Nehaniv. Cambridge, MA, MIT Press.

Brick, T. and M. Scheutz (2007). *Incremental Natural Language Processing for HRI*. HRI'07, Arlington, VA.

Brooks, R., C. Breazeal, et al. (1998). The Cog Project: Building a Humanoid Robot. *Computation for Metaphors, Analogy and Agents*. C. Nehaniv, Springer-Verlag. LNCS**1562**.

Brooks, R. A. (1986). "A Robust Layered Control System for a Mobile Robot." *IEEE Transactions on Robotics and Automation* **2**(1): 14–23.

Brooks, R. A. (1991/1997). Intelligence without representation. *Mind Design II*. J. Haugeland. Cambridge, MA, The MIT Press. 395–420.

Brooks, R. A. (1999). *Cambrian Intelligence: The Early History of the New AI*. Cambridge, MA., A Bradford Book/MIT Press.

Brooks, R. A. (2002a). *Flesh and Machines: How Robots Will Change Us*. New York, Pantheon Books.

Brooks, R. A. (2002b). "Lord of the Robots." *Technology Review* **105**(3): 78–83.

Brooks, R. A. and L. A. Stein (1994). "Building Brains for Bodies." *Autonomous Robots* **1**(1): 7–25.

Bruce, B. (1999) Educational Reform: How Does Technology Affect Educational Change? *Journal of Adolescent and Adult Education.* Accessed Nov. 14, 2006 from: http://www.readingonline.org/electronic/jaal/9-99_Column.html.

Brucell, V., M. Burton, et al. (1993). "Sex Discrimination: how do we tell the difference between male and female faces?" *Perception* **22**: 131–152.

Buchanan, B. G., G. L. Sutherland, et al. (1969). Heurstic DENDRAL: A program for generating explanatory hypothesis in organic chemistry. *Machine Intelligence.* B. Meltzer, Michie, D., and Swann, M. Edinburgh, Scotland, Edinburgh University Press. **4**: 209–254.

Castañeda, C. and L. Suchman (2005). Robots Visions. Accessed April 25, 2007 from: http://www.comp.lancs.ac.uk/sociology/papers/***.pdf

Castells, M. (1996). *The Rise of The Network Society.* Malden: MA, Blackwell Publishers.

Castells, M. (2001). *The Internet Galaxy: Reflections on the Internet, Business, and Society.* Oxford: UK, Oxford University Press.

Chalmers, D. J., R. M. French, et al. (1992). "High-level Perception, Representation, and Analogy." *Journal of Experimental and Theoretical Artificial Intelligence* **4**(3): 185–211.

Chemero, A. (2000). "Anti-Representationalism and the Dynamical Stance." *Philosophy of Science* **67**: 626–647.

Chomsky, N. (1957). *Syntactic Structures.* The Hague, Mouton.

Chrisley (2002). Artificial Intelligence. *The Oxford Companion to the Mind.* R. Gregory. Oxford, Oxford University Press.

Christiansen, M. H. and N. Chater (1999). "Connectionist Natural Language Processing: The State of the Art." *Cognitive Science* **23**(4): 417–437.

Churchland (1997). On the Nature of Theories: A Neurocomputational Perspective. *Mind Design II.* J. Haugeland. Cambridge, MA, MIT Press: 251–292.

Churchland, P. M. (1989). On the Nature of Theories: A Neurocomputatoinal Perspective. *Mind Design II.* J. Haugeland. Cambridge, MIT Press.

Clancey, W. J. (1997). *Situated Cognition: On Human Knowledge and Computer Representations.* Cambridge, UK, Univeristy of Cambridge.

Clapin, H., Ed. (2002). *Philosophy of Mental Representation.* Oxford, Oxford University Press.

Clark, A. (1997). *Being There: Putting Brain, Body, and World Together Again.* Cambridge, MA, A Bradford Book/MIT Press.

Clark, A. (2001). *Mindware.* Cambridge, MA, MIT Press.

Clark, A. (2003). *Natural-Born Cyborgs: Minds, Technologies, and the Future of Human Intelligence.* Oxford, Oxford University Press.

Clark, E. V. (1993). *The Lexicon in Acquisition.* Cambridge, UK, Cambridge University Press.

Clynes, M. E. and N. S. Kline (1960). "Cyborgs and Space." *Astronautics* (Sept. 1960): 33–42.

Cohen, D. I. A. (1997). *Theory of Computer Theory.* New York, John Wiley and Sons.

Cohen, H. (1995). "The Further Exploits of AARON, Painter." *Stanford Humanities Review* **4**(2).

Cohen, P. R. and A. E. Howe (1988). "How Evaluation Guides AI Research." *AI Magazine* **Winter 1988**: 35–43.

Collins, G. (1989). Coach. *Inside Case-based Reasoning*. C. Riesbeck and R. C. Schank. Hillsdale, NJ, Lawrence Erlbaum.

Collins, H. (1990). *Artificial Experts: Social Knowledge and Intelligent Machines*. Cambridge, MA, MIT Press.

Collins, H. (1992). "Hubert L. Dreyfus, Forms of Life, and a Simple Test for Machine Intelligence." *Social Studies of Science* 22: 726–39.

Collins, H. and M. Kusch (1998). *The Shape of Actions: What Humans and Machines Can Do*. Cambridge, MA., MIT press.

Collins, H. and T. Pinch (1998). *The Golem: What everyone should know about science*. Cambirdge, Cambridge University Press.

Cope, D. (1991). *Computers and Musical Style*. Madison: WI, A-R Editions, Inc.

Cope, D. (2001). *Virtual Music: Computer Synthesis of Musical Style*. Cambridge, MA., MIT Press.

Copeland, J. B. (1997). "CYC: A case Study in Ontological Engineering." Retrieved April 2003, from http://phil.indiana.edu/ejap/1997.Spring/copeland976.2.html.

Cottrell, G. W., C. Padgett, et al. (2000). Is all face processing holistic? The View from UCSD, ScientificCommons.

Crevier, D. (1993). *The Tumultuous History of The Search for Artificial Intelligence*. New York, NY, Basic Books.

Cussins, A. (1998). Nonconceptual Content of Experience and Conceptual Content of Thought. Unpublished manuscript.

Cussins, A. (in press). "Content, Embodiment and Objectivity – The Theory of Cognitive Trails." Unpublished manuscript.

Dartnall, T., Ed. (2002). *Creativity, Cognition, and Knowledge*. Perspectives on Cognitive Science. Westport: CN, Praeger.

Davidson, A. (1990). Closing Up the Corpses. *Meaning and Method*. G. Boulos. Cambridge: MA, Harvard University Press.

Davis, M. (1988). Mathematical Logic and the Origin of Modern Computers. *The Universal Turing Machine: A Half-Century Survey*. R. Herken. Oxford, UK, Oxford University Press.

Day, R. (2005). "Clearing up "implicit knowledge": Implications for Knowledge Management, information science, psychology, and social epistemology." *Journal of the American Society for Information Science and Technology* 56(6): 630–635.

Dell, G. S. (1986). "A spreading-activation theory of retrieval in sentence production." *Psychological Review* 93: 283–321.

Dell, G. S., M. F. Schwartz, N. Martin, E. M. Saffran, D. A. Gagnon (1997). "Lexical access in aphasic and nonaphasic speakers." *Psychological Review* 104(801–939).

Dell, G. S., F. Chang, Z. M. Griffin (1999). "Connectionist models of language production: Lexical access and grammatical encoding." *Cognitive Science* 23: 517–542.

Dell, G. S., C. Juliano, et al. (1993). "Structure and content in language production: A theory of frame constraints in phonological speech errors." *Cognitive Science* 17: 149–195.

DeLong, H. (1970). *A Profile of Mathematical Logic*. Reading, MA, Addison-Wesley.

Dennett, D. (1998). "Revolution, no! Reform." *Behavioral and Brain Sciences* 21(5): 636–637.

Dennett, D. C. (1990). Cognitive Wheels: The Frame Problem of AI. *The Philosophy of Artificial Intelligence*. M. A. Boden. Oxford, UK, Oxford University Press: 147–170.

Dennett, D. C. (1991). "Real Patterns." *Journal of Philosophy* **88**(1): 27–51.

Dennett, D. C. (1995). *Darwin's Dangerous Idea*. New York, Simon and Schuster.

Dennett, D. C. (1997). True Believers: Intentional Strategy and Why It Works. *Mind Design II*. J. Haugeland. Cambridge, MA., MIT Press: 57–79.

Dennett, D. C. (1977). *Brainstorms*. Cambridge, MA, MIT Press.

Descartes, R. (1979). *Meditations on First Philosophy*. Indianapolis, IN, Hackett Publishing Company.

Dewey, J. (1920/1948). *Reconstruction of Philosophy*. Boston, MA., Beacon Press.

Dewey, J. (1938). *Logic: The Theory of Inquiry*. Carbondale, IL., Southern Illinois University Press.

Dewey, J. (1950). *Common Sense and Science*. Carbondale, IL, Southern Illinois University Press.

Dietrich, E. and A. B. Markman (1998). "All information processing entails computation." *Behavioral and Brain Sciences* **21**(5): 637–38.

Dretske, F. I. (1994). If You Can't Make One, You Don't Know How It Works. *Midwest Studies in Philosophy*. P. French and T. Uehling. Notre Dame, IN., University of Notre Dame Press: 468–482.

Dreyfus, H. L. (1972). *What Computers Can't Do?* New York, Harper Collins.

Dreyfus, H. L. (1991). "Response to Collins, Artificial Experts." *Social Studies of Science* **22**: 717–726.

Dreyfus, H. L. (1992). *What Computers Still Can't Do? A critique of Artificial Reason*. Cambridge, MA, The MIT Press.

Dyer, F. C. and T. D. Seeley (1989). "On the evolution of the dance language." *The American Naturalist* **133**(4): 580–590.

Edelman, G. M. (1987). *Neural Darwinism: The Theory of Neural Group Selection*. New York, Basic Books.

Edwards, P. N. (1996). *The Closed World: Computers and The Politics of Discourse in Cold War America*. Cambridge, MA, The MIT Press.

Ekbia, H. R. (2001). *Once Again, Artificial Intelligence at A Crossroads*. Annual Meeting of the Society for Social Studies of Science, Boston, MA.

Ekbia, H. R. (2002a). *The Two Senses of "Common Sense."* 13th Midwest Artificial Intelligence and Cognitive Science Conference, Chicago, IL.

Ekbia, H. R. (2002b). *AI's Disparity Syndrome*. Annual Meeting of the Society for Social Studies of Science, Milwaukee, WI.

Ekbia, H. R. (2006). Taking Decisions into the Wild: An AI Perspective on the Design of iDSS. *Intelligent Decision-Making Support Systems (I-DMSS): Foundations, Applications and Challenges* J. Gupta, G. Forgionne and M. More. Berlin, Springer-Verlag.

Ekbia, H. R. (forthcoming). "Informational Artifacts as Quasi-Objects."

Ekbia, H. R. and L. Gasser (forthcoming). "Common Ground: For a Sociology of Code."

Ekbia, H. R., J. Goldberg, D. Landy (2003). Starting Large or Small? An Unresolved Dilemma for Connectionist Models of Language Learning. *Bootstrapping in Language Acquisition: Psychological, Linguistic and Computational Aspects*. Bloomington, IN.

Ekbia, H. R. and N. Hara (2005). Incentive Structures in Knowledge Management. *Encyclopedia of Knowledge Management.* D. Schwartz. Hershey, PA, Idea Group.

Ekbia, H. R. and R. Kling (2003). *Power in Knowledge Management in Late Modern Times.* Academy of Management, Seattle, WA.

Ekbia, H. R. and A. Maguitman (2001). *Context and Relevance: A Pragmatic Approach.* 3rd International Conference on Modeling and Using Context, Dundee, UK, Springer Verlag.

Elman, J. L. (1990). "Finding structure in time." *Cognitive Science* 14: 179–211.

Elman, J. L. (1993). "Learning and development in neural networks: The importance of starting small." *Cognition* 48: 71–99.

Enfield, N. J. and S. C. Levinson (2006). *Roots of Human Sociality: Culture, Cognition and Interaction.* Oxford, Berg.

Epstein, J. M. (2005). Remarks on the Foundations of Agent-Based Generative Social Science. *The Brookings Institution: CSED Working Paper.* Washington DC.

Falkenheiner, B., K. D. Forbus, et al. (1990). "The structure-mapping engine." *Artificial Intelligence* 41(1): 1–63.

Farah, M. J., K. D. Wiilson, et al. (1998). "What Is "Special" About Face Perception?" *Psychological Review* 105(3): 42–498.

Fauconnier, G. (1994). *Mental Spaces: Aspects of Meaning Construction in Natural Language.* Cambridge, UK, Cambridge University Press.

Feigenbaum, E. A. and A. Barr, Eds. (1982). *The Handbook of Artificial Intelligence.* Reading, MA., Addison-Wesley.

Fikes, R. E., P. E. Hart, et al. (1972). "Learning and Executing Generalized Robot Plans." *Artificial Intelligence* 3(4): 251–288.

Fodor, J. and Z. Pylyshyn (1997). Connectionism and Cognitive Architecture: A Critical Analysis. *Mind Design II: Philosophy, Psychology, Artificial Intelligence.* J. Haugeland. Cambridge, MA, The MIT Press: 309–350.

Fodor, J. A. (1980). Methodological Solipsism Considered as a Research Strategy in Cognitive Psychology. *Representations: Philosophical Essays on the Foundations of Cognitive Science,* The Harvester Press.

Forbus, K. D., D. Gentner, et al. (1998). "Analogy just looks like high level perception: why a domain-general approach to analogical mapping is right "*J. EXPT. THFOR. ARTIF. INTELL* 10: 231–257.

Forrest, S., Ed. (1991). *Emergent Computation.* Cambridge: MA, MIT Press.

Forsythe, D. E. (2001). *Studying Those Who Study Us: An Anthropologist in the World of Artificial Intelligence.* Stanford, CA., Stanford University Press.

Foucault, M. (1977). *Knowledge and Power: Selected Interviews and Other Writings.* New York, Pantheon Books.

Foucault, M. (1994). *The Order of Things: An Archaelogy of the Human Sciences.* New York: NY, Random House/Vintage Books.

Foundalis, H. (2006). Phaeaco: A Cognitive Architecture Inspired by Bongard's Problems. *Computer Science Dept.* Bloomington, Indiana University.

Friedman, M. (1999). *Reconsidering Logical Positivism.* Cambridge, UK, Cambridge University Press.

Funt, B. V. (1980). "Problem-Solving with Diagrammatic Representations." *Artificial Intelligence* 13.

Gadamer, H.-G. (1976). *Philosophical Hermeneutics*. Berkeley, CA, University of California Press.

Gallistel, C. R. (1998). Symbolic Processes in the Brain: The Case of Insect Navigation. *An Invitation to Cognitive Science: Methods, Models, and Conceptual Issues*. D. Scarborough and S. Sternberg. Cambridge, Mass., MIT Press/A Bradford Book.

Gasser, L. (1991). "Social conceptions of knowledge and action." *Artificial Intelligence* **47**(1): 107–138.

Gasser, M. and E. Colunga (2000). *Babies, Variables, and Relational Correlations*. 22nd Annual Conference of the Cognitive Science Society, Philadelphia, Lawrence Erlbaum.

Gazzaniga, M. S., R. Ivry, et al. (1998). *Fundamentals of Cognitive Neuroscience*. New York, W.W. Norton.

Gee, J. P. (1999). *An Introduction to Discourse Analysis*. UK, Routledge.

Gell, A. (1998). *Art and Agency: An Anthropological Theory*. Oxford, Oxford University Press.

Genter, D. (1983). "Structure-Mapping: A Theoretical Framework for Analogy." *Cognitive Science* 7(2): 155–170.

Gerschenfeld, N. (1999). *When Things Start to Think*. New York, Henry Holt.

Gibson, J. J. (1978). "The Ecological Approach to the Visual Perception of Pictures." *Leonardo* 11(3): 227–235.

Giere, R. N. (1999). *Science without Laws*. Chicago, The University of Chicago Press.

Gieryn, T. F. (1999). *Cultural Boundaries of Science: Credibility on the line*. Chicago: IL, Univeristy of Chicago Press.

Gilbert, N. (2004). Agent-Based Social Simulation. *Center for Research on Social Simulation*. Guilford: UK.

Gilbert, N. and K. G. Troitzsch (2005). *Simulation for the Social Scientist*. Berkshire: UK, Open University Press.

Goodman, N. (1976). *Languages of Art*. Indianapolis, IN, Hacket Publishing Company.

Govindarajan, K. K., S. Grossberg, et al. (1994). A neural network model of auditory scene analysis and source segregation. *Technical report*. Boston, MA.

Graubard, S. R. (1988). *The Artificial Intelligence Debate: False Starts, Real Foundations*. Cambridge, MA, MIT Press.

Greenberg, K., Ed. (2000). *The Robot in the Garden*. Cambridge: MA, MIT Press.

Grossberg, S. (1976). "Adaptive pattern classification and universal recoding: Part I. Parallel development and coding of neural feature detectors." *Biological Cybernetic* **21**: 121–134.

Grossberg, S. (1987). "Competetive Learning: From Interactive Activation to Adaptive Resonance." *Cognitive Science* 11(1): 23–63.

Grossberg, S. (1995). "The Attentive Brain." *American Scientist* **83**: 438–449.

Grossberg, S. and C. W. Myers (1999). The Resonant Dynamics of Conscious Speech. *Technical Report*. Boston, MA.

Grover, L. (1996). *A Fast Quantum Mechanical Algorithm for Data base Search*. 28th Annual ACM Symposium on the Theory of Computing.

Hacking, I. (1979). "What is logic?" *The Journal of Philosophy* **LXXVI**(6): 285–319.

Hacking, I. (1983). *Representing and Intervening: Introductory Topics in the Philosophy of Natural Science*. Cambridge, Cambridge University Press.

Hacking, I. (1999). Making Up People. *Science Studies Reader.* M. Biagioli. New York and London, Routledge: 161–171.

Hammond, K. J. (1989). *Case-Based Planning: Viewing Planning as a Memory Task.* San Diego, CA., Academic Press.

Hammond, K. J., T. M. Converse, et al. (1995). "The Stabilization of Environments." *Artificial Intelligence* **72**(1–2): 305–327.

Haraway, D. (1991). *Simians, Cyborgs, and Women: The Reinvention of Nature.* New York, Routledge.

Haraway, D. (1997). *Modest_Witness@Second_Millenium.FemaleMan_Meets_ OncoMouse*™. New York, Routledge.

Haraway, D. (2003). *The Companion Species Manifesto: Dogs, People and Significant Others.* Chicago, Prickly Paradigm Press.

Haraway, D. J. (1989). *Primate Visions: Gender, Race, and Nature in the World of Modern Science.* New York and London, Routledge.

Harnad, S. (1990). "The symbol grounding problem." *Physica D* **42**: 335–346.

Haugeland, J. (1978/98). The Plausibility of Cognitivism. *Having Thought.* J. Haugeland. Cambridge, MA., Harvard University Press.

Haugeland, J., Ed. (1981). *Mind Design I.* Cambridge, MA, A Bradford Book/MIT Press.

Haugeland, J. (1985). *Artificial Intelligence: The Very Idea.* Cambridge, MA, Bradford/MIT Press.

Haugeland, J., Ed. (1997). *Mind Design II: Philosophy, Psychology, Artificial Intelligence.* Cambridge, Mass., A Bradford Book/MIT Press.

Haugeland, J. (1998). *Having Thought: Essays in the Metaphysics of Mind.* Cambridge, Mass., Harvard University Press.

Hayes, P. J. (1973). *Computation and Deduction.* 2nd Mathematical Fooundations of Computer Science Symposium, Czechoslovakian Academy of Sciences.

Hayes, P. J. (1990). The Naive Physics Manifesto. *The Philosophy of Artificial Intelligence.* M. A. Boden. Oxford, UK, Oxford University Press: 171–205.

Hayles, N. K. (1999). *How we became posthuman: Virtual bodies in cybernetics, literature, and informatics.* Chicago, Chicago University Press.

Hayles, N. K. (2005). "Computing the Human." *Theory, Culture & Society* **22**(1): 131–151.

Hebb, D. (1949). *Organization of Behavior.* New York, Wiley.

Hempel, C. G. and P. Oppenheim (1948). "Studies in the Logic of Explanation." *Philosophy of Science* **15**: 135–175.

Hempel, C. G. and P. Oppenheim (1949). Studies in the Logic of Explanation. *Aspects of Scientific Explanation.* C. G. Hempel. New York, Macmillan.

Hennessy, J. L. and D. A. Patterson (1996). *Computer Architecture: A Quantitative Approach.* San Francisco, CA., Morgan Kaufmann Publishers.

Hertz, J., A. Krogh, et al. (1991). *Introduction to the Theory of Neural Computation.* Redwood City, CA, Addison-Wesley.

Hinton, G. and T. Sejnowski (1986). Learning and relearning in Boltzmann machines. *Parallel Distributed Processing.* D. Rumelhart and J. McClelland. Cambridge, MA, MIT Press. **1**: 282–317.

Hirsh-Pasek, K. and R. M. Golinkoff (1996). *The Origins of Grammar: Evidence from Early Language Comprehension.* Cambridge, MA., MIT Press.

Hofstadter, D. R. (1979). *Gödel, Escher, Bach: an Eternal Golden Braid.* New York, N.Y., Basic Books.

Hofstadter, D. R. (1985). *Metamagical Themas: Questing for the Essence of Mind and Pattern*. New York, N.Y., Basic Books.

Hofstadter, D. R. (1985b). Waking Up from the Boolean Dream, Or, Subcognition as Computation. *Metamagical Themas: Questing for the Essence of Mind and Pattern*. New York, Basic Books.

Hofstadter, D. R. (1995). *Fluid Concepts and Creative Analogies*. New York, N.Y., Basic Books.

Hofstadter, D. R. (1997). *Le Ton beau de Marot: In Praise of the Music of Language*. New York, Basic Books.

Hofstadter, D. R. (1999). Moore's Law, Artificial Evolution, and the Fate of Humanity. *Festschrift in Honor of John Holland's 70th Birthday*. M. Mitchell.

Hofstadter, D. R. (2001). Analogy as the Core of Cognition. *Integration of Theory and Data from the Cognitive, Computational, and Neural Sciences*. K. J. Holyoak, Gentner, D., and Kokinov, B. Cambridge, MA., MIT Press.

Hofstadter, D. R. (2002). Staring Emmy Straight in the Eye – and Doing My Best Not to Flinch. *Creativity, Cognition, and Knowledge*. T. Dartnall. Westport: CN, Praeger: 67–100.

Hofstadter, D. R. and D. C. Dennett (1982). *The Mind's I: Fantasies and Reflections on Self and Soul*. New York, Basic Books.

Hofstadter, D. R. and D. Moser (1989). "To Err is Human: To Study Error-Making in Cognitive Science." *Michigan Quarterly Review* 28(2): 185–215.

Holland, J. (1975). *Adaptation in Natural and Artificial Systems*. Ann Arbor, Michigan, University of Michigan Press.

Holland, J. (1995). *Hidden Order: How Adaptation Builds Complexity*. Reading, MA., Addison-Wesley.

Holland, J. H. (1986). Escaping Brittleness: The Possibilities of General-purpose Learning Algorithms Applied to Parallel Rule-based Systems. *Machine Learning: An Artificial Intelligence Approach*. R. S. Michalski, J. G. Carbonell and T. M. Mitchell. Los Altos, CA., Morgan Kaufmann. **II:** 593–623.

Hölldobler, B. and E. O. Wilson (1990). *Ants*. Cambridge, MA, Belknap Press of Harvard University Press.

Holyoak, K. J. and P. Thagard (1995). *Mental Leaps: Analogy in Creative Thought*. Cambridge: MA, MIT Press/Bradford Books.

Hopfield, J. (1982). *Neural Networks and Physical Systems with Emergent Collective Computational Abilities*. National Academy of Sciences, USA79.

Hume, D. (1739). *A Treatise of Human Nature*. London, Penguin Books.

Hummel, J. E. and K. J. Holyoak (1997). "Distributed Representations of Structure: A Theory of analogical access and mapping." *Psychological Review* **104**: 427–466.

Hurlbert, A. and T. Poggio (1988). "Making machines (and artificial intelligence)." *Daedalus* 117(1): 213–239.

Huskey, V. R. and H. D. Huskey (1980). "Lady Lovelace and Charles Babbage." *Annals of History of Computing* 2: 299–329.

Hutchins, E. (1995). *Cognition in The Wild*. Cambridge, Mass., MIT Press.

James, W. (1907/1998). *Pragmatism and The Meaning of Truth*. Cambridge, MA., Harvard University Press.

Johnson-Laird, P. (1988). *The Computer and the Mind: An Introduction to Cognitive Science*. Cambridge, MA, Harvard University Press.

Jordan, M. I. (1986). *Attractor Dynamics and Parallelism in a Connectionist Sequential Machine*. 8th Annual Conference of Cognitive Science Society, Hillsdale, NJ, Lawrence Erlbaum.

Joy, B. (2000). "Why the future doesn't need us?" *Wired* **8**(4).

Joyce, J. (1996). When/why/of what is less more? *Center for Cogntive Science*. Edinburgh, University of Edinburgh. **M.Sc. Dissertation**.

Kail, R. (1984). *The development of memory*. New York, W. H. Freeman.

Kaipainen, M. and R. F. Port (unpublished). Speech Cycling.

Kanerva, P. (1988). *Sparse Distributed Memory*. Cambridge, MA., MIT Press.

Karmiloff-Smith, A. (1992). *Beyond modularity: a developmental perspcetive on cognitive science*. Cambridge: MA, MIT Press/Bradford Books.

Keller, E. F. (2007). Booting up baby. *Genesis Redux Essays in the History and Philosophy of Artificial Life*. J. Riskin. Chicago, University of Chicago Press: 334–345.

Kelso, J. A. S. (1995). *Dynamic Patterns: The Self-Organization of Brain and Behavior*. Cambridge, MA., MIT Press.

Kennedy, J. and R. C. Eberhart (2001). *Swarm Intelligence*. New York, Morgan Kaufmann.

Kintsch, W. (2000). "Metaphor comprehension: A computational theory." *Psyhonomic Bulletin and Review* **7**: 257–266.

Kirsh, D. (1991). "Today the earwig, tomorrow man?" *Artificial Intelligence* **47**: 161–184.

Kling, R. (1980). "Social analyses of computing: Theoretical perspectives in recent empirical research." *Computing Surveys* **12**(1): 61–110.

Kling, R. (1997). Hopes and Horrors: Technological Utopianism and Anti-Utopianism in Narratives of Computerization. *Computerization and Controversy: Value Conflicts and Social Choices*. R. Kling. San Diego, CA, Academic Press: 40–58.

Kling, R. (1999). What is Social Informatics and Why Does it Matter? *D-Lib Magazine*. **5**.

Kling, R. and S. Iacono (1995). Computerization movements and the mobilization of support for computerization. *Ecologies of knowledge*. L. S. Star. New York, SUNY: 119–153.

Knuth, D. (1983). *The Art of Computer Programming*. Reading, MA., Addison-Wesley.

Koestler, A. (1964). *The Act of Creation*. New York: NY, Macmillan.

Kohler, R. (1999). Moral Economy, Material Culture, and Community in Drosophilia Genetics. *The Science Studies Reader*. M. Biagioli. New York and London, Routledge: 243–257.

Kolodner, J. L. (1996). Making the Implicit Explicit: Clarifying the Principles of Case-Based Reasoning. *Case-Based Reasoning: Experiences, Lessons, and Future Directions*. D. B. Leake. Menlo Park, CA., AAAI Press/MIT Press: 349–370.

Kolodner, J. L. and D. Leake (1996). A Tutorial Introduction to Case-Based Reasoning *Case-Based Reasoning: Experiences, Lessons and Future Directions*. D. Leake. Cambridge, MA, MIT Press: 31–65.

Kowalski, R. A. (1977). Algorithm=Logic+Control. *Memorandum, Imperial College*. London, UK.

Kuhn, T. (1962). *The Structure of Scientific Revolutions*. Chicago, University of Chicago Press.

Kurzweil, R. (1999). *The Age of Spiritual Machines: When Computers Exceed Human Intelligence*. New York, N.Y., Viking.

Laham, D. (1997). *Latent Semantic Analysis approaches to categorization.* 19th annual meeting of the Cognitive Science Society, Erlbaum.

Lakoff, G. (1987). *Women, Fire and Dangerous Things.* Chicago, University of Chicago Press.

Landauer, T. K., Foltz, P. W., & Laham, D. (1998). "Introduction to Latent Semantic Analysis." *Discourse Processes* **25**: 259–284.

Landauer, T. K., Laham, D., & Foltz, P. W. (1998). "Learning human-like knowledge by Singular Value Decomposition: A progress report. In M. I. Jordan, M. J. Kearns & S. A. Solla (Eds.), Advances."

Landauer, T. K. and S. T. Dumais (1997). "A solution to Plato's problem: the latent semantic analysis theory of acquisition, induction, and representation of knowledge." *Psychological Review* **104**: 211–240.

Landauer, T. K., D. Laham, et al. (1997). *How well can passage meaning be derived without using word order? A comparison of Latent Semantic Analysis and humans.* 19th annual meeting of the Cognitive Science Society, Erlbaum.

Landes, D. (2000). *Revolution in Time: Clocks and the Making of the Modern World.* London, Viking Press.

Langton, C. G. (1989). *Artificial Life.* Redwood City, CA., Addison-Wesley.

Lanier, J. (2000) One Half of A Manifesto: Why stupid software will save the future from neo-Darwinian machines. *Wired*: 8(12).

Larkin, J. and H. A. Simon (1987). "Why a Diagram is (Sometimes) Worth Ten Thousand Words." *Cognitive Science* **11**(1): 65–100.

Latash, M. L. (1993). *Control of Human Movement.* Champaign, IL., Human Kinetics: 1–48.

Latour, B. (1987). *Science in Action.* Cambridge, MA., Harvard University Press.

Latour, B. (1993). *We Have Never Been Modern.* Cambridge: MA, Harvard University Press.

Latour, B. (1999). *Pandora's Hope: Essays on the Reality of Science Studies.* Cambridge, MA., Harvard University Press.

Latour, B. (2005). *Reassembling the Social: An Introduction to Actor-Network Theory.* Oxford, Oxford University Press.

Leake, D. B., Ed. (1996). *Case-Based Reasoning: Experiences, Lessons, and Future Directions.* Menlo Park, CA., AAAI Press/MIT Press.

Leclerc, J. and F. Gosselin (2004). *Processes of artistic creativity: The case of Isabelle Hayeur.* Twenty-Seventh Conference of the Cognitive Science Society, Mahwah: NJ, Erlbaum.

Leclerc, J. and F. Gosselin (2005). *ACE: A Model of the Cognitive Strategies of a Contemporary Artist.* Twenty-Seventh Conference of the Cognitive Science Society, Mahwah: NJ, Erlbaum.

Lenat, D. B. (1997a). From 2001 to 2001: Common Sense and the Mind of HAL. *Hal's Legacy: 2001's Computer As Dream & Reality.* D. G. Stork. Cambridge, Mass., MIT Press.

Lenat, D. B. (1997b). "The Dimensions of Context Space." Retrieved April, 2003, from www.cyc.com.

Lenat, D. B. (2002). Cyc Workshop. *Presentation.*

Lenat, D. B. and E. A. Feigenbaum (1991). "On the Thresholds of Knowledge." *Artificial Intelligence* **47**(1–3): 185–250.

Lenat, D. B. and R. V. Guha (1990). *Building Large Knowledge-Based Systems*. Reading, Mass., Addison Wesley.

Lenat, D. B., M. Prakash, et al. (1986). "Using common-sense knowledge to overcome brittleness and knowledge acquisition bottlenecks." *AI Magazine* 7: 65–85.

Levelt, W. J. M. (1989). *Speaking: From intention to articulation*. Cambridge, MA., MIT Press.

Lewis, D. (1971). "Analog and Digital." *Nous* 5(3): 321–327.

Lewontin, R. C. (1998). The Evolution of Cognition: Questions We Will Never Answer. *An Invitation to Cognitive Science: Methods, Models, and Conceptual Issues*. D. Scarborough and S. Sternberg. Cambridge, MA., A Bradford Book/MIT Press. 4: 107–132.

Lloyd, E. A. (1994). *The Structure and Confirmation of Evolutionary Theory*. Princeton, N.J., Princeton University Press.

Llyod, G. (1999). Science in Antiquity: The Greek and Chinese Cases and Their Relevance to the Problems of Culture and Cognition. *Science Studies Reader*. M. Biagioli. New York and London, Routledge: 302–316.

Loy, G. (1989). Composing with Computers: A Survey of Some Compositional Formalisms and Music Programming Languages. *Current Directions in Computer Music Research*. M. Mathews and J. R. Pierce. Cambridge: MA, MIT Press.

Mackay, W. A., D. J. Crammond, et al. (1986). "Measurements of human forearm viscoelasticity." *Journal of Biomechanics* 19: 231–238.

Manna, Z. and R. Waldinger (1985). *The Logical Basis for Computer Programming*. Reading, Mass., Addison-Wesley.

Maris, M. and R. T. Boekhorst (1996). *Exploiting physical constraints: Heap formation through behavioral error in a group of robots*. IEEE/RSJ International Conference on Intelligent Robots and Systems.

Marr, D. (1982). *Vision*. San Francisco, CA, Freeman.

Marshall, J. and D. R. Hofstadter (1997). "The Metacat Project: a self-watching model of analogy-making." *Cognitive Studies: The Bulletin of Japanese Cogn.Sci.Soc.* 4(4).

Marshall, J. B. (1999). Metacat: A Self-Watching Cognitive Architecture for Analogy-Making and High-Level Perception. *Computer Science Dept*. Bloomington, Indiana University.

Mataric, M. J. (1992). "Intergation of reprenstation into goal-driven behavior-based robots." *IEEE Transactions on Robotics and Automation* 8(3): 304–312.

Mazlish, B. (1993). *The Fourth Discontinuity: the co-evolution of humans and machines*. New Haven, Yale University Press.

McCarthy, J. (1980). "Circumscription – A Form of Non-Monotonic Reasoning." *Artificial Intelligence* 13: 27–39.

McCarthy, J. (1986). "Applications of Circumscription to Formalizing Commonsense Knowledge." *Artificial Intelligence* 28(1): 89–116.

McCarthy, J. and P. J. Hayes (1969). Some Philosophical Problems from the Standpoint of Artificial Intelligence. *Machine Intelligence*. B. M. D. Michie. Edinburgh, UK, Edinburgh University Press. 4.

McClelland, J. and D. Rumelhart (1986). *Parallel Distributed Processing*. Cambridge, MA, MIT Press.

McCorduck, P. (1979). *Machines who think*. San Francisco, CA, W. H. Freeman.

McCorduck, P. (1991). *Aaron's Code: meta-art, artificial intelligence and the work of Harold Cohen*. New York, Freeman.

McCulloch, W. S. and W. H. Pitts (1943). "A Logical Calculus of the Ideas Immanent in Nervous Activity." *Bulletin of Mathematical Biophysics* **5**: 115–133.

McDermott, D. (1976). "Artificial intelligence meets natural stupidity." *SIGART Newsletter* **57**: 4–9.

McDermott, D. (1982). "A Temporal Logic for Reasoning about Processes and Plans." *Cognitive Science* **6**: 101–155.

McDermott, D. (1987). "A Critique of Pure Reason." *Computational Intelligence* **3**(1): 151–160.

McDonough, R. (2002). Emergence and Creativity. *Creativity, Cognition, and Knowledge.* T. Dartnall. Westport: CN, Praeger: 282–301.

McGraw, G. and D. R. Hofstadter (2002). Letter Spirit: Perception and Creation of Diverse Alphabetic Styles. *Creativity, Cognition, and Knowledge.* T. Dartnall. Westport: CN, Praeger: 251–266.

McLeod, P., K. Plunkett, et al. (1998). *Introduction to Connectionist Modelling of Cognitive Processes.* New York, Oxford Univeristy Press.

McNeal, C. (1998). *The Medieval Art of Love.* New York, N.Y., Gaimann & King Ltd.

Mead, G. H. (1934). *Mind, Self, and Society from the Standpoint of a Social Behaviorist.* Chicago, Chicago Univeristy Press.

Meglicki, Z. (2000). "Introduction to Quantum Computing." Retrieved May 1, 2003, from http://www.ovpit.indiana.edu/B679.

Menzel, P. and F. D'Aluisio (2000). *Robo sapiens.* Cambridge: MA, MIT Press.

Minsky, M. (1975). A framework for representing knowledge. *The Psychology of Computer Vision.* P. H. Winston. New York, McGraw-Hill: 211–277.

Minsky, M. (1985). *The Society of Mind.* Cambridge, MA., MIT Press.

Minsky, M. (1995). "Future of AI Technology." *Toshiba Review* **47**(7).

Minsky, M. (2005). The Emotion Machine. Accessed November 28, 2006 from: web.media.mit.edu/~minsky/.

Mitchell, M. (1993). *Analogy-Making as Perception: A Computer Model.* Cambridge, MA, MIT Press.

Mitchell, M. (1996). *An Introduction to Genetic Algorithms.* Cambridge, MA., MIT Press.

Mitchell, M. (1998). "Theories of structure versus theories of change." *Behavioral and Brain Sciences* **21**(5): 645–46.

Moravec, H. (1998). *Mind Children: The Future of Robot and Human Intelligence.* Cambridge and New York, Cambirdge University Press.

Morris, W. C., G. W. Cottrell, et al. (1999). "A Connectionist Simulation of the Empirircal Acquisition of Grammatical Relations." *Cognitive Science.*

Mortensen, C. (1989). Mental Images: Should Cognitive Science Learn From Neurophysiology. *Computers, Brains, and Minds: Essays in Cognitive Scienc.* P. Slezak and W. R. Albury. Dodrecht, Kluwer Academic Publishers.

Nagel, T. (1974). "What is it like to be a bat?" *Philosophical Review* **4**: 435–450.

Neumaier, O. (1987). A Wittgensteinian View of Artificial Intelligence. *Aritificial Intelligence: The Case Against.* R. Born. London, Croom Helm: 132–174.

Newborn, M. (1997). *Kasparov versus Deep Blue: Computer Chess Comes of Age.* New York, N.Y., Springer.

Newell, A. (1990). *Unified Theories of Cognition.* Cambridge, MA., Harvard University Press.

Newell, A., J. C. Shaw, et al. (1960). *Report on a General Problem-Solving Program.* Proceedings of the International Conference on Information Processing, Paris.

Newell, A. and H. A. Simon (1961). GPS, a program that simulates human thought. *Lernende Automaten.* H. Billing. Munich, Oldenbourg: 109–124.

Newell, A. and H. A. Simon (1976). "Computer Science as Empirical Inquiry." *Communications of the ACM* **19**(3): 113–126.

Newport, E. L. (1990). "Maturational constraints on language learning." *Cognitive Science* **14**: 11–28.

Noble, D. F. (1977). *America by Design: Science, Technology, and the Rise of Corporate capitalism.* Oxford, UK, Oxford University Press.

Noble, D. F. (1984). *Forces of Production: A Social History of Industrial Automation.* New York, NY, Alfred A. Knopf.

Norton, A. (1995). Dynamics: An Introduction. *Mind as Motion.* R. F. Port and T. v. Gelder. Cambridge, MA., MIT Press: 45–68.

Oyama, S. (2000). *Evolution's Eye: A Systems View of the Biology-Culture Divide.* Durham, NC, Duke University Press.

Peirce, C. S. (1905/1940). Critical Common-Sensism. *The Philosophy of Peirce: Selected Writings.* J. Buchler. New York: Harcourt, Brace & Company: 290–301.

Petitot, J., F. J. Varela, et al. (1999). *Naturalizing Phenomenology: Issues in Contemporary Phenomenology and Cogntive Science.* Stanford, CA., Stanford University Press.

Petroski, H. (1989). *The Pencil: A History of Design and Circumstances.* New York, Knopf.

Pfeifer, R. and C. Scheier (1999). *Understanding Intelligence.* Cambridge, MA., MIT Press.

Piaget, J. (1952). *The Origins of Intelligence in Children.* New York, International University Press.

Pinker, S. (1984). *Language Learnability and Language Development.* Cambridge, MA., Harvard University Press.

Pinker, S. (1991). "Rules of Language." *Science* **253**: 530–535.

Pinker, S. and A. Prince (1988). "On Language and Connectionism: Analysis of a parallel distributed processing model of language acquisition." *Cognition* **28**: 73–193.

Plate, T. (1995). Holographic Reduced Representations. *Department of Computer Science.* Toronto, University of Toronto.

Plunkett, K. and P. Juola (1999). "A Connectionist Model of English Past Tense and Plural Morphology." *Cognitive Science* **23**(4): 463–490.

Plunkett, K. and V. Marchman (1991). "U-shaped learning and frequency effects in a multi-layered perceptron: Implications for child language acquisition." *Cognition* **38**: 43–102.

Poincaré, H. (1952). *Science and Hypothesis.* New York, Dover Publications.

Poincaré, H. (1982). *The Foundations of Science: Science and hypothesis, the value of science, science and method.* Washington, DC, University Press of America.

Polanyi, M. (1958). *Personal Knowledge: Towards a Postcritical Philosophy.* Chicago, Chicago University Press.

Popper, K. R. (1972). Two Faces of Common Sense. *Objective Knowledge: An Evolutionary Approach.* Oxford, UK, Clarendon Press.

Port, R. F. and T. van Gelder (1995). *Mind as Motion: Explorations in the Dynamics of Cognition.* Cambridge, MA., A Bradford Book/MIT Press.

Pratt, V. (1994). "Visit to Cyc." Retrieved Accessed July 24, 2002, from http://boole.stanford.edu/pratt.html.

Preskill, J. (1997). "Lecture Notes for Physics 229: Quantum Information and Computation." Retrieved Accessed May 4 2000, from www.theory.caltech.edu/people/preskill/ph229.

Prinz, J. J. and L. W. Barsalou (2002). Acquisition and Productivity in Perceptual Symbol Systems: An Account of Mundane Creativity. *Creativity, Cognition, and Knowledge.* T. Dartnall. Westport: CN, Praeger: 105–126.

Pulvermüller, F. (1999). "Words in the Brain's Language." *Behavioral and Brain Sciences* **22**: 253–279.

Putnam, H. (1975). *Philosophical Papers: Mind, Language and Reality.* Cambridge, UK, Cambridge University Press.

Putnam, H. (1990). *Realism with a Human Face.* Cambridge, MA., Harvard University Press.

Pylyshyn, Z. W. (1984). *Computation and Cognition: Toward a Foundation for Cognitive Science.* Cambridge, MA, Bradford/MIT Press.

Quartz, S. R. and T. J. Sejnowski (1997). "The Neural Basis of Cognitive Development: A Constructivist Manifesto." *Brain and Behavioral Sciences* **20**: 537–596.

Quine, W. V. and J. S. Ullian (1978). *The Web of Belief.* New York, McGraw-Hill.

Reeke, G. N. and G. M. Edelman (1988). "Real brains and artificial intelligence." *Daedalus* **117**(1): 143–173.

Regier, T. and L. Carlson (2001). "Grounding spatial language in perception: An empirical and computational investigation." *Journal of Experimental Psychology: General* **130**: 273–298.

Rehling, J. (2002). Results in Letter Spirit Project. *Creativity, Cognition, and Knowledge.* T. Dartnall. Westport: CN, Praeger: 272–278.

Reid, T. (1785/1969). *Essays on the Intellectual Powers of Man.* Cambridge, MA., The MIT Press.

Restivo, S. (2001). *Bringing Up and Booting Up: Social Theory and the Emergence of Socially Intelligent Robots.* IEEE Conference on Robotics and Cybernetics, IEEE.

Rhode, D. L. T. and D. C. Plaut (1999). "Language acquisition in the absence of explicit negative evidence: how important is starting small?" *Cognition* **72**: 67–109.

Riesbeck, C. and R. C. Schank (1989). *Inside Case-based Reasoning.* Hillsdale, N.J., Lawrence Erlbaum.

Riesbeck, C. K. (1996). What Next? The Future of Case-Based Reasoning in Post-Modern AI. *Case-Based Reasoning: Experiences, Lessons, and Future.* D. B. Leake. Menlo park, CA., AAAI Press/MIT Press: 371–388.

Risan, L. (1997). Artificial Life: A technoscience leaving modernity? An Anthropology of subjects and objects. Accessed April 19, 2003 from: http://anthrobase.com/Txt/R/Risan_L_05.htm.

Riskin, J. (2007). *Genesis Redux: Essays in the History and Philosophy of Artificial Life.* Chicago, University of Chicago Press.

Roberts, S. and H. Pashler (2000). "How persuasive is a good fit? A comment on theory testing." *Psychological Review* **107**: 358–367.

Rochester, N., J. Holland, et al. (1956). "Test on a cell assembly theory of the action of the brain, using a large digital computer." *IRE Transactions on Information Theory* **IT-2**: 80–93.

Rosenblatt, P. (1958). "The Perceptron: A probabilistic model for information storage and organization in the brain." *Psychological Review* **65**: 386–408.

Roszak, T. (1994). *The Cult of Information: A Neo-Luddite Treatise on High-Tech, Artificial Intelligence, and The True Art of Thinking*. Berkeley, CA, University of California Press.

Rouse, J. (1987). *Knowledge and Power: Toward a Political Philosophy of Science*. Ithaca: N.Y., Cornell University Press.

Rouse, J. (1999). Understanding Scientific Practices: Cultural Studies of Science as a Philosophical Program. *The Science Studies Reader*. M. Biagioli. New York and London, Routledge: 442–456.

Rumelhart, D. E. (1989). The Architecture of Mind: A Connectionist Approach. *Mind Design II: Philosophy, Psychology, Artificial Intelligence*. J. Haugeland. Cambridge, MA., MIT Press: 205–232.

Rumelhart, D. E. (1997). The Architecture of Mind: A Connectionist Approach. *Mind Design II*. J. Haugeland. Cambridge, MA, MIT Press: 205–232.

Rumelhart, D. E., G. E. Hinton, et al. (1986). Learning internal representations by error propagation. *Parallel Distributed Processing*. D. E. R. a. J. L. McClelland. Cambridge, MA., MIT Press. **2**.

Rumelhart, D. E. and D. Norman (1982). "Simulating a Skilled Typist: A Study of Skilled Cognitive–Motor Performance." *Cognitive Science* **6**(1): 1–36.

Rumelhart, D. E. and D. Zipser (1985). "Feature discovery by competitive learning." *Cognitive Science* **9**: 75–112.

Russell, S. J. and P. Norvig (1995). *Artificial Intelligence: A Modern Approach*, Prentice Hall.

Saffran, J. R., R. N. Aslin, et al. (1996). "Statistical learning by 8-month old infants." *Science* **274**(5294): 1926–1928.

Santambrogio, M. and P. Violi (1988). Introduction. *Meaning and Mental Representation*. M. Santambrogio, P. Violi and U. Eco. Bloomington, IN, Indiana University Press: 3–23.

Scassellati, B. (1998). Imitation and Mechanisms of Joint Attention: A Developmental Structure for Building Social Skills on a Humanoid Robot. *Computation for Metaphors, Analogy and Agents*. C. Nehaniv, Springer-Verlag. **1562**.

Scassellati, B. (1999). A Binocular, Foveated Active Vision System, MIT, Artificial Intelligence Laboratory.

Scassellati, B. (2000). Investigating Models of Social Development Using a Humanoid Robot. *Biorobotics*. B. Webb and T. Consi. Cambridge, MA, MIT Press.

Schaffer, S. (1994) Babbage's Intelligence: Calculating Engines and the Factory System. Accessed April 14, 2004 from: http://www.wmin.ac.uk/mad/schaffer/schaffer01.html.

Schank, R. C. (1972). "Conceptual Dependency: A theory of natural language understanding." *Cognitive Psychology* **3**(4): 552–631.

Schank, R. C. (1982). *Dynamic Memory: A Theory of Learning in Computers and People*. Cambridge, UK, Cambridge University Press.

Schank, R. C. (1986). *Explanation Patterns*. Hillsdale, N.J., Lawrence Erlbaum Assoc.

Schank, R. C. (1995). Information Is Surprises. *The Third Culture: Beyond the Scientific Revolution*. J. Brockman. New York, Simon and Schuster.

Schank, R. C. and R. P. Abelson (1977). *Scripts, Plans, Goals, and Understanding*. Hillsdale, NJ, Lawrence Erlbaum Assoc.

Schank, R. C. and L. Birnbaum (1984). Memory, Meaning, and Syntax. *Talking Minds: The Study of Language in Cognitive Science*. Cambridge, MA., MIT Press: 209–251.

Schank, R. C. and A. Kass (1988). Knowledge Representation in People and Machines. *Meaning and Mental Representations*. U. Eco, M. Santambrogio and P. Violi. Bloomington and Indianapolis, Indiana University Press: 181–200.

Schank, R. C., A. Kass, et al. (1994). *Inside Case-based Explanation*. Hillsdale, N.J., Lawrence Erlbaum Assoc.

Schank, R. C. and D. B. Leake (2001). Natural Language Processing: Models of Roger Schank and His Students. *Encyclopedia of Cognitive Science*.

Schank, R. C. and C. Riesbeck (1981). *Inside Computer Understanding: Five Programs with Miniatures*. Hillsdale, NJ., Lawrence Erlbaum.

Scheutz, M. (2002). Agents with or without Emotions? Proceedings of the Fifteenth International Florida Artificial Intelligence Research Society Conference. 89–93.

Scheutz, M., P. Schemerhorn, et al. (2007). "First Steps toward Natural Human-Like HRI." *Autonomous Robots* **22**: 411–423.

Searle, J. (1992). *Rediscovery of The Mind*. Cambridge, MA, MIT Press.

Searle, J. (2002). I Married A Computer. *Are We Spiritual Machines? Ray Kurzweil vs. the Critics of Strong A.I.* J. W. Richards. Seattle, WA., Discovery Institute.

Searle, J. R. (1980). Minds, Brains, and Programs. *Mind Design II*. J. Haugeland. Cambridge, Mass., MIT Press.

Searle, J. R. (1984). *Minds, Brains, and Science*. Cambridge, MA., Harvard University Press.

Seidenberg, M. S. and M. C. MacDonald (1999). "A Probabilistic Constraints Approach to Language Acquisition and Processing." *Cognitive Science* **23**(4): 569–588.

Sejnowski, T. and C. Rosenberg (1987). NETtalk: a parallel network that learns to read aloud, Technical Report JHU/EECS-86/01, Johns Hopkins University.

Selfridge, O. (1959). *Pandemonium: A paradigm for learning*. Symposium on the Mechanization of Thought, London, HMSO.

Shanker, S. G. (1987). AI at the Crossroads. *The Question of Artificial Intelligence*. B. Bloomfield. London, Croom Helm: 1–58.

Shannon, C. (1950). "Programming a computer for playing chess." *Philosophical Magazine* **41**: 256–275.

Shapin, S. (1994). *A Social History of Truth: Civility and Science in Seventeenth-Century England*. Chicago: IL, University of Chicago Press.

Shimojima, A. (1996). On the Efficacy of Representation. *Philosophy*. Bloomington, Indiana University.

Shultz, T. R. and W. C. Schmidt (1991). *A Cascade-Correlation Model of Balance Scale Phenomenon*. 13th Annual Conference of Cognitive Science Society, Erlbaum.

Simon, H. A. (1969). *The Sciences of The Artificial*. Cambridge, MA, MIT Press.

Simon, H. A. (1995). "Artificial Intelligence: an empirical science." *Artificial Intelligence* **77**(1): 95–127.

Skinner, B. F. (1985). "Cognitive Science and Behaviourism." *British Journal of Psychology* **76**: 33–43.

Sloman, A. (2001). "Beyond Shallow Models of Emotion." *Cognitive Processing* **2**(1): 177–198.

Sloman, A. (2005a). AI in a New Millenium: Obstacles and Opportunities. *IJCAI*. Birmingham, UK.

Sloman, A. (2005b). Do Machines, Natural or Artificial, Really Need Emotions? *NWO Cognition Program*. Utrecht.

Smith, B. C. (1991). "The Owl and the Electric Encyclopedia." *Artificial Intelligence* **47**(1–3): 252–288.

Smith, B. C. (1996). *The Origin of Objects.* Cambridge, MA, The MIT Press.

Smith, B. C. (1997) One Hundred Billion Lines of C++. Accessed October 15, 2005 from: http://www.ageofsignificance.org/people/bcsmith/papers/smith-billion.html.

Smith, B. C. (1999). Situatedness. *MIT Encyclopedia of Cognitive Science (MITECS).* Cambridge, MA., MIT Press.

Smith, B. C. (2000). Indiscrete Affairs. *Vital Signs: Cultural Perspectives on Coding Life and Vitalizing Code.* L. Suchman and J. Fujimura. (in press).

Smith, B. C. (2002). Reply to Dennett. *Philosophy of Mental Representation.* H. Clapin. Oxford, Oxford University Press: 237–266.

Smith, B. C. (forthcoming). *The Age of Significance: Introduction.* Cambidge, MA, The MIT Press.

Smolensky, P. (1988). "On the proper treatment of connectionism." *Behavioral and Brain Sciences* **11**: 1–74.

Smolensky, P. (1999). "Grammar-based connectionist approaches to language." *Cognitive Science* **23**: 589–613.

Star, L. S., Ed. (1995). *Ecologies of Knowledge Work and Politics in Science and Technology.* SUNY Series in Science, Technology, and Society. New York: NY, SUNY.

Steedman, M. (1999). "Connectionist Sentence Processing in Perspective." *Cognitive Science* **23**(4): 615–634.

Steels, L. (1990). Cooperation between distributed agents through self-organization. *Decentralized AI.* Y. Demazeau and J. P. Muller. Amsterdam, North-Holland: 175–196.

Stewart, J. (1992). *Life = Cognition: The epistemological and ontological significance of Artificial Life.* First European Conference on Artificial Life, MIT Press.

Suchman, L. (1987). *Plans and Situated Actions.* Cambridge, UK., Cambridge University Press.

Suchman, L. A. (2007). *Human-Machine Reconfigurations.* Cambridge, Cambridge University Press.

Thelen, E. and L. B. Smith (1994). *A dynamic systems approach to the development of cognition and action.* Cambridge, MA., MIT Press.

Thompson, R. K. R., D. L. Oden, et al. (1997). "Language-Native Chimpanzees (Pan troglodytes) Judge Relations Between Relations in a Conceptual Matching-to-sample Task." *Journal of Experimental Psychology: Animal Behavior Processes* **23**: 31–43.

Toole, B. A. (1992). *Ada, the Enchantress of Numbers.* Mill Valley: CA, Strawberry Press.

Townsend, J. T. and J. Busemeyer (1995). Dyamic Representation of Decision-Making. *Mind as Motion.* R. F. a. T. v. G. Port. Cambridge, MA., MIT Press: 101–119.

Turing, A. M. (1936). *On Computable Numbers, with an Application to Entscheidungsproblem.* London Mathematical Society.

Turing, A. M. (1950). "Computing Machinery and Intelligence." *Mind* **59**: 433–460.

Turing, A. M. (1953). Digital Computers Applied to Games. *Faster than Thought.* B. V. Bowden. London, UK, Pitman.

Turkle, S. (1985). *The Second Self: Computers and The Human Spirit.* New York, NY, Simon and Schuster.

Turkle, S. (1995). *Life on the Screen: Identity in the Age of Internet.* New York, N.Y., Simon & Schuster.

van Gelder, T. (1998). "The dynamical hypothesis in cognitive science." *Behavioral and Brain Sciences* **21**(5): 615–628.

Varela, F. J., E. Thompson, et al. (1991). *The Embodied Mind: Cognitive Science and Human Experience.* Cambridge, Mass., MIT Press.

von Foerster, H. (1970). Thoughts and Notes on Cognition. *Cognition: A multiple view.* P. L. Garvin. New York, Spartan Books: 25–48.

Vygotsky, L. (1986). *Thought and Language.* Cambridge, Mass., MIT Press Translations.

Weizenbaum, J. (1976). *Computer Power and Human Reason.* San Francisco, CA, W. H. Freeman.

Wellman, B. (2001). "Computer Networks as Social Networks." *Science* **293**: 2031–2034.

Wellman, H. M. and S. A. Gellman (1992). "Cognitive Development: Foundational theories of core domains." *Annual Review of Psychology* **43**: 337–375.

Wiener, N. (1948). *Cybernetics.* New York, Wiley.

Wills, L. M. and J. L. Kolodner (1996). Toward More Creative Case-Based Design Systems. *Case-Based Reasoning: Experiences, Lessons, and Future Directions.* D. B. Leake. Menlo Park, CA., AAAI Press/MIT Press: 81–91.

Wilson, E. O. (1971). *The Insect Society.* Cambridge, MA., Harvard University Press.

Winner, L. (1986). *The Whale and The Reactor: A Search for Limits in an Age of High Technology.* Chicago, IL, University of Chicago Press.

Winograd, T. (1972). *Understanding Natural Language.* New York, Academic Press.

Winograd, T. and F. Flores (1986). *Understanding Computers and Cognition: A New Foundation for Design.* Norwood, N.J., Ablex.

Wittgenstein, L. (1953). *Philosophical Investigations.* New York, Blackwell.

Woods, W. A. (1975). What's in a link? Foundations for semantic networks. *Representation and Understanding: Studies in Cognitive Science.* D. G. Bobrow and A. M. Collins. New York, Academic Press: 35–82.

Woolgar, S. (1985). "Why Not a Sociology of Machines? The Case of Sociology and Artificial Intelligence." *Sociology* **19**(4): 557–572.

Woolgar, S. (1987). Reconstructing Man and Machine: A Note on Sociological Critiques of Cognitivism. *The Social Construction of Technological Systems.* T. H. W. Bijker, and T. Pinch. Cambridge, MA., MIT Press: 311–328.

Woolgar, S. (1995). Representation, Cognition, and Self: What Hope for the Integration of Psychology and Sociology? *Ecologies of Knowledge: Work and Politics in Science and Technology.* S. L. Star. New York State University of New York Press: 154–179.

Zipser, M. (2002). *Introduction to the Theory of Computation.* Boston, MA, PWS Publishing.

Author Index

Subject Index